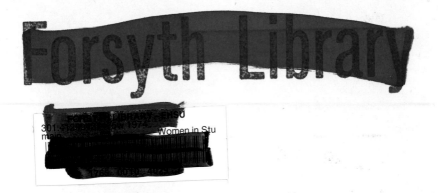

Women in Stuart
England and America

For my parents

Women in Stuart England and America

A comparative study

Roger Thompson
Department of English and American Studies
University of East Anglia

Routledge & Kegan Paul
London and Boston

First published in 1974
by Routledge & Kegan Paul Ltd
Broadway House, 68-74 Carter Lane,
London EC4V 5EL and
9 Park Street,
Boston, Mass. 02108, U.S.A.
Printed in Great Britain by
Butler & Tanner Ltd
Frome and London
© Roger Thompson 1974

ISBN 0 7100 7822 6

Library of Congress Catalog Card No. 73-93638

Contents

Preface

> You've come a long way, baby,
> To get where you've got to today!
> You've got your own cigarette now, lady!
> You've come a long, long way!

These immortal lines provided the refrain for one of the more urbane advertising campaigns on American television in recent years. The accompanying film sequences compared reckless Edwardian matrons, caught by scandalised husbands, secretly puffing in attics and gazebos, with cool contemporary cookies who demanded a slim, well-tailored cigarette, 'not the fat ones that men smoke'. The provision of Virginia Slims was seen by the advertisers as the climax of the liberation of American women which had begun with the suffragettes.

This book examines whether the commercial's 'long way' was not in fact a great deal longer than the copywriters claimed. Its approach is comparative. The situation of women in the seventeenth-century colonies is contrasted with that of women in England. Had women in America by the end of the first century of settlement come to enjoy a higher status in society and to perform different roles from those of their cousins in the old country? If so, what were the causes of this improvement in their lot? Finally, how was their emancipation manifested in the colonial culture, and was it a permanent feature of American life, or merely the product of the unsettling years of settlement?

Like Gaul, my attempt to answer these questions is divided into three parts. The first part of the book examines contemporary responses to the perennial 'woman question'. The second part looks at four major factors which could have contributed to the differences in women's treatment and opportunity between England and the colonies. The final part compares specific institutions and practices on the two sides of the Atlantic to see whether the four factors of contrast had their predicted effects.

One of the perennial fascinations of American history is the investigation of what national characteristics are distinctively

vii

American, and what are inherited from Old-World origins. The conflict between the nature and nurture schools is far from resolution. For instance, despite reams of research, some thought, and much polemic, there is little agreement about Turner's provocative assertion that 'American democracy was born of no theorist's dream; it was not carried in the *Sarah Constant* to Virginia, nor in the *Mayflower* to Plymouth. It came out of the American forest, and it gained a new strength each time it touched the frontier.'

The great majority of seventeenth-century colonists were English either by birth or by tradition. It would, however, be highly surprising if they had not been affected by their new and very different environment. (In order that environmental influences should have an opportunity to operate on colonial behaviour and outlook, this study has concentrated on the latter part of the century, that is the third or fourth generation of the earlier foundations.) It is precisely in this kind of discussion that the comparative approach can be so illuminating, the 'powerful magic wand' of Marc Bloch's description, if wisely and cautiously used. It is, I think, a matter of regret that comparisons so far have often been used in an impressionistic or jingoistic way. It is equally sad that, in other areas of study, they have not been used at all.

To prevent this study from becoming unduly ungainly and lasting a lifetime, I made the decision at a fairly early stage to limit my research in two ways. First, rather than attempt to analyse the position of women in all colonies in the seventeenth century, I would restrict myself to two which were reasonably mature by the year 1700, and which were representative of their sections. The two chosen were Massachusetts and Virginia: the former because I was working as a private researcher at Harvard, whose Houghton Library is a superb centre for colonial research; the latter because some fine work in the field had already been done, notably by Julia Cherry Spruill. The second limitation was more serious. The quantities of primary sources referring directly or indirectly to women in Stuart England are, I soon discovered, enormous. I therefore resolved with great regret to rely for the English side of the comparison on the work already done by scholars, which in itself is very considerable. While this inevitably weakens the authority of the comparisons, I do not feel that it invalidates the approach or the conclusions arrived at.

A second decision was about the scope of the study. Should it range broadly over a wide number of areas concerning women, or should it concentrate on a few aspects of the contrast, examined more exhaustively? The more I read, the more I became convinced that the most useful approach at this stage was the former, which would try to synthesise the many strands of recent research, and also to suggest new paths for study, particularly in a comparative way. For example, a great deal of original work has been done and is still in progress on demographic aspects of seventeenth-century history, much of which has a direct bearing on the problem of women in society. Other subjects under new or renewed examination include education, the family, local government, the franchise, superstition and witchcraft, legal and political rights, and illegitimacy, all of which are similarly relevant. The approach so far, however, has tended inevitably towards local or national studies. Much more needs to be discovered about all these fields, and in such other subjects as religion, democracy, social mobility, social control, and crime and vice patterns. Nonetheless, it has seemed to me a useful exercise to point out opportunities for further research and to suggest hesitantly some comparative hypotheses that could rewardingly be tested.

To write a book about the women of three areas over the period of a century is self-evidently a vainglorious exercise. In England alone at any one time there was probably something in the region of 2·5 millions of them. As any reader of social history knows, the material on the population tends to be in inverse ratio to class numbers: there is relatively plenty on the few aristocrats, only scraps on the masses. Gentlefolk speak for themselves, but humble people speak only through official or semi-official records; the biased words of dramatists or sermonisers or hacks; or their stray encounters with the more literate classes. This will be quickly obvious in the following pages. I have tried as far as possible to examine the situation lower down the social scale, but the balance is finally irredressable.

It is a pleasure to acknowledge the help of the following: the staffs of the Houghton and Widener Libraries at Harvard; Boston Public Library; Research Department, Colonial Williamsburg; University of East Anglia Library; Wayne Altree, David Fischer, Jane Goddard, John Hardy, Patricia Higgins, Sheila Hinchcliffe, Peter Laslett, Victor Morgan, Keith Thomas, Christopher Turner, Andrew Wheatcroft, and—last and most—Kit Thompson.

Part I

Introduction

Chapter 1

The Seventeenth-Century Scene

What used to be known by the unliberated as 'the woman question' is as old as Eve. There are plenty of descriptive, biographical and narrative studies on the state of play in seventeenth-century England and America.[1] The drama and poetry, sermons and family histories, legal records and diaries have been ransacked by generations of scholars. We shall not reiterate the excellent work that has already been done. Here our focus will be on the less well-worked areas of transatlantic comparison and the analysis of the causes and effects of differences in women's status and roles.

Most historical study and teaching has been rigidly national in scope. This inquiry will therefore begin with a brief sketch of England and the colonies in the Stuart period. The rest of the introduction will present a survey of published popular opinion on women on the two sides of the Atlantic; contrasts in career patterns; and the comments of travellers.

Stuart England

In the eighteenth century, Englishmen rather than Frenchmen or Italians had a European reputation for turbulence and political instability, and small wonder after the upheavals of the preceding century. The profound political and constitutional changes brought about by the Civil War, the Interregnum, and the Revolution of 1688–9 are what usually catch the historical headlines. Underlying these were less spectacular developments which are more crucial for the study of women's position in English society.

The first of these factors is that highly complex movement, the rise of capitalism, continuing from preceding centuries. On the one hand, this gave rise to a new class in English society, a bourgeoisie of commerce, business, industry and bureaucracy, mainly centred on larger towns and cities. These citizens and their wives were an important new element in English social life, something of a countervailing force to that of the entrenched aristocracy. It was a commonplace of social comment that the wives of citizens were freer than any other group of women in England, perhaps

3

in most of Europe. On the other hand, it has been argued that, in such a plutocracy, uselessness, which is the boast or bane of both sexes in an aristocracy, is a characteristic only of women.[2] Furthermore, some economic historians have deplored the removal of the wife from an economically productive business partnership with her husband, and her relegation to an ornamental role.[3]

The concept of 'possessive individualism' was intimately connected with the development of capitalism and with intellectual movements like the growth of scepticism and toleration. Assumptions like 'What makes a man human is freedom from dependence on the wills of others' cut right across cosmological theories like the great chain of being, and traditional patriarchalism in the family and the community.[4] If woman is subsumed in 'man', then accepted ideas about the natural inferiority of woman and her subordinate position in the family or communal team are in jeopardy. Significantly, the overthrow of autocratic monarchy in 1688 gave rise to comparisons with the autocratic paterfamilias, and produced demands—albeit literary ones—for compacts between equal partners in marriage.[5] There was, however, a less emancipating alternative. If possessiveness, rather than individualism, was stressed, then daughters or wives could be derogated into a species of property, to be bought and sold, or flashed around as a piece of ostentatious display.

The spread of calvinistic and post-calvinistic protestant dogma was linked in subtle ways with capitalism and individualism, and likewise affected the status of men, and contemporary opinion about them. This will be a major theme of succeeding chapters. Suffice it to say here that some strains in protestant and puritan thought worked in woman's favour—emphasis on an educated laity, for instance—while others, like the derivation of social attitudes from Hebrew traditions, may have worked against.

Foreign influences also played a part. The Dutchwoman of the seventeenth century was probably the most emancipated in the world. Those, like Sir Josiah Child, who sought to explain and emulate the economic and cultural 'miracle' of the Netherlands stressed women's role in it.[6] French influence was a vital factor in English cultural development in the seventeenth century. The example of the *Précieuses* was widely praised or lampooned, depending on the point of view, in English literature thereafter. Conversely, the oppressive treatment which women still received in such underdeveloped countries as Turkey or Russia may have had some marginal effects on their treatment in England.[7]

There were three periods in the seventeenth century when the 'woman question' emerged from the undergrowth of history: the second decade, the Civil War and Interregnum years, and the last two decades of the century. The first period witnessed a vigorous pamphlet war, fanned by the exposures of the Essex divorce scandal and the pretensions of some court and city women.[8] The middle years of the century saw profound social as well as political change. In this upheaval women took the stage in religious, political, legal and business affairs. Some commentators have detected in the latter decades the appearance of 'the new woman'.[9] It is true that protests by women against women's lot were made at this time. It is much less clear whether these represented the emergence of a new breed of Amazons, or total desperation at worsening conditions.

With the possible exception of the middle years of the century, there seems little doubt that the Stuart era was one of the bleaker ones for women, certainly a decline from that golden age of Renaissance flowering under the Tudors.

The Colonies

The expansion of Stuart England to the North American continent had a mixed bag of propellants—religious, economic, demographic, imperialist, missionary, to name a few. The earliest colony was Virginia, settled in 1607 and sponsored by the Virginian Company of London, a joint-stock enterprise. The economic motive was the most important in the founding of the old dominion, and its eventual success depended on the cultivation of the staple crop of tobacco. Economic and geographical conditions were responsible for the spread of the plantation system there, and the absence of large towns. The culture of tobacco was helped by the influx of large numbers of indentured servants and rather smaller numbers of African slaves. In the first century of settlement, land was fairly evenly divided among Virginians, though an aristocracy of large landholders had begun to emerge by the end of the century.

The financial problems of the Virginia Company led to the Crown taking over control of the colony in 1624. Henceforward the governor was appointed by the King. However, representative institutions, in the form of the House of Burgesses, were allowed to continue under royal government; the main unit of local government was the county. The Church of England was the established church of the colony, and power here tended to lie with the self-perpetuating vestries.

Because of royal authority, economic ties and the Anglican church, Virginia tended to be pretty closely related to England during the seventeenth century. Loyalist sentiment was strong there during the Civil War and the Interregnum, as symbolised by the outlook of its greatest Stuart governor, Sir William Berkeley, whose term of office ran from 1642 to 1677. The colony was more affected by prevailing English ideas and fashions than was New England, and its economy was threatened by the Navigation Acts. Politically, it was reasonably stable after the first generation of settlement, the one major exception being Bacon's Rebellion of 1676. The worst source of tension for much of the century was the Indian threat, which had been a leading cause of the uprising under Bacon.

In many ways Virginia was fairly typical of the other southern settlements of the Stuart period, Maryland and Carolina. Both of these developed staple economies reliant on England, though Maryland also served as a haven for persecuted Roman Catholics. Virginia's northern and southern neighbours were both propri-etorial colonies, rather than directly governed by the Crown. How-ever, what we shall be saying about Virginia in succeeding chapters will by and large be applicable to Maryland, which was one generation younger, and to Carolina, which was two.[10]

Efforts had been made from the start of the seventeenth century to settle the inhospitable coast of New England. The first success-ful attempt was that of the Plymouth Pilgrims in 1620. They were a group of about a hundred religious separatists who had already lived for a decade in exile in the Netherlands. Although important in folklore, and possibly for their religious organisation, their plantation on Cape Cod was historically less significant than neigh-bouring colonies. They never obtained a charter or colony status, and were merged with Massachusetts in 1691.[11]

The colony of Massachusetts Bay was the dominant settlement in seventeenth-century New England. Although economic motives were evident, the main impetus in its foundation in 1629 was religi-ous, and intimately linked with the Laudian persecution of puritan-ism in England. In the eyes of its sponsors, the Massachusetts Bay Company, the colony was to be a holy commonwealth, an exemplar to unreformed or backsliding protestantism in England and Europe. Its church polity was a form of congregationalism, and political and religious power was placed in the hands of the visible saints. During its first ten years it received a flood of some 16,000 refugees, who were organised in townships around the Bay and up the navigable rivers. Representative institutions were quickly, if not altogether willingly, granted, and for most of the century the central political authority was an elected governor, a court of assistants and a house of deputies, with the towns as the local unit of government.

Massachusetts tried to remain as independent as possible from England, although it owed its original charter of 1629 to the Crown. The only period of modest relaxation was during the post-Civil-War years. Although its puritan leadership persisted in trying to maintain provincial insularity from England, economic considerations pulled in the opposite direction. Most colonists practised subsistence agriculture, but a significant minority engaged, with increasing success, in trade based on the export of fish, timber products, and, later, rum. A flourishing merchant marine was based on such ports as Boston and Salem and plied coastal, trans-atlantic, West Indian and Mediterranean sea routes. Connections with English mercantile houses were a vital link in this commercial web, and militated against isolationism. The home rule of the Bay Company was successfully challenged by the new English imperi-alism of the Restoration, and in 1684 Massachusetts was forced to surrender its charter. The second charter, issued after the alarums of the Glorious Revolution in 1691, made Massachusetts into a royal colony and broke the grip of the godly on its political machinery.

Intellectually, Massachusetts had been by far the most cultivated colony of the Stuart period. It boasted Harvard College, a printing press, a remarkably well-educated clergy and laity with scientific, literary and scholarly—as well as theological—interests and achieve-ments. The initial utopian enthusiasm and purpose inevitably waned in the face of stability, prosperity, and a growing sentiment towards a measure of toleration. It retained, however, a purposeful sobriety and earnestness. It was undoubtedly one of the greatest achievements of seventeenth-century English puritanism, if not *the* greatest. Its neighbours, Rhode Island and Connecticut, were founded as more or less protesting offshoots, transfused with money and migrants from England. Though they developed certain indi-genous characteristics, they were profoundly influenced by the Bay Colony, far more than they usually cared to admit. When we subsequently analyse conditions in Massachusetts, then, we shall frequently reach conclusions applicable to all New England.[12]

The one section we shall only glance at spasmodically is the so-called middle colonies of New York, New Jersey and Pennsylvania. The first two were Dutch until their capture in 1664, and the latter was not founded until 1680. They were far more heterogeneous nationally and religiously than either Virginia or Massachusetts. In numerous ways—economic, social, theological and political, for instance—they occupied a transitional zone between north and south. Dutch influence was important in the social *mores* of the former New Netherlands, as were the Quaker and other sectarian faiths in William Penn's proprietory. I greatly regret having to omit them from this already lengthy work, for they are a most important area of study.

Finally, it is important to stress certain dissimilarities between England and her colonies, so that allowance can be made in com-parisons. The new settlements, for instance, had no great cities remotely comparable to London. Not only did this mean that the colonies lacked the benefits and evils of city life—and their effects on women—but they also lacked the influence that a great city exerts on its broad hinterland. Again, feudal institutions were never successfully established in British North America. Nor was there an aristocracy in the European sense, imposing its standards and economic and social control over the classes beneath it. These, and many other differences—economic, environmental, psychological, demographic, religious and social—which will be examined in subsequent chapters, must all be taken into account to prevent the mirror grossly distorting the picture.

Public Opinion about Women in England and the Colonies

The basis of any debate on the role and status of women in society rests upon the consideration of their innate capacities. This is rarely unanimous. Although women had their defenders in Stuart England, the great weight of public opinion deemed them mentally, morally, psychologically and physically inferior to men. Needless to say, the bulk of that view was formed and propagated by men, aided and abetted by many of the 'weaker sex'. Proponents of the 'better-half' ideal were also mainly male, though a few outspoken women defended the potentialities of their sex throughout the century.

It would be unreasonable to expect a radical change in the colonies. English opinions and traditions remained influential throughout the seventeenth century. Many opinion-formers there would tend to be conservative in their social thinking. Like educated Englishmen of their day, they were saturated with classical and biblical precedents which were not notably complimentary. None the less, a distinct amelioration of male attitudes is detectable in the colonies in the later part of the century, and this on the part of men of stature and influence, especially in Massachusetts.

This rapid and general survey will not pre-empt the complex and involved arguments of subsequent chapters. All that is intended here is to give a context to the discussion.

Popular stereotypes are a useful gauge to prevailing prejudices. In Stuart England calumniators painted several different caricatures labelled 'woman' with relish. One of the commonest, and most pervasive throughout all classes, was that of the woman who was all tongue: the straight blabbermouth, or the gossip and scandal-monger, or the shrew or scold. The first revealed in her vapid blatherings merely intellectual inferiority, but the others added to this a certain moral degradation as well. This failing was in the ascendant with the second common symbol of female inferiority, the Jezebel or Dalilah figure who tempted and ensnared innocent and well-intentioned men: the 'leaden swords in a velvet scabbard'. The adulteress was uniformly held to be more culpable than the adulterer. The seductive intentions of cosmetics and fashion were a major ground for criticism. A stock character of seventeenth-century literature was the woman who could not make up her mind, or was the feather-brained slave of fickle fashion. Women were frequently depicted as wastrels, spending recklessly what their husbands got, and more. As insulting in its way was the popular view of women as sex-objects, which transcended class. Treating women as things, to be exploited and discarded, is arguably the final degradation. To the seventeenth-century mind, however, witchcraft was a horrific crime, not only blasphemy, but in some cases lust, and the identification of women with devil-worship was symbolic of their general inferiority. One way or another the seven deadly sins were represented in these cartoon images.

This common belief in women's inherent inferiority was buttressed by social custom and philosophy. The great chain of being placed women in a lower degree to men, and domestic-conduct books,[13] sermons, and parental homilies all preached the need for wifely obedience and subordination. Woman's place was in the home, her role that of breeder and housekeeper. In gentle society she was naturally excluded from circles of male society. Her inferior education and lack of Latin usually cut her off from much of contemporary culture. It was hardly surprising that the double standard should thrive or that women should be treated as mindless ornaments or a species of property. The aims of conventional upbringing were to make daughters pliable and to give them superficial 'breeding'. Husbands were counselled to be understanding of feminine frailties and failings, but a woman who transgressed the narrow role prescribed for her was regarded as some kind of unnatural monster. Women who sought intellectual pursuits were ridiculed, their motives ascribed to lust or pride. Spinsters were objects of amused pity. Men were frequently warned against the machinations of widows. Faced with such a prevailing attitude, the prospects of being disposed of to a suitor by her parents and of ensuing frequent pregnancies, girls of Stuart England can hardly be blamed for developing a certain passive fatalism. Significantly, the commonest symbols employed to describe wives in the seventeenth century were moons, flowers which followed the sun, or mirrors.

At this stage it will be enough to give a few illustrations to demonstrate that conventional English ideas about women were transported across the Atlantic.

The essentially passive qualities which Edward Taylor praises in his wife,[14]

> As wife, a Tender, Tender, Loving Meet,
> Meeke, Patient, Humble, Modest, Faithfull, Sweet
> Endearing Help she was; Whose Choicest Treasure
> Of earthly things she held her Husband's pleasure,

were echoed or envied by numerous male memorialists and homilists. Sermons on the subject of women reflected the injunctions of English conduct-books. Gags and ducking-stools were prescribed punishments for female scolds, and adulteresses were more severely treated than adulterers. John Winthrop was not alone in thinking intellectual pursuits a likely cause of a woman's insanity, and Thomas Parker informed his sister that 'printing a book, beyond the custom of your sex, doth rankly smell'. Edward Johnson condemned a group of females who tried to take an active part in religious life in Massachusetts as 'silly women laden with diverse lusts' and 'phantasticall madnesse'.[15] In Virginia the ideal of wifely subordination ran so deep that an Anglican court supported a Quaker husband against a disobedient Anglican wife. A Virginian gentleman opined that women have 'nothing in the general view, but the heady contest at home. It began with poor Eve & ever since then has been so much of the devil in women'.[16]

Seventeenth-century women in England and America did not entirely lack apologists. In a period famed for both group and interpersonal violence among men, women's pacific qualities were stressed. Their civilising and stabilising attributes were praised by grateful husbands as well as by liberal preachers and pamphleteers.[17] 'Howses where no woemen bee, are lyke deserts or untilled land' was a popular proverb. Puritan writers, particularly, dwelt on the benefits of companionship and a happy home life as a basis for worldy and other-worldly success.[18] A stock character of drama, inherited from the Middle Ages, was the 'patient Grissel' the woman whose stamina and capacity for suffering finally won through.[19] The hostile environment was an obvious target. 'Custome is an Idiot' argued the author of *Haec Vir* (1620) with typical bluntness.[20] Education in which women were 'beat not *for* but *from* the Muses' made them 'Education's, not Nature's Fools'.[21] The basic asssumptions of the double standard were turned on their head: ' Women not proving bad till bad men make them so'.[22] In friendlier circumstances, like the golden age of the sixteenth century, or the world of the French salons, women's gifts had amply disproved male prejudices. The example of the great Elizabeth was frequently cited to demonstrate female potentialities and achievements. Progressive theologians stressed the spiritual equality, even superiority, of the 'better half'.

Much of the rest of this book will be taken up with demonstrating the relative emancipation of women in the American colonies. Here, then, a few points will suffice. 'She was good, not brilliant, useful not ornamental, and the mother of 15 children.'[23] Certainly in the first generations of settlement up to 1700 there is little evidence from either Massachusetts or Virginia that a swarm of female drones had developed. All hands, including feminine ones, were needed; without women the population would not grow to fill the empty lands. Where puritanism dominated opinion, as in Massachusetts, more liberal views on women's spiritual, moral and mental capacities could be expected to thrive. Though men fresh from England, like John Winthrop or Edward Johnson, might perpetuate English prejudices, it is noticeable that the third generation—Cotton Mather, for instance, or Benjamin Wadsworth or Benjamin Colman—concurred in the view that woman was 'a necessary good'.[24] The considerable migration from England after the Restoration may have added the liberal attitudes of the Interregnum to the domestic trend. The admiration expressed by influential men for Anne Bradstreet's verse contrasted starkly with prevalent English prejudice against female creativity.[25] Women's greater dedication to the faith was reflected in Cotton Mather's 'There are three Maries to one John', and in neither of the two colonies were the injustices and distortions of the double standard accepted as a matter of course. Women's legal rights were more consistently safeguarded in the Bay Colony and the old dominion, especially the former. The dispersed nature of settlement in the South inhibited the development of male exclusiveness and cultural apartheid, and fostered marital companionship and mutuality. The absence of large towns sustained a certain refreshing innocence in relations between the sexes. There was no overt feminist movement in the colonies in the seventeenth century, in contrast with the admittedly spasmodic and diverse protests in later Stuart England. This could represent a cowed second sex, but is more likely to mean a reasonably contented acceptance of women's situation.

Even with sophisticated modern techniques, the gauging of public opinion is notoriously difficult. It is infinitely more taxing for an age less given to scientific analysis, when the great bulk of the population was inarticulate, including the vast majority of the women themselves. The rest of this study will be given over to the sifting of evidence only alluded to in this rapid introductory survey of attitudes, and to evaluating the contention that in England the hand that held the bull-horn was male and more or less misogynist, with protesting voices scattered around the edge of the crowd, but that the environment in the colonies was noticeably more encouraging.

Female Career Patterns

Catalogues of women who succeeded in business, medicine or estate management have already explored the available evidence, which does not need duplicating here. We are, anyway, dealing with only a tiny minority of womankind: those who, through wealth, education or some other fortunate circumstance, were able to transcend the norm. However, the ways and situations in which such women were encouraged or inhibited, and the kinds of women who left some mark on history—however fickle and arbitrary the chances of its survival may be—could well give important clues to social conventions affecting women.

One area in which a considerable number of English women participated was that of letters. Several of those who now occupy small niches in literary history intended their work to remain private; such were Katherine Phillips ('The Matchless Orinda'), Dorothy Osborne, Lucy Hutchinson, Lady Halkett and Lady Fanshawe. For all those women who wrote then, the niches are never more than small; their work was either conventionally mediocre, or downright bad.

One characteristic that emerges from an analysis of these authoresses is the number with puritan or nonconformist backgrounds. This would place them, except for the middle years of the century, outside the dominant strain of English opinion. It is noticeable that several of them came from comparatively ordinary families; the puritan faith may well have given them the spur, and the tools, to transcend their conventional situation.

A second similarity, even more marked, is the way that many of these *lettristes* shared a common strain of abnormality, be it sexual, social or familial. 'Orinda', Mary Astell and Mary Manley were, for instance, all sexually odd; the first had lesbian leanings,[26] the second was a man-hating recluse[27] and the third one of the most notorious *demi-mondaines* of her day.[28] Many others wrote when either unmarried, or in marriages which were atypical. Catherine Trotter, Dorothy Osborne and Mary North gave up creative writing when they 'fell under the government of another',—that is, married.[29] Elizabeth 'Philomela' Singer and Anne Murray both married unusually late in life, as did Mrs Centlivre.[30] Anne Murray wrote only as the dowager Lady Halkett. The marriages of Mrs Pix, Mrs Centlivre and Margaret, Duchess of Newcastle ('Mad Madge'), were virtually all childless. Mary Astell, Elizabeth Elstob, the great Anglo-Saxonist, and Dudleya North were all unmarried.[31] In fact, a significant segment of the women who wrote were in some way or another free from the restraints which would normally have inhibited them from writing at all. Their creativity does not really argue any great freedom of intellectual endeavour for women in seventeenth-century English society. Mrs Evelyn and Dorothy Osborne appear to have had talents equal to or greater than many of them, but, as normally married women, they were forced by custom to eschew the life of the pen and, to a great extent, the life of the mind.

In this context, the contrasting situation of Anne Bradstreet, the only colonial woman to achieve comparable fame, is highly instructive. Her most recent biographer supports the claim that she was 'the first serious English poetess' by arguing that 'much of the passion and determination that went into what she wrote in New England would have been lacking, or largely watered down by the traditional confinements and artificial multiplicity of the kind of life she would have led in the mother country', perhaps better defined as the fatherland. In New England, 'the masculine dependence on women for devotion, encouragement, shared planning and maintenance of the home and community led to a new respect for courage and faithful endurance of the supposedly delicate creatures'. Those who survived the trials of colonial life 'looked at one another as tested human beings, rather than as members of a superior and inferior sex'.[32]

A considerable proportion of the Englishwomen who left a mark on the seventeenth century did so during the Civil War and Interregnum period. They distinguished themselves on both sides of the conflict and came from all classes of society. Some, like Brilliana, Lady Harley, or the Countess of Derby, or the besieged women of Gloucester or Bristol, saw active service.[33] Others like Jane Lane or Anne Murray performed remarkable feats as couriers or agents.[34] Yet others managed their absent husbands' estates, or persistently petitioned the parliamentary committees to salvage family properties. Elizabeth Lilburne was as determined an advocate as was Margaret, Duchess of Newcastle. The voice which cried out loudest against the trial of Charles I was feminine. Many men would have echoed Dr Denton's statement of 1646, 'Women were never soe usefull as now.'[35]

Such activity among Englishwomen was unparalleled before or after the Civil War period. It was largely caused by the sudden unsettling of traditions and the removal of societal, and particularly male, restraints on women's roles. They rose remarkably to an unaccustomed challenge. Some even took the bit between their teeth and actively engaged in religious or political activity on their own account.[36]

In many ways the colonies, especially in the early generations of settlement, provided a similar kind of environment of opportunity and similar challenges. The upsets of migration and change were not psychologically all that unlike the upsets of civil strife and revolution.[37] The great difference was that the English Restoration restored male hegemony, whereas the scenario of challenge was a more permanent feature of American life.

Travellers' Tales

Considering the appalling hazards of transatlantic travel, a large number of people paid visits from America to England, or from England to America.[38] Their comments, plus the impressions of new settlers from the Old World, ought to provide an invaluable basis for making comparisons on the status of women. Unfortunately, very few left any record that has survived; few of those had much to say about women; and several of them were profoundly unreliable.

The two Englishmen with most to say on the subject of American women were John Dunton and Ned Ward. The former was a plagiarist, the latter had never visited North America.[39] The stray comments of men like John Josselyn, or the Labadists Sluyter and Danckaerts, or Francis Nicholson are not to be relied on.[40] Governor Shute opined that women in New England were less grasping and materialistic than his compatriots,[41] William Byrd II assumed that the hysteria of an Englishwoman newly arrived in Virginia was socially acquired rather than organic,[42] and John Barnard found English women shyer in male company than Americans.[43]

This paucity of comment is hardly encouraging. If this was all that people had to say, then the contrast would not seem to have been very striking, hardly worth the extended analysis that follows this introduction.

Yet there are mitigating factors. The first is that transatlantic voyagers only crossed the ocean for very specific purposes. They were, in America, intending settlers or prospectors for groups of intending settlers, returning natives, missionaries, government officials, or sea-captains and traders. Visitors from the colonies to England similarly had specific diplomatic, religious or commercial errands. There are many excellent accounts of ocean-crossings, which cease abruptly on arrival. Once they reached their destinations they were quickly immersed in their business. Samuel Johnson is a good example. This ex-tutor from Yale visited England in 1722 at the age of twenty-six. He kept a journal. We could reasonably expect from someone so able and perceptive all kinds of comments on the English scene. Yet there is nothing. The reason soon becomes clear. Johnson had left the Congregational church; the purpose of his trip was ordination in the Church of England. His departure from New England had been bitter; he was unsure about his reception in England and his future. Small wonder, then, that his journal records in the minutest detail his relations with the dignitaries of his new church, and little else.[44]

Many travellers gravitated to their own kind when abroad. New Englanders mingled with dissenters in London; Quaker missionaries moved from one colonial cell to the next; merchants consorted with merchants; and so on. This would reduce the contrasts to a minimum.[45]

The art of factual social comment was itself in its infancy. General accounts, like those of Josselyn or Beverley,[46] are full of topographical information and abstruse pieces of natural history, but virtually devoid of sociological matter. When William Byrd II returned to Virginia after a four-year absence in London, instead of recording old friends met, old haunts rediscovered and changes remarked, his diary flows on in its accustomed way, noting the petty details of daily life.[47] It would be foolhardy, however, to conclude from this that Westover was the same as the West End of London.

Notes

1 Among the best on England are: Elisabeth Jean Gagen, *The New Woman* (New York, 1954); Maurice Ashley, *The Stuarts in Love* (London, 1963); Wallace Notestein, 'The English Woman 1580–1650' in J. H. Plumb, ed., *Studies in Social History Presented to G. M. Trevelyan* (London, 1955); M. Phillips and W. S. Tomkinson, *English Women in Life and Letters* (Oxford, 1927); Alice Clark, *The Working Life of Women in the Seventeenth Century* (New York, 1920); Louis B. Wright, *Middle-Class Culture in Elizabethan England* (Chapel Hill, 1935); Carl Bridenbaugh, *Vexed and Troubled Englishmen* (New York, 1968); Chilton Latham Powell, *English Domestic Relations 1487–1653* (New York, 1917); Ada Wallas, *Before the Bluestockings* (London, 1929); Myra Reynolds, *The Learned Lady in England 1650–1760* (Boston, 1920); Doris, Lady Stenton, *The English Woman in History* (London, 1957); Patricia M. Higgins, 'Women in the Civil War' (unpub. M.A. thesis, Manchester, 1965). Those on American women in the colonial period include: Julia Cherry Spruill, *Women's Life and Work in the Southern Colonies* (Chapel Hill, 1938); A. W. Calhoun, *A Social History of the American Family* (Boston, 1918); A. B. Hart, ed., *The Commonwealth History of Massachusetts* (Boston, 1928–9) vols I, II; Edmund S. Morgan, *The Puritan Family* (New York, 1966); Eric John Dingwall, *The American Woman in History* (London, 1957); Alice Morse Earle, *Colonial Dames and Goodwives* (Boston, 1895); Edmund S. Morgan, *Virginians at Home* (Chapel Hill, 1952); Annie L. Jester, *Domestic Life in Virginia in the Seventeenth Century* (Jamestown, 1957); Elizabeth A. Dexter, *Colonial Women of Affairs* (Boston, 1924).
2 Bertrand Russell, *In Praise of Idleness* (Harmondsworth, 1960), p. 15;

Therstein Veblen, *The Theory of the Leisure Class* (London, 1925), pp. 71–2, 81–3, 178–82, 352–3.

3 Clark, op. cit., pp. 9, 36, 38, 291–306.

4 C. B. Macpherson, *The Political Theory of Possessive Individualism* (Oxford, 1962), *passim*.

5 Richard B. Schlatter, *The Social Ideas of Religious Leaders 1660–88* (London, 1940), pp. 15–22; Gagen, op. cit., pp. 155ff.; cf. Locke's *Second Treatise*, ch. 7.

6 *Brief Observations Concerning Trade and the Interest of Money* (London, 1665).

7 Richard Baxter, *Christian Directory* (London, 1675), vol. II, pp. 395–8; Roger North, *Lives of the Norths*, ed. Augustus Jessopp (London, 1890), vol. II, p. 15.

8 Wright, op. cit., ch. 13.

9 Gagen, op. cit., *passim*, esp. chs 9, 10.

10 Good introductory narratives are Richard Morton, *Colonial Virginia* (Richmond, Va, 1960), and Wesley Frank Craven, *The Southern Colonies in the Seventeenth Century* (Baton Rouge, 1949).

11 George Langdon, *Pilgrim Colony* (New Haven, 1966); G. Willison, *Saints and Strangers* (New York, 1945).

12 There is a mass of writing on seventeenth-century Massachusetts, much of which will be cited in subsequent chapters. A useful introduction is A. B. Hart, op. cit., vols I, II.

13 Powell, op. cit., *passim*.

14 Thomas H. Johnson, ed., 'Topical Verses of Edward Taylor', Colonial Society of Massachusetts Publications, vol. 34 (1942), p. 537.

15 John Winthrop, *Journal: History of New England*, ed. J. K. Hosmer (New York, 1946), vol. II, p. 225; Morgan, op. cit., p. 44; Edward Johnson, *Wonderworking Providence of Sion's Saviour*, ed. J. F. Jameson (New York, 1937), p. 28.

16 Quoted by Robert E. and B. Katherine Brown, *Virginia 1705–1786: Democracy or Aristocracy?* (East Lansing, 1964), p. 55.

17 Notestein, op. cit., pp. 77–98; Ashley, op. cit., pp. 45ff; Reynolds, op. cit., p. 312.

18 James T. Johnson, 'English Puritan Thought on the Ends of Marriage', *Church History*, vol. 38 (1969), pp. 429–36; Morgan, op. cit., pp. 45–6; Calhoun, op. cit., vol. I, p. 92.

19 Powell, op. cit., pp. 196ff.

20 Wright, op. cit., p. 496.

21 Mary Astell, *Reflections on Marriage* (London, 1706), preface; Lady Winchilsea, quoted in Reynolds, op. cit., p. 154.

22 Samuel Rowlands, *An Apologie for Women*, quoted by Wright, op. cit., p. 499.

23 Alistair Cooke, *Talking About America* (New York, 1969), p. 130; the epitaph is on Mary Randolph Keith, buried at Washington, Kentucky. She was the mother of Chief Justice John Marshall.

24 Cotton Mather, *Ornaments for the Daughters of Zion* (Boston, 1691); Benjamin Wadsworth, *The Well-Ordered Family* (Boston, 1712); Jonathan Mitchell, *Nehemiah on the Wall in Troublesome Times* (Boston, 1671), esp. p. 6; Ebenezer Turell, *Life and Character of Dr. Benjamin Colman* (Boston, 1749). The phrase is John Cotton's.

25 Elizabeth Wade White, 'The Tenth Muse', *William and Mary Quarterly*, Third Series (hereafter *3 WMQ*), vol. VIII (1951), pp. 355ff.

26 See her 'Orinda to Lucasia Parting'. She had no children for ten years after the death of her first-born. I owe these points to Professor John Broadbent.

27 Reynolds, op. cit., p. 304; Wallas, op. cit., ch. 4.
28 Gwendolyn B. Needham, 'Mrs Manley—Eighteenth Century Wife of Bath', *Huntington Library Quarterly*, vol. XIV (1950-1), pp. 271-83.
29 Reynolds, op. cit., pp. 109, 60.
30 *D.N.B.*
31 Wallas, op. cit., chs 4, 5; *D.N.B. sub* William North.
32 White, op. cit., p. 375.
33 Higgins, op. cit., *passim*.
34 R. L. Ollard, *Escape of Charles II after the Battle of Worcester* (London, 1966), pp. 58-70, 80-93; Stenton, op. cit., pp. 160-1.
35 Higgins, op. cit., p. 187.
36 Ibid., *passim*; Keith Thomas, 'Women and the Civil War Sects' in Trevor Aston, ed., *Crisis in Europe 1560-1660* (London, 1965).
37 Bernard Bailyn, *Education in the Forming of American Society* (Chapel Hill, 1960), p. 21.
38 W. L. Sachse, *Colonial Americans in England* (Madison, 1956).
39 John B. Nichols, ed., *Life and Errors* (London, 1818), pp. 89ff.; *John Dunton's Letters from New England*, ed. W. H. Whitmore (Boston, 1867); the full extent of the plagiarism was uncovered by Chester N. Greenough, 'John Dunton's Letters from New England', Colonial Society of Massachusetts Publications, vol. XIV (1912), pp. 221ff.; the originals are in the Bodleian, Rawlinson MSS, Misc. 71, 72. Ward's *A Trip to New England* (London, 1699) along with J.W.'s *Letter from New England* is in George P. Winship, ed., *In Boston in 1682 and 1699* (Providence, 1905). See Howard W. Troyer, *Ned Ward of Grub Street* (Cambridge, Mass., 1946).
40 John Josselyn, *An Account of Two Voyages to New England Made during the Years 1638 and 1663* (London, 1674), in Massachusetts Historical Society Collections (hereafter Mass. Hist. Soc. Colls) Third Series, vol. III (1833); on his bias, see Fulmer Mood in *Dictionary of American Biography* (*D.A.B.*). Peter Sluyter and Jasper Danckaerts were prospecting for a Labadist settlement in the New World; they were strongly anti-English. *Journal*, ed. and trans. Henry C. Murphy (Brooklyn, 1867). On Nicholson's comments, see Fairfax Downey, 'The Governor Goes A-Wooing', *Virginia Magazine of History and Biography* (hereafter *Va Mag.*), vol. 55 (1947), p. 16.
41 When the diarist Samuel Sewall was moaning about the demands of Massachusetts women, he said sourly 'New England brooks its name', to which Shute replied 'they are not quite so bad here'. Samuel Sewall, *Diary*, in Mass. Hist. Soc. Colls, Fifth Series, vols V-VII (hereafter Sewall, *Diary*, vols I-III), vol. III, p. 270.
42 Louis B. Wright, ed., *The Secret Diary of William Byrd of Westover 1709-12* (hereafter *Westover Diary*) (Richmond, Va, 1941), p. 322.
43 Mass. Hist. Soc. Colls, Third Series, vol. V (1836), pp. 203-4, 199. Barnard's visit was in 1709.
44 E. Edwards Beardsley, *Life and Correspondence of Samuel Johnson* (New York, 1874), pp. 18-53.
45 E.g. Barnard stayed with Calamy in London; Dunton was a nonconformist sympathiser. Farmer and Woolman moved from Quaker household to Quaker household.
46 Robert Beverley, *History and Present State of Virginia* (originally published, London, 1705; ed. Louis B. Wright, Chapel Hill, 1947).
47 Louis B. Wright and Marion Tinling, eds, *William Byrd of Virginia: The London Diary and Other Writings* (New York, 1958), *sub* 1719; hereafter *London Diary*.

Part II

A New World

In this section we turn to some of the factors which, prima facie, might be expected to have contributed to differences in attitudes and opportunities, and to have made the American environment more fertile ground for women to achieve greater personal freedom and higher social esteem. In some instances they are peculiar to one colony. They usually vary in effectiveness between different colonies, between different areas of colonies, or between different generations. None the less, as a whole, they do combine to make a strong causal case. In the final section of the book this case will be tested against various contrasts in the social *mores* of the English and American cultures.

Chapter 2
The Sex Ratio

The ratio between the sexes in any population is often expressed as the number of males per hundred females. Thus 'the normal sex ratio of live births of 105·5' means that for every hundred girls that are born live, there are 105·5 boys. When the sex ratio is described in this chapter as being high, this means that there is an excess of males over females, and vice versa.

All things being equal, nature has so ordered the statistics of male and female births that there will be a balance between the sexes. The slight imbalance in live births should normally be ironed out by the slightly greater vulnerability of male children. The slightly longer expectation of life among women should similarly be balanced by the women victims of childbirth. Unfortunately, however, all things are all too rarely equal. Wars, for instance, usually take a far greater toll of men, as do industrial accidents. After the First World War there was, in all the major combatant countries, a large surplus of widows and marriageable women. Where there is large-scale geographical mobility affecting one sex more than the other, a similar imbalance will be created. This is true of both the place of origin and the destination of migrants. Large numbers of young men left New England for the West in the early nineteenth century. There was thus created a high sex ratio in the West, and a low one in the New England states. The same is true of the modern movement away from the country to the cities. In contemporary America the tendency of more women than men to migrate to the urban areas has produced a low sex ratio there, and a high one in country districts.[1] In certain agricultural areas of the United States, there are townships where there are virtually no marriageable women and large numbers of bachelors.

Where the *mores* of a society encourage males to lead a fast or furious life, drinking excessively, duelling or risking their lives to prove their manhood, the sex ratio may well be low. It is, moreover, not always enough to talk about the sex ratio as a generality. The total ratio may appear to be balanced in a society, but the figure of 100 may conceal grave imbalances in different age groups

—a large number of aged widows, for instance, offsetting statistically, but not satisfying romantically, a surplus of marriageable bachelors. Generally speaking, 'the older a population group, the lower its sex ratio'.[2] J. Hajnal has pointed out other causes affecting the sex ratio. If there is a large difference in the ages at which men and women customarily marry, he argues, then the younger sex (almost always women) will stand less chance of finding a partner because more of the older sex will have died. Again, in a rapidly expanding population, where men tend to marry at a later age than women, the latter will again have less chance of marrying, because the birthrate when they were born would be greater than it was at the earlier time when the (older) men were born.[3]

What particularly concerns us in this chapter—once the evidence for the imbalance of the sex ratio has been presented—is the effects that such a disproportion might have, especially on the position of women in society. In *The Growth of Cities in the Nineteenth Century*, A. F. Weber wrote: 'All social life is affected by the proportions of the sexes. Wherever there exists a considerable predominance of one sex over the other, in point of numbers, there is less prospect of a well ordered social life.' Hans von Hentig put it more bluntly: 'Unbalanced numbers inexorably produce unbalanced behaviour.'[4] The sort of effects that sociologists expect of societies with a low sex ratio—that is, an excess of women—are listed by Greenberg: an upthrust of extreme patterns of feminism, emphasis on careers for women, the creation of women's organisations and pressure groups, higher divorce rates and love triangles, new folkways bearing on family philosophies, concubinage, lesbianism, polygyny and an increase in extra-marital sexuality (to which might be added a growth in prostitution in certain underdeveloped urban communities). There seems also some evidence to suggest that crime-rates are higher where there is a low sex ratio. It is also argued that, in ages of faith, an excess of women may lead to the growth of mysticism and quietist religious sects, as well as more extravagant offshoots which advocate polygyny under the cover of religious sanction.[5] What we should expect to find, in short, in a society with a low sex ratio is a general undervaluing of women, exploitation of the weaker sex by men, and various expedients on the part of the oppressed sex to escape their fate and give their lives some kind of meaning and justification. Greenberg makes one other important point: 'Women's behavioural characteristics are more closely related to sex ratio and exhibit greater variation with this phenomenon than do men's.'[6]

Where there is a surplus of males, however, a quite different set of characteristics is to be expected, even though man's behaviour will be less drastically affected by a shortage of women. The amount of change in a community will obviously depend on how great the shortage of women is—it is commoner to have male groups almost completely devoid of females than vice versa. The all-male society is exemplified by the mining-camp or the cow-town of the nineteenth-century West, graphically described by Edward Allsworth Ross:[7]

> In the male community law is weak, public opinion scarcely exists, and each does what is right in his own eyes, save insofar as he is checked by respect for the other man's gun. Life—one's own as well as another's—is held cheap, and is staked on small issues. Suicide is often frequent, because 'nobody cares'. The daredevil spirit prevails. Men resort gleefully to a saloon which calls itself 'The Bucket of Blood'. Few pay any attention to religion. It used to be said in the North-west, 'No Sunday west of Bismarck and west of Miles City no God'. Everyone thinks of making his 'pile' and getting away. There will be time enough then, he thinks, to look after his soul.

The only woman in this extreme kind of unbalanced society is the prostitute or the masculine Annie Oakley type. Where, however, there is a reasonable number of women, though in an overall minority, we could expect this nasty, brutish and short existence to be considerably modified. The violence, the excess and the rawness of life would likely be replaced by a desire for permanent settlement, for calm, for respectability and steady prosperity rather than a quick 'killing'. Uncouth and unkempt males would put away their guns and their decks of cards and use instead their combs and spongebags in order to attract not molls but wives. The saloon or the tavern loses custom as the lure of a home, of security and comfort rises as a counter-attraction. Men could be expected to treat women with great respect and forbearance, being aware of their own weak bargaining power. Within the family, women could expect a greater sense of equality in the making of decisions and the control of finances and the upbringing of children. The unlucky or unattractive men might have to resign themselves to a life of bachelorhood, but a far more respectable bachelorhood than in the all-male society. Some might be driven to perversions by their plight, to sodomy or buggery, to miscegenation, or to rape or pederasty. Others might adopt different creative channels, or might just leave in search of wives in a more promising area. For women, on the other hand, life, though it might be materially hard, would hold many attractions. Not only would marriage be easy to achieve, but the marriageable girl could reasonably expect to be able to choose among rivals, and to make conditions before accepting. She might well be freer of parental restraints on her choice of partner, and could hope to rise socially through marriage. Widows could likewise expect to find themselves courted, and the poor or ugly or simple girl would have a chance. Older women might even hope to break the social taboo against marrying younger men, and the 'fallen' woman would not necessarily be irredeemably lost where male beggars could not be choosers. The age at which girls married might be assumed to decrease as the demand for wives exerted itself on the market.[8]

We have been discussing imbalances between the sexes and their social results in very general terms. The question remains: 'How rare' or 'How superfluous.' At what sort of point on the scale of imbalance does the sex ratio become an effective factor? So far as I know, this is not a question which demographers or social scientists have been eager to grapple with, for the reasons that the sex ratio is only one in a complex set of factors in any given situation, and that data are often faulty or incomplete.

One way to attempt a rough answer to this important problem would be to take examples of societies in which female or male behaviour was somehow apparently abnormal, and try to correlate this with the sex ratio. In four such situations of apparent female aberration from conventional behaviour, namely the spiritual wife and polygamy movements connected with the Burned-over District in the 1830s, the 'redundant woman' problem of Victorian England in the 1860s, female participation in New England abolitionism in the 1830s, and the flapper phenomenon of the English 1920s, the sex ratio of marriageables ranged from 86 to 94. From my very cursory study, it would appear that the sex ratio has only to be quite slightly low before contributing towards 'imbalanced' behaviour.[9]

Aberrant male behaviour, by contrast, would appear to occur only in situations of severe imbalance, when the sex ratio exceeded the 200 mark. Where the ratio was only slightly high, that is between 100 and 125, as, for instance, in post-famine Ireland, nineteenth-century China, or Utah in 1850, then the abnormalities in masculine behaviour would be hardly noticeable, and female emancipation commensurately slight.[10] I advance these suggestions in the most tentative way, because firm conclusions would require far deeper examination than I have been able to give. They are at least worth bearing in mind as we consider the sex ratio in England and the colonies, and the effects that may have resulted from a disproportion between the sexes.

Massachusetts and Virginia

The men of the seventeenth century who were charged with enumerating the population at intermittent intervals did not, unfortunately, have an eye to the future. When the population of England at the end of the century is still a matter of controversy, we must plainly approach the question of the sex ratio with great caution.

It would be reasonable to expect the sex ratio in the colonies to be high, except in areas which were not subject to continuing influxes of mainly male migrants from Europe. Here, after the initial wave of settlers, the natural sex ratio would gradually take over, creating a balance or near balance, provided of course that there was no internal migration to unbalance the sexes locally. Such places would be pretty rare, though some of the New England colonies approach nearest to this kind of society.

What would be more usual, however, would be for the far larger numbers of male migrants coming into the colonies to be constantly unbalancing the ratio, constantly placing what women there were in the privileged position of rarity. Furthermore, we could expect those males who arrived in the colonies to be young and of marriageable age. It has been normal throughout history for this group to predominate in large-scale population movements, and the evidence of the great surge to the West in nineteenth-century America certainly bears this out.[11]

Fortunately, some very acute pioneering work on the colonial sex ratio has been done by Herbert Moller, whose essay 'Sex Composition and Correlated Culture Patterns in Colonial America' appeared in 1945.[12] In this section we shall follow his work closely. Moller's main tool in attempting to compute the sex ratio in the colonies is the surviving passenger lists of ships carrying settlers to the New World. These he treats as a representative sample from which to deduce the sex ratio as a whole. It is, of course, very difficult to prove that the lists are indeed representative, and impossible to assess that demographer's nightmare, omissions.[13]

An initial disparity between Virginia and Massachusetts arose from the fact that the former was settled by an overwhelmingly male first wave, whereas the great migration to Massachusetts Bay from 1629 to 1640 was far more a movement of whole families. Therefore in the first generation in the Chesapeake colony the sex ratio was alarmingly high, much like the Wild West of 250 years later.[14] Sir William Berkeley accounted for the slow growth of the colony on these grounds: 'Of those that came, there was not one woman to thirty men, and *populus virorum* is of no long duration anywhere.'[15] A generation later Robert Beverley made a similar point in his *History and Present State of Virginia*: 'Those that went over to that country first, were chiefly single men, who had not the incumbrance of wives and children in England.'[16] The Virginia Company in London tried to amend this situation by sending consignments of maids—140 in all—'an extraordinary choice lot' in 1620 and 1621.[17]

This shortage is borne out by the remarks of the authors of promotional tracts. Richard Eburne's *A Plain Pathway to Plantations*, published in London in 1624, contains a long discussion between the proponent of emigration, Enrubie, and an objector, Respire, on the subject 'women are unwilling to go'. Respire, who loses every argument with monotonous regularity, argues that 'My wife will not hear to go anywhither beyond sea, and therefore for her sake, though I were willing myself, I must be content to abide at home.' The anagrammatical promoter brings out his heavy artillery to counter this attack, firing off five reasons against the enemy, including biblical and historical exemplars who upped sticks for new parts.[18] The needs of early Virginia had permeated to the seamier quarters of English society. A letter from Sir Edward Hexter, a Somerset J.P., to the Privy Council, dated 19 October 1618, recounts the activities of one Owen Evans, who, 'under cover of being a messenger of the Chamber' had ordered the constable to press five maidens for Virginia in the hundred of Whiteleighe, had given 5/– to another to press six maidens, 1/– to Jacob Pryste to press his own daughter, and had received 10/– protection money from Ottery to keep away. Such was the terror that 'forty maidens fled out of one parish'.[19]

Despite all these enterprising efforts, by 1624–5 the inhabitants of Virginia, discounting 107 children, consisted of 873 white males and only 222 white females, making a sex ratio of 393.2 or virtually four adult males to every adult female. Women were not spared in the Indian massacres of 1622 and 1644, when, in all, some 850 settlers were killed.[20] Though less spectacular, the ravages of plague were, in the early 1620s, far more disastrous to population growth. There is, however, little reason to believe that women's immunity was as marked in Virginia as it was in London.[21]

In the 1630s, immigration continued to be male-dominated. Working from lists from twenty ships reaching Virginia between 1634 and 1635[22] Moller arrived at a migrants' sex ratio of 603.7 for those over sixteen years of age, and 613.5 for those under sixteen. He argues that the majority of boys under sixteen would probably be from thirteen to fifteen years old, that is, about to swell the demand for wives. Working on the figures for emigration from Bristol between 1654 and 1686[23] he arrives at a sex ratio of immigrants into Virginia of 308.3. The same sort of story emerges from

Hotten's figures of the exodus from Barbados to North America.[24] Between 1678 and 1679, 523 men left the island, compared with a mere 60 women.

These figures are highly suggestive. However, statistically Moller's article is largely concerned with the sex ratio of immigrants, rather than that of the total population within each colony.

The sources needed to arrive at any reliable and usable computation of the sex ratio at a given time are either listings of inhabitants, preferably giving ages and marital status, or censuses which differentiate inhabitants by age—or age-group—and sex. So far as I have been able to discover, neither exists for seventeenth-century Virginia, even on a local scale. This makes the checking of Moller's hypothesis extremely difficult. All we have to go on at the moment are crude and sometimes contradictory figures.

Estimates of the population of Virginia in 1665 place the total white population in the region of 38,000. Of these, 15,000 are men who can be mustered, that is, over sixteen years of age. Of this group, 5,000 are masters, and 10,000 servants. This leaves a total of some 23,000 women and children. If the total number of women over the age of sixteen was equal to that of the men, i.e. a sex ratio of 100, this would leave only 8,000 children under sixteen, which, from what we know of the colonial population, seems far too low. If, however, there were twice as many adult males as females, this would produce a figure of 15,500 for children under sixteen. Some demographers compute colonial population figures on the basis that the numbers under sixteen are roughly equal those over sixteen, and if this were true for mid-century Virginia, then even the sex ratio of 200 would be too low, and something like 4,000 women to 15,000 men, a sex ratio of 375, would be nearer the mark. If the sex ratio were 200 or above, as seems highly likely, the indentured servants in the colony, the great majority of whom would be recent immigrants of marriageable or near-marriageable age, could be expected to form the major part of the adult population, and thus to have very marked effects upon the sex ratio in the most sensitive age-range.[25]

The 1665 figures may be less reliable than some given by Governor Berkeley in 1671. He estimated that there were '6,000 Christian servants for a short time' (presumably indentured servants or redemptioners) in a total white population of 38,000. If the free white population was equally distributed in the over- and under-sixteen age groups, and if the sex ratio of free white adults was 100, then, if the great majority of servants, say 5,000, were male, the overall adult sex ratio would be 144, that is, 13,000 men to 9,000 women. The chances are, of course, that the free adult sex ratio was well above the hundred figure.[26]

A similar crude computation is possible for the year 1702, when, according to a census,[27] there were 25,000 tithables out of a total population of about 60,500 in Virginia. Tithables were males over sixteen and all negroes, and the nearest estimate for the latter is around 7,000. If two-thirds of the remaining 35,500 of the population were under sixteen, which is probably too low an estimate, then there would still be 18,000 adult white males to under 12,000 females, a sex ratio of 150. If the white population over sixteen was equal to the white population under sixteen, i.e. 26,250 each, then the number of adult females would have to be dropped to 8,250, or a sex ratio of 218.

To come to any acceptable conclusion about the sex ratio of the colony, it is obviously vital to establish the relationship between the rate of immigration into the colony and the indigenous natural increase. The former pressure would tend to tip the scales into a male-surplus, female-rarity angle, while the latter would steady them into a position of balance.

As we have seen, one way of discovering an immigration rate in seventeenth-century Virginia is through the destinations given by those who left England as indentured servants. This has been tried with great skill and pertinacity by Abbot Emerson Smith in his *Colonists in Bondage*.[28] Only Bristol has records over a long enough period—thirty-two years—to arrive at any very reliable average, and, even here, there is the possibility of under-recording. The annual average emigration to Virginia from 25 September 1654 to 12 June 1686, according to the Bristol Tolzey Book, is about 152. Smith estimates that the probable emigration to Virginia from London and its environs in the year 1 September 1683 to 31 August 1684, was around 250, but there is no way of telling how typical this figure is. Finally, from Liverpool emigration figures from 1698 to 1700, if the proportion of those destined for Virginia was similar to Bristol's, there would have been an annual total of around 90. If these annual figures are accurate and typical—and this is, of course a very big if—then the three major 'exporting ports' of England were sending something approaching 500 migrants each year to Virginia. Smith advances reasons for suspecting that these figures would tend to be on the low side.[29] First, he argues, 'during the seventeenth century, the largest movement of servants to the colonies was in the period just before and after the Restoration'.[30] Second, he claims that 'after about 1689 there was a great falling off in migration from Britain'. The first 'boom' would not, of course, be reflected in either the London or Liverpool figures, but the latter might well be much lower than they would have been a generation earlier. Our notional total of around 500 per annum does not take into account under-recording at Bristol;

migrants from other ports; those who did not go through the formal channels; or migrant servants from other countries or other colonies. It is perfectly feasible that, taking these considerations in mind, the average annual arrival-rate of servants in Virginia for much of the seventeenth century might have been 750 or even a thousand, of whom 600 to 750 would have been male, and even this would not include those single men who migrated at their own expense.[31]

If we assume a birth rate of forty per thousand per annum, which is almost certainly too high because of the shortage of women of child-bearing age, then annual births, the great equalising factor, would be under 1,000 in the 1660s and around 1,337 at the start of the eighteenth century. In other words, the increase in the number of girls would be almost totally offset by the persistence of a largely male-dominated immigration from outside the colony.[32]

It seems, then, reasonable to conclude that, within the estimated total population of Virginia of around 60,000 in 1702, there was a very considerable surplus of males, or as Defoe put it, 'Virginia did not yield any great plenty of wives.'[33]

The situation in Massachusetts was less spectacular partly because the initial great migration of around 16,000 was largely familial, and partly because succeeding movement to the colony was markedly smaller. None the less, Moller shows that in the early years, 1620–38—including Plymouth—from a sample of 17 per cent of all migrants, taken from the lists of forty-six ships collected by Banks, the sex ratio was 157·2, or three men to every two women arrivals. It is conceivable that this initial shortage of women may have had more permanent effects on New England's social *mores*. The more reliable sources at the end of our period agree that there were comparatively few indentured servants in Massachusetts.[34] The Bristol figures of indentured servants bound for Massachusetts between 1654 and 1686 show a predictably lower figure than Virginia—165 compared with 4,924—but the sex ratio of these migrants is 650·5, or 143 males to 22 females.[35]

The figures available for Massachusetts highlight the effects of internal migration within the colony. By the end of the century there is little doubt that there was actually a surplus of women in the larger towns of the colony, especially in Boston.[36] On the other hand, the regions nearer to the frontier, to which more single young men would likely be attracted than women, seem to have persisted in having a high ratio. The urban surplus is reflected in various satirical newspaper items. In the *Boston Gazette* for 16 May 1734, there appeared a letter from 'Amorous Bridegroom', writing on 9 August 1734, from 'Hymen's Castle', commenting on a scheme to dispose of unmarried British virgins by lottery that had appeared earlier that year in the *Boston Evening Post* (16 May): 'Such a scheme would be of no less advantage to this part of the world,' he wrote, 'since the circumstances of our young Women, in point of Marriage, do unhappily resemble those of Great Britain.' He refers later to 'a declining condition (especially in the Metropolis) in this respect'.[37]

Other factors at the end of the seventeenth century may have helped to exacerbate this situation in the more established parts of the colony. A. W. Calhoun reports that some 600 men died in King Philip's War (1675–6).[38] This may have been as much as a tenth of the total adult male population of the colony, and an even larger proportion of those of marriageable age. Secondly, the coast towns would contain a significant proportion of men engaged in abnormally hazardous occupations, like seamen, fishermen or whalers. Such vocations might furthermore tend to encourage roving, prolonged absence, or permanent desertion.

What population figures we have for Massachusetts in the 1690s tend to support the contention that the overall sex ratio would be around the 100 mark. The generally accepted figures for this decade give a total population of between 40,000 and 50,000, with a militia of about 10,000 men. If there were a similar 10,000 women between the ages of sixteen and sixty, this would leave a residue of children and the aged of about 25,000, the sort of total we should theoretically expect.[39] Such a balanced ratio would not, however, rule out an imbalance within different areas of the colony.

In general terms, then, we can accept the tentative conclusion that Moller arrives at, namely that, apart from the relatively few urban areas, more than three men to every two women were unmarried, but of marriageable age, throughout the colonies. This ratio was probably higher in some areas, and there is every likelihood that Virginia was one of these areas. In the eighteenth century, which was relatively worse for women than the seventeenth, 'the chances of marriage and remarriage among women were much better' than among men, 'a considerable number' of whom would 'have to forego marriage altogether'.

By the time that the first extant 'enumeration' was made in Massachusetts in 1764 and early 1765 this internal imbalance was clearly visible.[40] The sex ratio for the colony as a whole is 96·8, compared with 96·0 in the first federal census of 1790. The counties of greatest female surplus, however, are the three eastern ones of Suffolk, Essex and Middlesex. Boston had 7,622 white females to only 7,050 males. In the western counties, however, although population is obviously much thinner, the males predominate. Great Barrington, in the Berkshire Hills, had 276 men to 255 females; a similar male surplus is found in Cumberland and Lincoln counties.

The position of women may not have been anything like so desperate as these crude figures for the more settled regions suggest. The life expectancy of women seems to have been higher.[41] As early as 1698, Boston was described as being 'full of widows and orphans, and many of them helpless creatures'. Cotton Mather declared that one-sixth of the communicants at his church were widows.[42] The breakdown of the 1764 figures for Boston bears this out; though women over sixteen outnumber men 3,612 to 2,941, the figures for under sixteen are 4,010 to 4,109, a male surplus of 99. Computing the sex ratio of the marriageable, rather than the total, population from a New Hampshire census of 1767, Moller arrived at a ratio of three men to two women, which is more meaningful when we discuss the social effects of the sex ratio, than the overall New Hampshire figure of 102·1.[43]

England

If we are right in assuming that the sex ratio in the colonies in the seventeenth century was abnormally high, we might reasonably expect that the ratio in the supplying country would be correspondingly low. If England conformed to the normal pattern, we would further expect that the sex ratio would be lowest in the cities, somewhat higher in the rural areas.

The most reliable figures on English population that have survived are those presented by Gregory King in his *Natural and Politicall Observations and Conclusions upon the State and Condition of England*.[44] King concluded from his work on the enumerations that were made for the so-called Marriage Act of 1694 (6–7 W. & M., c. 6.) that the sex ratio in London was ten men to every thirteen women, a sex ratio of 77; in 'other cities and market towns' it was eight men to every nine women or 88, and that in villages and hamlets—which according to Glass would be his most unreliable material—100 men to 99 women or 101. In total numbers, King calculated that there were 2·8 million women in England to 2·7 men.[45] What this figure hides, however, is that the number of males under sixteen is in fact in excess of the number of females by 1,122,000 to 1,118,000. This makes a sex ratio of 94·8 for those over sixteen, compared with the total sex ratio of 99·4.

King himself had some interesting comments on the apparent anomaly that, though more male children than female were born, the overall sex ratio was low. This point had been raised by Harley in a letter querying statements in the *Observations*. 'To the Age of 16 the males exceed the Females', he wrote, '& after the Females exceed ye Males.' 'Are adult Females more durable than Males? The Accidents from Childbearing is after 16 generally.' King replied:[46]

> Upon a serious consideration I have adventured to state it (the sex ratio of births) at . . . 14 Males to 13 Female Births or thereabouts; accordingly in 190,000 annual Births, there should be 98,500 males, & 91,500 Females, vizt. A Surplus of 7000 males which number is not much more than equal to the males carried off extraordinary by wars, the Sea, & the Plantations, in wch Articles the Females are very little concern'd. On the other side the numbers of co-existing Males is less than the Females in general by 1 in 28. or rather 2 in 28, as I have since more carefully collected them from the Assessm^{ts}. on Marriages Births & Buryalls . . . The Accident of dying in Childbed strictly speaking Grant[47] states but 1 in 200. So that it signifies little to the many occasions wch. expose the lives of the males, beyond that of the Females, even from 3 or 4 years old to the end of their days, wch. We may estimate at abt. 9 in 200.

Glass has also analysed some of the detailed figures for the Marriage Act enumeration for London within the walls. Taking a sample of forty out of the ninety-seven parish returns, he comes to a grand total of 15,262 women to 13,236 men, a sex ratio of 87. Within this total were 9,915 single women to 8,571 single men—including children—and 4,418 married women to 4,392 married men. Widows outnumbered widowers to the tune of 929 to 273.[48] In the seven richest parishes of his sample Glass found that the sex ratio had risen to 97, mainly because of a larger number of male servants and apprentices.[49]

This situation in the capital is certainly corroborated by Defoe, who knew his London well. One of the major reasons that the ingenuous Moll Flanders gives for her various amorous plights is the alarming shortage of men in London. 'The market is against our sex just now,' says a gentlewoman, 'the men play the game all into their own hands.'[50]

How far this surplus of women in the capital existed earlier in the century it is difficult with any accuracy to say. John Graunt's 'Table of Males, and Females, for London' gives the total of male and female burials and christenings for each year from 1629 to 1664. Male burials outnumber female by 235,246 to 214,658 and christenings by 156,750 to 146,231.[51] E. A. Wrigley has shown that the population of the city was growing extremely rapidly throughout the century, from around 200,000 in 1600, to around 400,000 in 1650, to something like 575,000 in 1700.[52]

This rise was brought about by immigration into the city rather than by natural increase. If modern behaviour is anything to go by, there may well have been more female immigrants into London than male. The stereotype of the innocent country girl arriving in a centre of vice, made immortal by Hogarth in *The Harlot's Progress*, was already well established in drama by the end of the century.[53] In real life we know of several examples of girls like Joan Martindale who took it into their heads that life would be better in London and, despite opposition, made the break from the country. Joan travelled down from Yorkshire shortly after the Restoration, and was so poor after the plague that she contemplated selling her hair.[54] Louis B. Wright cites a mid-century ballad called 'The Wiving Age' which suggests that the man-shortage went back that far. It is subtitled 'A great complaint of the Maidens of London, who now for lacke of good Husbands are undone.'[55]

One factor which may have reduced the number of men in the capital in the first two-thirds of the seventeenth century was their greater vulnerability to the plague. According to Francis Hering, six or ten men died for every woman in the epidemic of 1603.[56] A recent study of one city parish bears out the assertion that the plague was a grimmer reaper for men than women. In St Botolph's without Bishopsgate, the sex ratio of adult burials was 200 in 1603 and 190 in 1625, compared with an average of 114·7 for the non-epidemic years from 1580 to 1605.[57] There is reason to believe that 'women outnumbered men substantially in St. Botolph's', in which case 'the true relative plague mortality' would be greater than the bald sex-ratio figures suggest. The reasons for the harsher victimisation of men remain somewhat speculative. The Hollingsworths suggest that 'women were (largely by accident) much less liable to attack from the bacillus by way of the flea or rat, because of greater cleanliness of person and dress, and because they did not go near places where most rats were to be found as frequently as did men'. If their findings are generally valid, as seems likely, then the effects of plague would be profound on the sexual balance of the population throughout the earlier part of the century, for, in the great outbreaks of 1603, 1625, 1636 and 1665, something in the region of a sixth of the total population of the metropolis was destroyed. If two or more men died for every woman when the total London death-rate ran at figures like 35,104, 41,313, 10,400 and 68,596, then there would be a very marked shortage of marriageable males. Not only this, but plague was hardly ever completely absent from London life; in the relatively quiescent years of 1606 to 1610, the annual plague mortalities were 2,124, 2,352, 2,262, 4,240 and 1,803. London was only the top of the plague league because of its uniquely vast size. The other cities and towns of England were also prone to the epidemic, and proportionately their populations sometimes suffered even worse than the capital's.[58]

Some other apparently reliable data on other towns has been discovered among King's papers and elsewhere by Glass. The Marriage Act enumeration for Bristol in the Bristol Archives Department shows that out of a total population count of 19,403 there were 10,625 females to 8,519 males, though in a seaport the apparent sex ratio might be higher because of male absence or death at sea. If we divide the unspecified 259 entries equally, these figures produce a sex ratio for 1695 of 80·4.[59] The fullest and most famous figures are from Lichfield, which was King's own home town, where the enumeration was carried out by a Mr Lamb under King's supervision. Glass quotes a letter of King's to Lamb dated 12 August 1695. Talking of apparent discrepancies in the number of males, he writes:[60]

> From 16 years they decrease to 6 of 22 (years old) and but 2 of 23 years, So that London for Apprentices, Gentlemens Services and ye wars seems to drain them of males those years for very few could be married before 23 years old (note that this acco[t] is all along of Bachelors). . . . I observed there are 1280 Males and 1560 Females, vizt. 280 Females more than males in these 3 Articles.

$$\left.\begin{array}{l}\text{50 Widowers}\\\text{190 Widows}\end{array}\right\}\text{diff. } 140 \quad \left.\begin{array}{l}\text{580 sons}\\\text{680 daurs}\end{array}\right\}\text{diff. } 100 \quad \left.\begin{array}{l}\text{Menservts 100}\\\text{Maids 140}\end{array}\right\}\text{diff. } 40$$

> Which seemed to be occasioned (1) by ye Women overliving the men: 2 more widows resort to great Towns for Conveniency of Living: 3[dly] Widowers oftener marry again Widows; 4 The Wars draw many Husbands away where they are slayn before their ordinary time. As to the Surplus of Daurs., London, Gentl. Services, & ye Wars drain ye males. As to Maid Servts All great Towns require more than Men Servts, ye Country otherwise

King's statistics for Lichfield give a sex ratio of 83·3. As Stone noted, 31 per cent of all women in the fertile age-group between the ages of twenty-five and forty-four were either widows or spinsters.[61]

A recent survey of seventy communities for the years 1574 to 1821 produces a sex ratio for the whole period of 91·3.[62] In Clayworth in 1676 there were twenty-four widows, compared with only seven widowers, though the eighteen bachelors exceeded the spinsters by two. Ealing in 1599 had 229 males to 197 females. The numbers under sixteen were ninety-one and sixty-eight respectively, leaving those over at 138 men to 129 women. Bearing in mind the greater longevity of widows, this might well have meant a low sex ratio for marriageables, which would conform with King's suggestions to Harley.[63]

Another study of a total of twenty-two parishes between 1688 and 1699, with a total population of 14,456, arrives at an overall sex ratio of 88·5. The ratio for nine London parishes and three provincial parishes with population over 1,000 is 87·5. The overall sex ratios for children, servants and single people are 83·1, 89·1 and 94·0 respectively. The last includes widows and widowers as well as the unmarried. The sex ratio of servants in twenty-two Kentish parishes in 1705 is 226, 448 menservants to 199 women. The servant sex ratio in Stoke-on-Trent in 1701, however, is only 59·7, thirty-seven males to sixty-two females.[64] It is possible that the very high Kentish figure was caused by the migration of young girls to nearby London. The low figure for Stoke may have been more typical of the provinces. The sex ratio for five Southampton parishes at the end of the century, a fairly full return for what was then a declining seaport of some 3,000 people, was 79·9.[65] Until we have more data it is foolhardy to generalise.

A hundred and twenty-six local censuses are known to have survived from the eighteenth century. Twenty-eight give details about sexes: twenty-six of them show a female preponderance. The twenty urban censuses show a sex ratio varying between 77 and 91; six of the eight rural ones vary between 95 and 98; and two show a slight male preponderance.[66] This accords with the broader trend. 'It is probable that in eighteenth-century Europe . . . the ratio of male to female population at the prime marriageable ages . . . was much less favourable to women's chances of marriage than in many non-Western populations.' It seems likely that this situation was also the rule for the preceding century.[67]

What the small and patchy information that we have cited in this chapter seems to say is that the sex ratio in England was low, especially in urban areas, throughout the century. The major causes of this surplus of women seem to have been man's greater vulnerability, and emigration to the colonies.[68] The greater longevity of women probably makes the ratio of marriageable women even lower than the totals suggest, and created a surplus pool even in rural areas.

Supporting Evidence—The Colonies

If the sex ratio in the colonies was indeed high, we should expect to find evidence in social practices to support this, like ease of marriage for girls and remarriage for widows, upward social mobility for women and a proportional reduction of male arrogance.

There is little doubt that marriage was a great deal easier to come by for girls in the New World than in the Old. The demand for wives, as we have seen, was strongest in the early years. In 1619 the newly-created House of Burgesses in Virginia, petitioning for grants of land for women along with their husbands, declared: 'in a newe plantation it is not knowen whether man or woman be the most necessary'.[69] The fortunes of the maids sent out by the Virginia Company is also instructive. By 1622 all of them were married, even though they cost their wooers 50 pounds' worth of tobacco, to defray the company's costs in sending them over. As Robert Beverley described the first planters a century later:[70]

When they were Settled, they grew sensible of the Misfortune of wanting Wives. . . . The single men were put to their shifts. . . . They had no hopes but that the plenty in which they lived might invite Modest women of small Fortunes. Those, if they were but moderately qualified in all other respects, might depend upon Marrying very well in those Days, without any Fortune. Nay, the first Planters were so far from expecting Money with a Woman, that it was a common thing for them to buy a deserving Wife at the price of 100 pound, and make themselves believe they had a hopeful Bargain.

There may have been a measure of sour grapes behind Beverley's apparently cynical tone. He himself had been married for only one year to William Byrd II's sister Ursula, who had died in 1698 in childbirth. Why this eligible widower of twenty-five never re-married is not known, but the reason could have been a lack of eligible girls. The same situation existed in Maryland, where George Alsop, admittedly a promoter, drew this tempting picture:[71]

The Women that go over into this Province as Servants, have the best luck here as in any place of the world besides; for they are no sooner on shoar, but they are courted into a Copulative Matrimony, which some of them (for aught I know) had they not come to such a Market with their Virginity, might have kept it by them untill it had been mouldy.

The celebrated case of Mrs Cecily Jordan is an excellent example of the bargaining power of women in the early years of colonisation in Virginia. In 1623, with her first husband hardly cold in the grave, she received advances from the Rev. Greville Pooley. They became engaged, but on the one provision that for decency's sake their rapid betrothal should remain a secret. Pooley could not keep his mouth shut, however, and Mrs Jordan promptly allied herself with another suitor. Pooley failed in a breach of promise suit against her. A year later Eleanor Spragg was ordered to repent before the congregation 'her offence in contracting herself to two several men at one time'. The danger of this kind of man-catching was viewed with such concern by the authorities that they ordered the clergy to announce that similar offences would be punished with whipping or fines.[72] That this state of affairs was common not just for the South is borne out by the remark that 'For maids they are soone gonne in this countrie' made of the New England settlement at Piscataqua.[73] Another northern example of rarity making the heart grow fonder was the scandalous proceeding of Governor Richard Bellingham with Penelope Pelham in 1641, only eleven years after the founding of Massachusetts Bay. Winthrop laconically described the case:[74]

> The governour Mr Bellingham was married. The young gentlewoman was ready to be contracted to a friend of his who lodged in his house, and by his consent had proceeded so far with her, when on a sudden the governour treated with her and obtained her for himself. He excused it by the strength of his affection, and that she was not absolutely promised to the other gentleman. Two errors more he committed upon it. 1. That he would not have his contract published where he dwelt, contrary to order of the court. 2. That he (as a magistrate) married himself contrary to the constant practice of the country.

Bellingham evaded an inquiry by refusing to go off the bench and then putting off discussion and remained married to his politic wife until his death.

Reminiscent of the Jordan case in Virginia was the action for breach of promise brought by Alex. Becke against Joyce Bradwicke during the first generation, 'for promiseing him marriage and nowe refuseing to perform the same' because she had switched to some more attractive suitor.[75] There were many such cases before the courts of the New England colonies. Also comparable was the first marriage which took place in Plymouth. This was between Edward Winslow, who had been a widower for three months, and Susannah White, whose husband had been dead for only two.[76] Heavy pressures of demand would also push down the age at which girls married. One of the first females to arrive in Virginia, Anne Burras, who came as the servant to Mrs Forrest in the second supply of 1608, was married within months of her arrival to John Laydon, although she was only fourteen. There are also cases of girls being married on the voyage over.[77]

The total population of any young colony would be made up almost entirely of immigrants among whom males would naturally predominate. There is, none the less, convincing literary evidence that women continued to enjoy rarity value throughout the seventeenth century, especially in the South, and to exploit it to their advantage.

Towards the turn of the century there are several cases which support this contention. One of the most famous is that of Sarah Harrison. She was courted by William Roscoe and was induced to sign an undertaking, which read:[78]

> These are to certify all Persons in the World, that I, Sarah Harrison, Daughter of Mr. Benjamin Harrison, do, and am fully resolved, and by these Presents, do oblige myself, (and cordially promise) to William Rascow, never to marry, or contract Marriage with any man during his Life, only himself. To confirm these Presents, I, the abovementioned Sarah Harrison do call the Almighty God to Witness, and so help me God. Amen. To these said Presents I set my Hand. Sarah Harrison. Test April 28, 1687.

This apparently watertight undertaking—and the need for one is surely pertinent—did not prevent her from marrying James Blair, at which ceremony she further made the sparks fly by three times refusing to utter the word 'obey'. Governor Nicholson himself came up against another strong-minded and choosey girl in his frustrated wooing of the sixteen-year-old Lucy Burwell. When this affair took place in 1699, Nicholson was a bachelor of forty-four, a key figure in the British colonial administration, and a man with justifiable self-confidence in his powers and prowess. Two points emerge with clarity. The first is the almost craven tone of the Governor's letter to a girl young enough to be his daughter. ' When I am so unlucky as to find you in the least discomposed, melancholy, or seemingly angry, I am in an agony of sorrow and grief', he writes on 'December 30th, about 2 o'clock in ye morning' (1700). Second, his jilter has at least two other eligible men dancing attendance, Archibald Blair, brother of the Commissary, and Edmund Berkeley, whom she later married in 1704. Not even the prestige of a governorship was sufficient, apparently, for the hard-to-get girls of Virginia.[79] A girl might even take the unconventional step of refusing marriage with any suitor because she considered none good enough. Such seems to have been Evelyn Byrd. Writing to his old friend the Earl of Orrery on 3 February 1728, her father says, 'One of the most Antick Virgins I am acquainted with is my daughter; either our young Fellows are not smart eno' for her, or she seems too smart for them, but in a little Time, I hope, they will split the difference.' She was at this time aged twenty.[80] The reputation of Virginia as a marriage market for undisposable girls—not unlike the British colonies in the nineteenth and twentieth centuries—seems to have become so notorious in the early eighteenth century that William Gooch's sister-in-law, Anne Stainton, who described herself as 'two and thirty years of Age, Ugly and Poor', thought it necessary to disclaim this as any reason for accompanying her sister to the colony in 1727. ' Cocky . . . openly declares she will never marry', wrote the Governor to his brother. ' This I imagine is rather her Pride than earnest, she constantly adding I did not come here for a Husband. I might have been married in England.' She herself wrote 'All the pritty Fellows here have a good tast, they like Youth, Beauty and Money, but I can tell them; If I had either of the three, I should think it hard fortune not to have a Love.'[81] Gooch's daughter-in-law, on the other hand, who was described by her father-in-law: 'I can't perhaps say she is the prettiest woman I ever saw, yet she is the finest shape, well bred and has good sense', still found a second husband among 'many admirers' after the tragic death of Billy Gooch. This, despite the fact that she had 'only the Interest of [her fortune, destined to her child] to tempt a second husband'.[82] William Fitzhugh's sister was forty-one when she arrived in Virginia in 1686. Yet this antiquity did not prevent her being married to Dr Ralph Smith within a year of her arrival, and then after his death marrying a second time in 1690 to a man fourteen years her junior.[83]

The evidence of ease of remarriage in Virginia is considerable. William Byrd I writing to 'His brother Rand' on 31 March 1685, stated 'My Coz Grendon (in ye flower of his Age) dyed ye 10 of 8br last at sea and the Old Woman (not indureing to lye alone) Marryed about ye latter end of Jan'ry to one Mr Edward Brain a stranger here.' She was, admittedly, wealthy, but so, it would appear, was her new husband, 'comeing into the country in Sepr with 30 servants [presumably indentured ones for sale] and 1000 or 1200 l worth of goods'.[84] The case of the Revd James Bulware, who sued Edward Danneline both for marriage fees and for the funeral-sermon fees that he had preached for Mrs Danneline's first husband, John Smith, was by no means unique; as with Gertrude, 'the funeral bak'd meats/did coldly furnish forth the marriage tables'.[85] The mother of Elizabeth Carter was married six times.[86] Jane Sparrow buried her husband on Tuesday, 11 September 1660 and married a merchant, William Rollinson, the following Sunday.[87] Lady Berkeley was married to three colonial governors consecutively.

We await the finding of demographic research on the age of marriage in Virginia in the seventeenth century. With such demand we would expect that it would be forced down, well below the average of England. There are many examples of girls, usually of

good families, marrying in their mid teens, like Ursula Byrd or
Betty Hansford, who at fifteen wooed a man old enough to be her
grandfather.[88] Bruce records the case of a prominent citizen of
Northampton County, not by all reports the typical adventurer of
romance, who ran off in 1622 with an heiress aged twelve from
Captain Jones's, where she was being educated.[89] In December,
1739, William Byrd II confided to his diary that 'Phil. Johnson
came and made proposals about Annie'. His daughter by his second
marriage was at that time only fifteen. Johnson was sent away 'with
a gentle denial' but Annie only waited another three years before
marrying Charles, a son of 'King' Carter.[90] These examples, which
could be multiplied, are at least suggestive of the pressures of male
demand.

We have so far spoken mainly of the wealthier classes, who would
normally both marry younger and tend to be more choosey about
marriage partners. But from what fragmentary evidence we have
at the present stage of published research it would appear that these
trends were probably true of the humbler walks of life in the
South as well. A Virginian law of 1642–3 enacted strong penalties
against secret marriages—the only sort of marriages possible
because of their agreements with their masters—for indentured
servants. The fact that the penalties for women were much tougher
than for men suggests once again that the sex ratio was operating
strongly in their favour in the marriage market.[91] After 1661, a
freeman who married an indentured maidservant had to pay her
master 1,500 pounds' worth of tobacco.[92] Laws of this kind are not
generally enacted in vacuo; we may reasonably presume that there
must have been a considerable number of indentured maidservants
married before their indentures were fully served, to cause such
enactments to be placed on the books of the colony. Gooch, writing
to his brother in 1730, reported 'Dalton is dead; his son is lately
married to a very young woman that they say has about £60 a year
in England.' The Daltons were not of the aristocracy.[93]

Girls could also expect to marry above themselves in Virginia.
John Hammond, who had lived for nineteen years in Virginia and
whose 'Leah and Rachel' impresses as a modest and accurate
account of conditions in the colony, gave the following advice to
women fare-payers going to Virginia or Maryland:[94]

> I advise them to sojourn in a house of honest repute, for by
> their carriage, they may advance themselves in marriage, by
> their ill overthrow their fortunes; and although loose persons
> seldome live long unmarried if free; yet they match with as
> dissolute as themselves, and never live handsomely or are ever
> respected.

Similarly, William Bullock, writing in 1649, said that 'Maidservants of good honest stock may choose their husbands out of the
better sort of people.'[95] Such was Margaret Edwards, an indentured
servant, who in the 1640s married Stephen Taylor, a planter, 'an
honest man and gave a great price' to redeem her indentures.[96] In
the next decade Colonel Henry Norwood, a cavalier seeking refuge
in Virginia, described some poor women who were shipwrecked on
Kickotank, part of the eastern shore. Thanks to help from the
Indians, they 'did soon arrive at perfect health, and lived (one or
both of them) to be well married, and bear children, and to subsist
in as plentiful condition as they could wish'.[97] Writing to a Mr
Pemberton in England, Robert Carter recalled, 'Twenty-odd years
ago you sent by Capt. Woodward . . . Margaret Upton, the best
woman servant I ever had in my family since I was a master of one.
She married very well after she was free.'[98] In a quarrel over cards
in *The Sotweed Factor* (1708), one Maryland planter's wife says to
her opponent:[99]

> Tho now so brave,
> I knew you late a four-years slave,
> What if for planter's wife you go
> Nature designed you for the hoe.

The price that poorer young men were prepared to pay seems
to bear out the opportunities which girls had for upward social
mobility. Complaining about the difficulty of keeping women servants, Bullock wrote that even[100]

> a poore silly Wench, made for a Foile to set of[f] beautie, and
> yet a proper young Fellow must needs have her, and being but
> new come out of his time and not strong enough to pay the
> charges I was at in cloathing and transporting her, was content
> to serve me a twelve Moneth for a Wife.

Thus, the conclusion that 'that man that's full of Children do keepe
his Sonnes in England, and send his Daughters to Virginia, by
which meanes he shall not give but receive portions for all his
Children'.

Further confirmation comes from the reaction of parents to a
daughter's marriage below her on the social scale. En route for
Mr Randolph's at Tuckahoe, William Byrd II met with Mrs
Fleming.[101]

> Here I learned all the tragical story of her daughter's humble
> marriage to her uncle's overseer. Besides the meanness of this
> mortal's aspect, the man has not one visible quality, except
> impudence, to recommend him to a female's inclinations. But
> there is sometimes such a charm in that Hibernian endowment,

that frail women can't withstand it, though it stand alone without any other recommendation. Had she run away with a gentleman or a pretty fellow, there might have been some excuse for her, though he were of inferior fortune; but to stoop to a dirty plebeian, without any kind of merit, is the lowest prostitution. I found the family justly enraged at it . . . so senseless a prank as this young gentlewoman had played.

Byrd, who perhaps significantly sought a second wife in England, rather than Virginia, speaks vehemently; wasted opportunity seems to have been the worst of Miss Fleming's sins.

There were, of course, exceptions. Francis Louis Michel, in Virginia in 1702 from Switzerland, reported that the four Lerber sisters, the eldest twenty-seven and the youngest seventeen, were all unmarried. However, they were foreigners in predominantly English Virginia, and furthermore Anabaptists of more than normal devotion to their faith.[102] Durand of Dauphiné was offered by Ralph Wormeley 'the widow of a wealthy citizen; that she was only 30 years of age, good looking, without children, and that he knew that she wanted nothing better than to marry a person of quality; that he had great influence with her; that she had a good house, a plantation of 1,000 acres of land, and plenty of servants and cattle of all kinds'. Ralph Wormeley, however, was here acting the role of real-estate agent in a buyers' market; as with glowing descriptions by modern property salesmen, one suspects that interpretation was nine-tenths of the law.[103]

If, as Nicholas Cresswell, visiting America in 1774, believed, the colonies were 'a paradise on Earth for women'[104] we might expect that the fallen woman might even enjoy a chance of rising again, that the double standard would be thrust aside by the more insistent demand for wives. We need not rely entirely for corroboration on the evidence of Moll Flanders. Michel mentions the death on board his ship of 'an English lady, of high family and great wealth. As she had been guilty of some indiscretion, her family were sending her to Virginia'.[105] Trollops accompanied Durand on his voyage, and fallen women in large numbers were shipped to the southern colonies, particularly Maryland, in the eighteenth century, yet evidence of large-scale immorality is hard to find in colonial Virginia. William Byrd, fresh from the fleshpots of London, searched Williamsburg in vain for a whore in November 1720. He also reported finding the daughter of a baronet serving at a friend's house; 'her complexion being red-hair'd inclined her so much to Lewdness, that her father sent her . . . to seek her fortune on this side of the Globe'.[106] Calhoun suggests that, because citizens were so precious in the undermanned colonies, a woman who successfully reared a bastard was considered to have atoned for her sin to society. He also mentions that women, though sullied, often quickly married.[107] Though we need not take the apocryphal speech of Polly Baker too seriously, the murder of bastards by their mothers seems to have been very uncommon in Virginia, if we are to judge by the letters of Spotswood to the Council of Trade.[108]

One would have expected that if there were such a shortage of women in Virginia in the seventeenth century, a considerable amount of intermarriage with either Indian or negro women might have taken place, as it did in New France, where there was a similar shortage.[109] Certainly in the early years the example of John Rolfe in marrying Pocahontas does not seem to have been an isolated incident. Governor Thomas Dale at the same time offered marriage to Pocahontas's younger sister, which her father Powhatan wisely rejected, particularly as Dale already had a wife in England. There was a strong element of policy behind this rush to matrimony, which was rewarded by relatively peaceful relations with the Indians while Powhatan lived. In 1609 the preacher of a sermon at Whitechapel thought it necessary to warn intending emigrants to Virginia against miscegenation, presumably because cases had already occurred in the first two years of settlement there. 'Abram's posteritie [must] keepe to themselves,' he declared. 'They may not marry nor give in marriage to the heathen, that are uncircumcised.'[110] Calhoun claims that marriage of white men to Indians was common[111] and Bennett describes 'an extensive trade in genes' between black and white in the seventeenth century, especially between white indentured servants and black slaves, who in the first two generations were treated very similarly.[112]

None the less, by the end of the seventeenth century there had developed a strong taboo, certainly against regular unions of this kind. Spotswood, writing in 1717 to officials in London who were keen to promote intermarriage, stated: 'Notwithstanding the long intercourse between ye Inhabitants of this Country and ye Indians, and their living amongst one another for so many years, I cannot Find one Englishman that has an Indian wife, or an Indian married to a white woman.'[113] Robert Beverley, writing in 1705, was highly sympathetic towards the Indians and claimed that 'the example of John Rolfe might well have been followed by other settlers to the vast improvement of the country'. It was not followed in the early days, he argued, 'on account of their being Pagans, and for fear that they shou'd conspire with those of their own Nation, to destroy their Husbands'. Currently, however, he gives the impression that the prejudice against intermarriage may have been exacerbated by white female feelings on the subject.[114] Our knowledge of the causes of colour prejudice is woefully inadequate and conflicting.

Yet if the argument of Wilbur J. Cash on the situation in the nineteenth and twentieth century South is anything to go by, there
would seem to be grounds for thinking that the absence of intermarriage by the end of the seventeenth century may have resulted
from pressure exerted by women. This, in turn, would represent
a very strong influence on social *mores* by the 'weaker' sex.[115] Whatever the cause, it achieved the maintenance of a rarity value among
women in the South, which it is hard to imagine did not affect the
relationship of the sexes to women's advantage.

What of southern manhood in the seventeenth century? We
have already seen certain members of the upper classes either seeking wives in Europe or not remarrying. Usually, where there is a
shortage of potential wives, members of the upper classes do proportionately better in finding mates than do their inferiors. There is
usually far less taboo against male members of the upper classes
marrying beneath them, or, for that matter, against older men
generally marrying younger, even much younger, women.

The extant evidence for the situation of humbler men seems to
bear out our expectation. A letter from Arthur Blackamore to
'J. D.', dated February 25, 1715, reads, 'I hope to live as easie without a Wife, as 'tis possible for me to do with any one, except her I
courted; and she has given me a flat denial.'[116] Patience might
end enforced celibacy. In 1685, Giles Webb, then aged twenty-
three, wooed Sarah Swann. Sarah, however, chose the son of Henry
Randolph instead. Randolph died in 1693, at which point Giles
Webb repeated his suit and, at the second time of asking, was
accepted.[117] On the frontier, where women would be in shortest
supply, old prejudices about the weaker sex might collapse.
William Byrd II gives several examples of this.[118]

> I told Harry Morris first to minister to correct his own errors,
> but likewise those of his wife, since the power certainly
> belonged to him in virtue of his conjugal authority. He
> scratched his head at this last admonition, from which I in-
> ferred that the grey mare was the better horse.

He used the same phrase of the wife of a Huguenot minister, 'and
the poor man submits to her vagaries for peace sake'.[119]

If men were frustrated by an absence of women of eligible age,
one might expect to find evidence of repressed energy building up
and occasionally exploding. Byrd reports that on 19 April 1712
'several of our young gentlemen were before Mr Bland for a riot
committed last night at Su Allen's and A-t-k-s-n's, but came off with
paying 10/– a piece.'[120] Three years earlier he sat himself in 'Court,
where a man was tried for ravishing a very homely woman. There
were abundance of women in the gallery.'[121] In the *London Diary*,

he himself quite frequently records his own sense of frustration as a Virginian widower.[122] It is, of course, in the nature of things almost impossible to tell how typical Byrd was in this. The negress and the indentured maidservant might well have been employed to dull the sharp edge of desire. None the less, there is little doubt that the sex ratio worked in women's favour in Virginia.

The situation in Massachusetts was a good deal less acute than it was in Virginia. None the less, there is a considerable amount of supporting evidence to suggest that women of marriageable age had a good deal of bargaining power even there.

Samuel Sewall reported in 1691 the death through choking of a woman of humble position; she was 'Hamlen, formerly Plats, before that, Crabtree, a middle-aged woman'. Oft-married women were quite common.[123] Sewall's daughter Betty, who does not come through the pages of the diary as being a particularly attractive catch, was none the less courted by two others before she finally accepted Grove Hirst.[124] Katherine Winthrop, the widow with whom poor Sewall had such trouble later, had already been married to John Eyre and Wait Still Winthrop when Sewall took up the hunt. Her first marriage took place when she was only fifteen.[125] Winthrop had been forced, very much against his inclinations, to remain a widower for ten years before remarrying. The sort of bargaining power that an eligible girl brought to bear is vividly brought out by a phrase in Sewall's account of the marriage of Deborah Byfield. '22 8er, (1696): Captain Byfield marries his daughter, Deborah to James Lynde, before Mr. Willard. Mr. Sparhawke would have had her.'[126] Cotton Mather was hardly exaggerating when he said that 'a virtuous woman of Boston will not be long without a good husband'.[127]

Massachusetts women could expect to rise socially through marriage. Benjamin Wadsworth in *The Well-Ordered Family* infers that men may be more often tempted to attack their wives for their lower birth or wealth than vice versa.[128] Michael Wigglesworth might incur the olympian wrath of Increase Mather when he proposed to marry his own young servant girl; none the less the match was made.[129] Compare the case of Hugh Hall, whose father had moved from New England to Barbados, but who had returned to Harvard before entering his father's West Indian business. After one unsuccessful attempt at matrimony in Boston, Hall wrote to a friend there:[130]

From the Satisfaction I take in a Batcheldors Life I am very maturely Deliberating whether I had best Commence the Matrimonial state or no, which if it should happen in the Affirmative, I Conjecture I shall be as much Plunged where to make my Application; for I shall be pretty Difficult under my present Circumstances, and much more if I Arrive to be a Ten Thousand pound Man, which I doubt not a few Years will Effect (GOD sparing my Life).

The choice facing Hall was either to give some poorer girl a lift up the financial scale, or to remain in a 'Batcheldors life'.

Although eighteenth-century Boston was becoming famous for its old maids,[131] the reception of the so-called Incest Bill suggests that this was a fairly new development. The bill forbade marriage with a deceased wife's sister, or deceased wife's niece, as being within the forbidden degrees. It passed in 1695 by only twenty-seven votes to twenty-four in the lower house of the General Court, and then only after the urging of the ministers of the Congregational Church. The reason for its narrow squeak is given by Sewall: 'Several have married their wives sisters, and the Deputies thought it hard to part them.'[132]

On the New England frontier, women were more obviously scarce. In the Pynchon Court Record we find evidence both for the rapid remarriage of widows and for the frustrations of men breaking out. Katharine Bliss, the widow of Nathaniel, a man of only very moderate fortune, married Thomas Gelbert on 23 May 1655, only three months after her first husband's death. In 1642 the widow of John Searle waited only two months. In 1659 Samuell Allin brought a case against John Bliss, both of Northampton, for unjustly stealing away the affections of his fiancée, Hannah Woodward. John Hobell was whipped for extracting promises of marriage from Abigail Burt, despite her father's prohibition in 1641.

The suggestions of male frustration vary. Samuel Terry was caught 'with his face to the Meeting House wall nere the corner of the meeting house chafing his yard to provoak lust even in sermon tyme'. Robert Lyman was charged with 'inticeinge' John Stebbins's wife 'severall tymes that he might ly with her, takeing her in his armes and otherwise venting his unchast desires'. Robert Bartlett tried to rape Sarah Smith while her husband was away in 1656.[133]

The Suffolk County Court Records for 1671–80 likewise contain several examples of male offences, from exposure to the offering of 'lascivious carriages towards 27 persons of the female kinde', which argue a certain strain of frustration among young men.[134] In the early days of New England's settlement, cases of sodomy and buggery were unduly common.[135] Five such offences were committed at Salem in 1629 before the migration proper had begun.[136]

Miscegenation, against which the authorities in Massachusetts seem to have taken a stronger line than further south, also posed a problem. In 1631, Winthrop records in his journal under 6 September that 'a young fellow was whipped for soliciting an Indian Squaw to incontinency'. Nearly a century later Zebulon Thorp was recorded by Sewall as dying before his trial for ravishing a negress.[137] Several other cases of this kind are recorded in the church and court records of seventeenth-century Massachusetts that have survived.[138] A law against intermarriage between the races was not passed in Massachusetts until 1705.[139] Sarah Knight reveals, in her comments on what she obviously considers the too familiar treatment of slaves in Connecticut, a deep-seated prejudice against blacks, which may help to explain the passage of the law in the same year that she wrote. She objects strongly to negroes being at the same table with their master, refers to the 'black hoof' going into the dish with 'the white hand' and to a negro as 'black face'.[140]

These examples from Massachusetts, taken together, provide strong support for the contention that women of marriageable age were in relatively short supply in many parts of the colony. This may not have been the sole cause for such aberrant behaviour, but a high sex ratio must surely have been a strong contributor.

Supporting Evidence: England

The beginning of this chapter described the sorts of behaviour which sociologists and social anthropologists expect in a society where there is an excess of women over men. The evidence in this section will demonstrate that this kind of deviancy did in fact occur, and that there are powerful, non-demographic data to support the view that women in England were in a very poor bargaining position in contrast with the colonies.

So far as marriage is concerned, we would expect to find the sort of situation that we have described in Virginia turned upside down, with men in the commanding position calling the tune. Lawrence Stone has shown that for the peerage in the seventeenth century the marrying-off of daughters was a matter of increasing difficulty and concern. The ratio between dowry or portion—that is the money which a bride's parents handed over with her at marriage—and her jointure—that is the amount guaranteed to her by her husband for her life if she outlived him—rose from four or five to one in the mid-sixteenth century to ten to one by the end of the seventeenth. In other words the intrinsic value of a peer's daughter decreased on average by more than half.[141] 'The principal cause of these striking changes,' he concludes, 'is the simple factor of supply and demand: the number of marriageable girls exceeded that of eligible boys.'

The position of the gentry does not seem to have been much

47

better. Sir William Morrice wrote in the year 1661: 'There are many merchants' daughters that weigh so many thousands that ours are commodities lying on our hands, who can't set them off with so great weight.'[142] On the eve of the Civil War Henry Oxinden wrote to his mother from Kent: 'Pray if my sister Elizabeth may marry well in London, not to neglect itt, for good husbands are hard to be gott here.'[143] The position for that class does not seem to have improved as time went on. The advice of Richard Allestree, probably author of *The Ladies Calling*, to 'superannuated virgins' was to turn to their spiritual bridegroom rather than imitating mutton dressed up as lamb in an attempt to catch a husband. We can infer from his section on this subject that he believed himself to be addressing a considerable audience of old maids.[144] Ned Ward described 'the exchange commodity broker— a kind of mongrel matchmaker' who carried 'a catalogue of women wanting marriage, some young, some not, all tame as a city cuckold chid by his wife'.[145] *The London Jilt* bewailed[146]

> The wretched condition of those women being old and ugly [who] abandon themselves to some young miserable bully; for they're no sooner joined together by the Bond of Marriage, than that these Sparks who only took this rank flesh for the conveniences wherewith it is attended, being to play the master with the Money, which others it seems have raked up for them, they seek out Wenches who are less in years and have more Charms than their old toothless Spouses.

When Jacques Fontaine was staying in the west country and was engaged to be married, he received a very strange proposal from a Mr and Miss Downes. It was suggested that Fontaine should break off his engagement and instead marry Miss Downes, whose main attraction at thirty-four was a dowry of £3,000, and that her brother, who claimed to be worth £10,000, should marry Fontaine's intended.[147] William Byrd's sister-in-law gives the impression that the difficulty of getting daughters well disposed of continued into the next century. 'My Sisters Marriages were boath much greater than I possibly could have hoped for. Beauty without Money seldom avails much in this prescent age [i.e. 1742].'[148] In this sentiment she all but repeats verbatim similar statements in Defoe's *Moll Flanders*.

For the poorer classes, especially for girls without portions, the position was probably even worse. Merryman in Sedley's *Bellamira* (1687) says, 'I shall not come home a get [i.e. to beget] girls, without I know where to get Portions for 'em; in this Age, they Soure and grow stale on their Parent's Hands.'[149] It is surely no coincidence that several charities were established in the century to provide dowries for poor girls.[150] Dorothy George has demonstrated for the beginning of the eighteenth century that there was an excess of female servants in London, and all the evidence points to this situation having persisted throughout our period also.[151] In the countryside the situation does not seem to have been all that much better. The Martindale family was scandalised when an oldest son married a girl worth only £40. 'The smallnesse of her fortune was a great prejudice to our family,' records Adam.[152] Roger Lowe, an apprentice grocer living in rural Lancashire, never seemed to lack for sweethearts. On one occasion he records that 'Anne Hasleden moved me sundry times to get Henry Lowe to woo her'.[153] Dorothy Osborne, describing her secluded life in Bedfordshire in a letter of 1653 to William Temple, mentions that 'a great many young wenches keep sheep and cows and sit in the shade singing of Ballads. . . . I talke to them and finde that they want nothing to make them the happiest people in the world, but the knowledge that they are so.'[154] Perhaps these participants in this pastoral idyll were unaware of the folk-song which was the fore-runner of 'Where are you going to, my pretty maid?' In the seventeenth century version the interrogatory squire has a similar kind of reaction to her 'My face is my fortune, Sir'; but this does not prevent him from suggesting a roll in the hay before he departs on his fortune-hunting way.[155]

Women married beneath themselves. The most famous case, which must also vie for the record in rapid remarriage, occurred in 1639, when a gentleman worth £500 in land brought his wife with him to London. He died there suddenly at 8 p.m., and his wife married at noon the journeyman draper who appeared the next morning to sell her mourning.[156] The dissenting preachers George Fox and Richard Baxter both married well above themselves on the social scale; Margaret Fox was a gentlewoman and the widow of a Lancashire J.P., and Margaret Baxter had been brought up by gentlefolk in Apperley Castle. Lionel Cranfield was not the first and by no means the last ambitious but poor young apprentice whose first step on the ladder of success was marriage to his master's daughter.[157] William Byrd attempted, among his literary exercises, a character of a female prude. This had most of the usual sallies, like her nervousness about her nudity at her resurrection; the punch-line was also something of a cliché by the early eighteenth century: 'She is now going to visit her child by her uncle's coach-man.'[158]

With such conditions in the marriage market, it is hardly surprising that the kind of women and female behaviour which social scientists have led us to expect in a low cycle of the sex ratio should make their appearance on the scene. There was the spate of mannish women who caused such official consternation with their yellow ruffs and their swords that James I ordered the ministers to preach against them from the pulpit. This, too, was the age of such semi-mythical masculine females as Moll Cutpurse and Long Meg, who may, on the stage, have reflected a similar aggressive type in real life.[159] Later in the century emerged that querulous feminism which is often associated with a surplus of marriageable women whose energies are channelled perforce into protest movements.[160] The hot-blooded pursuit of the available men was not open to many in that age of parentally-arranged matches. Yet the censorious Chamberlain mentions a widow who was quite plainly chasing Tom Hatton: 'I know not what to say of the widows of this age, nor what privileges they pretend,' he sniffily concluded— as though this were not uncommon.[161]

A scheme which recurs throughout the century, that of some kind of seminary for unmarried and unmarriageable women, corroborates the thesis that there was a serious surplus. First suggested in the 1630s by Lettice Cary, Lady Falkland, and advocated later by Mary Astell and Daniel Defoe, such institutions would take over the role from the dissolved convents of 'convenient stowage for their withered daughters', as Milton uncharitably put it.[162] Miss Astell pictured a potential inmate: the poor lady who fails to make a conquest; she becomes over-careful of her body to retain her attractiveness and so neglects her mind. Her beauty decays and she becomes increasingly terrified of the dreadful name of old maid. To avoid it she flies to a dishonourable match with some idle fellow with a race of beggarly children.[163] The creative side of Mary Astell's *Serious Proposal to the Ladies* tried to envisage a decent vocation for the unmarried gentlewoman, instead of the despised limbo of the useless old maid. 'The whole world', she wrote, 'is a single lady's Family, her opportunities of doing good are not lessen'd but encreas'd by her being unconfin'd. . . . And perhaps the Glory of reforming this Prophane and Profligate Age is reserv'd for you Ladies.'[164]

Another escape route lay in the direction of quietism, which, as Herbert Moller has suggested, flourished for this very reason in seventeenth-century Western Europe. Such devotion to the spirit was not limited to ladies of quality like Catherine Rich or Mary Godolphin. Quakerism appealed very strongly to humbler women. Roger Lowe reports the death of a poor maid in his village, Alice Leland, who had turned from hopes of marriage to man to visions of marriage with Christ.[165] It could even be that some of the more outlandish religious sects that sprang up during the Interregnum, like James Naylor's Quaker splinter-group, were a form of polygyny responding unconsciously to the problem of a shortage of men.

For the financially dependent, dishonour rather than death might be the only answer. For some gentlewomen, relatives might supply some form of employment in the dead-end occupations of governess or companion or barely tolerated semi-servant. Not all the prostitutes who swarmed in London came from the poorer classes, however. Byrd recounts how, on 30 March 1718, he and Lord Orrery visited two gentlewomen seen at play, and how 'my Lord rogered one of them, but I did nothing'.[166] Byrd had several assignations with women who appear to have been of faded gentility.[167]

Meanwhile, the men ruled the roost. Some might not even bother to marry at all—they could have their cake and eat it. According to Aubrey, Sir Henry Lee 'was never married, but kept a woman to read to him while he was in bed.' It would appear from his epitaph that reading was the least strenuous of her bedtime duties.[168] Others could afford to browse around the large field before choosing, and then he was a fool who did not pick a filly whose endowment included more than looks. 'My first inclination to marry', recollected Hyde, 'had no other passion than an appetite for a convenient estate.'[169] The tone of William Byrd's love-letters shows his sureness of his strong bargaining position.[170]

The existence of widespread prostitution in the century, well authenticated in London and probably widespread in the country-side too, is most likely to occur in societies with an unbalanced sex ratio. It arises from a sense of the inequality of the sexes, and is often a logical accompaniment of a patriarchal society. The male who patronises prostitutes tends to develop a depreciating attitude towards women and an exaggerated sense of self-importance.[171] While accepting that economic conditions also play their part, it can hardly be denied that the thousands of girls driven on to the streets probably represented a surplus on the slightly more honour-able marriage market. The letter from an emigrant to Carolina, which read:[172]

We have provided well for our single woman, who consisted of 13 persons. They have all been favourably married. In the old country they would not have had such good fortune . . . poor females who are of scanty means should come to America if they are virtuous and sensible. They will get along nicely inasmuch as all can make their fortune

was, in fact, addressed to a brother in Switzerland. But our evidence points to it being just as applicable for England. 'I greatly want a schoolmistress to them', wrote Robert Carter on 19 July 1720. 'I know there are a great many such to be met with in London that are hardly able to maintain themselves.'[173] Lucky the woman picked out for the job!

Notes

1 The 1940 figures were: Urban sex ratio: 95·5; rural: 107·8. See Joseph H. Greenberg, *Numerical Sex Disproportion* (Boulder, Colorado, 1950), p. 6.
2 Ibid., p. 5.
3 J. Hajnal, 'European Marriage Patterns in Perspective' in D. V. Glass and D. E. C. Eversley, eds, *Population in History* (London, 1965), p. 129.
4 Hans von Hentig, *Crime: Causes and Conditions* (New York, 1947). Both quotations are cited in Greenberg, op. cit., p. 1.
5 See Greenberg, op. cit., pp. 3, 60, 80; Herbert Moller, 'Sex Composition and Correlated Culture Patterns in Colonial America', *3 WMQ*, vol. II (1945), p. 146.
6 Greenberg, op. cit., p. 90.
7 E. A. Ross, *Outlines of Sociology* (New York, 1923), pp. 6–7, cited in Greenberg, op. cit., p. 55.
8 For graphic examples of these characteristics from the nineteenth-century West, see: Michael McGiffert, ed., *The Character of Americans* (Homewood, Ill., 1964), p. 110; W. P. Webb, *The Great Plains* (Boston, 1931), p. 248; George E. Probst, *The Happy Republic* (New York, 1962), pp. 136–143; A. W. Calhoun, *Social History of the American Family* (Boston, 1918), vol. II, pp. 104–5; John D. Hicks, *The Populist Revolt* (Minneapolis, 1931), p. 13; Lincoln Steffens, *Autobiography* (New York, 1958), p. 2; W. A. White, *Autobiography* (New York, 1946), p. 76; David Donald, *Lincoln Reconsidered* (New York, 1956), pp. 224–5. Cf. a seventeenth-century French West-Indian example in A. E. Smith, *Colonists in Bondage* (Chapel Hill, 1947), p. 302.
9 Whitney R. Cross, *The Burned-over District* (New York, 1965), pp. 84–8, 237, 351, 5; Fawn M. Brodie, *No Man Knows My History* (London, 1963), pp. 185, 186, 183, 401, 341, 335–7, 347; David C. Marsh, *Changing Social Structure of England and Wales* (London, 1965), pp. 20–2; J. A. and Olive Banks, *Feminism and Family Planning in Late Victorian England* (Liverpool, 1964), pp. 27–9, 37, 45; B. R. Mitchell, *Abstract of British Historical Statistics* (Cambridge, 1962), p. 6; B. R. Mitchell and H. G. Jones, *A Second Abstract . . .* (Cambridge, 1971), p. 12; David Donald, *Lincoln Reconsidered* (New York, 1956), pp. 28, 34; Charles Loch Mowat, *Britain Between the Wars* (London, 1955), p. 212.
10 Severe imbalance existed in Malaya among Chinese immigrants, producing major social problems of opium-smoking, gambling and crime. Victor Purcell, *The Chinese in Malaya* (Kuala Lumpur, 1967), ch. 9; Herbert Moller, 'The Social Causation of the Courtly Love Tradition', *Comparative Studies in Society and History*, vol. I (1958–9), pp. 137–63, discusses the severe situation in tenth-century Moslem Spain, troubadour France and Germany, and alludes to male concubinage in eighteenth- and nineteenth-century Polynesia. In all cases, the impression is that the ratio was very high. Purcell suggests that the Malayan situation was changing markedly when, in 1931, the ratio had been reduced to 195, compared with 1,000 in 1901. The sex ratio of California in 1850 was in the region of 1,117. On Ireland, see 'Commission on Emigration and Other Population Problems 1948–54', *Reports* (Dublin, n.d.), pp. 3, 16, 23, 63, 67, 71–2, 77, 101; K. H. Connell, *Irish Peasant Society* (Oxford, 1968), chs 2, 4; Conrad M.

Arensburg and Solon T. Kimball, *Family and Community in Ireland* (Cambridge, Mass., 1940), pp. 226–7, argue from 200 family histories in a Clare parish that girls tended to marry above their family station after 1864. The rural sex ratio in Ireland in 1901 was 109. For China, see Ping-ti Ho, *Studies in the Population of China, 1368–1953* (Cambridge, Mass., 1959), pp. 8, 12, 41–2, 57–8, 62, 68, 96; C. K. Yang, *The Chinese Family in the Communist Revolution* (Cambridge, Mass., 1959), pp. 7, 46, 66, chs 4, 6. On the situation in Utah in the early days of settlement, see P. A. M. Taylor, *Expectations Westward* (Edinburgh, 1965), pp. 146–8; Thomas F. O'Dea, *The Mormons* (Chicago, 1957), pp. 60, 142–3, 247, 249. I am grateful to Dr Neil Tranter and Mr Colin Raban for suggestions on this problem.

11 Recent research suggests that the age of twenty-five is the peak in the migratory urge during the human life cycle. See T. H. Hollingsworth, *Historical Demography* (London, 1969), pp. 187–8.

12 Moller, 'Sex Composition', pp. 113–53.

13 The two authorities on which he mainly relies are Charles E. Banks, *The Planters of the Commonwealth* (Boston, 1930), for Massachusetts, and John C. Hotten, *The Original Lists of Persons of Quality, Emigrants . . . who went from Great Britain to the American Plantations, 1600–1700* (New York, 1931).

14 Julia C. Spruill, *Women's Life and Work in the Southern Colonies* (Chapel Hill, 1938), ch. 1.

15 Sir William Berkeley, *A Discourse of Virginia* (London, 1663), p. 3.

16 Robert Beverley, *History and Present State of Virginia* (London, 1705), ed. Louis B. Wright (Chapel Hill, 1947), pp. 286–7.

17 See Spruill, op. cit., pp. 8–9; 'Maids for Wives', *Va Mag.*, vol. L (1943), p. 318; Annie L. Jester, *Domestic Life in Colonial Virginia in the Seventeenth Century* (Jamestown, 1957), Booklet No. 17 in the Jamestown 350th Anniversary Series, ed. Earl G. Swem, pp. 3–15, also enumerates the women in the colony before the supply.

18 Richard Eburne, *A Plain Pathway to Plantations* (London, 1624), ed. Louis B. Wright (Ithaca, N.Y., 1962), pp. 149–52.

19 *Correspondence Domestic, Jac. I*, vol. CIII, No. 42. For an account of the spiriting, trepanning and kidnapping of English women for the colonies later in the century, see Walter H. Blumenthal, *Brides from Bridewell* (Rutland, Vt, 1962), chs 2, 4.

20 Out of 328 identifiable names of victims in 1622, 52 were women. Susan M. Kingsbury, *Records of the Virginia Company of London* (Washington, 1933), vol. III, pp. 565–71.

21 R. Morton, *Colonial Virginia* (Richmond, Va, 1960), pp. 74–5, 84–5, 153. and above, pp. 33–4.

22 Hotten, op. cit., pp. 35–138.

23 In N. D. Harding and W. D. Bowman, eds, *Bristol and America: Record of First Settlers in the Colonies of North America* (Bristol, n.d.).

24 Hotten, op. cit., pp. 345–418; many of these would have gone to Carolina.

25 Evarts B. Greene and Virginia Harrington, *American Population before the Federal Census of 1790* (New York, 1932), p. 136.

26 Ibid.

27 Cited in ibid., p. 138.

28 A. E. Smith, op. cit., pp. 309–10.

29 Ibid., 335–6.

30 The 'Tolzey Book' of Bristol, for instance, shows a total of 1,265 servants destined for Virginia between 1659 and 1662, whereas for the same time-span ten years later the total is 696 (p. 309).

31 Smith, op. cit., concludes that 'not less than one-half, nor more than two thirds, of all white immigrants to the colonies were indentured servants or redemptioners or convicts' over the colonial period (p. 336). Thomas J. Werkenbaker, working from the evidence of land patents, arrived at an annual immigration rate of 1,500 to 2,000 indentured servants between 1635 and 1705. It seems likely, however, that his sources would tend to give an inflated total. See *The First Americans* (New York, 1927), p. 25.

32 The birthrate of 40 : 1,000 is further open to doubt since it was arrived at from sampling approach of twenty New England towns between the years 1720 and 1760. The important point is, however, that this rate is considered about the highest for a very fertile area and period. Robert Higgs and H. Louis Stehler III, 'Colonial New England Demography: A Sampling Approach', *3 WMQ*, vol. XXVII (1970), pp. 282–94. Lockridge found that the average birthrate for Dedham between 1638 and 1717 was 36 per thousand. 'The Population of Dedham, Mass., 1636–1736', *Economic History Review*, Second Series, vol. XIX (1966), pp. 318–44. J. Potter accepts a birthrate of 45 to 50 per thousand as being a possible hypothetical rate after 1700 for all colonies, but this would certainly seem too high for Stuart Virginia. 'Growth of Population in America 1700–1860' in Glass and Eversley, op. cit., esp. pp. 634–46. These computations do not, of course, take into account the prevailing death-rate, especially the infant and immigrant mortality-rates, or the possibility that one sex was more vulnerable than the other. All too little is known about the infant mortality-rate in Virginia, but the chances are that, though it was probably higher than that for New England, it was not high by English standards. There is some confusion over the death-rate among immigrants. In 1671, Governor Berkeley estimated that 80 per cent of the servants who managed to survive the voyage to Virginia perished shortly after landing, and Smith accepts that 'at least in the first years . . . fifty or seventy-five out of every hundred white servants died without ever having had a decent chance of survival' (pp. 254, 304). There are reasons to think, however, that this appalling mortality-rate declined sharply in the last quarter of the century. More effective cures for sub-tropical diseases, like the bark, were employed; 'seasoning' stresses and dangers were allowed for by owners who had, after all, invested considerable capital in their servants; and conditions of work and living had been improved (Smith, op. cit., pp. 254–5). This, none the less, must remain one of the larger question marks hanging over our conclusions. Finally, there seems little evidence to suggest that there was a particularly devastating male mortality-rate. It is to be hoped that the demographic research in progress will provide us with firmer figures.

33 Even at the first federal census in 1790—when the numbers of males omitted would probably be much greater than females—the sex ratio was still 105·6. Moller computes the sex ratio of South Carolina in 1703 as 152·4. *Moll Flanders* (Signet ed., New York, 1964), pp. 296–7.

34 Randolph, cited in Smith, op. cit., p. 316, reported to London c. 1676 that there were only 'a few who serve four years for the charge of being transported thither'. Governor Shute told the Board of Trade in 1718 that the number of servants arriving in the year following 29 June 1717 totalled 113 men and 13 women and that there had been 'no great difference for the seven years last past'. Ibid., p. 317. The percentage of white servants in the Rhode Island census of 1708 was likewise minimal—55 out of a total population of 7,181 (Green and Harrington, op. cit., p. 65).

35 Moller's figures come from Harding and Bowman, op. cit. Smith gives a total of 162, but does not differentiate sexes (p. 309).

36 At Ipswich, the male surplus only lasted to about 1657. Susan L. Norton,

'Population Growth in Colonial America', *Population Studies*, vol. XXV (1971), p. 446.

37 *3 WMQ*, vol. IX (1952), pp. 395–8. Cf. vol. XV (1958), pp. 373–4, which reprints Lady Mary Wortley Montagu's 'The Request of an Old Maid by the Declaration of her Passion' from the *Boston Gazette* 24–30 January 1937.

38 Calhoun, op. cit., vol. I, p. 116.

39 Greene and Harrington, op. cit., p. 14.

40 See Josiah H. Benton, jr, *Early Census-Making in Massachusetts* (privately printed in Boston, 1905); this contains a facsimile of the census and a description of earlier enumerations which have not survived.

41 Norton, op. cit., p. 441.

42 Alice M. Earle, *Colonial Dames and Goodwives* (Boston, 1895), p. 30.

43 This suggestion receives support from figures for the colony of New York around 1700. In Brooklyn, in 1698, as many as 15.3 per cent of all heads of households were women, presumably widows; the percentage for Dock Ward, New York city, in 1703 was 13.9. The sex ratios for certain New York localities were as follows: 1698, Flushing, 125.4; 1703, Dock Ward, 115.6; 1702, Orange County, 89.5; 1710, New Rochelle, 92.7; 1714, Dutchess County, 112.7. I owe these figures to Mr John R. Hardy, of Trinity Hall, Cambridge. I am much indebted to Mr Hardy for allowing me to use a copy of his informative and painstaking undergraduate thesis, 'A Cursory Investigation of Household Size and Structure in New York State, 1680–1780' (Cambridge University, 1970) and for discussing his findings with me. The sex ratio of free adults in Bristol in 1689, according to the census of that year, was 103. John Demos, 'Families in Colonial Bristol', *3 WMQ*, vol. XXV (1968), pp. 40–57.

44 London, 1696; reprinted under the editorship of George E. Barnett (Baltimore, 1936). For a masterly and favourable assessment of King's accuracy, see D. V. Glass, 'Two Papers on Gregory King', especially the second, in Glass and Eversley, op. cit., pp. 159–220.

45 Ibid., p. 211.

46 Ibid., pp. 206–7.

47 John Graunt, whom King regarded as his exemplar as a demographer.

48 Jordan found that one-seventh of the female philanthropists of London came from the country gentry. His assumption that these widows retired to the 'comfort and security' of the city is certainly in line with more recent behaviour. *The Charities of London* (London, 1960), p. 31.

49 D. V. Glass, 'Notes on the Demography of London at the End of the Seventeenth Century', *Daedalus*, vol. XCVII, No. 2 (Spring 1968), pp. 581–92.

50 *Moll Flanders*, ed. cit., p. 22; cf. pp. 62–8.

51 Charles H. Hull, *The Economic Writings of Sir William Petty* (New York, 1964), p. 411. Cf. pp. 372–8 for Graunt's comments on these figures.

52 E. A. Wrigley, 'A Simple Model of London's Importance in Changing English Society and Economics 1650–1750', *Past and Present*, No. 37 (July, 1967), pp. 44–6.

53 See, e.g., Thomas Middleton, *Michaelmas Term* (1607), II, ii; Edward Ravenscroft, *The London Cuckolds* (1681), II, iii; or Thomas Shadwell, *The Squire of Alsatia* (1688), II.

54 *Life of Adam Martindale*, ed. R. Parkinson (Chetham Society, 1845), pp. 6–7.

55 Louis B. Wright, *Middle-Class Culture in Elizabethan England* (Chapel Hill, 1935), p. 225.

56 Francis Hering, *A Modest Defence of the Caveat given to the Wearers of*

Impoisoned Amulets (1604), quoted in F. P. Wilson, *The Plague in Shakespeare's London* (London, 1963), pp. 3–4n.

57 Mary F. and T. H. Hollingsworth, 'Plague Mortality Rates by Age and Sex', *Population Studies*, vol. XXV (1971), pp. 131–46. In St Botolph's, the adults, that is people over fifteen, represent about 40 per cent of the total victims. In St Margaret's, Westminster, however, the proportions are much higher: in 1603, 794 over fifteen against 452 under, and, in 1665, 536 over against 207 under.

58 Wilson, op. cit., pp. 114, 118, 174; J. F. D. Shrewsbury, *A History of Bubonic Plague in the British Isles* (Cambridge, 1970), chs 7–9; in 1603, for instance, Norwich was estimated to have lost a quarter of its population, and York a similar or larger proportion in the following year, pp. 272, 275. Cf. Keith Thomas, *Religion and the Decline of Magic* (London, 1971), pp. 7–8.

59 Glass, 'Two Papers on Gregory King' in Glass and Eversley, op. cit., p. 192.

60 Ibid., p. 206.

61 L. Stone, 'Social Mobility in England 1500–1700', *Past and Present*, No. 33 (1966), p. 41. It is worth pointing out that nearly half of this group were spinsters aged from twenty-five to thirty inclusive. It is conceivable that family limitation might have accounted for this prolonged spinsterhood. See E. A. Wrigley, 'Family Limitation in Pre-Industrial England', *Economic History Review*, Second Series, vol. XIX (1966), pp. 82–107.

62 Peter Laslett, 'Household Size in England over Three Centuries', *Population Studies*, vol. XXIII (1969), p. 215.

63 E. A. Wrigley, ed., *Introduction to English Historical Demography* (London, 1966), pp. 193–203.

64 Hardy, op. cit., pp. 54–6.

65 Kindly given by Mr Peter Laslett.

66 C. M. Law, 'Some Eighteenth Century Censuses', *Population Studies*, vol. XXIII (1969), pp. 87–100.

67 Hajnal, op. cit., pp. 125–7.

68 On male interpersonal violence, see T. H. Hollingsworth, 'A Demographic Study of the British Ducal Families' in Glass and Eversley, op. cit., p. 359. Cf. Stone, op. cit., V, ii.

69 Quoted in Spruill, op. cit., p. 9.

70 Beverley, *History and Present State of Virginia*, ed. cit., pp. 286–7.

71 George Alsop, 'Character of the Province of Maryland' in *Narratives of Early Maryland*, ed. Clayton C. Hall (New York, 1910), p. 358.

72 Spruill, op. cit., p. 151.

73 Cited in Calhoun, op. cit., vol. I, p. 68.

74 John Winthrop, *Journal: History of New England*, ed. J. K. Hosmer (New York, 1946), vol. II, pp. 43–4.

75 George E. Howard, *History of Matrimonial Institutions* (Chicago, 1904), vol. II, p. 200.

76 Henry W. Lawrence, *The Not-Quite Puritans* (Boston, 1928), p. 85.

77 Jester, op. cit., p. 3.

78 *Papers Relating to an Affidavit made by his Reverence James Blair against Francis Nicholson, Esq. Governor of the said Province,* facsimile in Harvard College Library of an original in the John Carter Brown Library (hereafter *Papers Relating to an Affidavit*), p. 103.

79 Fairfax Downey, 'The Governor goes A-Wooing' in *Va Mag.*, vol. LV (1947), pp. 6–19.

80 'Letters and Literary Exercises 1696–1726' in Maude H. Woodfin, ed., *Another Secret Diary of William Byrd* (Richmond, Va, 1942) (hereafter *Another Secret Diary*), p. 381.

81 *Letters of William Gooch to his brother, Thomas, Bishop of Norwich* (hereafter *Gooch Letters*), transcript in the Research Department of Colonial Williamsburg, Inc., pp. 4, 16, 152.

82 Ibid., pp. 107, 131.

83 *William Fitzhugh and his Chesapeake World*, ed. Richard B. Davis (Chapel Hill, 1963), pp. 218, 313.

84 'Letters of William Byrd I', *Va Mag.*, vol. XXIV (1916), pp. 236, 250, 351.

85 Philip A. Bruce, *Social History of Virginia in the Seventeenth Century* (Richmond, Va, 1907), pp. 224ff.

86 *Va Mag.*, vol. II (1893), p. 237.

87 Spruill, op. cit., p. 158. See her ch. 6 for numerous other examples of rapid and frequent remarriages.

88 See Spruill, op. cit., ch. 6, for further examples.

89 Bruce, op. cit., p. 233.

90 *Another Secret Diary*, p. 15.

91 W. W. Hening, *Statutes at Large . . . of Virginia* (Richmond, Va, 1809–23), vol. 1, pp. 252–3.

92 Ibid., vol. II, p. 114. For a general discussion of this subject, see Howard, op. cit., vol. II, ch. 13.

93 *Gooch Letters*, p. 22.

94 John Hammond, 'Leah and Rachel' (London, 1656), reprinted by Peter Force in *Tracts*, vol. III, No. 14, p. 15.

95 Quoted in Calhoun, op. cit., vol. I, p. 251.

96 See Jester, op. cit., p. 49.

97 Force, *Tracts*, vol. III, No. 10, p. 33.

98 Dated 14 February 1721. Louis B. Wright, ed., *Letters of Robert Carter, 1720–27* (San Marino, 1940), p. 92.

99 Quoted in Calhoun, op. cit., vol. I, p. 250.

100 Quoted from *Virginia Impartially Examined* (1649) by Smith, op. cit., p. 302.

101 'A Progress to the Mines in the Year 1732' in *London Diary*, p. 624.

102 *Va Mag.*, vol. XXIV (1916), p. 116.

103 Durand, *A Frenchman in Virginia*, trans. and ed. by Fairfax Harrison (privately printed, 1923), pp. 55–6.

104 Nicholas Cresswell, *Journal, 1774–7* (New York, 1924), p. 271.

105 Michel, *Journal*, p. 12.

106 *London Diary*, p. 328. Quoted in Edmund S. Morgan, *Virginians at Home* (Williamsburg, 1952), p. 23. On convict transportation, see Blumenthal, op. cit., *passim*.

107 Calhoun, op. cit., vol. I, pp. 140, 150.

108 Polly Baker's speech, in which she defends herself before a bench of magistrates against a charge of bearing a fifth bastard, is reprinted as an Appendix to vol. II of *The Writings of Benjamin Franklin*, collected and edited by Albert H. Smyth (New York, 1907), pp. 463–7. She delivers a *coup de grâce* by claiming that the father in the present case is one of the justices, who had absented himself; one of his colleagues was so impressed with the plaintiff that he promptly made an honest woman of her, and sired fifteen children by her! R. A. Brock, ed., *The Official Letters of Alexander Spotswood* (Richmond, Va, 1882–5), vol. I, pp. 57–8, vol. II, p. 19.

109 See James Douglas, *New England and New France* (New York, 1913), ch. 11; Sigmund Diamond, 'An Experiment in "Feudalism": French Canada in the Seventeenth Century', *3 WMQ*, vol. XVIII (1961), pp. 3–34; Isabel Foulché-Delbosc, 'Women of New France', *Canadian Historical Review*, vol. XXI (1940), pp. 132–49.

110 Quoted in Lerone Bennett, jr, *Before the Mayflower* (Baltimore, 1968), p. 243.
111 Calhoun, op. cit., vol. 1, p. 323.
112 Pp. 242–7, citing Carter Woodson's 'The Beginnings of the Miscegenation of Whites and Blacks', *Journal of Negro History*, vol. III (1918). One of the descendants of Oppechankanough, the Queen of Pamunkey, had a child by an English colonel. T.M. (almost certainly Thomas Mathew), *'Bacon's Rebellion'*, Force, *Tracts*, vol. I, No. 8, p. 14.
113 Leonidas Dodson, *Alexander Spotswood* (Philadelphia, 1932), p. 91.
114 Beverley, *History and Present State of Virginia*, ed. cit., pp. 286–7; p. 38; Book III, Section 7, *passim*.
115 Wilbur J. Cash, *The Mind of the South* (New York, 1960), pp. 85–9.
116 Martha W. Hiden and Henry M. Dargan, 'John Gibbon's MS. Notes Concerning Virginia', *Va Mag.*, vol. LXXIV (1966), p. 16.
117 'Letters of the Byrd Family', *Va Mag.*, vol. XXVI (1918), p. 21. Cf. *Another Secret Diary*, pp. 219–20; *Gooch Letters*, p. 18, letter dated 7 January 1729/30.
118 *London Diary*, p. 616.
119 Ibid., p. 626. Cf. the newly-uxorious Spotswood, p. 628.
120 *Westover Diary*, p. 517.
121 Ibid., p. 95.
122 E.g. entries for 18 November, 28 August, 22 August, 9 December 1720.
123 Sewall, *Diary*, vol. I, p. 355; Earle, op. cit., pp. 31–41.
124 Sewall, *Diary*, vol. I, pp. 490ff.
125 Ibid., p. 482, n.2.
126 Ibid., p. 436.
127 Cotton Mather, *Ornaments for the Daughters of Zion* (Boston, 1691), p. 33.
128 Benjamin Wadsworth, *The Well-Ordered Family* (Boston, 1712), pp. 38–9.
129 E. S. Morgan, *Puritan Family* (New York, 1966), pp. 55–6.
130 Ibid., p. 56. Cf. J. C. Jeaffreson, *A Young Squire of the Seventeenth Century* (London, 1878), p. 263.
131 Calhoun, op. cit., vol. I, p. 57.
132 Sewall, *Diary*, vol. I, p. 407.
133 For these and other examples, see *Colonial Justice in Western Massachusetts (1639–1702)*, ed. Joseph H. Smith (Cambridge, Mass., 1961), pp. 103, 209, 212, 233, 242, 248, 290, 310, 390, 389.
134 *Collections of the Colonial Society of Massachusetts*, vol. XXX, part II (Boston, 1933), pp. 604, 605, 626, 674, 697, 786, 807, 912, 914n.
135 See Bradford's *History 'of Plimouth Plantation'* (Boston, 1898), pp. 459–77.
136 See Cotton Mather, *Magnalia Christi Americana* (London, 1702) (hereafter *Magnalia*), Book VI, pp. 35–8; Francis Higginson, *Journal*, in Alexander Young, ed., *Chronicles of the First Planters* (Boston, 1846), p. 231; Calhoun, op. cit., vol. I, pp. 134–5.
137 Sewall, *Diary*, vol. I, p. 128.
138 See Emil Oberholzer, *Delinquent Saints* (New York, 1956), p. 134.
139 Howard, op. cit., vol. II, p. 218.
140 Sarah Knight, *Journal*, ed. George P. Winship (New York, 1935), p. 38.
141 L. Stone, *Crisis of the Aristocracy 1558–1641* (Oxford, 1965), pp. 637–45. His whole chapter on marriage, 11, is illuminating.
142 Quoted in M. Ashley, *The Stuarts in Love* (London, 1963), p. 49.
143 Quoted in C. Bridenbaugh, *Vexed and Troubled Englishmen* (New York, 1968), p. 33.
144 Part II, 2nd ed. (London, 1673).
145 *The London Spy (1698–1700)*, Folio Society ed., p. 58.
146 By Alexander Oldys(?) (London, 1683), p. 100.

147 Ann Maury, ed., *Memoirs of a Huguenot Family* (New York, 1872), pp. 128–32.
148 'Byrd Family Letters', *Va Mag.*, vol. XXXVII (1929), p. 113.
149 III, i; cited in E. J. Gagen, *The New Woman* (New York, 1954), p. 152.
150 W. K. Jordan, *Charities of Rural England* (London, 1961), p. 50.
151 M. Dorothy George, *London Life in the Eighteenth Century* (London, 1925), p. 113.
152 *Life of Adam Martindale*, ed. cit, p. 16.
153 Roger Lowe, *Diary*, ed. W. L. Sachse (London, 1938), p. 49.
154 Quoted in M. Phillips and W. S. Tomkinson, *English Women in Life and Letters* (Oxford, 1927), p. 54.
155 See Iona and Peter Opie, *The Oxford Dictionary of Nursery Rhymes* (1952), pp. 282–3.
156 *HMC Gawdy*, X, 172, cited in Bridenbaugh, op. cit., p. 34.
157 Alice Clark, *Working Life of Women in the Seventeenth Century* (New York, 1920), gives other examples. Shakespeare's father was a yeoman who married a gentleman's daughter, and there were many like him in the seventeenth century. Cf. Christina Hole, *English Home Life 1500–1800* (London, 1947), p. 59.
158 *Another Secret Diary*, p. 288.
159 Gagen, op. cit., pp. 109–11.
160 Above, p. 5.
161 W. Notestein, 'The English Woman 1580–1650' in *Studies in Social History Presented to G. M. Trevelyan*, ed. J. H. Plumb (London, 1955), p. 76.
162 Stone, op. cit., p. 646.
163 Ada Wallas, *Before the Bluestockings* (London, 1929), p. 123.
164 Ibid., p. 122.
165 Roger Lowe, *Diary*, p. 28.
166 *London Diary*, p. 100.
167 E.g. pp. 118, 140.
168 *Brief Lives*, ed. Oliver L. Dick (Harmondsworth, 1962), p. 263. See Ashley, op. cit., on this theme, p. 21.
169 Quoted in Ashley, op. cit., p. 26.
170 See 'Literary Exercises' in *Another Secret Diary, passim,* and esp. letter to 'Preciosa' on p. 270.
171 Paul H. Landis, *Social Problems* (Chicago, 1959), ch. 16.
172 Quoted by Spruill, op. cit., p. 137.
173 *Letters of Robert Carter*, ed. cit., p. 33.

Chapter 3
Economic Opportunities

This chapter explores two closely linked themes. It examines first the prevailing economic conditions of the areas under study, in an attempt to discover in general terms how widely prosperity and the symbols of affluence were spread. Second, it attempts to clarify the economic opportunities open to women, and the extent to which these expanded or contracted in England and America in the seventeenth century.

The first of the prerequisites which the sociologist Paul Landis prescribes for sexual equality is 'economic equality'.[1] This too is the underlying message of Calhoun's analysis of women's status in America. 'Economic independence', he writes, 'is the only sure basis of equality.'[2]

Phrases like 'economic equality' and 'economic independence' do not get us very far, however. A prostitute may be economically independent, and equality in poverty is not a very enviable state. At the base of the economic factor is the question of *opportunity*, and its twin, the question of *roles*. Equal pay for equal work is an empty slogan if women are deprived of the opportunities for equal work.

It is dangerously easy, as we shall see, to sentimentalise more primitive systems of production, like the domestic system, in comparison with advanced technological societies. None the less, whatever the economic disadvantages, there do seem to have been social compensations in a system where the wife shared in family production, rather than being 'kept', a wage slave, or an ornament.

Contrasting Economic Conditions

'Such as could not marry here [England], but hardly live and allow themselves clothes, do marry there and bestow thrice more in all necessaries and conveniences (and not a little in ornamental things too) for themselves, their wives, and children, both as to apparel and household stuff.' So wrote William Penn in *Some Account of the Province of Pennsilvania*.[3] What Penn called 'the future ease and plenty'[4] was the oft-repeated chorus of promotional writers from Captain John Smith to General James Oglethorpe. And, unlike so many of their other claims, this was substantially right. There were of course what Penn discreetly called 'present inconveniences', as the early settlers at Jamestown or Plymouth or Boston would have feelingly agreed. But once a colony was firmly established, there can be little doubt that the settlers could confidently hope to enjoy a considerably higher standard of living than they had had in the Old World. For the colonies of Massachusetts and Virginia, Robert and Katherine Brown have shown with a wealth of detail that the great majority of people were, comparatively speaking, prosperous.[5]

Contemporary statements on the thriving prosperity of Massachusetts and Virginia are not hard to come by in the seventeenth century, either. One of the refrains of the later part of Edward Johnson's *Wonder-working Providence of Sion's Saviour*, written around 1650, concerns the effects on zeal and morality of growing prosperity. Even once-poor indentured servants are now worth 'scores, and some, hundreds of pounds'. We hear, all too frequently, of 'heaps upon heaps of riches', of 'plenty of all things', of merchants 'taken up with the income of a large profit', of husbandmen's 'over eager pursuit of the fruits of the earth', of 'wages large' and 'gold and garments gay', 'the longing lust for gain' which helps 'every bird to feather his own nest'.[6] Ezekiel Rogers, the first minister of Rowley, seconds this lament about 'love of the world, not Thy Word'.[7] Needless to say both the Mathers, especially Cotton, charged the even greater prosperity of their time as a primary cause for the spiritual backsliding which they saw all around them.[8] Increase Mather pooh-poohed the excuse that tithes were falling because of poverty.[9]

> That the Allegation of the Countrys Poverty, is but a pretended reason for the Ingratitude that many are guilty of, is evident from this Consideration . . . that less than one half the Tenths would in many Towns with us honourably support the Ministry among them. Are there not some Towns in New-England in which the Inhabitants spend more at the Tavern, than they do to uphold the Publick Worship of God?

Ned Ward, copying John Josselyn's account, painted a picture of leisure, good food and plentiful drink, which must have seemed like a vision of the promised land to many of his London customers.[10] Robert Keayne, whose property was appraised at £2,569. 19s. 3d. in 1656, was but the most famous example of a man who had 'studied and endeavoured to redeem my time as a thing most dear and precious to me and have often denied myself in such refreshings that otherwise I might lawfully have made use of', to his very great personal profit.[11] The story that John Hull gave as his daughter Hannah's dowry her weight in pine-tree shillings may be legend, but it represents the general belief in the wealth that a Boston merchant of the later seventeenth century could amass.[12]

A similar picture is given for Virginia by such European visitors as Durand of Dauphiné. 'When a man has 50 acres of land, two men servants and a maid and some cattle, neither he nor his wife have ever anything to do except to make visits to their neighbours.' His description of the wedding feast of a mere overseer suggests the affluence: 'We were 80 at the first table and were served so abundantly of meat of all sorts that I am sure that there was enough for a regiment of 500 men.'[13]

What is important for the New World is that this prosperity seems to have been widely spread. As Kenneth Lockridge suggests, the pyramid of wealth was in the seventeenth century low in height and very broad-based. There were 'few very rich, and few poor'.[14] It is surely significant that there was remarkably little counter-migration back to England from New England, after the initial settling stage, for purely economic reasons, and that, as Bailyn has shewn, English merchants, especially after the Restoration, saw New England as a most tempting growth area.[15]

Widespread prosperity is also the conclusion which P. A. Bruce deduced from his thorough investigations into the seventeenth-century Virginian economy. 'All the descriptions of Virginia in the seventeenth century transmitted to us', he writes, 'go to show that the people of all classes in that age lived in the greatest abundance.' He quotes Robert Beverley's *History* (1705): 'Such was the geniality of the climate of Virginia and such the fertility of the soil, that no one there was so sunk in poverty as to be compelled to live by beggary.' This should be taken in consort with Beverley's belief that the Virginians were not over-industrious. William Bullock, author of *Virginia, Impartially Examined* (London, 1649), is also called as witness. Along with general statements of widespread prosperity, he describes how a hired labourer could turn his annual wages of £6 into £60 by shrewd investment within four years, and could make much more if he had his own tobacco patch.[16] After a careful comparison of prices in England and Virginia in the century, he concludes that the prices of basic foodstuffs rose in England but fell, often by as much as 50 per cent, in Virginia, so that by the end of the century, items like beef, butter and pork cost less than half the English average.[17] On wages he is more ambiguous, but it is almost certainly true that wages in Virginia were a good deal higher than in England.[18] He quotes Bullock as saying 'that by the expenditure' of £5 per annum, the standard charge for board, 'any one might live in a manner which in England would entail an outlay of £30'. He also gives numerous examples of artisans, coopers, carpenters, sawyers and shipwrights who, through their trades and the supplementary income from tobacco culture, grew very prosperous.[19]

It is true that, especially after the Restoration, tobacco prices fell, never to recover the boom levels of the 1620s and 1630s. It is unclear how this affected the living standards of ordinary planters. The easy acquisition of land would at least ensure a comfortable subsistence.

There is no need to labour the well-known fact that the situation in England was in the bleakest contrast to that in Virginia and Massachusetts. The rich might be getting richer, but the poor, a good half of the population, were getting progressively poorer. Gregory King believed that half the population in 1695 were in fact earning annually less than their keep. While prices tended to rise, wages of the mass of agricultural labourers failed to keep pace, as J. E. Thorold Rogers has conclusively shown.[20] The urban artisans do not seem to have been much better off. According to a preacher before the Virginia Company in 1622, they might rise early and go to bed late, eat only brown bread and cheese, and 'yet with difficulty they secured food enough to appease their hunger, or clothing sufficient to hide their nakedness'.[21] As David Ogg has written, 'neither contemporary nor modern economists can explain how they lived'.[22] The savage, employer-oriented Act of Settlement of 1662 struck an appalling blow at the agricultural labourer and the wage-earner generally, chaining him to his parish of birth, depriving him of the possibility of constant employment or the means of finding it, turning him 'into a serf without land'.[23] There is little reason to doubt the validity of Bruce's picture of the lot of the majority of Englishmen:[24]

> Confined to his native parish as to the limits of a prison; receiving wages which had been assessed by landowners who were interested in reducing them to the lowest point, wages which did not furnish an easy subsistence to his family even in years of plenty; compelled to purchase his supplies at prices set by the producers, and exposed to heavy penalties for the smallest infractions of the law.

In this welter of suffering humanity one class who suffered worst, as Mrs George points out, was the poor unmarried woman.[25] John Hammond, returned to London after nineteen years spent in Virginia, wondered 'how possibly a livelihood could be exacted out of' such predominantly female trades 'as to cry matches, smalcoal, Blacking, Pen and Ink, Thred Laces, and a 100 more suche kinde of trifling merchandises'.[26] The dame who said, 'It's little they pay, and it's little we learn 'em' was probably typical.[27] The wages of the spinster—a new usage coined in 1617, and possibly reflecting the growing number of female wage-slaves in the clothing industry[28]—were, renownedly, at the bottom of the national scale. The assumption is plain in 1640: 'Shee beinge very poore, getting her livinge by spininge'; by 1700 the average wage of an ordinary spinster was only 4d. per day without food.[29] The lot of women in domestic service was similarly poor; hours were long, employment uncertain, poverty imminent.[30] What Thomas Powell described as 'housewives trades' were dominated by women largely because the remuneration was so small.[31]

If we turn to what might be called the symbols of affluence and poverty, we find a similarly stark contrast between England and the two colonies. There is a whole cluster of factors, for instance, connected with marriage and the family, which are normally telling barometric readings of general social welfare. Most modern researchers agree that, certainly for Massachusetts and most probably for Virginia, the average age of marriage was lower for men and women than in England; expectation of life was higher; the survival rate for infants was higher and the size of nuclear families was larger, i.e. there were more children per marriage.[32] Franklin, it will be remembered, believed that 'this marrying early is encouraged from the prospect of a good subsistence'.[33]

For England the trends are all in the opposite direction. E. A. Wrigley has found strong evidence to suggest that family limitation was consciously practised in the second half of the century.[34] Among its other deleterious effects for the mass of the population, it is clear that the Act of Settlement of 1662 actively militated against the marriage of the humble, by preventing their permanent settlement in any other parish except that of their birth.[35] In his *Some Account of the Province of Pennsilvania* (1681) William Penn writes of servants in England, from an employer's point of view:[36]

> These people rarely marry, though many of them do worse; but if they do, 'tis when they are in age, and the reason is clear, because their usual keeping at their masters is too great and costly for them with a family at their own charge, and they scarcely know how to live lower, so that too many of them choose rather to vent their lusts at an evil ordinary [inn] than honestly marry and work; the excess and sloth of the age not allowing marriage and the change that follows, all which hinders the increase of our people.

There seems little doubt that high death-rate in London in the seventeenth century was largely due to the poverty of many of its inhabitants.[37] Even in the country at large the rise in population was very slow by American standards.[38]

Another obvious indicator of economic welfare is the presence or absence of a 'poor' problem. England undeniably had one throughout the century. The century began with Elizabethan parliaments grappling with the problem and ended with King estimating the number of paupers and cottagers as a quarter of the whole population. Commentators spoke throughout the century of swarms of idlers in London.[39] The curse, however, was on all England. The large-scale migration to London and the amount of geographical mobility during the century were almost certainly partially due to poverty and the search for work.[40] In the two colonies, on the other hand, although there were some poor, most of them seem to have fallen into the category of the handicapped—cripples, orphans, the aged—rather than the genuine unemployed. Bruce quotes the example given by Beverley of a bequest made to the poor of a Virginian parish which had not been used for nine years because no one qualified.[41]

A similar suggestive guide to the economic opportunities open specifically to women is the prevailing amount of prostitution. While figures are hard to come by for the seventeenth century, there is little doubt that prostitution was rife and rising in London, and probably was considerable throughout the country as a whole.[42] In the colonies, on the other hand, despite a shortage of women and thus a considerable class of unmarried men of marriageable age, I have been able to find hardly any evidence of the existence of the oldest profession. Though some women may choose this career many, many more are driven to it by the prevailing economic conditions.[43]

Diet and dress are also items of expenditure which reflect the prevailing economic conditions. Visitors to the colonies from Europe noted, sometimes with astonishment, the abundance of food which was set before them, and the open-handedness of the hospitality, especially in Virginia. We have already mentioned Durand at the overseer's wedding feast. Mrs Spruill gives ample evidence that this was not an isolated case; Virginia had become famous for its groaning boards as early as 1634.[44] Both Durand and Jacques Fontaine remark on the Virginians' refusal to accept any payment for hospitality to total strangers. Bruce comments on this: 'The ease with which a subsistence was secured . . . was the principal explanation of the hospitality for which the people were distinguished.'[45] Josselyn noted the hearty appetites of even the humble in New England.[46] The fact that visitors thought that colonial diet was worthy of comment suggests that it was considerably superior to that of ordinary people in England.[47]

Dress was a popular subject for both preachers and magistrates in Massachusetts. Their constant gripe was against people of the lower orders, especially women, who dressed above their station. Sumptuary laws were passed as early as 1634 in Massachusetts, and in 1640 the General Court, in forbidding silk or tiffany hoods and scarves to women of families with estates of less than £200, declared that 'intolerable excess and bravery hath crept in upon us'.[48] In the 1670s as the criticisms of declension from the godly grew in crescendo and seemed to second their attempts at reform by visiting New England with a succession of disasters, the courts attempted a purge. At Northampton, in 1676, thirty-eight women and thirty young men were hauled up for over-extravagant dress, specifically in some cases for wearing silks.[49] In Boston, Ruth Hemenway, Abigail Roberts and Alice Wright were similarly charged before the Suffolk County Court with exceeding their rank in their apparel.[50] None of it seemed to do any good. Cotton Mather fulminated against the continuing luxuriousness and inappropriateness of ordinary people's clothes in the 1690s.[51] When Sarah Knight stopped at Billings's Tavern on her outward journey to New York in 1702, the daughter of the proprietor put on several rings in order to impress the guest. In New York the middle-class women wore beautiful earrings and rings which fascinated Mrs Knight.[52]

In Virginia it does not seem to have been unusual for women from fairly ordinary walks of life to have ordered clothes from England.[53] Sumptuary laws and taxes seem to have been as ineffective as in the north.[54] For the wealthier, nothing less than the height of London fashion would do. When William Gooch's son was trying to fix a date for his wedding to a planter's daughter from Maryland, he was frustrated, because 'his Mistress, who, tho' everything has been long since agreed upon, had taken a sort of Resolution not to be married until the ships came in, unwilling to come into my family with the same cloathes she had the last summer'.[55] One can see the governor sympathising with Increase Mather's lament of 1676: 'A proud fashion no sooner comes into the country but the haughty Daughters of Zion in this place are taking it up, and thereby the whole land is at last infected.'[56]

In England, on the other hand, though the well-to-do might preen themselves like peacocks in the latest extravaganzas, there seems to have been much less trouble from ordinary people trying to ape their betters. This is hardly surprising when artisans complained about the difficulty of clothing themselves and their families in anything at all. When the wife of a Ludlow blacksmith appeared on the streets of the town in dress conventionally worn by a merchant's wife, she was hooted indoors by her neighbours.[57]

This would suggest conventional acceptance of sumptuary and class distinctions. Maidservants in England were distinguished by the darker colour and coarser texture of their clothing.[58]

Finally we might just allude to comments about leisure as an indicator. Several visitors to both Massachusetts and Virginia commented on the relative indolence of quite ordinary people in the colonies, in implicit contrast with their peers in England. Josselyn, Durand and Beverley all quoted specifically the ease of life at the end of the century. Hugh Jones likewise spoke of 'the laziness of the "common planters"', blaming it on their being 'climate-struck'.[59] All in all, there is little reason to doubt that for the ordinary run of people colonial life held out far greater hopes of prosperity and upward social mobility than the Old World, despite the real, but limited, improvements which Stone and others have detected for England in the seventeenth century.[60]

Economic Opportunities for Women in England and the Colonies

Did future ease and prosperity await women as well as men in the New World in contrast with the Old? Certainly the promoters thought so—Penn addressed his 'country*folks*' and Smith specifically named 'spinsters' as one of trades for the 'fatherlesse children of thirteene or fourteene years of age, or young maried people, that have small wealth to live on'.[61] The same tune was sounded in letters from settlers, which we have already recorded.

Plainly the greatest asset which the colonies held out to women from the Old World was sheer economic demand. While English 'economists' from Hakluyt to King worried about over-population, a phenomenon particularly affecting a surplus of women, 'women wanted' was a fitting sign for colonial settlements. We need not here dwell on the truism that in the colonies labour was short while land was abundant, whereas the reverse was true for England, but, clearly, women, as a major source of labour, could be expected to benefit or suffer depending on the state of the market. Not only could women expect, as we have seen, to rise socially through marriage where they were in short supply, but where labour in general was so short they could expect to breach male closed-shops so far as employment opportunities were concerned. Where the pool of labour was overcrowded, however, the reverse process of exclusion might be expected to operate.

The lot of the servant girl in England in the seventeenth century was unenviable. Even though the number of servants which the rich employed seems to have increased during the century, the state of the labour market remained against them.[62] Indeed this very

67

increase might well have resulted from the cheapness of the labour force. In such a situation there was very little protection for the employed against the employer. The runaway apprentice was a stock figure of letters, even though apprenticeship was the major avenue for many to the possibility of wealth. The Pepys household was probably not atypical. The maid who did the fortnightly wash was up in the early hours of the morning and was sometimes not finished until late at night. Pepys harried and beat the servant girls for what he considered their sluttishness. One he locked all night in the cellar. Deborah Willett was not immune from his more lecherous attentions. The life of the maids compares startlingly with the listless existence of that brainless butterfly Elisabeth Pepys.[63] This kind of treatment was not particularly new or particularly harsh. Bridenbaugh gives several examples from many in the Middlesex County Quarter Sessions Records of savage maltreatment of servants.[64] Those that ever got to the courts were probably only a small minority in that employer-oriented age. Mrs Marshall has gathered a collection of harrowing accounts of the conditions of work and cruel fates of poor girls at the end of the century. They tended to be apprenticed in treadmill trades to masters only interested in the premiums that a parish overseer of the poor might pay. Where a girl became pregnant, as was all too likely, she was often allowed to die through wanton neglect. Not only labour but also life itself was dirt cheap in England.[65] The rapid rise of the charity school movement at the end of the century was a response to the challenge of the unemployment problem. Most of the girls in the schools were trained in domestic service.[66] Hannah Woolley, who had courageously overcome terrible disadvantages herself, ran a registry for domestic service in London in the 1670s.[67] None the less, the competition among her clients for the good jobs must have been intense. Domestic service might not be the lot of the poor only. Thomas Shepard, the future minister at Cambridge, Mass., married Elizabeth Touteville when she was a servant in the household of Sir Richard Darley of Buttercrambe in Yorkshire. She was also his kinswoman. Ralph Josselin, the yeoman-vicar of Earls Colne in Essex, noted in his diary in August, 1644 'My sister Mary is come under my roof as a servant.' Mary Josselin was thirty-three and unmarried.[68] Hannah Woolley, who herself had a reasonable education which allowed her to become self-supporting as a dame at the tender age of fourteen, bewailed the fate of those gentlewomen fallen on evil times, who, because of their lack of vocational training, were unable to keep themselves as housekeepers or waiting-women, but were reduced to the mean status of chambermaids. Some, no doubt, sank even lower and swelled the army of prostitutes that was the last harrowing resort in a punitive economic system.[69] The slide was certainly slippery. Steele quoted a woman who had 'so much Indignation and Resolution as not to go upon the town, as the phrase is, but took to work for my Living in an obscure Place,' but 'a sett of Idle Fellows about this town' were constantly importuning her.[70]

For the country girl, the Act of Settlement, as we have seen, militated against the main career which she could hope for, marriage. Roger North, in his *Discourse upon the Poor*, written at the end of the century, described the effects of the 'War on the Cottages' which landlords and parish officials waged after the act to hinder the settlement of the poor in their domains:[71]

> Young men, intimidated by such cruel treatment, are unwill-ing to marry; and this leads them frequently to debauch young women and then leave them with child in a very hope-less condition.

Mrs Marshall goes farther. The Law, she says, 'broke the habit of chastity among the poorer classes . . . the habit of disregarding marriage became common.'

It would be foolish and unrealistic to paint an over-rosy picture of the condition of servants in the colonies. We know, for instance, that William Byrd took advantage of an English servant-girl whom he took back to Virginia with him from London in 1720[72] and that when he had half a chance he would do the same to others as well.[73] We are told by Sewall that when Mr Mather's maid was suddenly and unsuspectedly brought to bed of a child, he promptly turned her out of his house.[74] Bastards were born to maidservants in Massachusetts and Virginia, just as they were in England. To be a servant-woman was not a particularly enviable lot anywhere.[75]

None the less we would expect the laws of supply and demand to help. That servants were short in the two colonies seems un-deniable. When William Bradford, towards the end of his life— and his *History*—dolefully set about explaining 'how came it to pass that so many wicked persons and profane people should so quicly come over into this land, and mixe themselves amongst them? seeing it was religious men yt begane ye work, and they came for religions sake', one reason he gave was 'Men being to come over into a wilderness, in which much labour and servise was to be done aboute building & planting, &c., such as wanted help in yt respecte, when they could not have such as yey would, were glad to take such as they could.'[76] Winthrop's *Journal* is peppered with complaints about the servant problem.[77] Ezekiel Rogers, another early settler, of Massachusetts Bay, likewise looked back in 1658; it is 'hard to get a servant that is Glad of Catechising, or Family Duties: I had a rare blessing of servants in Yorkshire; and

69

those that I brought over were a blessing: But the Young Brood doth much afflict me.'[78] At the end of the century there was still a dearth of servants in a household like Cotton Mather's, which could be expected to have them if they were available.[79] The general scarcity is borne out by Edmund S. Morgan.[80] At Andover, Mass., in the second generation of settlement, one reason for the sons remaining at home even after marriage is thought to have been the need for their labour on the family holdings.[81]

The situation in Virginia was made more complex by the presence of slaves. How and why chattel negro slavery became institutionalised in the southern colonies is a matter of some debate. The Handlins argue convincingly that what set the negro apart from other servants in the mid-seventeenth-century South was the need for 'the peopling of the country' as a Virginia statute put it.[82]

To encourage immigration therefore, the colonies embarked upon a line of legislation designed to improve servants' conditions and to enlarge the prospect of a meaningful release, a release that was not the start of a new period of servitude, but of life as a freeman and landowner.

In this process the negro did not share; instead of being protected, safeguarded and liberated as were 'christian' servants, he dropped instead inexorably into a state of legalised chattel slavery. The merits of the case need not detain us here. What is significant for our purposes is that all the theses on the origins of legalised slavery concur in stressing the pressing need for labour in Virginia in the seventeenth century. The enormous influx of Africans into Virginia after the ending of the Royal Africa Company's monopoly on the slave-trade bears witness to this need, as does Gooch's report to the Board of Trade in 1730 that large numbers of white servants as well as black slaves had been imported in the previous decade. Twenty-two years before, Colonel Jenings had reported to the same body that the number of white servants in Virginia was so few that they need not be considered. Contemporary evidence suggests that this shortage was due to lack of supply rather than of demand. Writing of the maltreatment of a niece in 1745, Mary Ann Maury said, 'I did my best to get the poor girl away from her, but she was too serviceable.'[83] We have seen Robert Carter writing to London for a school-mistress for his children. Other planters likewise sent requests for domestic servants to England at the end of the century.[84] Where a planter like William Byrd had to use negro house-servants, it seems probable that this was because he could not get white ones, rather than from deliberate choice. Anyway, for our period, the number of negro slaves in Virginia could be counted in hundreds, and did not pose a serious employment threat to white servants.[85]

Given this colonial shortage, we would expect to find women who had emigrated as indentured servants taking advantage of their position. And we do, both in individual cases, and in statute. Edmund Morgan, who examines the position of servants in *The Puritan Family*, comes to the conclusion that they had the whip hand in Massachusetts. He records severe punishments against masters or their sons who took advantage of the girls bound for a period of years to their service. John and Joseph Harris, father and son, were given twenty stripes and a term of imprisonment for the seduction of their maidservant. In the Suffolk County Court in 1676 Judith Platts complained against John Mann, her master, 'for wanton & lascivious carriages towards her, and cruell beatings of her'.[86] Masters and mistresses were similarly vigilant against the stratagems of male servants. A pregnant maid was no maid; if, like Mr Mather's, she was turned out on to the street, there was no army of replacements, as might be on the books of Mrs Woolley's agency in London. Masters were similarly hamstrung against lesser offenders. If they handed them over to the authorities for punishment, they were punishing themselves as much as the culprit. There are several examples given by Morgan of female servants who showed scant respect to their masters. When Mehitable Brabrook was scolded for some fault, she responded, not with toadying penitence, but with a toad in the family's milk.[87] A Beverley maid was found guilty in 1674 of 'riding about the field astride her master's mare'. Another, when reprimanded by her master for beating his daughter would 'mock him to his face'.[88] Cotton Mather, reflecting perhaps on his own unfortunate domestic experiences, had few good words to say for servants in the *Magnalia*. Discussing 'the evils that abound amongst us', he laid much blame on 'servants, that are not kept in due Subjection, their Masters . . . especially being sinfully indulgent towards them'. Among the evils perpetrated by that class he found 'Pride in respect of Apparel. . . . Servants and the poorer sort of people are notoriously guilty in this matter, who (too generally) go above their Estates and Degrees'. Once freed, 'Day Labourers and Mechanicks are unreasonable in their demands.' It was such as these, no doubt, that Josselyn described as earning up to £20 a year. He quoted Ben Jonson's proverb: 'Whistle to a jade and he will pay you with a fart, claw a churl by the britch and he will shit in your hand.'[89] This evidence suggests that, despite other valid criticisms of his thesis, Bernard Bailyn's claim that, in seventeenth-century America, there was 'rampaging insubordination', with servants dishonouring their obligations by negotiation, force or fraud, and achieving their independence quickly and often, seems well-grounded.[90]

The situation seems to have been much the same in Virginia. This was to be expected in the early years of settlement when women were desperately short, but observers of the second and third generations go out of their way to stress the superior conditions of colonial employment as compared with those in England. One reason for this, of course, was that after the Restoration the competition for migrants increased. Carolina, Pennsylvania and the Jerseys were in the race now, not to mention the West Indies, which had taken a large share throughout the century.

This is perhaps one explanation for the stress that John Hammond lays on the fact that women were not normally '(as is reported) put into the grounde to worke, but occupie such domestique imployments and housewifery as in England'.[91] Beverley, writing fifty years later, and himself keen to encourage immigration, made the same point. 'White woman is rarely or never put to work in the ground, if she be good for anything else: And to Discourage all Planters from using any women servants so, their Law imposes the heaviest taxes upon female Servants working in the Ground, while it suffers all other white Women to be absolutely exempted.'[92] That this was not just advertisers' puff is borne out by surviving indentures, like that made between Margaret Broderick and William Fitzhugh in the 1680s.[93]

As we have already noted, the whole institution of indentured servitude came to be regularised by statute, and, as in Massachusetts, the female servant, who must never be put off the idea of Virginia, was safeguarded both by law and by the vigilance of the county courts, which were composed of employers who might suffer from a dearth of servants.[94]

That servants were not driven by their masters in Virginia seems beyond doubt. Beverley, who had reason to know, claimed that not even 'their slaves are worked near so hard, nor so many hours in a day, as the Husbandmen and Day-Labourers in England'.[95] Hammond stated that 'both men and women have times of recreations as much or more than in any part of the World besides'.[96] If the Byrd family is anything to go by, the white servants seem to have almost ruled the roost. In the opening pages of the *Westover Diary* we meet the children's nurse, who not only misbehaves with Daniel, but stays away all night at a relative's wedding, and when reprimanded for this breach of orders 'gave as good as got and was very impudent'.[97] Two years later, we hear of Tom L—d, who 'gave bad language to my wife and I gave chase with my cane but could not overtake him'.[98] One of the last entries of the diary reads: 'My wife had a great quarrel with her maid

Prue and with good reason; she is growing a most notable girl for stealing and laziness and lying and everything that is bad.'[99] That Byrd was not alone is borne out by another entry, in February 1712. 'Col. Duke and his maid were ready to quarrel several times, by which I told him it was plain he was too familiar at other times, but the Col. denied it stiffly.'[100] Even the Governor was not immune. Byrd records how in February 1711, Spotswood 'makes a bargain with his servants not to get drunk at his Ball, but the next day'.[101]

An ultimate sanction which servants had against unjust or slave-driving masters lay in running away. North Carolina, Byrd's Lubberland, or the Vale of Humility between two mountains of Conceit (Virginia and South Carolina) was a notorious haven for runaways by the early eighteenth century. Other masters, desperately in need of help, were not above encouraging promising servants to abscond or giving fugitives aid and employment. In a country so thinly settled it was not all that difficult to evade detection, and the costs of pursuit and recovery were often exorbitant, running up to as much as £10.[102]

Two facts argue that the lot of even the indentured servant—in theory little more than a temporary slave—was a good deal better in fact than that of an English servant. The first is the obvious one that so many thought it worth while to brave the unknown. The second is that there were very few conspiracies among servants, which could be expected if they were in fact badly treated. This compares very favourably with the numerous cases of unrest in city and country in England, such as the explosions of London apprentices, or the bread riots.[103]

Although indentured servants were not meant to marry, it would appear that maids were not infrequently courted by freemen. Not only would this mean that there would be no dowry forthcoming, but by various Virginian laws the freeman who married a maid-servant had to compensate the master for the loss of her services. The fact that such statutes were enacted suggests that they were necessary.[104] Whereas economic conditions militated against marriage for poorer people in England, the opposite seems to have been true in America. Hammond states that that great stumbling block in England, the portion or dowry, was available for almost all girls in Virginia. 'Few there are but are able to give some Portions with their Daughters, more or lesse, according to their abilities.'[105] Even that most pathetic Dickensian tear-jerker, the poor orphan girl, was not automatically bound for the streets, if she lasted that long. By law, girls were bound apprentice until they were eighteen, 'at which time, they who have taken any care to improve themselves, generally get well married, and live in plenty, though they had not a farthing of paternal Estate'.[106] That phrase 'improve themselves', forerunner of 'the self-made man', strikes an echo in Bailyn's *Education in the Forming of American Society* where he writes of 'the recognition that one's role in life had not been fully cast, that the immediate inheritance did not set the final limits, that opportunities beyond the expectation of birth lay all about and could be reached by effort'.[107]

Less is known about women who worked for wages, but it does not seem unreasonable to think that they too were far better off than if they had stayed in England. Although the Browns conclude from their study of Virginia in the eighteenth century that the wages of women were lower than those paid to men, they admit that for special trades women could command equality.[108] In his discussion of wages in Virginia in the preceding century, Bruce mentions Lord Culpeper's response to his 'Instructions' in 1681 concerning the encouragement of a silk industry, which would presumably employ a considerable number of women; the governor 'despaired of silk because of dearness of labour'.[109] He cites an agreement between Josephine Chowne and John Corbett in 1697, whereby Mrs Chowne was to be paid at the rate of £5 16s. 6d. per month; unfortunately neither Bruce nor the agreement specifies the work she was to do. From the examples he gives, the average payment to servants for domestic service at the turn of the century seems to have been between £3 and £5 per year, with full board, or up to 10d. by the day. This was certainly much more than would be paid in England, where prices were higher.[110]

We get an occasional glance at some of these employees. One such, Katherine Young, the housekeeper of the fledgling College of William and Mary, emerges from a paper war between Governor Nicholson and James Blair, Commissary and President of the College. That self-important cleric was moved to call her 'Impudent Hussy', not altogether without cause. [111]

Not only were conditions, comparatively speaking, worse in England, but as the century progressed, the economic opportunities for women deteriorated. This is the thesis of Alice Clark's survey, *The Working Life of Women in the Seventeenth Century*. This decrease in outlets she puts down to various causes, but the all-embracing villain to her is 'the blind force of capitalism'. This blundering destroyer worked on all classes indiscriminately. Among the landowning classes, nobility and gentry, it drove women from partnership with their husbands by emphasising the commercial aspect of landownership, and making estate management into a male-dominated business enterprise. It had a similar effect on bourgeois families by destroying the household unit of business or manufacture, and rendering the woman a mere consumer and ornament. Among the artisan classes, the limitation of the number of masters in various crafts led to a swelling of the number of employed journeymen working away from home. Their wives, who earlier might have hoped to be accepted as members of their husband's guilds and to help in production, were relegated either to 'unpaid domestic servants' or 'separate [and usually ill-paid] employment'. The 'blind forces' killed off Dame Margery Eyre and Ralph's Jane.[112] Miss Clark reports that even yeomen's wives were withdrawing from active, productive work on the farm. The lot of the great mass of agricultural labourers was also in decline, as we have seen. The landowning élite managed to create a class of 'landless serfs', the exploited day-labourers, whose wives could only help to keep the loitering wolf from the door by becoming the wage-slaves of the clothing industry, or domestic drudges. Soaring prosperity or plunging poverty allied to produce the same result. The old familial economic partnership of husband and wife was being undermined. The wife was being driven from her productive role. The concept of the husband supporting his family was replacing mutuality in earning power. In becoming a dependent, the wife lost her 'psychic and moral influence'; her place might still be in the home, but her husband was no longer an integral part of it. Even in fields which women had previously dominated, like brewing, or baking, or midwifery or the retail trade, specialisation tended to squeeze them out in favour of men. They were systematically excluded from 'all independent sources of information and from organisations for the pursuit of science, trade and education'. Significantly, their education went into eclipse; the accomplishments replaced Renaissance rigour. Vocational training for women became an introduction to domestic service or the distaff.[113] Though marred by determinism, Miss Clark's argument is supported by ample and compelling evidence. All in all, there is little doubt that, economically, women's lot did indeed decline in Stuart England.

On the other hand, there are strong reasons for arguing that the rot had not permeated so deeply in the colonies. The more even spread of prosperity is important. Thus, John Dunton, writing in the 1680s, could compare Boston women who were still their husband's partners with English women who were 'Lilies of the Field'.[114] Although such figures as the Parke sisters in Virginia were beginning to show signs of that languid ennui so marked among affluent Englishwomen after the Restoration, they were not entirely excluded from useful work and decision-making. Many of the rows which William Byrd so self-righteously chronicles were about the running of Westover and the plantation, about finances and servants. Though she might be incompetent, Lucy Parke Byrd

75

was none the less still the housekeeper, just as her husband was the manager of his estates, an active farmer and trader rather than a rentier and an absentee. Women who ran plantations with skill and efficiency are not uncommon.[115] Richard Morris has demonstrated in his important early work on colonial law that numerous tort cases show that women had still at the end of the century a close knowledge of their husbands' businesses.[116] Our point is well summarised by Professor Dexter:[117]

> As people become prosperous they desire to multiply their luxuries, and it has been demonstrated repeatedly that of all luxuries one of the most coveted is the possession of 'ladies', a class of woman, that is, who reflect credit upon their husbands and fathers in exact proportion to their uselessness. In pioneer conditions, a lady—using the word in this restricted sense—is as much out of place as a prize Pomeranian.

Perhaps more important than the spread of prosperity was the shortage of labour, which we have discussed in another context. Not only would this tend to increase the bargaining power of women wage-earners and servants, but it would also emphasise women's, including married women's, economic value to the family and the community. They were pairs of hands, not to hold a begging-bowl or a lady's mirror, but to help in production. Woman in America was a mate not just in bed but in work, too.[118] There was no need to make work, as Pepys did to keep Elisabeth from pining indolence; rather, as Boorstin suggests, the American had from the beginning to be a jack-of-all-trades.[119] The Boston merchant, the New England minister, the Virginia planter all had to be 'undifferentiated men' and their wives and daughters had to be undifferentiated women, too. There was no room in America for restrictive male practices. While men might be easing women out of medicine and gynaecology in England, a man could be fined in New England for 'presuming to act the part of midwife', possibly because he should have other tasks to occupy him.[120] Any skill was valuable whichever sex possessed it. A woman weaver could command a comparable wage to that of a man in Virginia; in England women were relegated to the lowly-paid toil of spinning.[121] There was scope enough for a Sarah Knight, an Eliza Pinckney or a Katie Mather to use their talents in the New World. In England, with few exceptions, 'there was no career open to women above the rank of servant'.[122] Moller points out that in America quietism did not flourish as it did among women in Europe.[123] While Englishmen might pour scorn on the idea of gentlewomen engaging in business,[124] and Josiah Child could be amazed at the role of Dutchwomen in commerce,[125] Sewall could ask business advice of Madam

Winthrop, John Custis discuss investments with his wife, and Cotton Mather advocate training in business for girls so that they could help their husbands.[126]

In her scholarly *Colonial Women of Affairs,* Mrs Dexter allows herself the speculation that 'conditions were worse [for women] in the early and middle parts of the nineteenth century than they had been in the previous century' and, by implication, in our period too. Mrs Spruill argues that women in the first century of settlement were tougher and more highly respected than their successors.[127] It is surely significant that the feminist protest which occurred in Restoration England, and was not unconnected with lack of economic opportunity, was not echoed in America for a century. It seems likely that John Adams's grandmother had less need than his wife to remind her husband to 'remember the ladies'.

Notes

1 Paul Landis, *Social Problems* (Chicago, 1959), p. 286.
2 A. W. Calhoun, *Social History of the American Family* (Boston, 1918), vol. II, p. 80.
3 William Penn, *Some Account of the Province of Pennsilvania* (London, 1681), reprinted in Merrill Jensen, ed., *American Colonial Documents to 1776* (London, 1964) (vol. IX in *English Historical Documents,* General Editor, David C. Douglas), p. 123.
4 Ibid., p. 128.
5 Robert E. Brown, *Middle Class Democracy in Colonial Massachusetts 1691–1780* (Ithaca, N.Y., 1955) and Robert E. and B. Katherine Brown, *Virginia 1705–1786: Democracy or Aristocracy?* (Madison, 1964).
6 Edward Johnson, *Wonderworking Providence of Sion's Saviour,* ed. J. Franklin Jameson (New York, 1937), pp. 252, 253, 254, 259ff.
7 Cotton Mather, *Magnalia,* Book III, p. 103.
8 E.g. ibid., Book V, *passim,* esp. p. 90. See also George P. Winship's Introduction to *In Boston in 1682 and 1699* (Providence, 1905), pp. ix–xxviii.
9 Increase Mather, *Discourse of Tithes* (1711), quoted in ibid., p. xix. On this subject, see also Ola Elizabeth Winslow, *Meetinghouse Hill* (New York, 1952).
10 Winship, op. cit., p. 52.
11 Bernard Bailyn, ed., *The Apologia of Robert Keayne* (New York, 1965), pp. x, 78.
12 On the general subject of mercantile wealth in New England, see Bailyn's *New England Merchants in the Seventeenth Century* (New York, 1964), *passim,* esp. chs 4–7.
13 J. Durand, *A Frenchman in Virginia,* ed. and trans. by Fairfax Harrison (privately printed, 1923), pp. 33, 97. Cf. Robert Beverley, *History and Present State of Virginia,* ed. Louis B. Wright (Chapel Hill, 1947) and Hugh Jones, *Present State of Virginia,* ed. R. L. Morton (Chapel Hill, 1956).
14 Kenneth Lockridge, 'Evolution of New England Society, 1630–1790', *Past and Present,* No. 39 (1968), pp. 62ff.
15 Bailyn, *New England Merchants,* pp. 110ff.

16 P. A. Bruce, *The Economic History of Virginia in the 17th Century* (New York, 1895), vol. II, pp. 255, 197, 50–1, 574–5. Cf. Thomas J. Wertenbaker's analysis of the 1704 rent-roll of the colony, which concludes that at least 90 per cent of the freeholders were 'the sturdy independent class of small farmers', with plantations of a few hundred acres mostly worked without slaves or labourers. *The Planters of Colonial Virginia* (Princeton, 1922), pp. 53–9.

17 Figures taken from J. E. Thorold Rogers's *History of Agriculture and Prices in England* (Oxford, 1887), vol. V, and W. W. Hening, *Statutes at Large . . . of Virginia* (Richmond, Va, 1809–23), vols I, II: Bruce, op. cit., vol. II, pp. 208–11.

18 Ibid., vol. II, p. 49.

19 Ibid., vol. II, pp. 203, chs 17, 18, *passim*.

20 Thorold Rogers, op. cit., vol. V.

21 Quoted in Bruce, op. cit., vol. I, p. 581.

22 Quoted in Christopher Hill, *A Century of Revolution* (London, 1961), p. 206.

23 See ibid., p. 207; the quotation is taken from Thorold Rogers; for extended discussions of the effects of the Act see Dorothy Marshall, *English Poor in the Eighteenth Century* (London, 1926), pp. 161ff.; and Bruce, op. cit., vol. I, pp. 577–8.

24 Bruce, op. cit., vol. I, pp. 580–1.

25 Dorothy George, *London Life in the Eighteenth Century* (London, 1925), p. 164.

26 John Hammond, 'Leah and Rachel', reprinted in Force, *Tracts*, vol. III, No. 14, p. 18.

27 Quoted in F. W Tickner, *Women in English Economic History* (London, 1923), p. 104. Cf. the fate of Elizabeth Elstob, the Anglo-Saxon scholar, who after her brother's death subsisted as a dame for many years; see Ada Wallas, *Before the Bluestockings* (London, 1929), ch. 5.

28 Christopher Hill, *Intellectual Origins of the English Revolution* (Oxford, 1965), p. 273.

29 Alice Clark, *Working Life of Women in the Seventeenth Century* (New York, 1920), pp. 114, 129.

30 See C. Bridenbaugh, *Vexed and Troubled Englishmen* (New York, 1968), pp. 169ff.

31 Ibid., p. 169.

32 See esp. John Demos, 'Life in Plymouth', *3 WMQ*, vol. XXII (1965), pp. 275–85; Philip J. Greven, jr, 'Family Structure in Seventeenth Century Andover, Massachusetts', *3 WMQ*, vol. XXIII (1966), pp. 236–56; P. A. Bruce, *Social History of Virginia in the Seventeenth Century* (Richmond, 1907); John R. Hardy, 'A Cursory Investigation of Household Size and Structure in New York State, 1680–1780' (Cambridge University thesis, 1970), *passim*; Edmund S. Morgan, *Virginians at Home* (Williamsburg, 1952); see also David J. Rothman, 'A Note on the Study of the Colonial Family', *3 WMQ*, vol. XXIII (1966), pp. 627–30. For a full discussion see below, pp. 125–7.

33 Quoted in J. Potter, 'Growth of Population in America, 1700–1860' in D. V. Glass and D. E. C. Eversley, eds, *Population in History* (London, 1965), p. 644.

34 E. A. Wrigley, 'Family Limitation in Pre-Industrial England', *Economic History Review*, Second Series, vol. XIX (1966), pp. 82–106.

35 See Marshall, op. cit., p. 167. 'The minister who marries a poor couple prays that they might be fruitful, but his parishioners hope otherwise,' comments Mrs Marshall.

36 Penn, op. cit., reprinted in Jensen, op. cit., pp. 123–4.

37 See John Graunt, *Natural and Political Observations . . . upon the Bills of Mortality* (London, 1662), pp. 27–9, reprinted in Charles H. Hull, ed., *The Economic Writings of Sir William Petty* (New York, 1964), pp. 352–3.

38 Graunt, op. cit., p. 59, Hull, op. cit., p. 371. See also E. A. Wrigley, 'A Simple Model of London's Importance in Changing English Society and Economy, 1650–1750', *Past and Present*, No. 37 (1967), pp. 44–70. Cf. Clark, op. cit., p. 306.

39 Bruce, *Economic History*, vol. I, p. 581; Graunt, op. cit., p. 27, Hull, op. cit., pp. 352–3.

40 See Bridenbaugh, op. cit., pp. 38ff.; Peter Laslett and John Harrison, 'Clayworth and Cogenhoe' in H. E. Bell and R. L. Ollard, eds, *Historical Essays 1600–1750 Presented to David Ogg* (London, 1963), pp. 170ff.

41 Bruce, *Economic History*, vol. I, p. 257.

42 For a fuller discussion of this subject see ch. 11.

43 Cf. Landis's figures for modern America: during the depression there were 100,000 prostitutes in Chicago alone; the count for the whole USA in 1951 was only 275,000, despite, of course, a significant rise of population in the intervening twenty years (Landis, op. cit., p. 301).

44 J. C. Spruill, *Women's Life and Work in the Southern Colonies* (Chapel Hill, 1938), ch. 4, 'Housewives and Their Helpers'.

45 Bruce, *Economic History*, vol. II, p. 202.

46 Josselyn, *Two Voyages to New England* (London, 1674), ed. Veazie (Boston, 1865), pp. 140, 142.

47 Both Durand and Fontaine had gone to America after domicile in England.

48 Harriet S. Tapley, 'Women of Massachusetts, 1620–89' in A. B. Hart, ed., *Commonwealth History of Massachusetts* (Boston, 1927–8), vol. I, pp. 295–6.

49 Henry W. Lawrence, *The Not-Quite Puritans* (Boston, 1928), pp. 4–7.

50 'Records of the Suffolk County Court 1671–80' (hereafter 'Records') in *Collections of the Colonial Society of Massachusetts*, vol. XXX, Part II (Boston, 1933), pp. 698, 751.

51 Cotton Mather, *Ornaments for the Daughters of Zion* (Boston, 1691), p. 57.

52 Sarah Knight, *Journal*, ed. George P. Winship (New York, 1935), pp. 7, 54.

53 Durand, op. cit., p. 99.

54 Bruce, *Economic History*, vol. II, pp. 186–8.

55 *Gooch Letters*, p. 73; letter dated 4 June 1740.

56 Increase Mather, *Earnest Exhortation to the Inhabitants of New England*, p. 6, quoted in Bailyn, *New England Merchants*, p. 141.

57 Quoted in C. V. Wedgwood, *The King's Peace* (London, 1955), p. 53.

58 M. Phillips and W. S. Tomkinson, *English Women in Life and Letters* (Oxford, 1927), p. 66.

59 Hugh Jones, ed. cit., p. 84.

60 See *Past and Present*, No. 33 for conference papers on social mobility in England, especially Stone's, 'Social Mobility in England 1500–1700', pp. 40ff.

61 *Description of New England* (1616) in Edward Arber, ed., *Travels and Works of Captain John Smith* (Edinburgh, 1910), Part I, p. 214.

62 Penn, op. cit., p. 123: 'The pride of the age in its attendance and retinue is so gross and universal that where a man of £1,000 a year formerly kept but four or five servants, he now [1681] keeps twice that number.'

63 See Phillips and Tompkinson, op. cit., pp. 74–144.

64 Bridenbaugh, op. cit., p. 172; cf. pp. 74–144.

65 Marshall, op. cit., pp. 196ff.

66 See Dorothy Gardiner, *English Girlhood at School* (London, 1929), ch. 14, for a good summary, and below, pp. 191–2.

67 Wallas, op. cit., p. 29.
68 Alan Macfarlane, *The Family Life of Ralph Josselin* (Cambridge, 1970), p. 129.
69 See above, p. 65, and below, pp. 240–4.
70 In *Spectator* No. 266, cited in Wallas, op. cit., p. 219.
71 North, cited in Marshall, op. cit., p. 206; her comments pp. 222ff.
72 *London Diary*, pp. 491ff.
73 Ibid., pp. 482, 500.
74 Sewall, *Diary*, I, p. 130; entry for 11 May 1686.
75 The best account is still Abbot Emerson Smith, *Colonists in Bondage* (Chapel Hill, 1947); see also Marcus Jernegan, *Laboring and Dependent Classes in Colonial America* (New York, 1960), Part I, ch. 3.
76 *Bradford's History 'Of Plimouth Plantation'* (Boston, 1898), p. 476.
77 Winthrop, *Journal: History of New England*, ed. J. K. Hosmer (New York, 1946), vol. I, pp. 104, 158, 175; vol. II, pp. 24, 38, 93, 97, 228, 307.
78 Quoted in *Magnalia*, Book III, p. 103.
79 Elizabeth B. Schlesinger, 'Cotton Mather and his Children', *3 WMQ*, vol. X (1953), p. 181.
80 E. S. Morgan, *The Puritan Family* (New York, 1966), pp. 125ff.
81 Greven, op. cit., p. 244.
82 Oscar and Mary Handlin, 'The Origins of the Southern Labor System', *3 WMQ*, vol. VII (1950), pp. 199–222. For another explanation not cited, see Bruce, *Economic History*, vol. II, ch. 11 and pp. 572–3; Winthrop D. Jordan, *White Over Black* (Baltimore, 1969), ch. 2, is a masterly account which modifies the Handlins' thesis.
83 *Memoirs of a Huguenot Family*, ed. Ann Maury (New York, 1872), p. 327.
84 See, e.g., R. B. Davis, ed., *William Fitzhugh and his Chesapeake World* (Chapel Hill, 1963), pp. 82, 205.
85 See Evarts B. Greene and Virginia Harrington, *American Population before the Federal Census of 1790* (New York, 1932), pp. 135–45; they give 2,000 negroes to a total population of 40,000 in 1665; of the 15,000 men that can be mustered in that year, two-thirds are servants and one-third masters. For 1705, the number of slaves was given at 9,000 in a total of over 60,000.
86 'Records', p. 807. She was later charged with fornication. Ibid., p. 1102.
87 Morgan, op. cit., pp. 112–33.
88 Cited by Tapley, op. cit., pp. 318–19.
89 Josselyn, op. cit., pp. 140, 96.
90 B. Bailyn, *Education in the Forming of American Society* (Chapel Hill, 1960), pp. 29–32.
91 Hammond, op. cit., p. 12.
92 Beverley, op. cit., p. 271.
93 Davis, op. cit., p. 205, n.
94 For a full description of the enlightened policy of the colony, with appropriate citations from Hening, see Bruce, *Economic History*, vol. II, ch. 10. Cf. A. E. Smith, op. cit., ch. 11.
95 Beverley, op. cit., p. 272.
96 Hammond, op. cit., p. 12.
97 *Westover Diary*, pp. 7, 28.
98 Ibid., p. 281.
99 Ibid., p. 583.
100 Ibid., p. 480.
101 Ibid., p. 296.
102 Bruce, *Economic History*, vol. I, pp. 19–29.
103 Ibid., vol. II, pp. 29–31. A. E. Smith, op. cit., pp. 260–2. Smith argues that

women had an easier time adapting to conditions in the colonies than men (p. 259).

104 Hening, op. cit., vol. I, 252–3, vol. II, 114; for a discussion of this legislation, see G. E. Howard, *History of Matrimonial Institutions* (Chicago, 1904), vol. II, pp. 231–6, and A. E. Smith, op. cit., p. 302.

105 Hammond, op. cit., p. 17.

106 Ibid., p. 260.

107 Bailyn, *Education*, p. 36.

108 Brown and Brown, *Virginia 1705–1786*, p. 55.

109 Bruce, *Economic History*, vol. I, p. 585.

110 Ibid., vol. II, pp. 49–50. On English wages and prices, see Thorold Rogers, op. cit., vol. V, pp. 664–71, 825–7, and the excellent diagrams based on these figures in Hill, *Century of Revolution*, Appendix C, pp. 317–19.

111 *Papers relating to an Affidavit made by . . . James Blair against Francis Nicholson*, p. 26. Cf. Mrs Dunn, the amanuensis of the Byrd household. *Westover Diary*, pp. 91, 106, 404, 504, 535, 574. *Another Secret Diary*, p. 290.

112 Dekker's *Shoemaker's Holiday*.

113 This summarises her argument on pp. 5–12 and 291–306.

114 John B. Nichols, ed., *Life and Errors* (London, 1818), p. 105.

115 See e.g. 'A Letter of John Clayton . . . to the Royal Society, May 12th, 1688', in Force, *Tracts*, vol. III, pp. 44, 26. Dexter, Spruill and Earle all have chapters on this subject.

116 Richard Morris, *Studies in the History of American Law* (New York, 1930), p. 199.

117 E. A. Dexter, *Colonial Women of Affairs* (Boston, 1924), pp. 170–1.

118 See H. Moller, 'Sex Composition and Correlated Cultural Patterns in Colonial America', *3 WMQ*, vol. II (1945), p. 141.

119 Phillips and Tomkinson, op. cit., 91. Daniel Boorstin, *The Americans: I: The Colonial Experience* (Harmondsworth, 1965), chs 30, 31, 32, 36, 40, 44, 54, 56.

120 Dexter, op. cit., p. 60.

121 Brown and Brown, *Virginia 1705–1786*, p. 55; Clark, op. cit., p. 104.

122 C. Hole, *English Home Life, 1500–1800* (London, 1947), p. 58.

123 Moller, op. cit., pp. 146ff.; cf. W. H. Blumenthal, *Brides from Bridewell* (Rutland, Vt, 1962), pp. 18ff.

124 See W. Notestein, 'The English Woman 1580–1650' in *Studies in Social History Presented to G. M. Trevelyan, ed. J. H. Plumb* (London, 1955), p. 84; Chesterfield, *Letters*, p. 91.

125 Josiah Child, *Brief Observations concerning Trade and the Interest of Money* (London, 1665), 'Seventh Reason'.

126 See Sewall, *Diary*, III, pp. 272–4; *Westover Diary*, p. 440; Cotton Mather, *Ornaments for the Daughters of Zion* (Boston, 1691), p. 82.

127 Dexter, op. cit., p. 170ff.; Spruill, op. cit., p. 242.

Chapter 4

Women and the Puritan Churches

' "The time has come", the Walrus said, to talk of puritanism and the puritans. I had hoped to get through this book without that disagreeable task of definition; but it cannot be done.'[1] If the redoubtable historian of Harvard and puritan intellectual life quails at the prospect, how much more should lesser mortals? If definition is disagreeable, an attempt to discover the social effects of puritanism plunges us into a sea of disagreement. Specifically, there is little concurrence among the experts about the effects which puritanism had on the role and status of women, either within the churches, or in society at large.

This chapter will be suffused with attempts at defining different areas of puritan thought. The term 'puritan' will be used in two, I hope easily distinguished, senses: first, as already used, in the generic sense, as the 'left wing' of protestantism, and incorporating the sects; second, with particular reference to the established Congregational church of Massachusetts, and in this sense very definitely excluding sectarian 'heretics'.

Just as the sex ratio appeared to exert greater influence in man-starved Virginia, so we would obviously expect any benefits from puritanism for women to be most effective in Massachusetts. Puritanism was the mainstream of the New England colony, the great cultural shaper, whereas in the old country, though undeniably influential, it was tributary to the dominant Anglican system. If, therefore, we find that puritanism did in fact contribute to women's emancipation, then they would reap the richest harvest in Massachusetts.

Puritan Social Orthodoxy

If we were to follow the party line of orthodox Massachusetts puritanism, or, for that matter, of the English dogma from which it developed, we would have to conclude that its liberating influence on women was negligible. In theory, at least, Massachusetts and staider English puritanism were strictly patriarchal.

That great authority, 'the Apostle', was apparently quite unambiguous on this point. 'As the church is subject unto Christ, so let the wives be [subject] to their husbands in everything.'[2] More specific was the message of the First Epistle to Timothy: 'A woman must be a learner, listening quietly and with due submission. I do not permit a woman to be a teacher, nor must women domineer over men; she should be quiet'. Furthermore, 'It is my desire that everywhere prayers be said by the men of the congregation, who shall lift up their hands with a pure intention.'[3] St Peter, often thought of as more liberal than the misogynist bachelor Paul, was in this equally firm.[4]

> Women must accept the authority of their husbands, so that if there are any of them who disbelieve the Gospel they may be won over, without a word being said, by observing the chaste and reverent behaviour of their wives. . . . Thus it was among God's people in days of old: the women who fixed their hopes on Him adorned themselves by submission to their husbands. Such was Sarah, who obeyed Abraham and called him 'my master'.

St Paul, of course, even appeared to believe that marriage itself was a second-best: 'Better be married than be burned with vain desire', but better still, keep cool and celibate.[5] To puritan patriarchs, the argument ended here. The most influential spokesmen of puritan dogma throughout the century emphasised the subordination of women. Winthrop and Johnson agreed on the absurdity of permitting women any religious independence. Cotton Mather, who was somewhat more sympathetic to women in the church, none the less admonished them that the best way to avoid errors, to which they were, he thought, peculiarly prone, was to follow the lead given by good men.[6] Such men would probably have sympathised with the quandary that the Virginian authorities faced over the Walker case, and would have agreed with the verdict. The problem which George and Ann Walker posed was that the husband was a Quaker, and therefore a heretic, while the wife was an orthodox Anglican, and therefore, presumably, much more suitable to control the upbringing of the Walker children in Anglican Virginia. The court, however, concluded that wifely subordination was a more important principle at stake than heresy, and by its judgment buttressed the husband's authority within the family.[7]

Not only were the preachings of Congregationalism clear on this point, but also some of its practices seemed to underline the doctrine of the inferiority of women. The common, though not universal, practice of receiving women's confessions in private was partly based on the assumption that women were weaker vessels who needed more delicate handling.[8] Though women might become members of churches, in some, at least, they seem to have only had second-class membership so far as the conduct of church affairs was concerned, being 'but mute observers'.[9] Rutman quotes a letter from Peter Bulkeley, pastor of recently-founded Concord to John Cotton, written in February 1642: 'may a woman seeking guidance', he queries, 'ask advice in a private assembly, or should a man undertake to ask for her?'[10] The puritan church organisation gave women no official role to undertake. It is true that Thomas Lechford, writing in 1642, mentioned the office of the Deaconess or Widow, and that, at that period, Cotton and Davenport both saw these older female members potentially as 'fit assistants to the Deacons, in ministering to the sick'.[11] However, there is no sign that this potential office was developed in Massachusetts. Officially subordinate, deprived of voice or official capacity, women can hardly be described as being positively nurtured by the larger puritan church organisations. Yet the fact remains that, despite this repressive party line, women of broadly puritan bent did make a remarkable impact on both religious and other affairs in the seventeenth century, in Massachusetts and in England. We need here only mention such Amazons as Anne Hutchinson or Mary Dyer in Massachusetts, or, in England, Margaret Fell or the sectarian women of the Interregnum. What we must now try to discover is whether there were inherent qualities in seventeenth-century puritanism which encouraged and emancipated women, and whether there were other factors affecting puritanism which led to similar results. We must conclude the chapter by asking whether puritanism had any particular attractions to women, over and above other creeds.

Puritanism and Emancipation

One of the most hackneyed catch-phrases about protestant doctrine is 'The Priesthood of All Believers'. This responsibility of the individual in seeking his own salvation has been traditionally contrasted with the role of the priest, the sacraments, and the church hierarchy in Roman Catholic theology. The reformers' emphasis on the personal conscience of the believer, and on his personal relationship with God, was central to the new dogma, and was, and is, an area which is vulnerable to heavy hostile attack. If such onus was to be placed upon the individual believer, it was charged, how could the convictions and conscience of one follower be weighed and evaluated against those of another, and how, in the last resort, could any meaningful church, let alone uniformity, be maintained?

These concepts and these problems were exported to Massachusetts in the 1630s and remained in England and baffle authority during the puritan hegemony of the 1640s and 1650s. In Massachusetts Congregationalism, the importance of the individual covenant for the church member is probably the most obvious manifestation of the dogma. What is important for our purposes is that that individual might well be a woman.

When a church was being founded in newly settled Dedham, Massachusetts, in 1637, one of the first necessities was to select from the settlers seven pillars or founder members. Among those short-listed was Joseph Kingsbury, an important member of the community who had already been appointed to a committee to 'contrive the Fabrik of a meetinghouse' which was to stand on part of his lot. Upon examination, however, he was found to be 'too much addicted to ye world', 'stiff and unhumbled', and was finally guilty of 'distempered flying out'. He was rejected, not only as a pillar, but also from church membership when ordinary members were chosen. His wife, however, 'a tender harted soule full of feares & temptations but truly breathing after Christ', was admitted to membership among the first intake. Joseph Kingsbury had to wait for four years before being admitted a member of the church at Dedham.[12] This case is not unique. In the *Records of the First Church of Boston*, it is not uncommon to find wives admitted to membership before their husbands.[13]

The full gravity of these cases can only be understood when the importance of membership is considered. To the puritan in Massachusetts, membership of the church was the most crucial hurdle in life. Acceptance was not just entry into a club, but joining 'a little bundle of eternal life'.[14] It meant the difference between heaven and hell in the life hereafter. It was not the approval of men that mattered, but the approval of God that the candidate must show. 'Election' was not human, but divine; man alone was powerless to achieve it. To number with the saints showed that you were predestined by God for salvation. It was the separation on earth of the sheep from the goats. When the dying wife of Thomas Shepard, minister of Cambridge, took the church covenant in 1636, 'she said to us she now had had enough; and we were afraid her feeble body would have at that time fallen under the weight of her joy'. She had, just in time, entered 'the marginal zone of safety'.[15]

What would have been the effect in the Kingsbury household of the wife's election and the husband's rejection from the 'visible saints'? Where excommunicants from the church covenant 'would meet either with black looks or with pitying ones [because] they had thrown away a precious jewel'[16] and where church membership was the key for citizenship,[17] how would a male, who was merely a member of the unregenerate congregation, feel about a wife who was a member of the church, numbered among the visible saints? How would Kingsbury's traditional authority within his family and community be affected by the fact that, when he reapplied for the coveted membership, his own wife would be one of the sisters who might uprise from their seats, while the brethren would show their hands, in voting?[18] Much the same, no doubt, as the many husbands who were excommunicated for offences while their wives remained members.[19] What the psychological and social effects of this situation were, it is, in the very nature of the case, almost impossible to discover. We can only speculate that New England puritanism, by being in this vital area no respecter of persons or of sexes, and thus subtly and unconsciously an underminer of that very patriarchalism it publicly championed, must inevitably have given women's morale and self-esteem a very considerable boost.[20]

It was one of the most irritating and, at the same time, dangerous of Roger Williams's traits that he tended to drive tentative or vulnerable puritan beliefs to their logical conclusion, irrespective of politics or practicality. It is therefore not surprising that this undermining of patriarchalism by puritan belief should have manifested itself most starkly in Williams's infant plantation of Providence, Rhode Island, in the controversial Verin case. Goodman Verin had not only 'refused to hear the word with us (which we molested him not for this 12 month)', but also forbade his wife to attend his neighbour Williams's lectures. When the case came up for official discussion, the traditionalist, Goodman Arnold, argued that 'when he consented to that order' for religious liberty, 'he never intended it should extend to the breach of any ordinance of God, such as the subjection of wives to their husbands'. Goodman Green told him flatly, however, 'that if they should restrain their wives etc., all the women of the country would cry out of them, etc.' Eventually, it was the Pauline husband, and not the disobedient wife, who was punished by the Council's sentence of disfranchisement in 1638.[21]

To the puritan, salvation did not come in neat family package-trips, but in single, non-transferable tickets, for man or for woman. 'She too had to go on a spiritual pilgrimage and make spiritual war, and she had to go on her own feet and fight her own battle.'[22] Preaching at Cambridge, Massachusetts, in 1671, Jonathan Mitchell said, 'Woman is lastly [i.e. ultimately] and as *Homo* (or one of mankinde) for God; but nextly and as *Mulier* (in her proper place and sex) for the man.'[23] It is this tension between *Homo* and *Mulier*, a tension inherent in puritanism, between church 'sister' and man's wife, that held the potential for greater female independence and individualism. In arguing that slaves in Spanish South America were better treated under the aegis of the Roman Catholic church than were their brothers in the North, Stanley Elkins uses a line analogous to our own. Catholics assumed that 'he was a man, that he had a moral nature, that he was not only as susceptible to sin but also as eligible for grace as his master—that master and slave were brothers in Christ'.[24]

Closely allied with this sense of equality in eligibility for grace is the tendency inherent in puritanism towards fissiveness, separatism, the splintering away of sects. Independency was not merely the name for a puritan group, it was also a state of mind which the creed encouraged. If there was to be a priesthood for all believers, it was not a very long stride to a church for every priest. Furthermore, the broad tenets of puritanism in England had been formed during its opposition to the Establishment. Its early dynamism was sustained by hostility to what was thought of as a half-baked reformation. It was weaned on attacks on Parker and cut its teeth on opposition to Whitgift and Bancroft. Its muscles had been developed in combat against Anglican errors and its health had been maintained by preserving a certain immunising distance from the disease-ridden Church of England.

But what would happen if the opposition became the government? How would the spirit of questioning and criticism, the tradition of exclusiveness, the obstinate sense of ownership of the one truth—how would these be accommodated in a new Establishment? And how secure would the new order be in its own orthodoxy? Would doctrines developed in opposition be rigid enough to stand the strains of ruling? These were problems faced both by the Congregationalists in their errand into the wilderness and by the mixed band of puritans who emerged victorious from the English Civil War. There was more than one architect aspiring to draw the plans and supervise the building of the city upon a hill, as there was for the holy commonwealth in England. Men like Winthrop, Williams, Wilson, Cotton, Wheelwright and Hooker engaged in open debate, swaying congregations like Salem, Boston or Cambridge with their schemes. The very multiplicity of experiments during the Interregnum, and Cromwell's frequent need to beseech opponents 'in the bowels of Christ' that they might be wrong, tell a similar story. On the personal level, how would the godly puritan respond to the justification that 'My God-given conscience tells me that what I do is right', especially when he himself had recently used just such an argument to support his opposition to Laudianism? In this general atmosphere of instability and uncertainty, women too might come into their own. They too had God-given consciences. Like the Catholic women of Elizabeth's reign, they too had first-hand experience of the dangers of the heretic-hunting Establishment. They had been active members of the puritan underground and might claim their due when it surfaced.

All these questions, of course, lead us to the disturbing Mrs Hutchinson, and not only to her, but also to a host of other women. In Massachusetts, for instance, they are signposts to Sarah Keayne, who was driven out of the First Church of Boston for 'hir Irregular prophesying in mixt Assemblys and for refusing ordinarily to heare in the Churches of Christ';[25] to Lady Deborah Moody, who questioned orthodox doctrine on baptism and earned the reputation from John Endicott of 'a dangerous woman';[26] to the 'devout *women*', followers of Roger Williams at Salem, who 'did embrace his opinions, and separated from the churches';[27] to Mrs Oliver of Salem, who disturbed the peace in church meeting because she was excluded from membership, but who 'was (for ability of speech, and appearance of zeal and devotion) far before Mrs Hutchinson';[28] to the Quaker missionaries like Mary Dyer— a sometime Hutchinsonian, who had followed her leader out of the Boston meeting-house when she was formally excommunicated— and to the women in Massachusetts and Virginia who were their converts.[29]

It seems highly unlikely that the emergence of Anne Hutchinson was unconnected with the fluid state of affairs in infant Massachusetts. The sense of release and exhilarating liberation surely helped in developing her revolutionary claims and in sustaining her movement. It also helps to explain the violent vindictiveness among men in authority that her actions excited.[30] Her achievement had breathtaking temerity. What she did was to usurp the leadership of the church of Boston from its pastor and to win over to her teachings such men as John Cotton and Governor Harry Vane, and the great majority of the men in the congregation. What, in effect, she claimed was equal authority in church matters with the traditional masters.

It is, of course, all too easy to fall into the trap of romanticising Anne Hutchinson, as Charles Francis Adams tended to do. Yet even if we accept that Mrs Hutchinson was a dangerous 'nihilist' threatening the cohesion of the infant colony, as Morgan argues, or that she was psychologically abnormal, afflicted with menopausal neuroses, bitterly intolerant, and supported by groups who were motivated not only by theological considerations, as Battis suggests, none the less we should not forget that her opponents were men with great educational, social and, most of all, traditional advantages as men; that she disproved customary masculine arguments about the weakness of women's intellect and courage; and that her impact was not just a nine-days' wonder in the ecclesiastical history of Massachusetts.[31] It is surely worth pondering, as Battis suggests, what she might have achieved if she had been born in a period more amenable to the views of women. What she did achieve, against an overwhelmingly hostile tradition, speaks not only for her striking personality, but also for the opportunities which an unsure puritanism could offer to women.

Much the same could be said of the rise of the sects in England, particularly of their most enduring group, the Quakers. The story of the role of women like Katherine Chidley, Dorothy Hazzard, Mary Cary or Mrs Attaway has been well and fully told by Keith Thomas and Patricia Higgins.[32] It will be enough here to cull a few examples of their actions, and to outline the main changes which they temporarily wrought.

Dorothy Hazzard lived in Bristol. In 1631, Anthony Kelly, a grocer, her first husband, died. 'After his death,' writes Miss Higgins, 'she seems to have developed into a forceful character.' In good puritan manner, she refused to close her shop at Christmas,[33] and was compared to 'a he-goat before the flock'. In 1639 she walked out of divine service in the Anglican church when the good Laudian who was preaching dared to justify pictures and images. Her second husband, Mr Hazzard, was a godly Anglican minister, but, after the ending of the Eleven Years' Tyranny, she moved more and more towards separatism. She refused to attend Common Prayer services, merely entering the church when her husband began to preach. In the 1640s she set up a separatist congregation at Broadmead, which had 160 members. Several other leading lights of this group were women.[34]

Dorothy Hazzard was one of many. The puritan Oliver Heywood's mother personally demolished 'relicks of superstition' in her parish church, and 'procured the settlement of godly ministers in places adjacent'. Mrs Chidley not only mothered a leading leveller son, but also preached and jousted in a tract tournament with the doughty Edwards of *Gangraena* fame. Having spread the word from London pulpits, she took herself and her 'poyson' off to Suffolk in the summer of 1646 to swell her following. Mrs Attaway was the most famous of the 'tubbers' in Coleman Street, London. Among other enormities, she commended 'Master Milton's Doctrine of Divorce, which she put into practice by running away with another woman's husband'. Elizabeth Avery, whose tract-writing so offended the nose of her New England brother, Thomas Parker, became a leading member of the Fifth Monarchy movement in Dublin in the 1650s. Women became famed as travelling preachers, religious controversialists, extempore exhorters, faith-healers, prophetesses, versifiers, tractarians, fasters and revelationists. They criticised male preachers with cries of 'Lies' and 'False Doctrine', 'Black Dog',

'Damned Dogg', 'God in his mouth and the Devil in his Heart' and 'Rather hear a carte wheel creake and a dogge barke'. They organised meetings of the young for godly instruction and were active, even aggressive, in the choice or dismissal of ministers. Little wonder that men like Prynne or Nalson or the Venetian ambassador reacted like Winthrop or Edward Johnson.[35]

'From the Montanist movement onwards, the history of enthusiasm is largely a history of female emancipation', wrote Ronald Knox in *Enthusiasm*.[36] Most important for us is the way that the sects both gave women a far greater role in church government and discipline, and also propounded freedom of conscience for women. Thomas cites John Brinsley, a hostile but perceptive observer, to explain the causes of female participation in the new groups: 'They were not allowed to concern themselves with the discipline and government of the Church "and hereupon they grow discontented, and fall into dislike with the present state of the Church; and that discontent lays them open to Satan's delusions" '. He also quotes Mrs Chidley and several others to the effect that a husband has no authority 'to be a Lord over her conscience'. Jane Adams, who failed to attend Baptist meeting at Fenstanton in 1658, got short shrift when she claimed that her husband would not let her come. Thomas sees the most important long-term role of the sects as that of undermining religious sanctions which buttressed the contemporary view of society. He writes:[37]

> Once the religious sanction was taken away or weakened, 'then the whole of society was subject to challenge and rescrutiny from a new point of view—that of reason, natural right, popular consent and common interest. . . . As another pamphleteer realised, 'If this principle were true, that all subjection and obedience to persons and their laws stood by virtue of their electing them, then . . . all women at once were exempt from being under government.'

The charge of usurpation bound Mrs Hutchinson to the English sectaries and levellers.

The doctrine of conscientious independence was taken one stage further by some of the more extreme sects. They argued that one of the regenerate, by being reborn into a new, saved, personality, was not required to remain yoked to a mate who was unregenerate. It was suggested in the Verin case that one solution would be that 'the church would dispose her to some other man who would use her better'.[38] This was a concept that found favour among such sectarians as Mrs Attaway in England, and with the Labadists in the Low Countries. Peter Sluyter made himself unpopular in America by twice enticing converts to his faith away from their wives, who remained unconverted.[39] In a limited way the orthodox puritans of New England also approved of such 'eugenics'. When, for instance, in 1658, Christopher Winter of the West Barnstaple church discovered an affection for a Mrs Cooper, who was 'vaine, light, proude ... and much given to scoffing', he was first warned by his co-members and then, when he failed to heed them, was excommunicated.[40] It is even possible that the serious discussions of polygamy which occurred in England in mid-century may have been connected with the fact that there were more female regenerates than male. The Muggletonians put such problems in their right perspective by decreeing that in heaven everyone would be male.[41]

There seems little doubt that the 'madness' of the Interregnum was thoroughly 'cured' by the Restoration. Both Anglicans and Presbyterians were throughout adamantly opposed to the opportunities which the sects gave to women. While those who remained faithful to the sects despite vigorous persecution tended to intermarry and form small islands of exclusivity, nonconformity developed a 'casuistry every bit as patriarchal as that of the more orthodox religious leaders before the Civil War'. Even the Quakers, whose 'contribution to women's emancipation was enormous', and the Baptists reverted to patriarchalism as they became institutionalised.[42] Apart from the nonconformist background which we have noted in several feminists, there seems little connection between Restoration emancipation movements and the teachings of the sects.

On the other hand, the separatist urge and its tendency to give opportunities to women seem to have persisted, despite masculine opposition, in New England. The inebriating example of Mrs Hutchinson died hard. Rhode Island, to which she fled, was, according to the hostile Johnson, festering with people,[43]

> among whom there were some of the female sexe, who (deeming the Apostle Paul to be too strict in not permitting a woman to preach in the publique Congregation) taught notwithstanding; they have their call to this office from an ardent desire of being famous, especially the grand Mistress of them all, who ordinarily prated every Sabbath day, till others, who thirsted after honour in the same way with herself, drew away her Auditors, and then she withdrew herself, her husband and her family also, to a more remote place.

In the second half of the century the Society of Friends, which had many affinities with Hutchinsonian antinomianism, had a significant number of female adherents, no doubt to some extent attracted by its doctrines of sexual equality. Apart from the early missionaries, like Mary Dyer, Anne Austin, or Mary Fisher, and the enthusiasts who disturbed the Congregationalists' peace by appearing naked in meeting or entering services covered with dirt, or barracking preachers,[44] there were less spectacular women who continued faithful and sustained the cells of believers. During his hectoring tour of the colonies on behalf of the Anglican Society for the Propagation of the Gospel, George Keith met many determined Quaker women who spoke at meetings and disputed with their stiff-necked visitor and critic.[45] Women often appear also in the frequent journals of Quaker missionaries to the New World.[46]

It may seem paradoxical after all this talk of persecution and hostility to advance as the third inherent quality of puritanism, which might help to emancipate women, the concept of toleration. None the less, it is not altogether illogical to link the ideas of the priesthood of all believers and of separatism with a gradual growth of the idea that the views of others, if not positively subversive, might best be borne with rather than mercilessly rooted out. Were this sense of live and let live extended by husbands and by society at large to women, then, plainly, a significant step forward in women's rights would have been achieved.[47]

Seventeenth-century puritans were not twentieth-century liberals. Their ideas of toleration were closely circumscribed. They could not be lenient to a fault. However, a reading of Winthrop's *Journal* does reveal a somewhat unexpected open-mindedness and charity on the part of the author. He, like other leaders, goes to endless pains to persuade, to reconcile differences, to achieve consensus, rather than to coerce and dictate. There are, of course, limits, and not all aspire to or even approve of even this flexibility. The obdurate, however, sustained blows from two directions in the 1660s: the humiliating failure of the persecutions to stop the Quaker plague—indeed the martyrdoms seem to have positively encouraged sympathy for the Friends—and the collapse of the consensus in the Half-Way Covenant controversy. Other, external, elements were also beginning to undermine zeal and orthodoxy, such as a growing commercialism, English tolerationist influences, and the dispersion of settlement. By the end of the century Nathaniel Ward's diatribe against indulgence for heretics would for many have had little more than archaic or literary interest.[48]

One benefit which women seem to have extracted from this modest relaxation consisted in a greater freedom of choice in the churches which they joined. On 1 April 1705, for instance, Sewall mentions that his daughter, who was married to Grove Hirst, had joined the Brattle Street Church, which could not have greatly pleased his orthodox soul.[49] Cotton Mather quite deliberately made no move about his daughters, Katey and Nibby, joining a church until they were fully grown, and could thus, presumably, make up their own minds.[50] This freedom accorded to women in matters of conscience at the end of the century is demonstrated by the Foxcroft family of Boston. Colonel Foxcroft was an Anglican and warden of the King's Chapel in Boston. His wife, however, remained a Congregationalist. A suggestion of the sort of influence that a godly mother might have is given by the fact that their son, Thomas, who graduated from Harvard in 1717, preferred to remain in his mother's faith rather than in his father's, and was ordained Assistant to the First Church.[51] Indeed, the very fact that so many more women than men attended churches at the end of the century argues that they were independent enough in their thinking not to be swayed by male indifference or complacency.

Feminine Zeal

None of the three factors inherent in puritanism has much relevance in an age of indifference. It remains to ask, therefore, whether women had a particularly strong commitment to puritanism, and whether this very zeal thereby subverted the patriarchal party line, and allowed women a greater involvement in the life of the churches.

Certainly women played important roles during the heroic phases of English puritanism, like the Laudian persecutions. To take but one example, when Thomas Shepard was on the run from Archbishop Neile's pursuivants in remote Hedden, Northumberland, it was two women of the town who maintained him and lent him a house in that poverty-stricken parish. When his first attempt to get to New England was foiled by shipwreck off Yarmouth in 1634, it was a Mrs Corbet of Bastwick who gave him shelter. Later, in London, he was hidden from the authorities by a succession of courageous puritan women.[52]

Furthermore, puritan Englishwomen had a reputation for overpowering zeal, particularly in the first half of the century. The 'she-precise hypocrite', who never missed a sermon, took notes on it assiduously, and would even 'dispute with the Doctors of Divinity at her own table', was a stock figure of fun on the Jacobean stage.[53] 'Shee overflows so with the Bible that she spills it upon every occasion and will not cudgel her maids without Scripture'.[54] Richard Hooker thought that the conversion of women was part of a puritan plot; because women were 'propense and inclinable to holiness', they would draw their menfolk after them into the cause. Certain churches with puritan preachers were heavily patronised by women.[55] In his studies of philanthropy, W. K. Jordan has demonstrated how from 1583 onwards 'formidably Puritan ladies' zealously endowed lectureships.[56] On a personal level, there were many puritan men, who, looking back to their youth, gratefully acknowledged the early instruction in godliness which they had received from their mothers.[57] There was, of course, considerable opposition from men to women taking any active part in religious life. Ralph Verney, for instance, was as strongly against his god-daughter learning shorthand, with which she might take down notes on sermons, as he was against her learning Latin. Fairly typical of this attitude was the counsel to women given by Richard Brathwaite in 1641: 'She desires not to have the esteeme of any shee-clarke . . . she had rather be approved of her living than learning.'[58] This may have been one of the causes for the detectable lapsing of women after the Restoration into a more mystical, devotional, quietist frame of mind, in which they spent hours in their private oratories or making endless entries in spiritual diaries.[59] It does not seem that English puritans or Anglicans in the seventeenth century ever really successfully harnessed and employed the religious zeal and energy of women.

The one general exception to this rule in England was the Society of Friends, in which women were accorded virtual equality and in which, certainly in the early years of the sect's history, they played a prominent and very active part. There were other reasons why Quakerism should be attractive to women. Its pacifism and practice of passive resistance, its spontaneity and lack of liturgical forms or complex theology—all these would be likely to appeal, not only to gentlefolk, but also to women of the poorer classes. The story of their often herioc role in the young movement has been well recorded already.[60] Significantly, it was in the very creed where there was no ministry, no traditional hierarchy and very little formality in meetings, that women did manage to make an impact.

We turn now to New England Congregationalism. We have already looked briefly at the official pronouncements and policy on the position of women in the churches, and singularly unencouraging they appeared to be. Nevertheless, puritan women in Massachusetts do not appear to have been unduly discouraged, certainly so far as their devotion to the church was concerned. The table of admissions to membership of the Boston church between 1630 and 1649 shows that 411 women were permitted to join the elect as opposed to 379 men. One, and probably the most telling, reason for this majority was 'the greater propensity of men to place the affairs of this world before those of the afterworld'.[61] In the latter part of the century, this propensity was much more marked, according to Cotton Mather: 'As there were three Maries to one John, so still there are far more Godly women in the world than Godly Men; and our Church Communions give us a little demonstration of this.' Among this feminine majority there were thirty or forty gracious young women who regularly came to communion.[62] Throughout the seventeenth century, Oberholzer has found no cases of women charged with sabbath-breaking, in striking contrast with large numbers of male offenders. One of the reasons which Madam Winthrop gave for not marrying Samuel Sewall was that, in joining his household, she would 'be so far from . . . the Lecture'.[63] It was Samuel Shrimpton's wife, not Shrimpton himself, that Edward Randolph had to assure 'that Nobody in your Colony will be disturbed in their worship'.[64] Mather illustrated the godliness of Boston women by citing the scandalous May case. Samuel May, a charlatan minister, was a cunning seducer in more than dogma. Yet his insinuations were smartly repelled by the young and attractive churchwoman he sought to tempt, and he was quickly reported to the authorities and deported from the colony.[65]

The Salem Witch-hunt reveals feminine zeal in two forms, one enviable, the other misguided and appalling. Often the women who were accused of witchcraft came out of the ordeal better than the men. Rebecca Nurse was not alone in her admirable bearing in the dock. Most of them were steadfast in denying their guilt, neither confessing, nor turning against their spouses like Giles Corey or William Good. They showed courageous scepticism towards the maniacal proceedings. No man followed Sarah Cloyse when she stalked out of Parris's vindictive hanging sermon against her sister, Rebecca Nurse. Not even George Jacobs could match the contemptuousness that Susannah Martin of Amesbury displayed towards her accusers. The convicted women died well—none asked for more time, like John Proctor. There was a magnificent disdain in Sarah Good's cursing response to the Revd. Nicholas Noyes's nagging on the scaffold: 'You are a liar. I am no more a witch than you are a wizard, and if you take away my life God will give you blood to drink.' Sarah Ingersoll had more insight than the wretched Noyes in sensing the falseness of Sarah Churchill's testimony at the height of the outbreak and persuading her to recant. Sarah Nurse dared publicly to depose against the fraud of one of the accusers at her mother's trial. The fifteen-year-old Margaret Jacobs faced almost certain re-accusation after recanting her confession which had incriminated that old buzzard, her grandfather. When the witchcraft spread to Andover, two leading men broke charity with their wives and urged them to confess. Goody Tyler had two lily-livered men to contend with. Her brother Bridges nagged at her all the way to Salem, and, when they arrived, John Emerson, cleric and schoolmaster, joined in the badgering to make her confess. Six Andover women withdrew their confessions, though fully aware of the probably fatal consequences. There is little doubt that the bearing of women such as these did as much to bring the madness to an end as did *Cases of Conscience*.[66]

The misguided zeal was, of course, that of the accusers, mainly women and girls, though it was men, one of them a son-in-law of Rebecca Nurse, who lodged the first complaints. Some of them, like Mrs Anne Putnam, had reputations for devotion to their church. It could be argued that their being victims of genuine clinical hysteria arising from fear of the devil shows that the teachings of the ministry had gone home to the feminine much more deeply than to the masculine subconscious. What is particularly remarkable about this confrontation of zeal with zeal is that men were sometimes edged right out of the lime-light, even though they might be prestigious magistrates like Hathorne, or ministers like Lawson.

A subsidiary explanation for the greater number of women church members than men in Winthrop's Boston is that if a parent failed to attain sainthood, or did not bother to attempt it, he or she was 'leaving their children in jeopardy for want of baptism', which was a privilege reserved for the offspring of members only. Oberholzer's account of members' confessions of fornication at a later period lends cogency to this, and supports the contention that women's zeal was markedly stronger than men's by the end of the century. He cites an, admittedly extreme, case at Danvers—formerly the Salem Village of the Witch-hunt—in 1710, where the wife appeared, confessed and showed signs of repentance, but the husband did not even bother to attend the hearing.[67] The act of confession restored the member 'to the privilege of transmitting baptism to his [or her] child, which by his fall he had cutt himselfe from'.[68] Especially after the introduction of the second charter in 1691, when excommunication would no longer automatically lead to male disfranchisement, it does not seem unlikely that the main impetus towards the regaining of church membership came from fallen wives rather than from fallen husbands. All these points add up to giving strong grounds for stating that the zeal of puritan women was sustained much more successfully throughout the century than was that of their menfolk.

In certain areas this zeal did achieve informal break-throughs for women. We should not expect too much. Even today the paradox persists that women, though the majority of worshippers in many denominations, are still not generally admitted to the ministry. It is, however, significant that in the mopping-up operations after the banishment of Mrs Hutchinson, a synod of elders decreed[69]

that they [women] might some few gather together to pray
and edify one another, yet such an assemblage as was then in
practice in Boston, where sixty or more did meet every week,
and one woman (in a prophetical way by resolving questions
of doctrine and expounding scripture) took upon her the
whole exercise, was agreed to be discreditable and without
rule.

From evidence available for the end of the century it seems clear
that women availed themselves of this outlet, not necessarily at all-
female gatherings, but assiduously at mixed ones. In December
1706, Cotton Mather noted an all-day meeting for Thanksgiving
organised by a group of devout women.[70] Sewall usually recorded
the weekday meetings which he attended for godly discussion and
edification, and they were often held at a woman member's house.
At a meeting on 15 January 1707, when the weather was bad, only
women braved the storm to come.[71] In 1713, on a bleak February
evening, there was a 'Privat Meeting at our house' and, Sewall
records with surprise, 'pretty number of Men'.[72] Hardly anything
is known about what actually went on at these meetings, but at
least women would in a small gathering have greater opportunity
of contributing to the proceedings.

Another area in which a modest advance was made in women's
participation in church services was in singing. At the end of the
century the Congregational church was riven with one of those
exotic disputes so hard to sympathise with or comprehend nowadays. It was between the new and old styles of singing at the
meetings and lectures. A subsidiary contest over women's right to
sing added fuel to the flames. With the victory of the new style,
'Women, who in many congregations had never been allowed to
sing, now moved into the liberated zone. "You have pleasanter
voices than men," the singing-lecturer told them. "God means you
to use them. Deborah and Miriam sang. Why not you? How will you
answer to God if you do not use this gift He has given you?" '[73] It
was not much, but it was a step ahead from mere mute observation.

Churches in Massachusetts undoubtedly varied as to the voice
that they gave women in their affairs. We would probably be safe
if we concluded that it was generally small. This makes the publication of the Manifesto of the Brattle Street Church on 17 November
in the last year of the century all the more important as a symbol
of progress and zeal rewarded. 'Finally,' it proclaimed, 'we cannot
confine the right of chusing a Minister to the Male Communicants
alone, but we think that every Baptised Adult Person who contri-
butes to the Maintenance, should have a vote in electing.'[74] The
circumlocution reveals that this was a contentiously liberal step,

and the founding of the church threw Boston orthodoxy into a great tizzy. Though the Mathers were finally brought round to public acceptance, in private they continued to regard the new church as a dangerous innovation and its pastor, Benjamin Colman, as little better than a heretic. The future, however, would go Colman's, not the Mathers', way. When in 1750 Jonathan Edwards sought to return the Northampton congregation to the rigours of the founding years of the colony, he was dismissed.[75]

We have discussed in this chapter only one aspect of puritanism and women: their role within the church. But puritanism was not merely a religion, it was a way of life. The doctrines affected every aspect of living. Particularly important to us were its influence on education and the upbringing of children; on courtship and marriage; and on family life and organisation in general. In all of these areas women were plainly deeply concerned and their role in society and their status affected. The influence of puritanism on these aspects cannot, however, be so clearly isolated and separately analysed. We have therefore deferred discussion of them to the third section of the book, where the results of the new environment are generally examined.

Notes

1 S. E. Morison, *Builders of the Bay Colony* (Boston, 1930), p. 54.
2 Ephesians, 1:33.
3 I Timothy, 2:11–12; 8.
4 I Peter, 3:1ff.
5 Corinthians, 7:1–9.
6 Cotton Mather, *Ornaments for the Daughters of Zion* (Boston, 1691), p. 53.
7 The case is described in some detail in Julia C. Spruill, *Women's Life and Work in the Southern Colonies* (Chapel Hill, 1938), p. 345.
8 Winthrop, *Journal: History of New England*, ed. J. K. Hosmer (New York, 1946), vol. I, p. 107.
9 Darrett Rutman, *Winthrop's Boston* (Chapel Hill, 1965), p. 65.
10 Ibid., p. 131.
11 *Plaine dealing: or Newes from New-England*, ed. J. Hammond Trumbull (Boston, 1867), p. 24, n. 14.
12 See Ola E. Winslow's excellent *Meetinghouse Hill* (New York, 1952), pp. 41ff.
13 *Colonial Society of Massachusetts Collections*, vol. 39, ed. Richard D. Pierce (Boston, 1961), p. 14, Margarette, the wife of Jeffery Ruggle; p. 17, Rebecka Merry and Lettyse Button; p. 21, Anne Burdon, are all examples from the first years.
14 Winslow, op. cit., p. 28.
15 Ibid., pp. 26–8.
16 Ibid., p. 194.
17 The franchise was restricted to church members in colonial, but probably not in local, elections.

18 Winslow, op. cit., p. 176. It is not clear whether women were allowed to vote on questions of the admission of members into the Dedham church. Although it was authoritatively stated in 1639 that 'women do not vote in our church concerns', there is the strong suggestion in Winslow that this was not universal practice.

19 See, for numerous examples, Emil Oberholzer, *Delinquent Saints* (New York, 1956), esp. pp. 124ff. Cf. Patrick Collinson, *The Elizabethan Puritan Movement* (London, 1967), p. 379, where he quotes a question to the Dedham Classis, 'Whether it were convenient a woman should pray, having a better gift than her husband.'

20 The puritan-supported movement towards the 'Spiritualisation of the Household', whereby the father/mother took on part of the role of minister with his family, would surely tend to exacerbate the situation further, if the 'minister' had been excluded or 'unfrocked'. See Levin L. Schücking, *The Puritan Family* (London, 1969), ch. 2; Christopher Hill, *Society and Puritanism* (London, 1964), ch. 13.

21 A. W. Calhoun, *A Social History of the American Family* (Boston, 1918), vol. I, p. 94.

22 W. and M. Haller, *The Rise of Puritanism, 1570–1640* (New York, 1938), p. 121.

23 *Nehemiah on the Wall in Troublesome Times,* cited in E. S. Morgan, *Puritan Family* (New York, 1966), p. 20.

24 *Slavery* (New York, 1963), p. 77.

25 *Records of First Church,* p. 46; see also a note on her in Edmund Morgan, 'A Boston Heiress', *Colonial Society of Massachusetts Transactions,* vol. XXXIV (1942), p. 500.

26 H. S. Tapley, 'Women of Massachusetts, 1620–89', A. B. Hart, ed., *The Commonwealth History of Massachusetts* (Boston, 1928–9), p. 311; Oberholzer, op. cit., p. 91.

27 Winthrop, op. cit., vol. I, pp. 168, 179.

28 Ibid., vol. I, pp. 285–6.

29 Spruill, op. cit., pp. 249ff., recounts the story of the defiance and punishment of Mary Tompkins and Anne Ambrose, missionaries to Virginia. Kai Erikson, *Wayward Puritans* (New York, 1966), pp. 114–36.

30 Cf., for instance, Winthrop's patient treatment of the infuriating Williams with his dictatorial bludgeoning of Mistress Hutchinson, described in E. S. Morgan, *The Puritan Dilemma* (Boston, 1958), chs 9, 10; Emery Battis, *Saints and Sectaries* (Chapel Hill, 1962), pp. 224ff.; Charles Francis Adams, *Three Episodes in Massachusetts History* (Boston, 1896), Part II; or the repeated remarks of Edward Johnson in *Wonderworking Providence of Sion's Saviour*, ed. J. F. Jameson (New York, 1937), pp. 28, 121, 127, 132, 134.

31 In 1638 and 1639 two or three Boston women were excommunicated from the First Church because they said that Anne Hutchinson had deserved neither her banishment nor her excommunication. 'Records', pp. 21, 25; Oberholzer, op. cit., p. 85; we have already mentioned Mary Dyer, who turned to the analogous faith of the Friends, and was martyred in Boston on 14 March 1661; two other cases, which may have been influenced by Mrs Hutchinson's example occurred at Barnstaple in 1649 and Reading in 1655. Oberholzer, op. cit., pp. 67, 64.

32 Keith Thomas, 'Women and the Civil War Sects' in Trevor Aston, ed., *Crisis in Europe, 1560–1660* (London, 1965), pp. 317–40; Patricia Higgins, 'Women in the Civil War' (unpub. M.A. thesis, Manchester University, 1965).

33 Cf. Sewall's frequent recording of this phenomenon in Boston later in the century.

34 I owe this account to Higgins, op. cit., pp. 76–80. Cf. Claire Cross, 'The Church in York during the Civil War', *Studies in Church History*, vol. IV (1967), p. 141.

35 Higgins, op. cit., pp. 68–108; cf. Thomas, op. cit., pp. 324–7.

36 Ronald Knox, *Enthusiasm* (Oxford, 1950), p. 20.

37 Thomas, op. cit., pp. 331, 333, 336; the pamphleteer is Thomas Edwards.

38 Calhoun, op. cit., vol. I, p. 94.

39 Jasper Danckaerts and Peter Sluyter, *Journal*, ed. Henry C. Murphy (Brooklyn, 1867), p. xxxvii.

40 Oberholzer, op. cit., p. 114.

41 Christopher Hill, *Intellectual Origins of the English Revolution* (Oxford, 1965), p. 275.

42 Thomas, op. cit., pp. 325, 334–5, 340.

43 Johnson, op. cit., p. 186.

44 See, e.g., Sewall, *Diary*, vol. I, p. 43 (1677); Ola E. Winslow, *Samuel Sewall of Boston* (New York, 1964), p. 26; *Magnalia*, Book VII, p. 24; Tapley, op. cit., p. 314; 'Records of Suffolk County Court', p. 843.

45 George Keith, *Journal of Travels* (London, 1706), *passim*.

46 E.g. *John Farmer's First American Journey*, ed. Henry J. Cadbury (Worcester, Mass., 1944), p. 7.

47 Such dangers were clearly seen by the Presbyterian Thomas Edwards in the 1640s. See Hill, *Society and Puritanism*, pp. 461, 463.

48 Nathaniel Ward, 'The Simple Cobbler of Agawam' (London, 1967) in Peter Force, *Tracts*, vol. III, No. 8.

49 Sewall, *Diary*, II, p. 128.

50 E. B. Schlesinger, 'Cotton Mather and His Children', *3 WMQ*, vol. X (1953), p. 183.

51 *Records of the First Church*, p. xl.

52 Alexander Young, ed., *Chronicles of the First Planters* (Boston, 1846), pp. 525–50. Similarly, Patrick Collinson, op. cit., pp. 82, 93, describes the women of London as 'the first line in defence of their preachers' during the purge which followed the Vestiarian Controversy of the 1560s. The same courage had been shown during the Marian persecutions a few years earlier. See P. Collinson, 'The Role of Women in the English Reformation', *Studies in Church History*, vol. II (1965), pp. 258–72, esp. pp. 258–260.

53 C. Bridenbaugh, *Vexed and Troubled Englishmen* (New York, 1968), pp. 338–9.

54 Earle, *Microcosmography*, quoted in D. Gardiner, *English Girlhood at School* (London, 1929), p. 270.

55 'The Role of Women in the English Reformation', Collinson, pp. 259–60. He quotes Lucien Romier on 'un zèle enflammé et une inflexible ténacité' among 'les huguenotes'.

56 W. K. Jordan, *The Charities of London* (London, 1960), p. 30.

57 Michael Walzer, *The Revolution of the Saints* (London, 1966), pp. 192–3. Cf. Johnson, op. cit., p. 100; Ebenezer Turell, *The Life and Character of Dr. Benjamin Colman* (Boston, 1749), p. 2.

58 Quoted in Gardiner, op. cit., p. 235.

59 H. Moller, 'Sex Composition and Correlated Culture Patterns in Colonial America', *3 WMQ*, vol. II (1945), pp. 146ff.; M. Reynolds, *The Learned Lady in England 1650–1760* (Boston, 1920), pp. 67–9, 92ff. Cosimo III, Duke of Tuscany, who visited England in 1669, commented nevertheless on the women he encountered, 'They are remarkably well-informed in the dogmas of the religion they profess'. Quoted in P. Woodham Smith, 'The Education of Englishwomen in the Seventeenth Century' (unpub. M.A. thesis, University of London, 1921), pp. 111–12.

60 Mabel Brailsford, *Quaker Women 1650–1690* (London, 1915).
61 Rutman, op. cit., p. 145.
62 Mather, op. cit., p. 47.
63 Sewall, *Diary*, vol. III, p. 274.
64 Michael Garibaldi Hall, *Edward Randolph and the American Colonies* (Chapel Hill, 1960), p. 85.
65 *Magnalia*, Book VII, p. 36.
66 G. L. Burr, ed., *Narratives of the Witchcraft Cases 1648–1706* (New York, 1946), pp. 180, 376–7; Chadwick Hansen, *Witchcraft at Salem* (London, 1970), *passim*. I have examined possible causes for female involvement in 'Salem Revisited', *Journal of American Studies*, vol. VI (1972).
67 Rutman, op. cit., p. 145. Oberholzer, op. cit., p. 137.
68 Ibid., p. 141.
69 Winthrop, op. cit., vol. I, p. 234.
70 Sewall, *Diary*, vol. I, p. 579.
71 Ibid., vol. II, p. 178.
72 Ibid., p. 369.
73 Winslow, op. cit., p. 159.
74 Samuel K. Lothrop, *History of the Brattle Street Church* (Boston, 1851), p. 25.
75 See Ola E. Winslow's Introduction to *Jonathan Edwards: Basic Writings* (New York, 1966), pp. xxiii–xxiv.

Chapter 5

Women and the Frontier

Frederick Jackson Turner's famous thesis that the American frontier was the major forger of American uniqueness has taken a fair beating from critics in recent years. However, few of the revisionists totally deny the influence of the frontier, as a threshold to economic opportunity, as a way of life and a state of mind, and as a transformer of traditional ideas.

For the colonists, the first frontier was 'the American strand'. In 1607, Jamestown was a frontier outpost; in 1630, Boston or Charlestown. Throughout the century the frontier was being doggedly driven inland from the coast. Edward Johnson described the process in 1651: 'Husbandmen, whose over-eager pursuit of the fruits of the earth made some of them many times run out so far into the Wilderness.'[1] But the pace of conquest was relatively slow in colonial times—two miles per year on average for the whole pre-revolutionary period. The influence of the frontier would, therefore, continue to be felt in the original seaboard settlements far longer than in Tocqueville's time, when the leading edge moved at an average of seventeen miles each year.[2] During King Philip's War, five decades after the first permanent settlement in New England, Indian braves advanced to within twenty miles of Boston. Similarly, frontier unrest had a rapid and shattering effect on Jamestown as late as 1676.

The meeting place of civilisation and the wilderness provided a magnificent, if daunting, challenge to women as well as men, a challenge, which, despite the difficulties of life in England, was surely unmatched there. In such a natural scenario for courage, endurance and effort, many individual women distinguished themselves. It is highly significant that we usually know of them through the pens of men. There can be little doubt that their achievements made a strong impression on colonial menfolk.

The act of migration and the transatlantic ordeal demanded fortitude. Winthrop singled out for praise the calmness of women passengers in the face of pirates, storms and childbirth.[3] Bradford recorded how the pilgrim women rejected the proffered chance of returning to England during the first hideous winter at Plymouth.[4]

When the wife of Boston's first pastor refused to cross to Massa-chusetts, Margaret Winthrop could only 'marvel at what stuff she is made of'.[5] The fearful wilderness so graphically described by William Bradford briefly daunted even Anne Hutchinson; 'when she came near within sight of Boston, and looking on the mean-ness of the place, [she] uttered these words, if she had not a sure word that England would be destroyed, her heart would shake'.[6] Mrs Forrest and her maid Ann Burras doubtless had to overcome similar fears on their pioneering voyage to Virginia in 1608, as would the Company's maids in 1619 and 1620.

Once landed, women must contribute to the survival and expansion of the bridgehead. Where manpower was so precious, women were not only a pair of hands, but also the reproducers of others. There was no time in these circumstances for rigid divisions of roles. Where a new world was being made women could not stick to the kitchen, let alone the boudoir.[7] Bradford pictured the wives of the early settlers helping their husbands planting out the corn in their family lots.[8] Johnson's description of the starving time in Massachusetts includes this passage:[9]

> The women once a day, as the tide gave way, resorted to the mussells, and clambankes . . . where they daily gathered their Families food with much heavenly discourse of the provisions Christ had formerly made for many thousands of his followers in the wildernesse. Quoth one, 'My husband hath travelled as far as Plimouth' (which is neere 40 miles) 'and hath with great toile brought a little corne home with him, and before that is spent the Lord will assuredly provide': quoth the other, 'Our last peck of meale is now in the oven at home baking, and many of our godly neighbours have quite spent all, and wee owe one loafe of that little wee have'; Then spake a third, 'My husband hath ventured himselfe among the Indians for Corne, and can get none, as also our honoured Governour hath distributed his so far, that a day or two more will put an end to his store, and all the rest, and yet methinks our children are as cheerful, fat and lusty with feeding upon those mussells, clambanks and other fish as they were in England, with their fill of bread, which makes mee cheerfull in the Lords providing for us.'

Women were co-workers in the pushing back of the frontier by the founding of new townships; they marched 'through the desart wildernesse' en route to Concord.

> Their hands were forced to make way for their bodies passage . . . their feete clambering over the crossed trees . . . to wade up to their knees . . . they had to endure the scorching plaine,

where ragged bushes scratch their legs fouly so that the blood
trickles down at every step . . . and the scent of the sweet ferne
made them very near fainting . . . and this not to be endured
for one day but many.

Once they had arrived, 'every one that can lift a hoe to strike it
into the Earth, standing stoutly to their labours, and teare up the
rootes and bushes, which the first yeare beares them a very thin
crop'.[10]

Such first-hand descriptions illuminate the realities behind bland
phrases. Thus, of the 'ancient maid', Elizabeth Poole, who helped
found the settlement of Taunton, Winthrop writes, 'She endured
much hardship.'[11] Judith Manigault settled in Carolina in 1685
and for four years 'worked like a slave'. For her, 'there was not
always food when wanted.'[12] To Edward Johnson, Mrs Sarah
Simmes was typical of the founding mothers:[13]

she came through perilous seas to war her warfare . . . indued
with graces fit for a wilderness condition, her courage exceeding her stature, with much cheerfulnesse did undergoe all the
difficulties of these times of straites.

Her typicality makes it less surprising that Leonard Calvert or
John Winthrop, jr, should leave their affairs in the hands of women
during their absences from their colonies.[14]

Once the initial crisis of settlement was painfully passed, the
problem of maintaining the bridgehead against the Indians had
to be faced, by women as well as men. In 1622, during the great
Indian massacre in Virginia, Mrs Procter, of Procter's Creek near
Richmond, then on the leading edge of settlement, defended her
plantation with pertinacity and bravery. Though described as a
'proper, civill, modest gentlewoman', she adamantly refused to
obey the orders of relievers to abandon her plantation until they
themselves threatened to put it to the torch.[15] New England women
were not backward, either, in courageous response to danger.
Hannah Bradley of Haverhill was understandably a paragon in
her own time, standing for the author of *A Memorial of the Present
Deplorable State of New England* as a fitting example of many
others. Having already been captured once, 'Behold, one of the
fierce *Tawnies* looked in, with a gun ready to fire upon them.' He
was floored, and Mrs Bradley despatched him with a libation of
boiling soap. A second brave received similar treatment, but not,
this time, fatally. Mrs Bradley and her sister fled their house, and
when cornered she gave herself up to the Indians in such a way as
to let her sister and child escape. There followed a hair-raising story
of trekking through the snow, giving birth to a child on the march,

eating only moosehide and soup thereof, sale to a French master in Quebec, and final ransom. This occurred in 1703, only six years after Hannah Dustin had earned a place in Sewall's *Diary* by not only escaping from her Indian masters, but also, with true Yankee canniness, returning to Boston with their scalps, for which she could claim a reward.[16] Mary Rowlandson, captured from Lancaster, Mass., in 1676 during King Philip's War, left a *Narrative* of her captivity and restoration, which was first published in 1682 and ran through thirty-seven editions up to 1930. In all she was forced to travel some 150 miles through appalling terrain heavily laden, wounded, and suffering the death of her six-year-old child.[17] These are but the most spectacular of many such exploits.[18]

Capture by Indians might well not have such glorious finales. At the beginning of the Pequod War in New England in 1636, as the savages descended on Hartford,[19]

> three woemankinde they caught, and carried away, but one of them being more fearfull of their cruell usage afterward then of the loss of her life at present, being borne away in the thickest of the company, resisted so stoutly with scratching and biting, that the Indian, exasperated therewith, cast her down on the earth, and beate out her braines with his Hatchet.

Knowledge of the fate that might await her makes the decision of Mrs Drummer, the wife of the pastor of York, and others, doubly courageous. Having been released from captivity she voluntarily surrendered herself again so that she could remain with her son.[20]

Symbolic of the breaching of conventional male attitudes is the identification of women with that masculine symbol *par excellence*: the gun. The print on the title page of Mary Rowlandson's enormously popular *Narrative* shows her firing a gun at her Indian assailants. Byrd described a Virginian frontier woman in 1710:[21]

> She is a very civil woman and shews nothing of ruggedness, or Immodesty in her carraige, yett she will carry a gunn in the woods and kill deer, turkeys, &c., shoot down wild cattle, catch and tye hoggs, knock down beeves with an ax and perform the most manful exercises as well as most men in these parts.

One reason given in the petition of the menfolk of Salem against being sent eleven miles from home to keep watch against Indians was the fact that they would be leaving their wives without arms or ammunition.[22]

The kind of tough individualism that frontier life developed is demonstrated by the active participation of women in Bacon's Rebellion in Virginia in 1676. The wife of one of his lieutenants, Anthony Havilland, was the first person to gather followers together, riding up and down the backcountry as Bacon's emissary. Sarah Drummond, the wife of William Drummond of Jamestown, truculently outfaced the governor's threats by taking up a stick and breaking it, saying, 'I fear the power of England no more than a broken straw.' After the death of the leader and the collapse of the uprising, a vindictive bloodletting set in. Lydia Cheisman, wife of one of the condemned ringleaders, pleaded for her husband's life to be spared and hers to be taken, as she had instigated him to rebel. Sarah, the wife of Colonel Thomas Grendon, jr, was the only woman excepted from the Act of Indemnity and Free Pardon of February 1677, as she had been 'a great encourager and assister in the late horrid Rebellion'.[23]

Less spectacular examples of women's influence and independence of mind in the frontier situation are not hard to find. In his surveying and speculating jaunts in frontier areas William Byrd frequently reports meeting with dominating females—in his phrase 'the grey mare was the better horse'. No doubt one reason for their hen-pecked husbands ignoring the diarist's urgings to assert their male authority was the need for companionship. This is certainly implied as a reason for Alexander Spotswood's conversion from bachelor chauvinism to a devoted uxoriousness.[24] Further north, frontier women showed equal spirit. While their husbands were away petitioning Boston for permission to erect a meeting-house, three women of Chebacco, near Gloucester, took the law into their own hands, and, with help, set about raising the structure themselves.[25] In young settlements quite ordinary women could exert great influence. In Beverley, for instance, Mary Dodge Woodbery[26]

> was a person of great decision of character, and her title of 'Madame Woodbery' indicates the position which she held in the community. It was her vote that ended a lengthy discussion of the men of the North Beverley Church, a vote in favour of extending a call to the Revd John Chipman to be their minister.

Similarly, to the islanders of Nantucket, Mary Starbuck in 1701 was 'esteemed as a Judge among them, for little of moment was done without her'.[27]

It can hardly be coincidence that Anne Bradstreet, who came to Massachusetts in the Great Migration and lived out her life in the remote settlement of Andover, should have penned these lines:[28]

> Now say, have women worth? or have they none?
> Or had they some, but with our Queen is't gone?

> Nay Masculines, you have thus taxt us long,
> But she, though dead, will vindicate our wrong.
> Let such as say our Sex is void of Reason,
> Know 'tis a slander now, but once was treason.

The frontier did not always act as an emancipator. William Byrd was not impressed with the chivalry of the men of Lubberland, as he called the northern Carolinian backwoods:[29]

> In truth the distemper of laziness siezes the men oftener than the women. These last spin, weave and knit, all with their own hands, while their husbands, depending on the bounty of the climate, are slothful in everything but getting of children, and in that only instance make themselves useful members of an infant colony.

The Revd Urmstone corroborated this description, and went on to bewail the immorality of such communities, with their wife-swappings and illicit liaisons.[30] Sarah Knight criticised 'stand-away' divorces which she heard about as she travelled through sparsely settled regions of Connecticut. She admitted, however, that in many cases women initiated the actions.[31] Furthermore, the northern part of Carolina was a notorious refuge for runaway servants and slaves and debtors, and it would be dangerous to generalise from its society that the frontier was a graveyard of morality.

If the analogy of the nineteenth-century West is anything to go by, it is highly likely that in general the presence of significant numbers of women in frontier communities actually debrutalised wilderness life. Where all-male groups settled, in early Virginia, for instance, or at Thomas Morton's Merrymount in New England, or in the remoter parts of New France, the rudeness and wildness of their existence stands out in stark contrast with more balanced communities.[32] As Lewis Mumford has written, domesticating 'woman was the chief enemy of the pioneer'.[33] The Virginia Company shipped out its consignments of maids for the pioneers, 'that their minds might be faster tyed to Virginia'.[34] Women were first given the vote in America, not because of their aggressive demands for it, but because men were impressed with their civilising effects in primitive areas.[35]

The frontier, we have said, was a transformer of received traditions. For instance, Johnson noted that 'in this wilderness-worke men of estates speed no better than others, and some much worse for want of being inured to such hard labour.'[36] It has been convincingly argued that the careers of Mrs Bradstreet and Mrs Hutchinson were at least facilitated by the changed environment of the New World.[37] The spirited response of so many ordinary women to the rigours of wilderness life would make prejudices about the natural inferiority of women hard to sustain.

Writing in 1705, Robert Beverley described how Sir Edmund Andros, on progress one summer, stopped for water at a poor man's house in Stafford County. He was met by a woman of seventy-six, who had a son of twelve, and who was lively and brisk. No doubt the story lost nothing in the telling; yet this was not only a conscious advertisement for the climate and fertility of Virginia, but also an unconscious tribute to the resilience and hardihood of its female inhabitants.[38]

Notes

1 E. Johnson, *Wonderworking Providence of Sion's Saviour*, ed. J. F. Jameson (New York, 1937), p. 253.
2 Marcus Cunliffe, *The Nation Takes Shape* (Chicago, 1959), p. 70.
3 J. Winthrop, *Journal: History of New England* ed. J. K. Hosmer (New York, 1946), vol. I, pp. 28, 33, 47.
4 *Bradford's History 'of Plimouth Plantation'* (Boston, 1898), p. 128.
5 H. S. Tapley, 'Women of Massachusetts, 1620–89' in *Commonwealth History of Massachusetts*, ed. A. B. Hart (Boston, 1928–9), p. 297.
6 S. E. Morison, *Builders of the Bay Colony* (Boston, 1930), pp. 42, 322. He quotes Hawthorne's inference that the 'horror of the wilderness life brought Lady Arbella Johnson to an early grave', and adds his own suspicion that 'some such thing lay behind the silence of Governor Bradford on the death of his young wife Dorothy, drowned from the Mayflower in Provincetown Harbor, after gazing for weeks on the desolate sand dunes of Cape Cod.' For similar reactions to the prairie frontier in the nineteenth century, see Walter Prescott Webb, *The Great Plains* (Boston, 1931), p. 506.
7 For examples of diversification of roles, see J. H. Smith, *Colonial Justice in Western Massachusetts (1639–1702)* (Cambridge, Mass., 1961), p. 389.
8 Bradford, op. cit., p. 162.
9 Johnson, op. cit., pp. 77–8. Cf. Winthrop, op. cit., vol. I, pp. 163, 168. Bradford, op. cit., pp. 111–14, 120–2, 131.
10 Ibid., pp. 112, 114.
11 Winthrop, op. cit., p. 51.
12 J. C. Spruill, *Women's Life and Work in the Southern Colonies* (Chapel Hill, 1938), p. 13.
13 Johnson, op. cit., p. 100.
14 Margaret Brent was Calvert's agent in Maryland; see Spruill, op. cit., p. 236. On Mrs Davenport, Winthrop's agent, see R. S. Dunn, *Puritans and Yankees* (Princeton, 1962), pp. 108ff.
15 *1 WMQ*, vol. XVI, p. 39.
16 Sewall, *Diary*, vol. II, pp. 59–62; ibid., p. 452.
17 See the edition edited by Frederick L. Weiss (Boston, 1930); Douglas E. Leech, 'The Whens of Mary Rowlandson's Captivity', *New England Quarterly*, vol. XXXIV (1961), p. 352.
18 See A. M. Earle, *Colonial Dames and Goodwives* (Boston, 1895), pp. 21–4; *Magnalia*, Book VI, p. 10.

19 Johnson, op. cit., p. 149.
20 James Douglas, *New England and New France* (New York, 1913), p. 287. Some Englishwomen 'went native'. Such was Eunice Williams, daughter of the minister of frontier Deerfield, or Mary Jemeson, the famous 'White Woman of the Genesee' in the eighteenth century. Sewall, *Diary*, vol. II, p. 374 and note.
21 Spruill, op. cit., p. 81.
22 Tapley, op. cit., pp. 299–300; E. A. Dexter, *Colonial Women of Affairs* (Boston, 1924), p. 132. Cf. Charles W. Ferguson, *The Male Attitude* (Boston, 1966), Part III.
23 An Cotton, 'Our Late Troubles in Virginia . . .' reprinted in Peter Force, *Tracts*, vol. I, No. 9; 'Narrative of the Indian and Civil Wars in Virginia in the Years 1675 & 6'; ibid., No. 11; *1 WMQ*, vol. XVI, p. 39; C. M. Andrews, ed., *Narratives of the Insurrections 1675–1690* (New York, 1943), p. 81. Sarah Drummond subsequently proved a persistent and highly successful petitioner, thus saving the family estate. Ibid., pp. 38–9.
24 *London Diary*, pp. 616, 622–3, 625, 626, 628.
25 O. E. Winslow, *Meetinghouse Hill* (New York, 1952), p. 128. Cf. the Quaker, Mary Dow, who persuaded her husband to return to his farm in frontier New Hampshire. Henry J. Cadbury, ed., *John Farmer's First American Journey 1711–14* (Worcester, Mass., 1944), p. 7.
26 Alice Lapham, *Old Planters of Beverley and their Lands* (Cambridge, Mass., 1930), pp. 68–9.
27 Alexander Starbuck, *The History of Nantucket* (Boston, 1924), p. 520.
28 John H. Ellis, ed., *Works of Anne Bradstreet* (Gloucester, Mass., 1962), p. 361.
29 *London Diary*, appendix.
30 A. W. Calhoun, *Social History of the American Family* (Boston, 1918), vol. I, p. 283.
31 Sarah Knight, *Journal*, ed. George P. Winship (New York, 1935), p. 39.
32 On Canada, see Sigmund Diamond, 'An Experiment in Feudalism: French Canada in the Seventeenth Century', *3 WMQ*, vol. XVIII (1961), pp. 3–34.
33 Lewis Mumford, *The Golden Day* (New York, 1926), pp. 87ff.
34 Spruill, op. cit., p. 3.
35 Alan P. Grimes, *The Puritan Ethic and Woman Suffrage* (New York, 1967), ch. 2; Andrew Sinclair, *The Emancipation of American Woman* (New York, 1966), ch. 19.
36 Johnson, op. cit., p. 113.
37 W. A. White, *Autobiography* (New York, 1946), p. 375; Emery Battis, *Saints and Sectaries* (Chapel Hill, 1962), p. 252; Larzer Ziff, 'Women in Colonial America and England', *British Association for American Studies Newsletter*, No. 22 (July 1970), pp. 18–20.
38 Robert Beverley, *History and Present State of Virginia*, ed. Louis B. Wright (Chapel Hill, 1947), p. 103.

Part III
Cultural Contrasts

In this third and final section, we shall be looking at certain differences in ways of life affecting women that seem to result from the changed environment of the New World in the seventeenth century. The first two chapters will examine the relatively intimate areas of courtship and marriage, and the family. After this we will investigate the more public areas of legal rights, educational opportunities and voting privileges afforded to women, and finally attempt to pinpoint important distinctions in the general tone of society on the two sides of the Atlantic.

Chapter 6

Courtship and Marriage

Courtship and marriage were vital events in that 'little common-wealth', the family, which was the basic social unit of both the Old and the New World.[1] This chapter will deal first with certain common assumptions about courtship and marriage that were, by and large, shared by the Old and New World. It will then trace certain subtle differences that developed in the New World within the framework of these shared assumptions, and finally will discuss certain sharp divergences in colonial opinion and practice, which, in some cases, would threaten the whole fortress of the traditional marriage lore of England.

First, however, we should note in passing that the laws and customs governing marriage were quite different from those in force either in England or America today. As this subject has been minutely covered by such authorities as G. E. Howard and C. L. Powell,[2] it is not necessary to delve into the differences in any great detail. Suffice it to say that the equivalent then of the modern engagement and marriage was roughly the spousal *de futuro* and the spousal *de presenti*. I say 'roughly' only, because, for instance, if intercourse occurred after the 'engagement', a binding, if irregular, marriage was then assumed to have been consummated.[3] Similarly, if one of the parties to a private, un-witnessed exchange of spousals *de presenti* then went off and publicly married someone else, that second marriage was adjudged adultery and its issue bastards. In other words, the 'I take thee, N, to be my lawful wedded wife . . .' of the common-prayer marriage service, which are the spousals *de presenti*, are what makes a marriage legal, and the minister's 'I pronounce thee man and wife' is merely the solemnisation, the public declaration, of an accomplished fact.

Escape from a marriage in seventeenth-century English ecclesiastical law could only be achieved (until the last years of the century, when private divorce bills began to be passed by Parliament) either by annulments or by separations. Powell cites ten causes which could justify annulments, and argues that the rich and persistent would have little difficulty in proving grounds for voiding an unhappy marriage. Plainly the possible private nature of spousals could provide ample opportunity for an unscrupulous rich man to argue either that he was already contracted by spousals *de presenti* to somebody else or that he had had intercourse with some other woman to whom he was betrothed. Indeed so scandalous was the practice of the ecclesiastical courts in these matters that they were popularly known as 'Bawdy Courts'.[4] None the less, such loopholes were open only to a tiny minority of the population, except on the most blatant grounds, and marriage was normally considered a 'till death us do part' affair, though death and parting might happen a good deal earlier than nowadays.

Modern legal historians know far more about the implications of the marriage laws then than did the contemporary man in the street. In the Stuart period, the whole question of the exact nature of matrimony had been obscured and confused by the reformation, or rather the partial reformation, that had occurred in the sixteenth century. English law and practice were a baffling blend of Roman and protestant thinking, of overlapping common- and ecclesiastical-law doctrines and of disagreements about the civil and the sacramental nature of the institution. It is, I think, wrong to credit the puritans with having revolutionised the institution. Rather they chose to stress the inherent civil aspects of the actual ceremony and laid emphasis on 'the unscrambling of the civil from the ecclesiastical powers and functions'. The underlining of the civil nature of the ceremony did not detract from the sacredness of the vows of the individuals taking part.[5]

Shared English and American Assumptions on Marriage

It would be extremely surprising if courtship and marriage had been revolutionised in the New World during the first three generations. Predictably, there were many marked similarities in custom and practice between the colonies and the mother country. First, both were marriage-oriented societies. Marriage was the normal expectation of both men and women, and bachelors and spinsters were objects of pity, curiosity, suspicion, or scorn. This was understandable when the family rather than the individual was the basic unit of society, when the person was conceived of as belonging to a group. Early ordinances prevented the granting of lots of land in Salem to unattached maids and required single persons to live under family government.[6] English society was hopelessly unequipped to offer much opportunity to unmarried women, especially of the gentler classes. There were no satisfying career prospects for a Dorothy Osborne or an Anne Murray. The alternative was either irksome dependence on parents or the frustration of talents, as with Elizabeth Elstob, the great Anglo-Saxonist.[7] Schemes for female seminaries were attempts to provide havens for single women, but they were predicably ridiculed by male contemporaries as serpentine means of finding husbands, or, at least, sexual satisfaction.[8] It would take more than the bitter complaint of Miss Astell to alter the assumption expressed in *The Lawes Resolutions of Women's Rights* (published in 1632, but basically a Tudor compilation): 'All of them [women] are understood either married or to bee married. . . . The Common Law here shaketh hand with Divinitie.'[9] Those 'to bee married' strained every nerve to attain that goal. 'The unmarried woman was a burden on her family, a living confession of failure.'[10]

The same pressures were at work on both sexes in the colonies. According to Dunton, who here has little reason for misinforming, virgins in their late twenties in Massachusetts Bay were popularly known as 'Thornbacks'. Sewall was very worried by his daughter Betty's apparent disinclination for matrimony.[11] Girls in America quickly learned that their main career in life was likely to be that of mother. Philip Fithian recorded that his charges at Nomini Hall, Fanny and Harriet, aged ten and six, having stuffed rags and lumber under their gowns, were 'prodigiously charmed at their resemblance to pregnant women'.[12] Neither was widow- or widower-hood a safe haven. Though Sewall, bereft of his first wife, might wonder 'in my mind whether to live a Single or a Married Life' and might have 'a sweet and very affectionat Meditation concerning the Lord Jesus . . . why did I not resolutely presently close with Him', his friends and neighbours by insinuations or open praise of likely candidates left the sexagenarian in no doubt about which state he should choose.[13] Similarly Cotton Mather, who felt strong 'temptations of widowhood', was warned by his father and match-making friends against such unconventional behaviour.[14] Old Increase was later to practise what he preached. In 1714, at the age of seventy-six, he was himself re-married, to a distant kinswoman.[15] Perhaps this was one reason why Cotton Mather counselled the women of Boston not to 'use any hasty method to get into the married Row'.[16] It is, I think, unnecessary to labour this point further. Certainly the Lady Sanpareil of the Duchess of Newcastle's imagination who asked her father to allow her to remain voluntarily celibate was a very rare bird indeed in the seventeenth century.[17]

The second area of general agreement in the English-speaking world was over the relationship of marriage and love. Perhaps no greater change has overtaken *mores* in the two countries than the injection of romance as a popular *sine qua non* of marriage. This is not to deny that falling in love was a factor in many seventeenth-century courtships and marriages, but it was emphatically not *the* factor—rather one of several.

It is true that there was a literary convention in the seventeenth century which required the courter to don all the paraphernalia of the distracted lover. This idea persists from the careless desolation described by Rosalind to Orlando in *As You Like It*[18] to the patently bogus ardour of William Byrd pursuing well-heeled nymphs in London in the early eighteenth century.[19] Such conventions were emphasised by the popular romances aimed at female readers. Here women were seen as goddesses, nymphs or shepherdesses, fit to 'inhabit the happy fields of Arcadia, rather than be wives and Mothers in old England'.[20] Occasionally these profuse professions of a debased courtly love have a ring of truth, as when William Temple threatened suicide if he could not marry Dorothy Osborne. Yet such genuine cases were rare.

More general were Osborne's sentiments: 'He that takes a wife wanting money is a slave to his affections, doing the basest of drudgeries without wages',[21] or his niece Dorothy's 'To marry for love were no reproachful thing if we did not see that of the thousand couples that do it, hardly one can be brought for an example that it may be done and not repented of afterwards.'[22] Most would have agreed with the advice of Hannah Woolley: 'Whatever you do, be not induced to marry one you have either abhorrency or loathing to',[23] but this was hardly romance. Few would go as far as the son of the Revd Stephen Bachiller of Massachusetts, who, when he sought a stepmother for his nine children, dropped a stick on the ground and followed it for forty miles until he met up with an eligible widow whom he eventually persuaded to take on him and his brood.[24] Yet George Monck, Duke of Albermarle, is reputed to have been hardly less offhand in his choice of a spouse. As he was setting sail in 1653, the brother of his mistress, Nan Clarges, a sempstress, came aboard to report a successful birth. 'Of what?' asked Monck. 'Of a son', came the reply. 'Why then, she is my wife', was the matter-of-fact conclusion.[25] 'Marrying for posterity' was neither rare nor shameful.[26]

Even people unencumbered by parental pressures towards marriage rarely mentioned love as a ground for attraction. Benjamin Colman, a widower, gave the following reasons for courting Sarah Clark:[27]

> It soon appeared to me that among the many virtuous single gentlewomen of the Town, Madam Sarah Clark, Relict of John Clark, Esq., must be the person to make me and my children happy, if married again. Her Piety, Gravity, Humil-

ity, Diligence, Cheerfulness, natural Love (long since) for my children, and theirs to her: besides her retired way of living and a small worldly Estate free from all Incumbrances, all concurred and moved me to make my Addresses to her.

He might as well have been discussing the hiring of a housekeeper. The same impression is gained from the famous letter of Michael Wigglesworth to the widow Avery. As Morgan comments, although the suitor was attracted by the widow (whom he had only met briefly) there is no suggestion that 'his was a case of love at first sight'. Most of 'the reasons were all directed to proving that it would be convenient and comfortable for her to marry him'.[28] To take a Virginian example, the Jones Family Papers contain letters written by Colonel Thomas Jones to the young, attractive and wealthy Widow Pratt, who was not without other admirers. Although the Colonel's letters have a uniform flatness and conventionality about them, without the slightest hint of passion, he it was who won the prize.[29] The speed with which marriages often took place after only brief meetings argues that passion or romantic attachment was not considered necessary.

It was a commonplace of the century on both sides of the Atlantic, that love, rather than being a God-given gift, a state that the eligible fell helplessly into, a mystical feeling towards the beloved, was, rather, a duty, a mode of behaviour required of the already married. As Mary Astell put it, modesty required 'That a Woman should not love before Marriage, but only make choice of one whom she can love hereafter; she who has none but innocent affections being easily led to fix them where Duty requires.'[30] By some writers, married love was equated with loyalty—a quality as much of the mind as the heart.[31] As the English adage had it, 'First he must choose his love, and then he must love his choice.'[32] Oberholzer epitomises the New England view 'To be a loving spouse was a divinely ordained obligation; it was more often the effect than the cause of marriage.'[33] Indeed passion, alias infatuation, alias lust, was seen throughout the century as a noxious ingredient, rather than a prerequisite yeast.[34] The examples of the Somerset scandal at the beginning of the century, of Charles I's infatuation with Henrietta Maria in the middle years, and of the tempestuous relationship of the Marlboroughs at the end were sufficient warning for many Englishmen. Sex and mere looks were especial snares, though 'sober contentation of sight' might be satisfied. In homelier language, 'there belongeth more to marriage than two payre of bare leggs'.[35] When Sewall and some of his cronies were gossiping about their courtships in 1698, 'we sat down at the Great Rock, and Mr. Taylor told me his courting his first wife, and Mr. Fitch his story of Mr. Dod's prayer to God to bring his Affections to close with a person pious, but hard-favoured'.[36] Powell believes that in the seventeenth century, the famous tombstone epitaph 'An ill-favoured thing, but mine own' was not atypical of many men's attitudes to their wives.[37] Paradoxically, it seems possible that the very submerged classes of society, who are imagined to be least capable of passionate wooing, and who have left virtually no evidence, may well have had the greatest freedom to indulge their romantic inclinations. Anthropological analogies, and the rare examples like Roger Lowe's diary, suggest that Eros had freer flight below than above stairs.

We need not labour the first corollary of this unromantic view of marriage: that, at least for yeomen upwards, marriage was regarded as a commercial arrangement between two families. How important a consideration in family finances this might be is strikingly illustrated in Alan Macfarlane's detailed breakdown of the Josselin family's expenditure on dowries during the lifetime of Ralph, a man hovering between yeoman and gentle status.[38] In England marriages were more often made at the attorney's table than in heaven.[39] Though marriages for money might be attacked as the primary reason for people going to hell[40] or as little better than bargain sales[41] or 'bargains to cohabit'[42], the evidence suggests that the commercial element was in fact on the increase in the seventeenth century in England.[43]

Despite certain mitigating factors, there is little doubt that the commercial assumptions were shared in the colonies. As Cotton Mather put it at the end of the century, it was 'silver with which women are often valued'.[44] If Sewall's attitude is typical of his class, and there is little reason to doubt it, finance played a major part in his courtships of the widows Denison (whose will he had helped previously to draw up), Ruggles, Tilley (whom he only visited three times before proposing), Winthrop, and Gibbs. His letters to the last, recorded in the *Diary*, read more like a company merger than a companionable union.[45] His haggling over a daughter's portion, even after her death, had precedents also.[46] For many families the marriage agreement was as important as the marriage ceremony. In matching her son James with Rebecca Cooper, Lucy Downing was so much more concerned with 'the estate very convenient' that, even when negotiations were far on, 'I think he hath not yet spoken to the mayd' about the proposal.[47] The same situation held in Virginia. The marriages of two afflicted brothers-in-law, William Byrd II and John Custis, would have been far less fraught if they had not been so obsessed with the division and proceeds of old Daniel Parke's estate. Their attitudes were almost certainly typical.[48] On both sides of the Atlantic in our period, the opinion which prevailed ensured that many girls, like Ben Franklin's Sylvia, were 'not wed but sold'.[49]

The second obvious and commonly held corollary was that marriage was much too important a business to be left to the marriers. At its most callous, the convention was based on the concept that the children were the parents' chattels.[50] Halifax, whose thought was very influential, tried to put it more kindly to his daughter:[51]

> It is one of the disadvantages of your Sex, that young women are seldom permitted to make their own choice; their Friends' Care and Experience are thought safer guides to them than their own fancies; and their Modesty often forbiddeth them to refuse when their Parents recommend, though their inward consent may not exactly go along with it.

In an era where age was equated with wisdom, and where it was the parents who put up the money, such a line was not altogether illogical. Few parents would go to the length of Sir Edward Coke, that champion of Englishmen's liberties, who, intent on hitching his wagon to the Buckingham star, had his daughter Frances 'tied to the bedposts and whipped till she consented to the Match' with the hideous John Villiers.[52] None the less, there were many who were prepared to use the more subtle instrument of financial control—disinheritance or withdrawal of portion, for instance—to achieve their ends.[53] Such conventions were reinforced by law in England and the colonies. The Massachusetts Statute of 1647 reads:[54]

> Whereas it is common practise in divers places, for young men irregularly and disorderly to watch all advantages for their evil purposes, to insinuate into the affections of young maidens, by coming to them in places and seasons unknown to their parents for such ends, whereby much evil hath grown amongst us, to the dishonour of God and damage of parties.... For prevention whereof for time to come: it is further Ordered, That whatsoever person from henceforth, shall endeavour directly or indirectly, to draw away the affection of any maid in this jurisdiction under pretence of marriage, before he hath obtained liberty and allowance from her parents or governors (or in absence of such) of the nearest magistrate, he shall forfeit for the first offence five pounds.

The evidence suggests that, on the whole, children tended to accept this 'parents know best' convention. Though John Bunyan might believe that 'It is too much the custom of young people now, to think themselves wise enough to make their own choice'[55] and though Plotwell in Jasper Mayne's *City Match* might argue that obedience to parental instructions was 'fit For none but farmers sons and milkmaids',[56] the conduct-books and Halifax were in this more influential than the dramatists.[57] Made marriages might well turn out to be mad marriages, but, certainly for the moneyed classes, there was too much at stake to leave such a decision to the madness of youth. FitzJohn Winthrop's 'What you shall please to direct for my waye of settlement I shall redily comply with your pleasure theirein',[58] may be unduly obsequious, but the furthest that many spirited young people dared to go was either to request the power of veto, or to wait out parents' or guardians' displeasure.[59]

Turning now from courtship to marriage itself, the assumption that the husband was the head of the family has already been discussed in some detail. A fundamental teaching of the common law, it was, furthermore, an integral part of the concept of the great chain of being, divinely instituted, and any upset promised a dire threat to social order. In a trivial way the dictum 'Let woman learn betimes to serve according to her lot' was emphasised by the common adoption of her husband's name; Sewall, for instance, easily fell into the habit of calling his daughter Betty 'my daughter Hirst' after her marriage to Grove Hirst.[60] The mental and physical cruelty which the Earl of Pembroke and Montgomery could with impunity inflict upon so spirited a woman as Anne Clifford, driving her to deep depressions and fears that she might be turned out without a roof to her head, illustrates the rightlessness of women in marriage.[61] Although the contract idea was, at the end of the century, directed towards marriage as well as constitutional law, and preachers did at times attempt to reconcile male claims to authority with the obligation to love, there is little evidence to suggest that husbands felt themselves in dire danger of being toppled from their pedestals.

People should marry within their class, and even within occupations.[62] In times of financial stress, hard-hit families of the nobility might deign to fish in mercantile waters, and daughters of farm labourers serving in yeomen's houses might hook a social superior. The line between depressed gentlefolk and affluent yeomanry might be hard to draw. Feminine beauty will always create its own exceptions. None the less, the evidence suggests that these were exceptions to the norm in England. Similarly, the well-known intermarriage of ministerial, mercantile and magisterial families in Massachusetts, and the 'one great tangled cousinry' which was the Virginian aristocracy in the eighteenth century, show that on the whole the rule held in the colonies too.[63]

The one acknowledged loophole in the general system was the position of the widow—a woman who, not being under male governance and in more than usually free control of her property, might be able to exercise greater freedom of choice. None the less, a husband might well try to exercise his authority from the grave by the dispositions contained in his will, and the pressure of a marriage-oriented society and such more personal considerations as loneliness or a sense of dependency might well drive a reluctant widow back to the altar—not to mention the insinuations and flattery of fortune-hunters.

American Erosion: Courtship

What we have been describing so far in this chapter is the 'party line' of both English and colonial society in the seventeenth century. This party line, however, which tended to operate against women's position in society, was less easily enforced or enforceable in the American environment. There was greater opportunity for women to marry for love or at least to marry their choice; the husband's despotism in marriage was strictly limited and the ideal of marriage was more of a partnership and a companionship than it was in England. Although colonial society allowed greater freedom in these areas, there was paradoxically less danger of exploitation, by, for instance, adventurers and male fortune-hunters.

We have already suggested in preceding chapters a whole cluster of causes which would tend to make choice of a marriage partner easier and freer for women. The advantageous sex ratio, the greater economic opportunities, the social philosophies of puritanism and the frontier ethos would all tend to operate in favour of women. Male plenty would make marriage a less crucial test of a young woman's eligibility, and diminish the desperation which certain English writers have noted. Though the *Spectator* might praise the English custom of a girl at first demurring when she was courted,[64] this might, according to Defoe, be a risky business, and the courter might take her at her word and move on to easier prey.[65] In Virginia, however, this custom was adopted by eligible girls with impunity. Miss Gagen, in attempting to show the emergence of a 'new woman' in the latter half of the seventeenth century, makes much of the proviso scenes of Restoration drama, which she sees as a development from the ploys employed by such as Shakespeare's comic heroines to force the gallant to declare his love before his nymph admits that she has succumbed. In such plays as Dryden's *Secret Beauty* (1667) or Shadwell's *Sullen Lovers* (1668) or Congreve's *Way of the World* (1700), this playing hard-to-get results

121

in the mistress extracting provisions from the ensnared gallant which would guarantee her freedom and mutuality in the ensuing marriage.[66] However, proviso scenes, and the preceding verbal duelling, gave dramatists a superb vehicle for witty conflict and suspense, and may well have served the deeper purpose of satirising the real-life enslavement of woman, rather than reflecting her contemporary emancipation. This is not to deny that in certain instances women were able to make stiff terms before marriage. Laura Norsworthy cites the conditions which Elizabeth Hatton extracted from Edward Coke in 1598: a private marriage, without banns, at night in Hatton House—these strange requirements were the result of sheer bravado, she thinks.[67] Phillips and Tomkinson reprint a fantastic letter of Eliza Spencer, heiress of a Lord Mayor of London, who had made a runaway marriage with Lord Compton. Her inheritance on her father's death in 1609 was large, but so were her demands, like £6,000 to buy jewels, or an annual allowance of £1,600, or the upkeep of two coaches.[68] These two women were great catches, however, abundantly worth humouring in the bush in order to get them into the hand. The great heiress was in England the exception which proved the rule, a rule quite different from the relative freedom which prevailed in the colonies. The comparison might be epitomised by citing the letter of Endicott, by no means the most permissive of New Englanders, in which he gives reasons why his ward, aged fifteen, rejects the suit of Emmanuel Downing's son:[69]

> 1st. The girle desires not to marry as yett. 2ndlie: She confesseth, which is the truth, herself to be altogether yett unfitt for such a condition, shee beinge a verie girle & but 15 yeares of age. 3rdlie: Where the man was moved to her shee said she could not like him.

This leisurely attitude contrasts strikingly with Stone's well-documented statement that an English girl of good birth who was not married off by the age of eighteen was in dire straits.[70]

This leads us on **to** the question of the comparative influence exercised by parents in their children's choice of marriage partner. Obviously, there are many subtle gradations, from the outright forcing of a child to the mild requirement that parents should give their blessing to their offspring's choice. The kind of pressure that parents would exert would depend on complex factors—their relationship with the particular child, for instance, and their psychological make-up. None the less, it is undeniable that the relative importance of economic factors would be bound to play an important part in determining parental attitudes.

There seems little doubt from the available evidence that the portion or dowry was rather less crucial in the colonies than it was in England, in all classes.[71] It was remarked upon as a difference by promotional writers and visitors to the colonies. The existence of greater economic opportunities meant, in Hammond's words, that 'Few there are but are able to give some Portions with their daughters, more or lesse, according to their abilities.'[72] Certainly there was little in the colonies to match the outcry against mercenary marriages that was endemic throughout the century in England.[73] No preacher, to my knowledge, in Virginia or Massachusetts, found it necessary to warn girls that in obeying their parents their motive should not be 'that of worldly prudence, fearing to displease your parents, lest they should diminish your intended portion, and so be a loser thereby.'[74] The control available to parents is implicit in this statement. Certainly Sewall's famous letter to his daughter Betty about her too frequent refusal of suitors, a letter couched in almost apologetic terms, compares very favourably with the actions of Englishmen like the Earl of Cork, Dorothy Osborne's brother, or Sir Edward Coke, or the Marquess of Dorchester when faced with daughters unwilling to do their father's will.[75]

Of course it was not only the fact that fathers were more able to afford dowries which altered the position in America. If the worst came to the worst, the prevailing economic optimism of the colonies would allow young couples to defy parental wishes with greater impunity. Although Philip Greven has argued that parents in Andover did use their financial whip hand in an 'English' manner to control their children, his argument is not supported by John Demos's inquiry in Plymouth, or by other available evidence.[76] Support for Demos's contention of the dispersion of the younger generation comes from the findings of Sumner Powell in his examination of the history of Sudbury, Mass. Here the younger generation of settlers moved out *en masse* when frustrated by their elders and set up a new township at Marlborough.[77] The 'inflexible rule' for Dedham from 1648 to 1700, according to Kenneth Lockridge, was 'continuity'. 'Most men lived their entire lives within this one village.' This might initially seem to support the Greven thesis of the younger generations remaining within the parental ambit, and thus being open to parental control of marriage partner. However, Lockridge himself admits that the death-rate for Dedham is under-recorded by as much as 56 per cent. This, he concedes, could be caused by 'the emigration of young men before they became taxable'. Moreover, the daughter towns of Medfield and Wrentham, incorporated in 1649 and 1673 respectively, might have acted as safety-valves for the younger generation, much as Marlborough did for Sudbury.[78]

Other pointers suggest limitations on parental control in the colonies. What Fitzjohn Winthrop described as 'the way and custome of the country for young folkes to choose, and where there is no visible exception everybody approves it'[79] was buttressed in Massachusetts by law. Lawrence cites a statute of 1641 enacted in Plymouth which reads: 'If any person shall wilfully and unreasonably deny any child timely and convenient marriage or shall exercise any unnatural severity towards them; such children shall have liberty to complain to authority for redress in such cases.'[80] While the laws of the Bay Colony allowed considerable powers to parents in the matter of courtship, they did insist that 'neither reason nor religion' allowed them 'to put force on their chldren'.[81] Provisos were also recorded against refusals motivated by 'the sinister end or covetous desire of a parent or guardian'.[82] An interesting case at Charlestown in 1679 remitted punishment of George Parminter and his wife for fornication, on the grounds that her parents had denied the contracting of the marriage for too long.[83] That a reasonably determined suitor might get his own way in the end is suggested by the case of the Quaker, Arthur Howland. Between 1660 and 1667 he was twice haled before the courts of Plymouth, charged with courting no less than the daughter of the Governor, Elizabeth Prince. Yet, despite this stern parental action, he finally married his choice in 1668.[84] Morgan cites the dilemma of Michael Wigglesworth, whose affections had come to centre on one girl when a letter arrived from his mother recommending another. He confessed himself to be in 'marvellous sorrow and perplexity more than I wel knew how to bear'.[85] The fact that his mother's letter presented him with a dilemma, rather than an overriding solution, bears out the generality of Winthrop's statement with which this paragraph opened.

It is, of course, true that there were cases in England where children got their own way through persistence. One of the most famous examples is that of the young John Reresby, who, despite his mother's opposition, finally wed Frances Brown, his own choice.[86] Furthermore, the English presbyterian, Daniel Rogers, argued that if parents were hard-hearted, their church or magistrate 'should reduce the parents into due order'.[87] Nevertheless, children in Massachusetts appear to have had greater safeguards in law and in common practice against parental domination, and to have made use of them to exercise a greater freedom of choice.

The legal situation in Virginia appears to have been much closer to that of England. By a law of 1632, parental consent was unnecessary for people over twenty-one seeking a licence to wed, but of course this apparent freedom of choice had no bearing on the much more important question of the financial arrangements. The evidence from statutes does suggest that the secret marriages of indentured servants, who were not normally permitted to marry while under articles, were not uncommon.[88] However, what we know from diaries and letters suggests that Lewis Burwell's riposte to the over-ardent Nicholson, 'I have left my daughter to make her own choice as to a husband,' was pretty typical of Virginian parental practice.[89] If the worst came to the worst, colonists in New England and Virginia had their Gretna Greens—New Hampshire and Maryland respectively.[90]

Another sign of greater freedom of choice may be the lower average age of marriage in the colonies than in England: may, rather than must, because a lower age of marriage could argue greater parental influence, and therefore less rather than more freedom of choice.[91] However, if lower age of marriage was a result of greater economic opportunities, as there is every reason to believe it was, and also a certain haste on the part of the many men to engage the few women of marriageable age, then the lower age would suggest that the young might well have a greater say in their own affairs. Greven writes that[92]

> The age of marriage is one of the most useful indices of economic, demographic and social change, both short and long term. For American colonial history, the age of marriage may prove to be of critical importance in measuring and evaluating the changes which transformed Englishmen and other Europeans into Americans during the seventeenth and eighteenth centuries.

The demographic evidence on marriage ages for England and the colonies is very patchy, but what we have got seems to be reasonably representative. The figures vary according to class. Stone shows that the average age for the eldest sons of peers marrying was twenty-one, while that for all children and grandchildren of noble families was twenty-five to twenty-six. Between 1550 and 1625 the average marriage age for daughters of upper-class families was twenty-one to twenty-two. For the lower orders, yeomen and below, males would have to wait till the age of twenty-seven or twenty-eight to marry and females till twenty-four or twenty-five. The reasons Stone adduces for this situation are all economic: the exigencies of apprenticeship or of living-in service, and the need to wait for a father to die or for a holding to fall vacant so that a new household could be set up.[93] E. A. Wrigley has even suggested that these relatively high averages may have gone up in the second half of the century, so far as the lower classes were concerned, and that as many as a third of women did not marry until they were in their thirties. Once again, economic considerations are advanced as the most likely causes of this attempt at family limitation.[94]

Similar figures for the colonies are at the moment harder to come by. Demos's findings from a sample of 650 persons in Plymouth plantation during the seventeenth century show that the mean age of marriage for men fell from 27·0 for men born before 1600 to 24·6 for men born between 1675 and 1700. For women the mean age rose with later generations. Women in his sample born between 1600 and 1625 married at a mean age of 20·6, that is seven years younger than the male mean for that generation, but women born between 1675 and 1700 had a mean marriage age of 22·3. Despite these slight fluctuations over the century, the average age of marriage in Plymouth was markedly lower than in England.[95] Greven's figures for Andover, Mass. tend to bear out this finding. The average marriage-age for second generation women there was 22·3, and for second-generation men 27·1. One-third of the sixty-six girls in this generation had married before they were twenty-one, and a further third between the ages of twenty-one and twenty-four. The average from 1680 to 1704 dropped below twenty-two.[96] Lockridge's figures for Dedham between 1640 and 1690 produce average marriage ages of 25·5 for men and 22·5 for women,[97] and Norton's for Ipswich from 1652 to 1700 a mean of 27·2 for men and 21·1 for women.[98] Sarah Knight found that in Connecticut, 'They generally marry very young: the males oftener as I am told under twentie than above.'[99]

The chances are that women married even younger in Virginia. One major reason advanced for domestic discord there was the immature age at which people married.[100] Durand of Dauphiné found the principals at a marriage feast he attended to be younger than was usual in his native land.[101] Certainly the impression of younger marriages in the colonies had permeated Grub Street by the time Ned Ward wrote his scurrilous report on Boston:[102]

> The *Women*, like Early *Fruits*, are soon *Ripe* and soon *Rotten*. A *Girl* there at Thirteen, thinks herself as well Quallified for a Husband, as a forward *Miss* at a Boarding-School, does here at Fifteen for a *Gallant*.

The effects of a lower marriage age would be considerable. Obviously this is one explanation for larger average size of family in the colonies than in England. Relations between parents and children who would be five or even ten years closer in age would probably be subtly affected. Likewise, the attitudes towards each other of spouses who had courted, married and conceived children in their young twenties or even late teens might well be distinctly different: more romantic, less quickly set, more adaptable. It is also worth while pondering on the kinds of effects that a longer expectation of married life might have. Such ingredients could well give a very different flavour to matrimony in the colonies.

Another intriguing hint comes to us through the custom of bundling, apparently quite common in rural New England in the seventeenth, eighteenth and even early nineteenth centuries.[103] The only study of this practice is the very inadequate one by Henry Reed Stiles.[104] This relies heavily on the notoriously unreliable Revd Samuel Peters, whose purpose was to contrast the respectability of the New World with the depravity of the Old. Bundling was a courtship custom similar to the Dutch *Queesting*, but not to be confused with 'tarrying', a primitive system of board and lodging in the host's bed. Anbury described it in his *Travels*:[106]

> When a young man is enamoured of a woman, and wishes to marry her, he proposes the affair to her parents (without whose consent no marriage, in this colony, can take place); if they have no objections, he is allowed to tarry with her one night, in order to make his court. At the usual time, the old couple retire to bed,[106] leaving the young ones to settle matters as they can, who having sat up as long as they think proper, get into bed together also, but without putting off their under garments, to prevent scandal. If the parties agree, it is all very well, the banns are published and they are married without delay; if not, they part and possibly never see each other again, unless, which is an accident which seldom happens, the forsaken maid proves pregnant, in which case the man, unless he absconds, is obliged to marry her, on pain of excommunication.

Apart from the misuse of 'tarry', and the limitation of the custom to one night, Anbury's description is substantially correct. Commenting on its implications, Calhoun sees the major reason for the custom as economic. 'Harsh economic conditions denied leisure for more seemly courtship and afforded but inadequate facilities for keeping houses warm.'[107] This, and the isolation of rural areas, would certainly go far to explain the custom, but there does remain the question of the parents of the girl leaving the unbetrothed couple unsupervised in a situation which even permissive modern parents would object to. Peters's conclusion seems unavoidable that 'this custom of bundling is attended with so much innocence in New England' that parents could rest assured that the courting couple would observe the strong social restraints of the time. The response of country women to attacks on bundling in the later part of the eighteenth century was that many more bastards were bred in the cities or towns than in the country districts. As a traditional song had it:[108]

> Now unto those that do oppose
> The bundling trade, I say
> Perhaps there's more got on the floor,
> Than any other way.

What is striking for our purposes is the amount of freedom which parents gave their children in the final choice of marriage partner, and the trust that they felt happy in allowing them. This is a far more liberal approach than the careful yeomen of England seem to have been prepared to adopt. Certainly there is no record of bundling having been practised in England in the seventeenth century.[109]

The impression, and it is only an impression, that women had far greater freedom and even initiative in courtship in the colonies is borne out by some well-known examples. Mrs Spruill sees courtship in the colonial South as having been far less formal, with more opportunity for a love-match, except perhaps among some of the very wealthiest families.[110] Certainly Nicholson implies in his letters that the youthful Lucy Burwell had been no shrinking violet; her initial complaisance perhaps justifies his frustrated rage later.[111] 'When you give me leave to kiss your fair hand, your pretty mouth, charming eyes and ravishing breasts, then I am in an extraordinary exstasie of joy and satisfaction and rapt up pleasure', he wrote in an insomniac outpouring.[112] Similarly the elderly Byrd reports the sudden marriage of his daughter Maria to Landon Carter on 22 September 1742: 'None of us thought of anything about it at ten in the morning, and by 3 the Gordian knot was tyed.'[113] In Massachusetts such prestigious individuals as Cotton Mather and Samuel Sewall were courted by young women. Mather with typical inward agonising passed up his wooer as she had a damaged reputation,[114] but Sewall's Harvard Commencement Address on the unpromising subject of 'Original Sin' so affected the eighteen-year-old Hannah Hull that she 'set her affection upon him from that hour', and he succumbed.[115] There were, of course, women in England who showed an equal determination, but their determination was something worthy of surprise or even anger, was often seen as a widowly trait, and was sometimes frustrated.[116] Calhoun quotes French visitors to America at the end of the eighteenth century, who 'were almost shocked at the freedom enjoyed by girls yet they admit that no harm came of it'.[117] What we know of the previous century suggests that this sense of freedom for 'young ladies' was no new acquisition. One is reminded of Josselyn's description of Boston, published in London in 1674: 'There is a small but pleasant common where the gallents a little before sunset walk with their marmalet madams as we do in Moorfields &c., till the nine o'clock bell rings them home.'[118] This freedom contrasts strikingly with the precautions that were taken in England. Benjamin Colman, who was himself a bit of a gallant, was surprised to find that the father of Elizabeth Singer, Philomela the puritan poetess, guarded her like Argos, with 'a hundred eyes upon his daughter'.[119]

What Mr Singer was protecting his daughter from was the possible roué who might, by elopement or clandestine marriage or some other confidence trick, inveigle her into a most undesirable alliance which would almost certainly result in financial loss for the family and dishonour for the victimised daughter. That the hundred eyes of Argos were none too many is borne out by the English evidence of the seventeenth century. Though a statute was passed in 1598 to remove benefit of clergy from 'those who force women with substance against their will'[120]—presumably into matrimony—no effective prevention seems to have been enacted until Lord Hardwicke's Marriage Act of 1754.[121] The Canons CII and CIII of 1604 attempted to close some of the more notorious loopholes, but Christopher Hill has shown that the Ecclesiastical or Bawdy Courts did a brisk trade in countenancing evasions throughout the century.[122] While the practice of the country followed the teaching that spousals *de presenti* made a marriage, and while certain churches and clergymen were permitted to act independently of authority, the exploitation of girls by adventurers was bound to continue. Miss Wedgwood gives several examples of the forcible abduction of heiresses, including the case of Sarah Cox, in 1637. She was snatched from a party of schoolgirls walking on Newington Common by a young gentleman, and forcibly married.[123] A young heiress from the city had no difficulty, after her elopement with a poor Scots laird, in getting herself married to him at Greenwich the same night.[124] When Sir Nathanial Brent visited the diocese of Lincoln in 1634 as part of Laud's campaign of enforcing 'thorough' in his province, he found much evidence of clandestine marriages being solemnised. One Edward Collingwood, the curate of Stow, 'would marry them with gloves and masks on'.[125] Such churches as St Paul's Covent Garden, Trinity Minories, St Pancras or St James's Duke's Place, which claimed to be outside the visitation of the Bishop of London, were notorious for their lack of scruple in performing marriages. Between 1664 and 1691, it is estimated that 40,000 usually illicit unions were solemnised—sometimes as many as forty a day. The scandal of Fleet marriages is similarly well-attested.[126] Now some of this number may, it is true, have reflected the harsh control which English parents exerted over their children's choice of spouse. Nevertheless, it is not hard to imagine that in many cases the victims of such liaisons would be the women. In analysing comedies of the Restoration period, Alleman has found eighty-eight examples of tricked marriages. It is interesting that in only twelve of these are the victims of the deceit female. In the rest, it is the women, usually maids, mistresses or prostitutes, who are the deceivers. However, in this case there seems good reason to infer that this was not a reflection of society but rather criticism by contrast with the true, male-oriented, state of affairs. Both Mrs Centlivre and Mrs Behn favoured the tricked marriage as a dramatic device, and in their cases it is the folly of the fops that they seek to underline.[127] Miss Gagen argues, from her findings that the incidence of elopements in Restoration drama rose, that feminine protest against parental control is here involved. While this could be supported by the arguments used by the characters in some of the plays she cites, it could equally well be taken to show that elopements were becoming more common in real life. A stage elopement, anyway, is a magnificent dramatic device, and it can be questioned how far dramatists, particularly in this period, reflected public opinion.[128] Rather more substantial as evidence of the dangers in which young women of quality went is Mary Astell's proposal for setting up a seminary. This would be a sanctuary where women would be safe from the inveiglements, 'the Fustian Complements' [sic] and 'Fulsome Flatteries' with which too often, according to Miss Astell, men took them in.[129] Evidence of the sort of precautions that a parent thought necessary is provided in William Byrd's *London Diary* and his letters of his unsuccessful courtship of Miss Smith. The ever-eager Byrd was required to use all the guile of a master-besieger to mine and sap even the outer works constructed against such as him.[130]

There is no denying that irregularities did occur in the colonies. One of the charges which James Blair made in his feud against Governor Francis Nicholson at the turn of the century was that he had granted a governor's marriage licence to Robert Snead, 'an idle man of no Estate nor bred to any Calling, to marry [Margaret Simson] a young orphan, & Heiress of York County, by the means whereof that young orphan' was married and ruined, contrary to the consent of her Guardian'. Nicholson denied this charge, with counter-affidavits, but none the less the marriage and ruination had undeniably taken place.[131] In 1699 the Virginian Council received complaints against a minister who abetted a runaway marriage in Maryland.[132] Advertisements appeared quite regularly in eighteenth-century Virginian newspapers formally refusing all responsibility on the part of parents of errant girls.[133] Similarly, things sometimes went awry in Massachusetts. If the laws of the colony are anything to go by, unauthorised courtship was not uncommon.[134] It would appear that Benjamin Colman's daughter eloped with one Albert Dennie.[135] The colonies were not spotless.

Where they did differ, however, was in their determination to try to prevent such irregularities. Writing of the matrimonial institutions in force in Virginia in the colonial period, Howard descries two major contrasts with England. First, the administration of the law was in the hands of the county officials, who were likely to be far more inquisitive and pernickety about irregularities. Second, the laws governing matrimony were far more carefully drawn and revised to provide comprehensive protection against exploiters.[136] A paradigm of the contrast is the case of Parson Waugh. This minister was in some ways not unlike the shady clergy who skulked around the Fleet. He was responsible for more than one clandestine marriage being solemnised over the border in Maryland, without banns being called or licence obtained from the county authorities in Virginia.[137] Not only did the council of Virginia itself take action against this 'notorious offender', but also, in 1705, an Act was passed against 'Ministers who go out of the province and marry there, with out Banns or license or consent of parents'.[138] This action compares most strikingly with the complacent English acceptance of scandals until the middle of the eighteenth century. It need hardly be added that the detailed marriage laws of the puritan colony were very tightly administered by the magistrates under whose sole purview they came for most of our period.[139]

American Erosion: Marriage

If we turn now to the actual institution of marriage rather than customs governing preliminaries, we find again evidence which suggests that conditions in America were a good deal more favourable to wives, despite the semblance of agreement on the 'official' level. Of course, any division between courtship and marriage must introduce artificialities into our discussion. If it is granted, for instance, that women in the colonies had a greater opportunity to marry for love, then it should follow that there was a greater chance of happiness within resultant marriages, and also that the wives, having had an element of choice of partner, would enjoy greater equality after their choice had been sealed.

There was an important distinction in the social purpose of marriage in the New and the Old Worlds. The American colonies, like most early settlements, were in desperate need of manpower. While the abundance of land and the shortage of labour can be

exaggerated—especially at the expense of the need for capital—
the resources of the New World did need plentiful supplies of
hands for rapid and effective exploitation.[140] This being so, the
role of women as 'fruitful vines by the sides of the house'[141] was of
enormous value to the colonial community. Mather himself quotes
with obvious pride the large numbers of children which certain
Massachusetts women had borne.[142] The resultant high esteem for
marriage—normally advantageous for women—was shared in the
southern colonies, where the marriage age was probably lower,
and thus multiplication even greater. Although Franklin's claim
that there were twice as many marriages and twice as many children
per marriage and that the American population doubled every
twenty years[143] has been shown to be something of an exaggeration,
none the less it is not too far from the truth.[144] In the same spirit,
he obviously felt that the point that he put into Polly Baker's
mouth was a valid one for the colonial experience:[145]

> I have brought five fine children into the world, at the risque
> of my life. . . . Can it be a crime (in the nature of things, I
> mean) to add to the king's subjects, in a new country, that
> really wants people? I own it, I should think it rather a praise-
> worthy than a punishable action. . . . The duty of the first
> and great command of nature and nature's God [is] *encrease
> and multiply*; a duty, from the steady performance of which
> nothing has been able to deter me.

Modern demographic evidence for the colonies implies that family
size was around double that in England, and that the survival rate
of children was a good deal higher.[146] The economic need for
population growth was given strong supplementary impetus, especially in the puritan colonies of New England, by the need and the
duty to maintain and increase the numbers of the godly.[147] All this
is in stark contrast with the situation in England, where children
might reasonably be considered a much more mixed blessing, and
where marriage and women might consequently be held in much
lower esteem.[148]

Not only did marriage serve a vital purpose in peopling a new
country, but also, in the colonies, despite a public concurrence
both legally and practically, with the axioms of English society,
matrimonial mutuality and companionship were stressed far more.

The legal restraints on husbandly authority are too well known
to need lengthy comment. Not only was a husband specifically
forbidden by the 1641 *Body of Liberties of Massachusetts* from in-
flicting 'Bodily Correction or Stripes . . . unless it be in his own
Defence' upon his wife, but the County Court records that have
survived show that this was taken extremely seriously and rigor-

ously enforced by the authorities.[149] Other, less physical, forms of cruelty were also checked.[150] Clerical opinion supported this legal protection for women against the unfettered authority of their husbands, a protection unknown in English law.[151]

To a considerable extent the environment, especially in rural districts in New England and in Virginia, forced a sense of companionship on husbands and wives. William Byrd II spent so much time with his wife, playing billiards, or walking, or reading, or card-playing, or even rowing, because there was no one else of similar class and education available. The same was probably an ingredient in the strong mutual regard between Anne and Simon Bradstreet at Andover, Mass. Even where there were hatred and mutual contempt in a married relationship, as with John and Frances Custis, their final and familiar agreement to live and let live had the alternative of isolation and loneliness behind it. The preamble of an agreement between George and Rachel Potter concluded in the last month of the century has this element in it. 'By his consent and in hope of more peaceable liveing, [Rachel had] withdrawn herself and removed to Boston for some time: and now finding it uncomfortable so to live and I being desirous to come together againe, doe here for her further incouragement and to prevent after strifes and alienations propose thes Artikles.'[152] The same spirit lies behind the covenant signed by the Revd Caspar Stoever and his wife Magdalena in 1734, to 'totally forget and bury in oblivion' past differences.[153]

Yet while the threat of loneliness might make a Cotton Mather or a Thomas Hooker companionable and concessive towards their wives,[154] these men were but practising what they and their fellow-clergy preached. Rather than the common English idea that marriage made men brutes, American puritans told their congregations that men who maltreated or tyrannised over their wives were brutes.[155] In general, the contrast between New and old England boiled down to a difference of emphasis between the male's authority and his love. Even the hard-liner Halifax mentions the need for mutuality in marriage[156] but in his order of priorities it is depressed below the need for a wife to obey. With New England writers, however, the obligations of the husband and the constant need for forbearance and affection on his part are more frequently stressed.[157] In *A Little Commonwealth*, John Demos speculates on the apparent paradox in Plymouth of a scarcity of court cases dealing with matrimonial or familial discord (despite the cramped conditions in which the early generations of settlers there had to live), and the relative frequency of disputes between neighbours. He conjectures that the strains of forbearance vital to smooth marital relations under such conditions were taken out on the outside world. Certainly some of the women who appeared as defendants in Plymouth cases do not suggest that meekness and humility were the causes of family peace.[158]

The question of sexual relations within marriage is hard to plumb. The only intimate account of which I am aware is contained in William Byrd's *Westover Diary*. In his stormy first marriage, the oft-recorded flourishes and rogerings serve more subtle purposes than 'great ecstacy and refreshment'. They were also means of reconciliation after quarrels, accompaniments of Byrd's home-comings from Williamsburg or further afield, or celebrations of mutual regard during the sunnier periods of the marriage. It was often Lucy Byrd who called the sexual tune. She, for instance, kept her husband in bed in the morning rather than getting up to read some Greek or Italian, and she was often the prompter of the peace-making bouts. There are also hints that she used the device, well-known in dramatic proviso scenes of the Restoration, of withholding sexual pleasure from a lusty husband who had displeased her. How common this kind of behaviour was it is impossible in the nature of the case to tell. One supposition can, however, be made. The deployment of this kind of sexual weaponry by women would become ridiculous if society condoned, and husbands could find, alternative sources of pleasure.[159]

Radical Changes: Massachusetts

We turn now to those very marked differences in custom and outlook which had developed in the colonies by the end of the century. These distinctions were most marked in the case of Massachusetts, but had certain dimmer reflections in the South.

First, marriage was regarded in New England law as a civil contract, not a sacrament, as in Anglican thinking. The ceremony was performed before a magistrate rather than a clergyman, and civil, rather than ecclesiastical, law governed the institution.[160] Henry Barrow, the independent, a seminal influence on this subject, compared church weddings to two businessmen who went along to the priest to have a deal blessed. As there was no biblical precedent, it was argued, the role of the church was superfluous. The Massachusetts authorities insisted on civil control to the extent of forbidding Hubbard of Hingham to preach at a Boston wedding in 1647, and charging a Huguenot *émigré* with solemnising marriages in 1685.[161] The contractual idea leads to the puritan corollary that under certain conditions the contract may be terminated. Few puritans—Milton was an exception—were capable of the ultimate conclusion, divorce by mutual consent, and even here Milton was unable to divest himself of preconceptions about male superiority.[162] The possibility, however circumscribed, of terminating the civil contract of marriage would plainly sow the seeds of a revolutionary change in that institution. It would also tend to give women greater safeguards and increased equality in marriage. When a woman entered into a legal contract, rather than 'dwindled into a wife', *mutual* obligations and rights were legally recognised, and the old medieval concept of the *femme covert* undermined.

Virginia was a different case. There the Anglican church retained its authority and doctrines. On the other hand, because ecclesiastical courts were never established in the colony in the seventeenth century, control of marriage law did tend to devolve on the county court officials. In practice, this made Virginia veer towards the New England concept of a civil contract under the supervision of the civil laws. Although divorce was not officially recognised, there is evidence that lay officials were in practice a good deal more liberal towards wives than were the ecclesiastical courts in England.[163]

A second major difference in the colonies, and again particularly in Massachusetts, was the degree of social control that was exerted over marriages. There is a danger of exaggerating the differences here. While accepting Richard B. Morris's point that the small-town environment of colonial America made private or secret vice almost impossible, compared with the opportunities which the larger English cities might afford, none the less it is worth remembering that the majority of the English population lived in villages, and that the frontier settlements, especially in North Carolina or New Hampshire, might provide as good a chance for immoral practices as the teeming tenements of London.[164] Little has been published about the activities of such English disciplinary bodies as archdeacons' courts.[165] However, it is unlikely that they exerted the same sort of social pressure as was used in New England and, to a lesser extent, in Virginia.[166] Furthermore, as Perry Miller has pointed out, civic-mindedness and social welfare were deeply embedded in puritan theology. The so-called 'social covenant', apart from being a weapon against Stuart authoritarianism, also accepted Gouge's famous dictum that 'a family is a little commonwealth, and a commonwealth is a greate family'.[167]

The puritan was not only responsible for himself; he was also responsible for his neighbours, both as members of a church, and as members of a body politic. This tended to invest authority in Massachusetts with greater justifiable powers of social supervision than Anglicanism or lay authority claimed in England over the private lives of citizens. That this power was fully implemented during the seventeenth century is amply shown by even a casual glance through either the laws of the colony or the records of the county courts. The Englishman's home in Massachusetts was not his castle, nor was his bed curtained.[168] Not only were courts interested in matrimonial discord and husbandly cruelty, but also they frequently acted when things had gone from bad to worse, and husband or wife had left home. Calhoun records the rather bizarre case of the Revd Stephen Batchelor who, in 1650, at the age of ninety, was ordered to live with his third wife.[169]

The Massachusetts authorities were insistent that at the earliest opportunity unaccompanied men should return to England to fetch their wives and families.[170] This and similar kinds of official involvement in matrimony were further buttressed by the concern which churches took in the matrimonial affairs of both saints and mere members of the congregation. In certain cases, churches claimed a say in the choice of marriage partner. When a member of the Barnstaple church insisted on marrying an unsuitable woman, he was excommunicated.[171] Sewall has several examples of churches or ministers intervening in marital problems, admonishing people for living apart from their spouses, warning against the choice of a particular individual, or against marital misbehaviour. When his daughter Judith was being courted, the approbation of Benjamin Colman, her minister, was obviously an important element in the proceedings.[172] *The Records of the First Church of Boston* likewise show a church intervening in difficult marital situations. In most cases, by the time an entry is recorded, the conflict has become so bad that one or other of the spouses is excommunicated. The implication of several entries is that this was a last resort after other attempts at reconciliation had been tried and failed.[173] When young Sam Sewall had trouble with his wife Rebecca, their minister, Mr Walter, played a prominent part in attempting a reconciliation.[174] After studying most of the extant New England church records, Emil Oberholzer comes to the conclusion that the church's marriage-guidance record was pretty poor.[175]

There were a relatively large number of failures in churches' attempts to restore harmony in discordant homes. . . . The coldness of the law prevailed over the empathetic understanding which the churches should have shown to those members whose family lives were in danger of disintegration.

This seems to be rather a harsh judgment. One wonders 'relative to what', and if the bald church records tell all the story of efforts to ameliorate the situation. Certainly, community concern, however authoritarian it might have been, must have done something to stabilise marriages, and since, in the prevailing official view, women were more likely to suffer from marital warfare than men, this would have helped to safeguard the female position.

The third important difference, again particularly between Massachusetts and England, was in the question of the double standard. Although in certain areas there might be lingering vestiges of doctrines of male superiority,[176] puritans generally were no respecters of sexes, so far as licence was concerned.[177] As Christopher Hill points out, monogamy was highly prized by the puritans.[178] Possibly the increased emphasis of all Calvinists on the all-seeing deity may have had additional effect here. Many domestic conduct-books taught that God was watching every move in the marriage (and outside it), and that Satan was always busy preparing ambushes for the unwary.[179] Thus Samuel Sewall, in 1704, prayed that 'Satan may not buffet me and my wife' as he was later to buffet son Sam and *his* wife Rebecca.[180] There was, furthermore, a common feeling among puritans that marriages were literally made in heaven, that is to say that the Almighty had a hand in the selection of partners. A good wife was 'God's gift'. 'It was God that first gave Adam his wife, and it is God that giveth every man his wife to this day.' There was 'a more speciall providence of God oft carrying things in these cases' or 'there is the finger of God here'.[181] This sense of divine intervention made it virtual blasphemy on the part of husbands as well as wives, to wreck part of His grand design.

Apart from prevailing popular opinion in England, there were certain technical reasons why the double standard was fostered there. Gellert Alleman has shown that the English ecclesiastical laws about separations and annulment were a positive encouragement to male immorality. The enormous difficulty and expense and embarrassment involved in obtaining a parliamentary divorce at the end of the century would have condoned extra-marital relations. The laws about alimony, even when a woman might technically be the guilty party, might well encourage gallants to seduce the wives of wealthy husbands. As one of Mrs Centlivre's characters put it in 1711, 'A wound in the Reputation of an English woman, they say, only lets in Alimony.'[182] Dramatists' interest in these problems increased markedly towards the end of the century, but, of course, the cuckolding activities of gallants had been a leading literary convention throughout the century.[183] Another invitation to the fortune-hunting roué lay in the annulment laws, which were so complex that any half-competent, crooked lawyer could find some loophole for an unscrupulous client. Thus the marriage of an adventurer to an heiress could be declared invalid by an ecclesiastical court, but the adventurer would be able to pocket the fortune that he had married. This was the fate of the famous Mrs Manley, and of other less voluble innocents.[184]

Yet when all is said and done, it was the general contempt, however masked, in which women were held by English society which was the greatest spur to the double standard.[185] How else would the Earl of Dorset have justified in his own mind his bringing of his mistress, Lady Penistone, to Knole and forcing his wife to entertain her?[186] How else could Halifax argue that a wife should 'affect ignorance' of her husband's infidelities?[187] How else could a Pepys or Byrd defend their petty and squalid immoralities? How else could the cynical Elias Ashmole have conned a woman twenty years his elder into marriage?[188]

It would only be when marriage, and thus women, were recognised as a positive good, a 'queen of friendships', and potentially the most exalted state for man, that the double standard would be effectively undermined. As we have tried to suggest in this and preceding chapters, this state of affairs was far more likely to occur in the colonies than it was in England during the seventeenth century, or indeed, in the centuries that followed.[189]

Notes

1 We have examined some of the conditions which Harriet Martineau would later hail in her account of American marriage: 'If there is any country on Earth where the course of true love may be expected to run smooth, it is America. It is a country where all can marry early, where there need be no anxiety about a worldly provision, and where the troubles arising from conventional considerations of rank and connexion ought to be entirely absent.' *Society in America,* ed. and abr. S. M. Lipset (New York, 1962), p. 296.

2 G. E. Howard, *History of Matrimonial Institutions* (Chicago, 1904); C. L. Powell, *English Domestic Relations 1487–1653* (New York, 1917), and 'Marriage in Early New England', *New England Quarterly*, vol. I (1928), pp. 323–34. Cf. G. S. Alleman, *Matrimonial Law and the Materials of Restoration Comedy* (Wallingford, Pa, 1942).

3 Powell, *English Domestic Relations*, p. 4, cites the marriage between the Duchess and Antonio in *The Duchess of Malfi* as an example of this kind of binding union.

4 Christopher Hill, *Society and Puritanism* (London, 1964), ch. 8.

5 Powell, *English Domestic Relations*, pp. 57ff.

6 A. W. Calhoun, *Social History of the American Family* (Boston, 1918), vol. I, pp. 67ff.

7 See Ada Wallas, *Before the Bluestockings* (London, 1929), ch. 5.

8 Ibid., ch. 4; Myra Reynolds, *The Learned Lady in England 1650–1760* (Boston, 1920), p. 304.

9 Quoted in C. Bridenbaugh, *Vexed and Troubled Englishmen* (New York, 1968), p. 28.

10 M. Ashley, *The Stuarts in Love* (London, 1963), p. 52.

11 E. S. Morgan, *Puritan Family* (New York, 1966), p. 84.

12 Quoted in E. S. Morgan, *Virginians at Home* (Chapel Hill, 1952), p. 20.

13 Sewall, *Diary*, vol. III, pp. 165ff.

14 Barrett Wendell, *Cotton Mather: The Puritan Priest* (New York, 1963), pp. 151ff.
15 Ibid., p. 185.
16 Cotton Mather, *Ornaments for the Daughters of Zion* (Boston, 1691), p. 82.
17 E. J. Gagen, *The New Woman* (New York, 1954), pp. 33ff.
18 *As You Like It,* III. ii; cf. the burlesque of the fond lover in the person of Malvolio in *Twelfth Night.*
19 See his 'Literary Exercises' in *Another Secret Diary*; thus, he asks 'Panthea' why she '(so enchantingly) rejects his Inclinations?' and signs his pleading, abject, letter 'Your slave' (*c.* 1702-3), p. 197.
20 Wallas, op. cit., p. 216.
21 Francis Osborne, *Advice to a Son* (London, 1656), quoted by Ashley, op. cit., p. 19.
22 Quoted in C. Hole, *English Home Life 1500-1800* (London, 1947), p. 55.
23 Wallas, op. cit., p. 35.
24 H. S. Tapley, 'Women of Massachusetts, 1620-89' in A. B. Hart, ed., *Commonwealth History of Massachusetts* (Boston, 1928-9), p. 301.
25 John Aubrey, *Brief Lives,* ed. Oliver L. Dick (Harmondsworth, 1962), p. 276.
26 Cf. Ashley, op. cit., p. 25.
27 E. Turell, *Life and Character of Dr. Benjamin Colman* (Boston, 1749), p. 207.
28 Morgan, *Puritan Family,* p. 53.
29 *Va Mag.,* vol. XXVI (1918), pp. 162ff.
30 Quoted by Wallas, op. cit., p. 119.
31 Ibid., pp. 39ff.
32 Quoted by W. and M. Haller, 'The Puritan Art of Love', *Huntington Library Quarterly,* vol. V (1940-1), p. 255. The chosen must be lovable rather than already loved. Indeed the period between betrothal and nuptials was seen as a time when a couple could get to know each other, *after* the decision.
33 E. Oberholzer, *Delinquent Saints* (New York, 1956), p. 111.
34 Cf. Henry Smith's description of unhappy marriage as 'Two poysons in a Stomacke'. W. and M. Haller, op. cit., p. 258.
35 Ibid., pp. 259ff.
36 Sewall, *Diary,* vol. I, p. 482.
37 Powell, *English Domestic Relations,* p. 129.
38 Alan Macfarlane, *The Family Life of Ralph Josselin* (Cambridge, 1970), Appendix B.
39 Ashley, op. cit., p. 49; cf. Joel H. Hurstfield, *The Queen's Wards* (London, 1958), pp. 155, 166-7.
40 In *Tell-Trothes New-Yeares Gift* (1593) the author had Robin Goodfellow returning from hell to tell mortal man the main causes of its over-population. Cited in Louis B. Wright, *Middle Class Culture in Elizabethan England* (Chapel Hill, 1935), p. 209.
41 Gagen, op. cit., p. 128.
42 *Tatler,* No. 149, quoted in Wallas, op. cit., p. 217.
43 Ashley, op. cit., p. 35; L. Stone, *Crisis of the Aristocracy 1558-1641* (Oxford, 1965), p. 197.
44 Mather, op. cit., p. 55.
45 Sewall, *Diary,* vol. III, 172-232, 262-76, 289-306.
46 Ibid., vol. II, p. 336. Cf. James Ford, 'Social Life', ch. 10 in Hart, op. cit., vol. I, p. 280, and Morgan, *Puritan Family,* pp. 56ff.
47 Ibid., p. 58.
48 Cf. Annie L. Jester, *Domestic Life in Colonial Virginia in the Seventeenth Century* (Jamestown, 1957), pp. 42ff.; J. C. Spruill, *Women's Life and Work in the Southern Colonies* (Chapel Hill, 1938), ch. 7.

49 'On Sylvia The Fair—A Jingle' quoted in Calhoun, op. cit., vol. I, p. 58. Franklin's Dulman with his gold reminds one of John Verney, a returned Turkey merchant, who conspired with a prospective girl's father to inspect her without her knowledge. Ashley, op. cit., p. 49.

50 R. B. Schlatter, *The Social Ideas of Religious Leaders 1660–88* (London, 1940), p. 13; Wallas, op. cit., p. 39.

51 Ibid., p. 65.

52 Laura Norsworthy, *Lady of Bleeding Heart Yard* (New York, 1936), p. 39.

53 Elizabeth Duke, for instance, who married the Virginian rebel Nathaniel Bacon in England, was disinherited by her father. Spruill, op. cit., p. 145, has several examples. Philip Greven, 'Family Structure in Seventeenth Century Andover, Massachusetts', *3 WMQ*, vol. XXIII (1966), pp. 244ff., suggests that the same leverage was used by parents in Andover, Mass. See also the veiled threat employed by Ralph Josselin against his recalcitrant son, Macfarlane, op. cit., p. 123.

54 *General Laws of Massachusetts Bay Colony* (Boston, 1814), pp. 151–2.

55 Quoted in Schlatter, op. cit., p. 15.

56 Mayne, *City Match*, II. vii (1639).

57 Cf. W. Notestein, 'The English Woman 1580–1650' in *Studies in Social History Presented to G. M. Trevelyan*, ed. J. H. Plumb (London, 1955), p. 99. W. K. Jordan argues that London merchants so arranged their wills that their widows found it 'at once difficult and unrewarding' to remarry outside the livery 'company of her late spouse', *The Charities of London* (London, 1960), p. 28.

58 Quoted in Morgan, *Puritan Family*, p. 84; written in 1661.

59 For some well-documented examples, see Notestein, op. cit., pp. 84–5; A. F. W. Papillon, *Memoirs of Thomas Papillon of London, Merchant (1623–1702)* (Reading, 1887), ch. 2; W. Notestein, *Four Worthies* (London, 1956), p. 131; M. Phillips and W. S. Tomkinson, *English Women in Life and Letters* (Oxford, 1927), pp. 48–54; Turell, op. cit., pp. 209ff. The normally liberal Benjamin Colman automatically assumed that the unhappiness of his daughter Abigail's life should have arisen from her defiance of his wishes over marriage; Byrd, *Another Secret Diary*, pp. 175, 298ff.; *London Diary, passim,* for Byrd's thwarted courtship of Mary Smith and others; E. B. Schlesinger, 'Cotton Mather and His Children', *3 WMQ*, vol. X (1953), p. 187; Sewall, *Diary*, I, pp. 424, 490–503; II, pp. 91, 250–63, 378–405; *Va Mag.*, vol. CXXIV (1966), p. 13.

60 Sewall, *Diary*, vol. II, p. 128.

61 Notestein, *Four Worthies*, p. 147.

62 W. K. Jordan, op. cit., p. 28.

63 B. Bailyn, *New England Merchants in the Seventeenth Century* (New York, 1964), pp. 135–7; idem in J. M. Smith, ed., *Seventeenth Century America* (Chapel Hill, 1959), p. 111; Morgan, *Puritan Family*, pp. 161ff.

64 12 June 1711, cited by Spruill, op. cit., p. 149.

65 *Moll Flanders* (Signet ed.), p. 62; 'If any young lady had so much arrogance as to counterfeit a negative, she never had the opportunity of denying twice, much less of recovering that false step and accepting what she had seemed to decline.'

66 Gagen, op. cit., pp. 139ff.

67 Norsworthy, op. cit., ch. 1.

68 Phillips and Tomkinson, op. cit., pp. 68–9.

69 Tapley, op. cit., p. 309.

70 L. Stone, 'Marriage among the English Nobility', *Comparative Studies in Society and History*, vol. III (1960–1), p. 195.

71 H. Moller, 'Sex Composition and Correlated Culture Patterns in Colonial America', *3 WMQ*, vol. II (1945), p. 141.

72 John Hammond, 'Leah and Rachel', in Force, *Tracts*, vol. III, No. 14, p. 17.

73 Cf. Wallas, op. cit., p. 216.

74 Hannah Woolley, quoted by Wallas, op. cit., p. 38.

75 See Howard, op. cit., pp. 167–9; *Home Life of Ladies in the Seventeenth Century*, by the author of *Magdalen Stafford* (London, 1860), pp. 136–48, paraphrasing the record of the early life of Mary (Boyle), Countess of Warwick; Robert Halsband, *The Life of Lady Mary Wortley Montagu* (London, 1961), ch. 2.

76 Greven, op. cit., pp. 224ff.; J. Demos, *A Little Commonwealth* (New York, 1970), pp. 119ff.

77 Sumner Powell, *Puritan Village* (New York, 1963), chs 7, 8.

78 K. Lockridge, 'The Population of Dedham, Massachusetts, 1636–1736', *Economic History Review*, Second Series, vol. XIX (1966), pp. 318–44.

79 Morgan, *Puritan Family*, p. 85.

80 H. W. Lawrence, *The Not-Quite Puritans* (Boston, 1928), p. 35; he also records a case brought by a suitor against a girl's father, which was won by the plaintiff.

81 Morgan, *Puritan Family*, pp. 79ff.

82 Howard, op. cit., vol. II, p. 163.

83 Ibid., p. 163.

84 Ibid.

85 Morgan, *Puritan Family*, p. 86.

86 Andrew Browning, ed., *The Memoirs of Sir John Reresby* (Glasgow, 1936), pp. 82–94.

87 *Matrimonial Honour* (London, 1642), p. 81, cited in the Hallers, op. cit., p. 255; cf. Powell, *English Domestic Relations*, pp. 90–2.

88 On this whole question, see Howard, op. cit., vol. II, ch. 13.

89 F. Downey, 'Governor goes A-Wooing', *Va Mag.*, vol. LV (1947), p. 14.

90 Howard, op. cit., vol. II, p. 231; Calhoun, op. cit., vol. I, p. 60.

91 This is the conclusion for pre-famine Ireland suggested by K. H. Connell, *The Population of Ireland 1750–1845* (Oxford, 1950), ch. 3.

92 P. Greven, 'Historical Demography and Colonial America', *3 WMQ*, vol. XXIV (1967), p. 446.

93 L. Stone, 'Social Mobility in England 1500–1700', *Past and Present*, No. 33 (1966), pp. 40–1. These conclusions are in general borne out by subsequent findings by such demographers as Laslett and Hollingsworth.

94 E. A. Wrigley, 'Family Limitation in Pre-Industrial England', *Economic History Review*, 2nd Series, vol. XIX (1966), pp. 82–106.

95 Demos, op. cit., p. 193.

96 P. Greven, *Four Generations* (Ithaca, 1970), pp. 116–21.

97 Lockridge, op. cit., p. 330.

98 Susan Norton, 'Population Growth in Colonial America', *Population Studies*, vol. XXV (1971), p. 446.

99 Sarah Knight, *Journal*, ed. George P. Winship (New York, 1935), p. 37.

100 Spruill, op. cit., chs 3, 7, 8.

101 Durand, *A Frenchman in Virginia*, ed. and trans. by Fairfax Harrison (privately printed, 1923), p. 32. Cf. J. Potter, 'Growth of Population in America 1700–1860' in D. V. Glass and D. E. C. Eversley, eds, *Population in History* (London, 1965), p. 660.

102 Ned Ward, *A Trip to New England* (London, 1699), p. 53.

103 Oberholzer, op. cit., describes bundling as being very common in the Colonial period, especially on Cape Cod (p. 141).

104 Henry Reed Stiles, *Bundling* (privately printed, 1871).
105 Anbury, *Travels*, vol. II (London, 1781), pp. 37–40, quoted by Stiles, op. cit., p. 70.
106 It is worth pointing out that this retirement would not necessarily give the courters the privacy that the phrase implies nowadays. The girls' parents would probably not go upstairs, and might not even leave the room.
107 Calhoun, op. cit., vol. I, p. 129; untypically, he also has a useful list of references, the most useful of which is to Mass. Hist. Soc. Proceedings, Second Series, vol. VI, pp. 503–10.
108 Quoted by Stiles, op. cit., pp. 55, 99.
109 Howard, op. cit., vol. II, pp. 181–5, has a good summary.
110 Spruill, op. cit., p. 147.
111 Fairfax Downey discovered the following scrawled in the flyleaf of a book: 'Lucy Burwell is the devil. If not the devil, she is one of his imps' (op. cit., p. 10).
112 Ibid., p. 11.
113 *Another Secret Diary*, p. 31.
114 Wendell, op. cit., pp. 150–1.
115 Ola E. Winslow, *Samuel Sewall of Boston* (New York, 1964), p. 52. The year was 1674.
116 See Notestein, 'The English Woman', pp. 75–6; Doris, Lady Stenton, *The Englishwoman in History* (London, 1957), p. 160.
117 Calhoun, op. cit., vol. II, p. 71.
118 Macfarlane, op. cit., p. 124.
119 Turell, op. cit., p. 35.
120 G. B. Harrison, *The Elizabethan Journals* (Garden City, New York, 1965), vol. II, p. 10.
121 See Alleman, op. cit., p. 5.
122 Ibid., p. 18; Hill, op. cit., ch. 8.
123 C. V. Wedgwood, *The King's Peace* (London, 1955), p. 50.
124 Ibid.
125 Alleman, op. cit., pp. 65–6, quoting William H. Hutton, *The English Church from 1626 to 1714*, p. 65.
126 Alleman, op. cit., pp. 47–8.
127 Ibid., pp. 82–101.
128 Gagen, op. cit., pp. 120ff.
129 Wallas, op. cit., ch. 4.
130 *London Diary*, p. 28, and entries for 1718 and 1719 *passim*.
131 *Papers Relating to an Affidavit*, p. 88.
132 *Exec. Journ. Council Col. Va*, II, 31; quoted in R. Davis, *William Fitzhugh and his Chesapeake World* (Chapel Hill, 1963), p. 98.
133 Spruill, op. cit., pp. 179–80.
134 See Lawrence, op. cit., pp. 28–9; Howard, op. cit., vol. II, p. 154.
135 Turell, op. cit., pp. 208ff.
136 Howard, op. cit., vol. II, pp. 228–37, with full citations of the relevant statutes from Hening.
137 Davis, op. cit., p. 98.
138 Howard, op. cit., vol. II, p. 231.
139 Cf. the fuss, already described, over Governor Bellingham's evasion, above p. 37. For a general discussion, see Howard, op. cit., vol. II, ch. 6.
140 See C. Ver Steeg, *The Formative Years* (London, 1965), pp. 23, 54.
141 Mather, *Magnalia*, Book III, ch. 29, § 11.
142 Ibid.
143 Albert H. Smyth, ed., *The Writings of Benjamin Franklin* (New York, 1907), vol. III, pp. 63–5.

144 J. Potter, op. cit., pp. 643ff.

145 Smyth, op. cit., vol. II, pp. 465-7.

146 Demos, op. cit., p. 192, shows that the average number of children per family at Plymouth rose from 7·8 for the first generation to 9·3 in the third, and that, of these, children reaching their majority rose from 7·2 to 7·9 by the third generation. Cf. Greven on Andover, 'Family Structure', pp. 236-8. Lockridge's figures (p. 330) for Dedham and Watertown are considerably lower. The average for 1636–1703 is 4·45 children per family. For literary evidence in support of these figures see Lawrence, op. cit., pp. 86-7. For England, see Peter Laslett, 'Household Size in England over Three Centuries', *Population Studies*, vol. 23 (1969), pp. 215ff.

147 Ernst Troeltsch, *The Social Teaching of the Christian Churches*, trans. Olive Wyon (London, 1931), p. 809.

148 Above, p. 64.

149 Morgan, *Puritan Family*, pp. 39ff.

150 Ibid., Calhoun, op. cit., vol I, pp. 93ff., 142-4. An entry in the *Westover Diary* suggests that society in Virginia likewise strongly disapproved of physical violence against wives, p. 322.

151 B. Wadsworth, *Well-Ordered Family* (Boston, 1712), pp. 25, 37; O. E. Winslow, *Meetinghouse Hill* (New York, 1952), p. 80.

152 Calhoun, op. cit., vol. I, p. 96.

153 Quoted in Spruill, op. cit., pp. 169-70.

154 Wendell, op. cit., pp. 200-1; Morgan, *Puritan Family*, p. 61.

155 Wadsworth, op. cit., p. 25; *Another Secret Diary*, p. 249.

156 Reynolds, op. cit., p. 321.

157 Morgan, *Puritan Family*, pp. 46-7, 50-3; Ashley, op. cit., pp. 20, 43; Mather, op. cit., p. 89; John Winthrop, 'Modell of Christian Charity' in Edmund S. Morgan, ed., *The Founding of Massachusetts* (Indianapolis, 1964), p. 199. James T. Johnson has argued that the priority placed on mutuality in marriage can be traced through a series of puritan writers from Perkins to Baxter, and that it represents a 'major strand in the puritan tradition [which] runs counter to the marriage doctrine expressed in the Book of Common Prayer'. 'English Puritan Thought on the Ends of Marriage', *Church History*, vol. XXXVIII (1969), pp. 429-36.

158 Demos, op. cit., pp. 50-1.

159 *Westover Diary*, pp. 211, 265, 278, 463, 482, 527, 533.

160 Powell, *English Domestic Relations*, pp. 37-58; also article in *New England Quarterly* mentioned in note 2.

161 Winthrop, vol. II, p. 330; Sewall, op. cit., vol. I, p. 98.

162 Powell, *English Domestic Relations*, pp. 92-8; Howard, op. cit., vol. II, pp. 85-92. We will discuss the incidence of divorce in a later chapter.

163 Howard, op. cit., vol. II, p. 229.

164 Morris, *Studies in the History of American Law*, p. 21; Spruill, op. cit., pp. 176, 183; Winthrop, *Journal: History of New England*, ed. J. K. Hosmer (New York, 1946), vol. II, pp. 28, 45, 218, 317-18.

165 For some examples of social control in England, see George Lee Haskins, *Law and Authority in Early Massachusetts* (New York, 1960), pp. 83-4, 196.

166 Hill, op. cit., ch. 8; P. E. H. Hair, 'Bridal Pregnancy in Earlier Rural England Further Examined', *Population Studies*, vol. XXIV (1970), pp. 67-70.

167 P. Miller, *The New England Mind: The Seventeenth Century* (Boston, 1961), p. 416.

168 See, for instance, 'Records of Suffolk County Court', Part II, 1675–80, pp. 754, 837-41, 867, 914, 1063, 943, 1023, 1161. Cf. Haskins, op. cit., pp. 79-81.

169 Morgan, *Puritan Family*, pp. 39–40, has several other references to similar orders.On pp. 61–3, he cites clerical authorities insisting on cohabitation, and records Edward Pinson's slander suit against Richard Dexter for saying 'That he Brock his deceased wife's hart with Greife, that he wold be absent from her 3 weeks together when he was at home, and wold never come nere her, and such Like.' Sewall, vol. III, p. 288, records the case of Ames Angier, recently elected school-master of Boston, and his wife, whose serious tiff led to the informal intervention of the magistrates to restore the peace, and obtain Mrs Angier's return to the home.

170 Morgan, *Puritan Family*, p. 39.

171 Oberholzer, op. cit., p. 114. Schlatter, op. cit., p. 15; on this subject in general, see also Haskins, pp. 90–1.

172 Sewall, vol. I, pp. 212–13, 347, 354, 410; vol. III, p. 243.

173 E.g. Anne Hett's '*stubborn* unrulinesse with her husband' (my italics); pp. 37, 62, 70, 72.

174 Sewall, *Diary*, vol. II, pp. 371, 400, 414; vol. III, pp. 40, 172.

175 Oberholzer, op. cit., p. 126.

176 See, for instance, Milton's attitude towards divorce, Howard, op. cit., vol. II, pp. 85–92; cf. Schlatter, op. cit., p. 24.

177 Keith Thomas, 'Double Standard', *Journal of the History of Ideas*, vol. XX (1959), p. 318.

178 C. Hill, *Intellectual Origins of the English Revolution* (Oxford, 1965), p. 273.

179 Powell, *English Domestic Relations*, p. 142.

180 Sewall, *Diary*, vol. II, p. 95.

181 All these quotations from Thomas Gataker are taken from the Hallers' essay 'The Puritan Art of Love', in op. cit., p. 263.

182 *Marplot in Lisbon,* cited by Alleman, op. cit., p. 118.

183 Ibid., pp. 107–18.

184 Ibid., pp. 119–23.

185 Powell, *English Domestic Relations*, pp. 124–5.

186 Notestein, *Four Worthies*, p. 143.

187 Spruill, op. cit., p. 216.

188 Hole, op. cit., p. 64.

189 Calhoun, op. cit., vol. II, pp. 111–12.

Chapter 7

The Family

'The whole of our history and of our civilisation depends on the family. And yet the historian . . . has so far ignored its humble history.' So wrote the eminent economic historian, Joan Thirsk, as recently as 1964.[1] It is paradoxical that historians are currently responding to this challenge, just at the time when the family as an institution is being seriously questioned.

Any study of the seventeenth-century family must start with the awareness that individualism was then only beginning to bud. For many Englishmen the family was the smallest recognisable unit of society. They identified not through the individual ego, but through membership in a family group. The effects on outlook were subtle but profound—as though modern man were *permanently* a member of a rowing eight, lacking any meaningful identity if parted from the rest of the crew.

This chapter looks at the specific question of parental control within the 'little commonwealth'. Were American colonial parents more permissive than their English counterparts? If the evidence suggests that they were, the results for women would be extremely important. Greater parental permissiveness might well argue that the mother played a greater role in family government than in a more patriarchal, authoritarian society. Daughters more permissively raised would thereby develop considerably greater independence than those kept firmly under the parental thumb. Such independence would affect the daughter's outlook when she graduated to being a wife and an adult member of her community.

Parental Control in the Colonies

There were certainly many in the colony of Massachusetts who believed that parental control was almost criminally neglected. This complaint is heard clearly in the 1650s and slowly rises to a crescendo by the end of the century. Before examining this, some caution is called for. It is, first of all, probably inevitable for at least some members of an older generation to criticise its successors. Any change leads to the lament that 'things ain't what they used to be'. Only totally static societies can avoid some kind of generation gap. Second, the planting of Plymouth and the Bay Colony was an act of high idealism. The heady pioneering zeal of the first generation could hardly be maintained, once stable settlement had been achieved.[2] This apparent back-sliding would increase the nostalgia and the querulousness of conservatives. The literary sources, furthermore, are stacked very heavily on the clerical side; many are sermons. Such a weight of monitory material may give a misleading impression of the actual situation. Finally, faults which might by contemporaries have been blamed on parental slackness may well have had far more complex causes.

Calhoun demonstrates that the by now marked differences between English and American child-rearing were remarked quite early by some English observers in America. A clerical school-master in North Carolina in 1772, for instance, bewailed 'the excessive indulgence of American parents and the great difficulty of keeping up a proper discipline'. By the early nineteenth century, which Calhoun, little imagining life in Spockland, saw as 'the century of the child', there are a host of comments on American indulgence.[3]

Although there are no surviving transatlantic contrasts for the seventeenth century, the evidence of domestic critics suggests that the two shores diverged in the matter of familial discipline. It was as early as the 1640s in Massachusetts that criticisms of the younger generation began to be made. John Cotton alleged that 'the younger generation were coming of age without coming into their fathers' spirit, and young men were manifesting their irreverence by wearing their hats when the Word was read in the congregations.'[4] Among the last entries in Winthrop's *History* is one telling of the drowning of the only son and a daughter of a couple, who 'confessed they had been too indulgent towards him, and had set their hearts overmuch upon him'.[5] To Edward Johnson, writing about 1650, one of the main causes of 'God's controversy with New England' was the indiscipline of the young.[6] Cotton Mather quotes a letter of Ezekial Rogers[7] to similar general effect, written in March 1658:[8]

I find greatest trouble and grief about the Rising Generation; young people are little stirred here; but they strengthen one another in Evil, by Example, by Counsel. Much ado I have with my own family; it is hard to get a servant that is glad of Catechising, or Family Duties . . . the Young Brood doth much afflict me. Even the Children of the Godly here, and elsewhere, make a woful Proof.

When the General Court, in the toils of the 'Half-Way Covenant' problem, proclaimed a Day of Humiliation in 1659, one crucial reason given was 'the sad face of the rising generation'.[9] Richard Mather, one of the oldest survivors of the first generation, who cast himself somewhat in the role of the conscience of the colony, had, according to his grandson, 'strong doubts concerning the younger generation' in whom he saw 'a flighty spirit, an ill use made of temporal prosperity, &c'.[10] Of the same generation, Peter Bulkeley was also concerned about the disobedience of children and servants, who sallied 'abroad in the nights' and were guilty of 'sinful miscarriages'. 'It is time to begin with more severity than hath been, unless we will see a confusion coming upon all.'[11]

This kind of criticism, containing either implicit or explicit condemnation of over-lenient parents, built up to a climax at the end of the 1670s, when in 1679 the great reforming synod met to consider the causes for the series of disasters that had befallen the colony. Aided by such pointers as Increase Mather's 'Whence is all that rising up, and disobedience in Inferiors towards Superiors, in Families, in Churches, and in the Commonwealth, but from unmortified Pride', the synod came without too much difficulty to the conclusion that a major cause of 'God's controversy with New England' was that 'parents neglect the discipline of their children'.[12] Yet the solemn warnings, and the measures taken by the synod, do not seem to have had very long-lasting effects.[13] If Cotton Mather is to be trusted, things were little improved in the 1680s and the 1690s. 'Blasphemy, cursing, prophane-swearing, lying, unlawful gaming, Sabbath-breaking, Idleness, Drunkenness, Uncleanness' were all charged to the younger generation.[14] The cause, according to Mather, was 'the shameful want of due Family Instruction' and parents who were 'out of measure *indulgent* to their children'. He concluded, 'As to what concerns Families and Government therof, there is much amiss. . . . Nay, Children and Servants . . . are not kept in due Subjection. . . . Most of the Evils that abound amongst us, proceed from Defects as to Family Government.'[15] Many of the more spectacular crimes which Mather obsessively records are blamed by the young criminals on their disobedience to their parents. Hugo Stone, speaking from the gallows before being hanged for murdering his wife, implored his audience to 'Observe the Rule of Obedience to your Parents'.[16]

But we need not rely entirely on the evidence of the Mathers. The concern of Boston was mirrored by the magistrates of Springfield in the 1670s and 1680s.[17] Samuel Sewall also concurred with the Mathers' dire view of the times. He quotes with apparent approval the remark of John Colman in a case about an insolent servant: 'Mention'd that scripture Obey in all Things ' 'The boy would do well', said his master, 'with good correction, words he directed to the Mother'.[18] Of a new judge, Sewall considered 'keeping good order in's family' a strong recommendation, as though this were not altogether usual.[19] A mother, under a premonition of death, wrote a letter of instructions to her children: 'Be sure you carry well to your father, obey him, love him, follow his instructions and example, be ruled by him, take his advise [*sic*] and have a care of grieving him.' This repetitive insistence suggests that obedience was not expected to be automatic.[20] Sarah Knight mentions in passing the bullying lack of respect she noticed in a young girl towards her father.[21] The antics of the young girls in the winter before they became involved in the witchcraft craze at Salem also suggest that discipline in even the minister's house was less strict than it ought to have been.[22] The delegates who joined in the condemnation of permissive parents in 1679 came from churches all over the colony. Church records throughout the colony also contain many cases of disobedient children, whose disrespect towards their parents sometimes reached such heights as trying to bribe a father to leave the colony because he was marrying again, threatening murder as well as offering abuse; or charging a mother with witchcraft. Other misdemeanours like drunkenness, fornication, incest and stealing are often linked with disobedience to parents.[23]

A strange phenomenon of Massachusetts in the seventeenth century was the number of children of morally exemplary parents who went wrong. We have already mentioned the indiscretions detected in the Parris children at Salem Village. Much earlier, Winthrop reports the case of the sons of Nathaniel Ward and Thomas Welde, who in 1644, while undergraduates at Harvard College, were convicted of stealing £15. He also describes an incident in 1635, when 'a Godly minister, discovered to the magistrates some seditious speeches of his own son, delivered in private to himself'. This excessive zeal Winthrop handled with his customary good sense.[24] The Cotton family did not escape without slur. John Cotton, son of 'the uncrowned pope', was found guilty by the First Church of Boston in 1664 of 'lascivious uncleane practises with three women' and lying.[25] Cotton Mather not only had a maid, who, totally unsuspectedly, gave birth to a bastard, but also his son Increase—or 'Cressy'—turned out a thorough scapegrace. Having fallen into the company of a group of rakes, in 1717, according to his father, 'an Harlot, big with a Bastard, Accuses my poor son Cressy, and Lays her Belly to him.' Cressy finally died at sea.[26] Thomas Dudley in the early years of the colony had accused Winthrop of undue leniency,[27] yet his son Joseph found the boot on the other foot when his daughter, Rebecca Sewall,

gave birth to an illegitimate child. 'Govr Dudley mention'd
Christ's pardoning Mary Magdalen; and God hates putting away;
but did not insert *sine causa*, as Pareus notes.' From hints in the
Diary it does not sound as though young Sam was an altogether
adequate husband, although his indulgent mother took his part
in a great quarrel with her daughter-in-law.[28] Sewall's troubles
were not over. In 1724 his grandson, Sam Hirst, was a cause of
'great Vexation'. On 15 March, he 'got up betime in the morning,
and took ben Swett with him and went into the Common to play
at Wicket. Went before any body was up, left the door open;
Sam came not to prayer; at which I was much displeased.' Two
days later: 'Did the like again, but took not Ben with him. I told
him he could not lodge here practising thus. So he lodged elsewhere. He grievously offended me in persuading his Sister Hannah
not to have Mr. Turall, without enquiring of me about it. And
play'd fast and loose with me in a matter relating to himself,
procuring me great Vexation.'[29] No wonder it was considered
necessary that a fast be kept 'to pray for the pouring out of God's
Spirit on New England, especially the Rising Generation'.[30]
Benjamin Colman, for all his liberal instincts, would probably
have heartily condoned Sewall's vexation, after his own experiences with his disobedient daughter Abigail.[31]

Before looking into possible causes for this situation, we should
take a side glance at Virginia. Although there is nothing like the
chorus of criticism and complaint from the southern colony, there
is some evidence to suggest that children there were indulged. The
tone of some of the Jones family letters suggests that the Joneses
at least had their share of spoilt brats. Thomas Jones records
winning an argument with his ten-year-old son, as though it were
a contest of equals, and Catesby's four-year-old niece displays an
appalling precocity.[32] Some of the quarrels which the spoilt
William Byrd had with his spoilt wife were about treatment of
the children. In May 1710, for instance, the diarist was 'out of
humour with my wife for forcing Evie to eat against her will'.
In January, he 'quarrelled with my wife for being cruel to Suky
Braine, though she deserved it'.[33] A sidelight gained from the
celebrated contest between Commissary James Blair and Governor
Nicholson is the indiscipline of the scholars in the newly-founded
College of William and Mary. In December 1701 there was a sit-in,
when 'they shut the school doors, against their Masters, in order
(as I understood) to obtain leave to break up sooner'. This was far
from being a mere schoolboy prank, and the College was in a state
of virtual siege; the governor was called in because of the serious-
ness of the situation.[34] Byrd's attitude to youthful hooliganism
in Williamsburg is, as with his own family, one of tolerance.[35]

Governor Gooch also came into contact with strong-willed youth, this time his son Billy and his fiancée. The governor capitulated.[36] Mrs Spruill argues that after the enormous expansion in the number of slaves in the South at the beginning of the eighteenth century, children would tend to become even more spoilt. She points out that Eliza Pinckney, for instance, had six slaves to look after her before she married.[37] This evidence, along with that cited in earlier chapters on such subjects as choice of marriage partner or economic opportunities, suggests, I think, that parents were probably as permissive in Virginia as they appear to have been in Massachusetts. The main difference between the two colonies was that Virginia had not been founded with quite the same sense of high idealism as Massachusetts, and thus the 'declension' was less noted and less bewailed.

It is, of course, possible that these aberrations were the not unnatural response of spirited youngsters against an excessively repressive older generation, especially in New England. We are reminded of Sewall's daughter Betty who had 'painful pangs' because of sermons she had heard like 'You shall seek me and shall not find me', which 'terrified her greatly', or Sam, who could not sleep because he feared death.[38] A child with a greater streak of rebelliousness might well cleave to the very vices that he had been incessantly warned against. Manses have produced their crop of loose women. To the puritan, the child was the symbol not of innocence, but of fallen man. This small adult provided living-space for the devil, who had to be threatened or whipped out.[39] It could, then, be argued that these offspring of champions of the 'New England Way' were but casualties of the front line in the cosmic conflict between God and the Devil.

Alternatively, it has been argued that the suppression of what Erikson calls the child's 'autonomy' could lead to a state of shame or doubt in later life. This underlying sense of guilt could, it is suggested, have led to, say, Cressy Mather's or Rebecca Dudley's waywardness.[40]

The most likely possibility, however, is permissiveness. Two eminent authorities on the period, Edmund Morgan and Bernard Bailyn, both suggest this explanation, arrived at by very different routes. Morgan comes to it through a discussion of the purpose of the 'economically unnecessary removal of children from home', like the wealthy Sewall's placing of a daughter with a family at Rowley. His suggested answer is:[41]

> that Puritan parents did not trust themselves with their own children, that they were afraid of spoiling them by too great affection . . . a child learned better manners when he was

brought up in another home than his own. . . . At the same
time the child would be taught good behaviour by someone
who would not forgive him any mischief out of affection for
his person.

Morgan's suggestion seems to be borne out by some initially unlikely examples. Increase Mather, for instance, wrote to his children
that they were 'all of you so many parts of myself and dearer to me
than all things which I enjoy in this world'. Their mother was not
only 'a Tender Mother (if there was such an one in the world)'
but also, because her husband 'kept close to my study & committed
the management of the affairs of the family to her', a vital formative
influence on the young Mathers.[42]

Similarly, Cotton Mather himself was a fond parent. 'Affection
glowed in this home as brightly as the fire upon the hearth, its
gentle light softening the grim, religious pattern of life. It pene-
trated to the heart of the old Puritan, quickening the love of a
father who playfully called his "little birds" by pet names.' He
opposed the use of force or anger or corporal punishment against
his children. He encouraged 'facetious' as well as 'instructive' table-
talk. Perhaps, after all, it was this mild rule which led Cressy into
'night riot with some detestable rakes of the town' and the big-
bellied harlot's appalling charge.[43] Sewall was 'always very sympathetic with his children in their religious trials'. When the sensitive
Betty wept when reading 'the 24. of Isaiah. . . . Sympathy with her
drew Tears from me also'.[44] Mrs Sewall was dead set against young
Sam's returning to his wife, even though the minister recommended
it. Previously, she had given every impression of the doting mother
in the conflict between son and daughter-in-law.[45] Of a lower class,
but also remarkably lenient, was Josiah Franklin, according to
his son's recollections. When Ben and some friends removed some
stones to build themselves a wharf, he 'convinced me that nothing
was useful which was not honest'. Fearing that his youngest son
would follow the example of Josiah, jr, and go to sea, the father
'sometimes took me to walk with him, and see joiners, bricklayers,
turners, braziers, etc., at their work, that he might observe my
inclination, and endeavour to fix it on some trade or other on
land'. After Franklin, who admits that he may have been 'too
saucy and provoking', had run away from Boston and found work
in Philadelphia, he returned home for a visit after an uncommuni-
cative seven months' absence. 'My unexpected appearance sur-
priz'd the family; all were, however, very glad to see me, and made
me welcome.' His mother attempted to reconcile an elder brother
with him. His father, who disapproved strongly of his actions, was
none the less tolerant and reasonable. The Franklin parents were

pillars of their church in Boston.[46] Most of these examples of relaxed parental attitudes come from the end of our period. It may
be relevant, however, to cite here an entry from Winthrop in 1647,
referring to Ezekiel Rogers, already quoted for his disappointment
with the younger generation. 'Mr. Rogers, preaching to the Synod
. . . reproved . . . also the call for the reviving the ancient practice
in England of children asking their parents' blessing upon their
knees etc.' It is arguable from this that a less formal relationship
between parents and their children had quasi-official sanction even
in the first generation.[47]

Bailyn's thesis, in many ways contradictory to Morgan's, none
the less comes round to much the same conclusion on the subject
of parental control.[48] He is concerned with the social changes which
migrations cause. He quotes the findings of Margaret Mead on
contemporary responses to rapid change: 'Children of five have
already incorporated into their everyday thinking ideas that most
elders will never fully assimilate.'[49] This, according to Bailyn, is
what happened in the new settlements in the seventeenth century.
Whereas in the traditional society of England, age and experience
had been equated with wisdom and automatically deferred to, in
the New World, youth, because of its greater flexibility and greater
adaptability and energy, became the guide. The world was turned
upside down, and a major casualty was the patriarchal family. Just
as Claude Brown's 'Mama, Dad and Papa' were, compared with
him, helpless innocents in modern Harlem, so were English parents
thrown up on the Atlantic coastal wilderness three centuries ago.[50]
Filial piety went overboard even during the voyage out—a journey
whose culture-shock made the modern jet-age variety seem the
mildest of tremors.

Bailyn's analogy has come under steady fire in the last decade.
His assumption that the extended family was the rule in England,
while America quickly adopted the nuclear pattern, has been
shown to be generally invalid by English and American historical
demographers. Laslett, Harrison and Lockridge have also advanced
the suggestion that English society may have been geographically
more mobile than colonial America in the seventeenth century.[51]
Demos has argued that 'the family's power to withstand the
challenge of a new physical setting and an increasingly fluid social
structure is at least as impressive as the concessions it made', and
has shown that, from the ages of people who were elected to office
in the plantation, it was 'not a community which conferred an
unusual degree of power and position on youth'.[52]

Yet, despite the stress by modern demographers on aspects of
traditionalism in colonial life, the evidence of generational conflict which we have cited remains, and, even bearing in mind our

earlier caveats, it is treated by contemporaries as too general a phenomenon to be dismissed as exceptional.[53] Both Bailyn and Morgan agree in depicting a situation in which parents either could not or would not control their teenagers, and this was a marked divergence from English familial conventions.[54]

Parental Control in England

There is some evidence that at the end of the century English manners had declined. The maunderings of Thomas Tyndale, who died in 1672 at the age of eighty-four, include 'Alas! O' God's will! It was not so in Queen Elizabeth's time: then youth bare Respect to old Age.' Yet what Tyndale is attacking in Aubrey's account is the whole 'corruption' of the Restoration world. To him 'All this is now lost'; he laments England's lost virility. He sounds as though he would have made a natural club bore.[55] Richard Allestree's *The Ladies Calling* also has something to say of the disobedience of the young. Presenting the character of a virgin, he writes:

> Now-a-days she that goes with her Parent (unless it be a Parent as wild as herself) thinks she does but walk abroad with her Gaoler. But the right of the Parent is so undoubted, that we find God himself gives way to it, and will not suffer the most holy pretence, no, not that of a Vow, to invade it, as we see in Numbers XXX. How will He then resent it, to have this Law violated upon the impulse of a gay passion, and an amorous fancy?[56]

In this case, however, the author is in fact generalising from a very specific contemporary problem, that of girls marrying without their parents' consent, or against their wishes. This problem may well have been exacerbated by the very considerable migration to the cities, which, as Bridenbaugh suggests, was one of the factors undermining the family in the seventeenth century.[57] The highly-paternalistic Allestree may also have been seeking to restress the importance of the financial side of matrimony, which had come under some fire during the Restoration period. The diarist Evelyn was nostalgic for the 1640s:[58]

> The virgins and young ladies of that Golden Age put their hands to the spindle, nor disdained they the needle; were helpful to their parents, instructed in the management of a family, and gave promise of making excellent wives.

Chilton Powell listed other Jacobean plays which followed the *Romeo and Juliet* theme. However, in every case he cites, the parents are, like the Montagues and Capulets, so blatantly unattractive and wrong-headed, that these dramatic examples can hardly be cited as a sign of a full-scale revolt against parental authority.[59] Notestein concedes that there were families that 'gained great pleasure from their children', and mentions the complaints of Stubbes and Hall that children were spoilt; he none the less concludes that in general in the first half of the century such adages as 'Spare the rod and spoil the child' and 'Little children should be seen and not heard' were more generally followed. He quotes Aubrey's statement that 'in his young manhood parents were as severe as schoolmasters, and schoolmasters as masters in houses of correction'. 'The child perfectly loathed the sight of his parents'. Aubrey also mentions that 'at Oxford (and I doe believe the like at Cambridge) the Rod was frequently used by the Tutors and Deanes on their pupills; even till Bachelaurs of Arts; even gentlemen-Commoners'.[60] Another of Aubrey's yarns gives a humorous sidelight on father-and-son relations:[61]

> Sir Walter Raleigh, being invited to dinner with some great person, where his son was to goe with him: He sayd to his Son, Thou art such a quarrelsome, affronting creature that I am ashamed to have such a Beare in my Company. Mr. Walt humbled himselfe to his Father, and promised he would behave himselfe mightily mannerly. So away they went. . . . He sate next to his Father and was very demure at leaste halfe dinner time. Then sayde he, 'I this morning not having the feare of God before my eies, but by the instigation of the devill, went to a whore. I was very eager for her, kissed and embraced her, and went to enjoy her, but she thrust me from her, and vowed I should not, *For your father lay with me but an hower ago.'* Sir Walt, being so strangely supprized and putt out of his countenance at so great a Table, gives his son a damned blow over the face; *his son, as rude as he was, would not strike his father* [my italics], but strikes over the face of the Gentleman that sate next to him, and sayed, *'Box about, 'twill come to my Father anon.'*

Notestein stresses the formality and distance between parents and children. Praised by Stubbes, this austere treatment was blamed by Sir William Davenant for frightening children out of their wits.[62] Stone discusses the campaign of the early part of the century in which the proponents of breast-feeding attacked the normal practice of putting children out to nurse. The new, and far more intimate, system was, however, 'still sufficiently unusual among the landed classes in the seventeenth century to be something to boast about'.[63] For whatever reasons it was perpetuated, the ancient tradition of boarding-out children in other households was hardly calculated to encourage intimacy between parents and adolescent children. In wealthier families, it was quite usual for children to address their parents from their knees. As late as the early eighteenth century, so spirited a woman as Lady Mary Wortley Montagu went on her knees when making a request to her father.[64] At meals children often stood behind their parents and could eat only what their parents passed to them. Only the father was permitted to wear his hat in the household. Grown children bared their heads when addressing him.[65] When a daughter married up the social scale, the roles were reversed. When a merchant's daughter, for instance, married into the nobility, her father bared his head when in her company.[66] Though 'many children be found sometimes to exceed their fathers in wit and in wisdom, yea, and in all gifts of body and mind', wrote John Stockwood in 1589, 'yet is this no good reason that they should take upon them their fathers authoritie'.[67] Clarendon implies that parental authority was restored in 1660. In the Interregnum, 'Children asked no blessing of their parents . . . parents had no manner of authority over their children.'[68] The popularity of Halifax's parental tract suggests that the later Stuart period was still a highly patriarchal age. Sir Robert Filmer, whose *Patriarcha* was significantly first published posthumously in 1680, made great play with the commandment 'Honour thy father and mother'. As Laslett points out, his views led him to advocate the burning of adulterous wives. 'If England was ever patriarchal', he comments, 'it was so in Sir Robert Filmer's generation'.[69] In this kind of set-up the role of the mother was reduced, a role which in more favourable circumstances might have softened male harshness.[70] The legal guardian of the children of a widow was not their mother, but, if he survived, their paternal grandfather. This was the fate of Anne Saville, who had married Piers Legh of Lyme after his father had for seven years refused his permission to the match. When Piers died, the four children were taken over by old Legh; their mother was only rarely allowed to see them, and wrote pathetic letters to her father-in-law asking after 'littell Peter'.[71]

What Christopher Hill has called 'The Spiritualisation of the Household' increased if anything the patriarchal authority of the father.[72] The Reformation, Hill argues, undermined the authority of the priest; into his place stepped the father. As the Mass gave way to the reading of the word as the central act of worship, the church likewise tended to lose ground to the domestic hearth. Thomas Taylor, in 1653, counselled the father/master 'to make his house a little church'. The puritans, particularly, but not exclusively, laid great emphasis on domestic catechising, which the father was responsible for, though in many puritan families the wife shared the instruction. When the State, unlike Massachusetts, did not support the parental creed, parents could, paradoxically, wield more dictatorial powers within their heterodox homes. Of course, the great stress laid by the Hebrews on the patriarchal family in the Old Testament and the Fifth Commandment lent added weight to paternal claims of authority. 'The word "Father" is an epitome of the whole Gospel', said R. Sibbes.

We have already seen that the family was regarded as the basic unit of political as well as religious society: it was a little common-wealth as well as a little church. It was common among seventeenth-century English commentators to compare the paterfamilias with the monarch in his power and authority. Toleration was objected to on the grounds that it would destroy family equilibrium: fathers 'should never have peace in their families more, or ever have command of wives, children, servants', prophesied the hard-liner Thomas Edwards. It was also argued that all the household was 'virtually represented' by the father, even by such a radical as Gerrard Winstanley. His attempt to incorporate an element of consent is grotesque. The authority wielded by a father was, among the ruling classes, a training-ground for higher things. James II's adviser, Father Petre, was judged inadequate for lofty responsi-bilities, because he 'Ne'er was master of a family'.[73]

So far as we can tell, then, England in the seventeenth century did not see a similar decline in parental authority to that which hit Massachusetts and to a lesser extent Virginia. When we appreci-ate the *plenitudo potestatis* that the father/master was invested with in English thought, it makes the semi-hysteria of transplanted Englishmen in New England the more understandable. The growth of permissiveness was not just an unwelcome trend to nostalgic conservatives; it was a threat of domestic revolution. It raised that most ticklish question of authority, which so exercised the rulers of Massachusetts in Winthrop's account of its early history.[74] The failure of the father's authority in the family was akin to that spectre of democracy so loathsome to the colony's leaders. This helps to explain why so many exemplary victims of God's providential wrath that Winthrop and Cotton Mather described were servants or children who had been disobedient to the just rule of their superiors.[75]

The increased freedom which women, as both daughters and wives, seem to have enjoyed in our two colonies is most probably a direct cause of this slackening over the century of the traditional chains of authority. For instance, the greater freedom of choice of husbands that girls seem to have enjoyed would result in part from the lessening of parental insistence. When the traditional English dogma of making daughters 'pliable' was relaxed, a chain reaction extending down the generations would be released. Self-willed daughters would make self-willed wives.[76] It may also be the case that women as mothers positively contributed to the more liberal relationship between parents and children. Traditionally throughout most of recorded history mothers have brought a softening influence to bear on the family, and particularly on its menfolk. They are probably the more permissive of the parents, the givers of unqualified love, the merciful forgivers and forgetters. The role of the woman in the family tended to be extended both by puritan dogma and by the exigencies of the colonial environment. In the well-ordered family of the puritans of Massachusetts, the mother had a large role in the upbringing of the children, in their early religious and secular education as well as their physical welfare. Similarly on the isolated plantations of Virginia, the mother, perforce, was an important manager of what had to be to a large extent a self-sufficient community. As we have seen, puritan writers were more used to the idea of a marriage partnership and fellowship between husband and wife than were English Anglicans. It does not, therefore, seem unreasonable to think that women may have been not only the beneficiaries, but also one of the causes, of the more permissive parenthood that the colonies seem to have fostered.

Notes

1 Joan Thirsk in *Past and Present*, No. 27 (1964), p. 116.
2 Cf. P. Miller, *The New England Mind: The Seventeenth Century* (Boston, 1961), p. 59 and ch. 16.
3 A. W. Calhoun, *Social History of the American Family* (Boston, 1918), vol. II, ch. 2, 'The Emancipation of Childhood'.
4 Miller, op. cit., p. 471.
5 J. Winthrop, *Journal: History of New England*, ed. J. K. Hosmer (New York, 1946), vol. II, p. 354.
6 E. Johnson, *Wonderworking Providence of Sion's Saviour*, ed. J. F. Jameson (New York, 1937), p. 225.
7 Minister of Rowley.
8 Cotton Mather, *Magnalia*, Book III, p. 103; cf. similar comments in 1642 by William Bradford, *History 'of Plimouth Plantation'* (Boston, 1898), pp. 459–61, 474–7.
9 Quoted by B. Bailyn, *New England Merchants in the Seventeenth Century* (New York, 1964), p. 109; his ch. 4, 'The Legacy of the First Generation' has much additional evidence on this theme, including some pointed comparisons between fathers and sons. Cf. P. Miller, *From Colony to Province* (Boston, 1961), chs 6, 7.
10 *Magnalia*, Book III, p. 130.
11 Quoted in H. S. Tapley, 'Women of Massachusetts, 1620–89', in A. B. Hart, ed., *Commonwealth History of Massachusetts* (Boston, 1928–9), p. 308.

12 Quoted in Miller, *From Colony to Province*, p. 35.
13 The expanded powers accorded to the Tithingmen, i.e. officials responsible for ten families, at this time, may be a further argument to suggest that parents could not be relied upon to take a tougher line against the disorders of the young. H. W. Lawrence, *The Not-Quite Puritans* (Boston, 1928), p. 128.
14 *Magnalia*, Book IV, p. 97; G. P. Winship, ed., *In Boston . . .* (Providence, 1905), pp. ix–xxviii.
15 *Magnalia*, Book V, pp. 88–9, 92–3; Book VI, p. 35.
16 Ibid., Book VI, pp. 39, 45, 47.
17 J. H. Smith, ed., *Colonial Justice in Western Massachusetts (1639–1702)* (Cambridge, Mass., 1961), pp. 103ff.
18 Sewall, *Diary*, vol. II, p. 155.
19 Ibid., p. 350.
20 Tapley, op. cit., p. 300.
21 Sarah Knight, *Journal*, ed. George P. Winship (New York, 1935), pp. 27–8.
22 Marion Starkey, *The Devil in Massachusetts* (London, 1963), chs 1, 2.
23 E. Oberholzer, *Delinquent Saints* (New York, 1956), pp. 39–41, 123, 124–5; Charles Francis Adams, *Some Phases of Sexuality in Colonial New England* (Boston, 1891), pp. 9–11; cf. Lawrence, op. cit., p. 170.
24 Winthrop, op. cit., vol. I, p. 126; vol. II, pp. 169–70.
25 'Records', p. 60.
26 Sewall, *Diary*, vol. I, p. 136; B. Wendell, *Cotton Mather: The Puritan Priest* (New York, 1963), p. 196.
27 Winthrop, op. cit., vol. I, p. 87; see also the Haynes charges, ibid., pp. 170–4.
28 Sewall, *Diary*, vol. III, p. 137; vol. II, p. 372.
29 Ibid., vol. III, p. 372.
30 Ibid., p. 309.
31 E. Turell, *Life and Character of Dr. Benjamin Colman* (Boston, 1749), pp. 210ff.
32 *Va Mag.*, vol. XXVI (1918), pp. 288ff.
33 *Westover Diary*, pp. 181, 282; there are also arguments over Mrs Byrd's frequent physical violence against her servants.
34 *Papers Relating to an Affidavit*, pp. 26ff.
35 *Westover Diary*, p. 517.
36 *Gooch Letters*, p. 73.
37 J. C. Spruill, *Women's Life and Work in the Southern Colonies* (Chapel Hill, 1938), p. 77.
38 Sewall, *Diary*, vol. I, pp. 420, 308–9.
39 Calhoun, op. cit., vol. I, p. 40; E. S. Morgan, *Puritan Family* (New York, 1966), pp. 87–96.
40 J. Demos, *A Little Commonwealth* (New York, 1970), pp. 135–42.
41 Morgan, op. cit., pp. 77–8. A. Macfarlane, discussing the apprenticeship of the children of the English puritan divine, Ralph Josselin, agrees that 'physical space to separate the generations at a time when they might threaten one another' was a major justification for the system, *The Family Life of Ralph Josselin* (Cambridge, 1970), p. 92 and Appendix B. Cf. Katharine Whitehorn's remarks on the merits of the system today (*Observer*, 13 December 1970).
42 K. B. Murdock, *Increase Mather* (Cambridge, Mass., 1926), pp. 72–3.
43 E. B. Schlesinger, 'Cotton Mather and his Children', *3 WMQ*, vol. X (1953), pp. 181, 183–4.
44 Morgan, op. cit., p. 137.
45 Sewall, *Diary*, vol. II, p. 372; vol. III, p. 40.

46 Benjamin Franklin, *Autobiography* (World's Classics edition), pp. 13, 16, 28, 40, 41–2.
47 Winthrop, op. cit., vol. II, p. 324.
48 Cf. David J. Rothman, 'A Note on the Study of the Colonial Family', *3 WMQ*, vol. XXIII (1966), p. 627.
49 Bailyn, *Education in the Forming of American Society* (Chapel Hill, 1957), p. 48 and list of references under Mead.
50 Claude Brown, *Manchild in the Promised Land* (Signet edition), pp. 289–290.
51 P. Laslett and J. Harrison, 'Clayworth and Cogenhoe' in H. E. Bell and R. L. Ollard, eds, *Historical Essays 1600 1750 Presented to David Ogg* (London, 1963), pp. 170ff.; K. Lockridge, 'Population of Dedham, Massachusetts, 1636–1736', *Economic History Review*, Second Series, vol. XIX (1966), pp. 318–44; cf. P. Greven, *Four Generations* (Ithaca, 1970), p. 265. On the other hand, Peter Spufford claims that apart 'from the great flow of people to London, all this intense movement was restricted to a very limited distance'. 'Population Movement in Seventeenth Century England', *Local Population Studies Magazine and Newsletter*, No. 4 (1970), pp. 41–50.
52 Demos, op. cit., pp. 190, 173–4. Cf. Greven, op. cit., pp. 98–9.
53 Demos, who finds no evidence for 'difficult adolescence' in Plymouth, none the less concurs that it seemed a problem in Massachusetts, op. cit., p. 146.
54 It is perhaps significant that Macfarlane tends to a similar conclusion for English puritans. 'If Josselin is typical,' he writes (op. cit., p. 125), 'Puritan fathers were less austere and less able to exert control of their children than some children would have us believe.'
55 John Aubrey, *Brief Lives*, ed. O. L. Dick (Harmondsworth, 1962), p. 355.
56 Richard Allestree, *The Ladies Calling* (London, 1673), section II, part i.
57 C. Bridenbaugh, *Vexed and Troubled Englishmen* (New York, 1968), p. 38; cf. E. A. Wrigley, 'A Simple Model of London's Importance in Changing English Society and Economy, 1650–1750', *Past and Present*, No. 37 (1967), pp. 44–70.
58 Quoted by M. Phillips and W. S. Tomkinson, *English Women in Life and Letters* (Oxford, 1927), p. 70.
59 C. L. Powell, *English Domestic Relations 1487–1653* (New York, 1917), pp. 201–3.
60 Quoted in Christopher Hill, *Society and Puritanism* (Panther edition), p. 447; Aubrey, op. cit., p. 15. Aubrey was born in 1626.
61 Ibid., pp. 318–19.
62 W. Notestein, 'The English Woman 1580–1650' in *Studies in Social History Presented to G. M. Trevelyan*, ed. J. H. Plumb (London, 1955), pp. 84, 106; cf. L. Stone, *Crisis of the Aristocracy 1558–1641* (Oxford, 1965), pp. 591–2; L. L. Schücking, *The Puritan Family* (London, 1969), pp. 74–5.
63 Stone, op. cit., pp. 592–3.
64 R. Halsband, *The Life of Lady Mary Wortley Montagu* (London, 1961), p. 126.
65 Hill, op. cit., p. 447.
66 C. V. Wedgwood, *The King's Peace* (London, 1955), p. 53.
67 John Stockwood, *A Bartholomew Fairing for Parents* (1589), quoted by Powell, op. cit., p. 131.
68 Quoted in Stone, op. cit., p. 670.
69 P. Laslett, 'Sir Robert Filmer: The Man versus the Whig Myth', *3 WMQ*, vol. V, p. 545. Filmer wrote in the late 1630s or early 1640s and died in 1653.
70 Notestein, op. cit., pp. 84–5; cf. Schücking, op. cit., pp. 85–8, who quotes Daniel Rogers's *Matrimonial Honour* on the role of the mother when a

child was to be flogged: 'She holdes not his [her husband's] hands from due stroakes, but bares their [children's] skins with delight, to his fatherly stripes' (p. 299).

71 C. Hole, *English Home Life 1500–1800* (London, 1947), p. 58. Governor Gooch, when faced with the same situation in Virginia through the sudden death of his son, wrote to his brother: 'My grandson, a very fine child, is another bar to such hopes [of coming home] for I can't leave him, and to take him from his mother would be cruel.' *Gooch Letters*, p. 115.

72 Schücking, op. cit., p. 83, argues that 'the spread of pietism had caused ideas about children's rights to become not more liberal, but actually more narrow'.

73 My debt to Christopher Hill's *Society and Puritanism*, ch. 13, for the last two paragraphs will be obvious.

74 See, for instance, Winthrop, op. cit., vol. I, pp. 288–90, 303; vol. II, pp. 229–45.

75 For cases of the former see ibid., vol. I, pp. 82, 103–4, 288–90; vol. II, pp. 9–11.

76 Cf. Notestein, op. cit., p. 85.

Chapter 8

Women's Legal Position and Rights

The way in which the law treated women in England and America in the seventeenth century is a useful barometer of society's attitudes. It is not necessarily accurate down to the last degree, not only because the law can be an ass, but also because it may well lag behind, or more rarely oustrip, popular sentiment. None the less, both statute and case law do give us considerable insight.

The problems of comparison are aggravated by certain marked differences between the Old World and the New. Some legal institutions were not carried over to either Massachusetts or Virginia by the migrants. There were, for instance, no courts of wards or chancery, nor ecclesiastical courts—all of which, in some way or other, had cognizance over cases dealing with women's rights. Nor did the specialised profession of the law migrate to the new colonies, though the widespread distrust and hatred of lawyers did.[1] Thomas Lechford, who fell foul of the Massachusetts authorities in the early days of settlement, was a practising lawyer, and his discomfiture was not altogether divorced from his profession. John Winthrop himself was a lawyer. However, Lechford hoped, vainly, to *practise* the law in Massachusetts, whereas Winthrop did not seek profit from it there. Nathaniel Ward, though trained as a lawyer, had long since given up its profession before migrating in 1634. For most of the century the legal systems of both Massachusetts and Virginia were in a state of some flux. Although the charters of both colonies insisted that their laws should be conformable to the laws of England, there were many reasons for deviations. Conditions in newly settled plantations were radically different, and in most cases magistrates and legislators were ignorant of the finer points of English law. There were also areas of the English common laws to which leading settlers were hostile. Added to this, the authorities who established the legal pattern in Massachusetts used Mosaic law and biblical precedents as a complementary and alternative guide.[2] The general results of this sea-change were that legal practice tended to become simplified, more flexible and more equitable in the New World. In this general improvement, women reaped considerable advantages.

161

In this chapter I propose to concentrate on two subjects not already covered: women's property rights, and divorce and separation laws.

Women's Property Rights

In seventeenth-century English common law there were two time-honoured traditions which governed most of the usage concerning women's property rights. The first was the concept of the *femme covert*, that is, of the total dependence of the wife upon her husband, and the vesting of all legal rights in him. A wife was a 'jural minor'.[3] *The Lawes Resolutions of Women's Rights*, a Tudor compilation first published in London in 1632, expatiated on the legal justification:[4]

> In this consolidation which we call wedlock is a locking together. It is true, that man and wife are one person; but understand in what manner. When a small brooke or little river incorporateth with Rhodanus, Humber, or Thames, the poor rivulet looseth her name; it is carried and recarried with the new associate; it beareth no sway; it possesseth nothing during coverture. A woman as soon as she is married, is called *covert*; in Latine *nupta*, that is, 'veiled'; as it were, clouded and overshadowed; she hath lost her streame. I may more truly, farre away, say to a married woman, Her new self is her superior; her companion, her master. . . . All of them [women] are understood either married, or to be married, and their desires are to their husbands, I know no remedy, yet some can shift it well enough. The common laws here shaketh hand with divinitye.

More tartly, the author summed up the lesson: 'That which the husband hath is his own. That which the wife hath is the Husband's'.[5] This argument was reiterated in *Baron and Femme: A Treatise of Law and Equity concerning Husbands and Wives*, and in other influential legal treatises and opinions of the century.[6] It was the fact that 'wives in England are entirely in the power of their husbands, their lives only excepted'[7] which spurred the Widow Blackacre in Wycherley's *Plain Dealer* to expostulate that 'Marriage to a woman is worse than excommunication, in depriving her of the benefit of lawes'.[8]

The consequences of coverture were sweeping. It meant that a husband had sole administration of all his wife's property, both personalty and realty, so that, for example, there are numerous examples of husbands specifically bequeathing wifely jewels to their widows.[9] It meant furthermore that a wife could not make a contract, could not sue or be sued in tort, since she had no proprietary capacity.[10] According to Blackstone, the wife had no legal right over her own children. Their father could dispose of them in his will at his pleasure.[11] In criminal law, it also led to some weird rulings. If a wife committed a crime in the presence of her husband, it was normally presumed that she was 'under compulsion' and that the husband was therefore responsible for her actions.[12] Even where a wife had committed a crime on her own, her husband might be required to give bond for her good behaviour.[13] Most humiliating of all, he might have to pay the fine or bond levied for his own wife's adultery.[14] Needless to say, since husband and wife were conceived of as one legal person, they were incapable of making contracts with or suing each other.[15] Even unmarried girls were thought of as being under their father's authority. Thus when a maid was seduced, her father might have to bring an action of trespass against the seducer.[16] Morgan records two cases where parents even instituted divorce proceedings against a husband on behalf of their daughter.[17]

Although the common law imposed certain liabilities on the husband—and we should not forget the liability to support his wife[18]— none the less, the disabilities under which a wife laboured were much the greater. These can be illustrated by a Virginian case. Susannah Cooper, a woman of some means, had married the improvident Isles Cooper in 1717. Having squandered most of her wealth, he then left her, with what was left of her estate encumbered by his debts. More than twenty years after his desertion, she petitioned the House of Burgesses for relief of her disabilities. Although she had managed to recoup her fortunes, she could not sell her property, being still officially under coverture. She had no redress against trespassers or people who refused to perform their contracts with her. She was unable to will her estate to her son. She was, to all intents and purposes, rightless at law.[19]

What we have been describing in general was the pretty rigid position held by the *common law* in England during the seventeenth century. It plainly reflects the low status of women in society in general. However, there was some amelioration to this usage. This came from the Court of Chancery, an equity court, which did in two areas admit a proprietary capacity to women. These consisted of the recognition of the contracts made between the betrothed before marriage—antenuptial contracts—and of the trust as a means of conferring a proprietary capacity on married women.[20] There were other exceptions to the hard rule of the common law. Certain corporation by-laws allowed women who, though married, traded on their own account, to be treated as *femme sole* traders, with certain proprietary and legal rights independent of their husbands.[21] On the other hand, Miss Clark argues that the decline of customary law in the seventeenth century in the face of the rise of the 'man-made' common law 'deprived married women and children of the property rights which customs had hitherto secured to them.'[22]

The second convention of the common law was that concerning dower rights. These 'thirds' were the medieval and early-modern equivalent of the modern widow's pension. Roughly speaking, they were a legally guaranteed interest in one-third of the husband's estate after his death. The dower rights normally attached upon marriage, and after that the husband could not unilaterally alienate dower lands, nor could he will them elsewhere. The husband's creditors had no claim on these dower lands. The only ways in which dower rights could be forfeited by a wife were either by her voluntary surrender, or because of her desertion or divorce for adultery. The one alternative arrangement was the antenuptial settlement, which could cancel dower rights.[23]

I have twice mentioned antenuptial agreements, often known as marriage settlements. These were, in the seventeenth century, accepted as alternatives to the common-law regulations governing property. They were usually only entered into by the well-to-do with large estates at stake, and also by widows who, of course, had a life interest in their dower and possibly other property as well. Jurisdiction over these settlements was in the hands of the Court of Chancery, which in the seventeenth century heard many disputes. These bargains between families—often arranged by their attorneys—dealt with the dowry, which the bride's family would contribute, and the jointure, a settlement by the bridegroom's family of certain property upon the wife. The jointure was in fact an alternative to the dower right, and might be vital to the bride if the groom's land was entailed and therefore barred his wife's dower.[24] It was assumed that there should be some currently accepted ratio between the dowry (or portion) and the jointure. In England, according to Lawrence Stone's calculations, the ratio of dowry to jointure rose from 4 or 5 : 1 in the mid-sixteenth century to something like 10 : 1 in the latter part of the seventeenth century.[25] In other words a bride in 1700 would only be getting £100 settled on her for every £1,000 of her dowry, instead of £200 or £250 in 1550. In most cases of first marriage, the antenuptial agreement was a subject for haggling between the two sets of parents or guardians. But where it prefaced a second marriage for a widow, it could win for her rights in marriage outrageous to the common law.

This, then, was the position in English legal practice in the seventeenth century. What we must now examine is the extent to which these rules were bent or broken in the colonies. It would be foolish to expect any spectacular gains for women who, it could well be argued, were very generously treated in their dower rights. In the main, Virginia tended to stick closely to the English pattern; the biblical precedents cited in Massachusetts were not notably liberal towards Jezebel and Dalilah, the daughters of Eve. None the less, Richard B. Morris—for long the authority on this subject— does detect several areas of improvement in the status of women before the law.[26] The reasons that he suggests for these changes— apart from those already mentioned—are 'the anarchical state of the law of remedies which prevailed in the colonial courts in the seventeenth century'; economic changes and the frontier outlook; and a greater sense of humane paternalism on the part of the colonial authorities. A further liberating factor, frequently implied throughout his essay, is that of Dutch law, both from New York and imported as an influence into Plymouth by the Pilgrims.

What these factors add up to is an increasing tendency to treat women as individuals before the law, in both a proprietary capacity and an evidential one. Firstly, there is a significant number of cases concerning property, where a wife is treated as an equal partner with her husband, or more rarely as an independent individual, rather than as a *femme covert,* subsumed in her husband's person. Morris cites a case in Plymouth in 1667 where Sarah, the wife of Thomas Howard, jr, was given a grant of land, and other cases where women acted for their husbands in defending or prosecuting their legal or economic rights, suing on husband's contracts and tort claims, and defending suits brought against them. He also mentions several cases where husband and wife brought joint actions, rather than the husband alone, as in common-law proceedings.[27]

Antenuptial agreements were a second area of advance. Whereas in England the equity courts handled cases arising out of contested marriage settlements, the colonial common-law courts assumed jurisdiction and extended women's proprietary rights in marriage by certain decisions, 'in derogation of the common law', and 'not clearly recognised by the Court of Chancery'. These decisions particularly covered wives' rights to administer their own property independently of their husbands, according to an antenuptial settlement.[28] It is well known that colonial women could be very hard hagglers in marriage settlements. John Demos cites the contract between John Phillips and the widow Faith Doty of Plymouth Plantation, agreed in 1667:[29]

> The said Faith Doty is to enjoy all her house and land, goods and cattles, that shee is now possessed of, to her owne proper use, to dispose of them att her owne free will from time to

time, and att any time as she shall see cause. . . . The children
of both the said parties shall remaine att the free and proper
and onely disposal of theire owne naturall parents, as they
shall see good to dispose of them.

There are numerous other examples of hard bargains being driven
by women as diverse as Katherine Winthrop, whose price finally
proved too high for the cagey Sewall, to Elizabeth Alford of
Virginia, whose intended agreed lamely not to meddle with his
wife's property.[30] What all these examples suggest is that, with the
backing of the courts, such settlements were striking at the very
basis of the *femme-covert* concept of wifely subordination before
the law. This diagnosis is borne out by the terrible time which
the brothers-in-law Custis and Byrd had in their attempt to dispose
of some of the lands of their wives' father, Colonel Daniel Parke,
to pay off his debts after his death. Lucy and Frances were anything but *femmes coverts* in their reactions to the scheme.[31]
A convention which was unknown in England but accepted in
the colonies was the postnuptial agreement. At common law such
a contract was inconceivable, simply because husband and wife
were considered as one. But it was used both in separation agreements, and in reconciliation agreements, in America, of which that
between the turbulent Custises is best known. Among other things
it was agreed that 'all business properly belonging to the wife
shall be solely transacted by her' without his 'intermeddling'.[32]
Of a postnuptial agreement made in Massachusetts between George
and Rachel Potter on their reconciliation in 1699, Calhoun comments, 'Such an agreement suggests an approach to equality, freedom and mutuality between husband and wife.'[33]
Cases are also recorded in colonial court records where married
women acted as though they were *femmes soles*. The best-known
occurred in Massachusetts in 1702, when Margaret Pastree appealed
against a decision to return some silk to one Sanders, who was a
creditor of her husband's. She appealed in her own name, and
won her case.[34] There were also instances when women were sued
in tort on their own, although married, and where they were permitted to give evidence both on behalf of and against their husbands—practices which would have made any English lawyer's wig
stand on end.[35]
We have already mentioned the relative generosity of the English
common law over the wife's and widow's dower rights. These rights
were not only fully supported by colonial courts and legislatures,
but were also extended in certain areas.[36] For instance, a wife's
dower might suffer if part of the property earmarked at marriage
were sold with her apparent permission, though force had been

applied privately by her husband. All colonial courts, according to
Morris, took steps to ensure that the real approval of the wife was
given. In Virginia, even infirm wives were catered for if they could
not come to court. The first *Lawes and Libertyes of Massachusetts*
in 1641 contained a requirement that any land alienated or con-
veyed by a married woman must have the ratification of the General
Court.[37] Demos argues that in Plymouth 'the widow's customary
"thirds" was not a mere dole; it was her *due*'. Courts there were
not above altering the terms of deceased husbands' wills, where
they seemed to be inequitable to the widow.[38] Virginia laid it
down in 1658 that a legacy by her husband was no bar to a widow's
dower, and Massachusetts made special arrangements for the support of the widows of murderers, whose property would be forfeit.[39]
Finally some colonial authorities 'marked a notable advance over
the contemporary English practice' by allowing a widow 'the right
to sue for damages for the death of her husband as a result of a
wrongful act attributable to the defendant in certain situations'.[40]
My colleague, Dr Christopher Turner, who has worked inten-
sively on Massachusetts wills, particularly those of Essex County,
concurs in the view that widows' rights were more fully protected
there than in England. He has also pointed out to me a marked
difference in arrangements made in wills for widows, caused by the
problem of the lack of labour. Rather than concentrating on the
specific lands in which the widow shall have a life interest, the tendency of Massachusetts wills was for minute provisions to be made
to guarantee the supply of goods and services—grain, firewood,
the use of a horse, etc.[41]

Before leaving the question of women's property rights, there
is one final point of importance connected with the transmission
of wealth. This is the fact that, whereas primogeniture, whether
or not arranged within the legal device of the strict settlement, was
the general rule of inheritance in England in the seventeenth
century, it seems to have fallen into decline in the colonies by the
time of the third generation.[42] Along with primogeniture, 'its
helpful companion, entail' seems also to have fallen into disuse,
or much less common use, by about 1700. As a result, Keim finds
that in Virginia 'numerous cases are on record in which daughters
did share [in the estates], even when there were several sons in
the family'. Where, as in the majority of cases, daughters did not
inherit real estate, it did not mean that 'the daughters' legacies
were necessarily much less valuable than those of the sons who
received lands'. Even when daughters received an inconsiderable
part of the estate in their fathers' wills, they 'often received a
valuable marriage portion and were deeded lands and slaves during
the life of the father'. Although daughters did not usually receive

equality of treatment,[43] none the less, the impression given by Keim is that in Virginia they were far more generously treated than in England.[44] This conclusion is corroborated by Habakkuk's work on English practice, especially for the earlier part of the century. If the father was still alive, he could economise in the interests of the eldest son and the estate by stinting the other childen; if the elder son were in possession, his economic interests would be likely to overcome any feelings of generosity or responsibility he might have towards his siblings. Habakkuk quotes Thomas Wilson's *The State of England*:[45] 'The elder brother must have all, and all the rest [of the children] that which the cat left on the malt heap, perhaps some small annuity during his life or what please our elder brother's worship to bestow upon us if we please him, and my mistress his wife'.[46]

An entry in Sewall's *Diary* suggests that Virginia's liberal example was followed in Massachusetts. 'Govr. Saltonstall sued for his Father's estate as eldest son and therefore sole Heir. I said 'twas contrary to our Law, the Law of Nature and the Law of GOD. It went against the Govr. in all the three Causes.' The editors in a note point out the divergence between the law in New England and England. In a dispute over the estate of John, son of Wait Still Winthrop, a Connecticut court ordered that the property be shared between the surviving son and daughter. On appeal to England, the King in Council gave all the land to the son 'declaring him the sole heir of all the landed estate'.[47] Dr Turner confirms this general picture by pointing out that in intestate probate cases in Essex County, Massachusetts, the courts granted significant amounts of the fathers' property to unmarried daughters 'as their portions'.[48] Hugh Peter, 'the strenuous puritan' in both Massachusetts and England, argued that 'if daughters were ingenious and would work, they ought to have equal portions with sons'.[49] Sewall's dictum, plus the fact that there was a campaign against primogeniture after the Civil War, suggests that there may have been a connection between more equitable inheritance patterns and puritanism.[50]

Plainly a major cause for this difference was the contrast between availability of land in the New and the Old World. Whereas in England, as the researches of Stone and Habakkuk show, the prime energies of the landed classes were bent on maintaining the family estates through such legal agencies as primogeniture, entails and the strict settlement, in the New World such obsessive land-mindedness was less necessary, and might, as Keim suggests, be positively harmful where soils were rapidly exhausted.[51] The great clans of collateral kin, brothers and cousins virtually equals, which Bailyn describes in eighteenth-century Virginia, could not develop in the same way in England, where the 'stem family' sucked up the lion's share of the nutriment, leaving younger sons, and daughters, but little to feed on.[52] Of course, as Macfarlane makes clear, the problem of inheritance patterns cannot be divorced from the practice over daughters' dowries. If a girl had received a sizeable portion from her father, she could hardly expect more than nominal bequests in his will.[53] There has been very little research on this subject, but it is probable that, as the value of dowries *vis à vis* jointures was declining in the seventeenth century, English women were also getting a poorer and poorer share of inherited family wealth.[54]

Separation and Divorce

In England for most of the seventeenth century, the termination of a regular marriage was impossible. As Justice Windham said in the King's bench in the case of *Terry* v. *Browne* in 1660, 'When they are once married, all the world cannot dissolve the marriage; for an Act of Parliament in this sense, against the Law of God, is void.'[55] The only two escapes for spouses that the ecclesiastical courts, which had sole jurisdiction over matrimonial causes, could offer were either *Divortium a vinculo matrimonii*—annulment— or *Divortium a mensa et thoro*—separation from bed and board. Annulment, then as now, meant that the marriage had never legally and regularly taken place, and that therefore the children of the 'union' were illegitimate. The kinds of grounds for which annulments could be granted were marriage within the forbidden degrees of kinship, or after spousals *de presenti* with another spouse, or, like the notorious Essex divorce, for impotence.[56] They were not all that difficult to obtain, at a price.[57] The chances of a pretended wife, though the innocent party, regaining her property after an annulment were, however, slight.[58]

Grounds which ecclesiastical courts accepted in awarding legal separations were, first, adultery, though they tended to be much harsher on female sins in this area than on male. The argument behind this was that by committing adultery a woman both disobeyed her husband's God-given authority, and, by the possible introduction of a cuckoo in the nest, robbed the rightful heirs of their inheritance. Few would doubt that the double standard also played a leading, if non-speaking, part.[59] Cruelty was not considered sufficient[60] though *extreme* cruelty, or cruelty *and* (male) adultery might occasionally be accepted.[61] Whether desertion was accepted as a ground for legal separation, or even for the right to remarry, is a moot point. Certainly the protestant reformers considered it a valid cause, with good Pauline precedent. In certain very specialised cases, the ecclesiastical courts seem to have granted rights to the deserted spouse to remarry. However, desertion is not mentioned as one of the grounds dissolving a marriage in any of the compilations reproduced by Powell.[62]

Apart from the adverse publicity which parties to separation proceedings incurred,[63] and the delay and large expense, the chief drawback to separation was the fact that neither of the parties, even if one was plainly innocent, was allowed by Canon Law to remarry.

The whole issue of remarriage had been agitated in the 1590s and early 1600s by such preachers as Bunny, Dove, Rainolds, Howson, and Pye.[64] The Canons of 1604, however, actually made legal separation more difficult by ordaining that collusion—which included an innocent party having sex with a guilty party after adultery was discovered—or lack of witnesses, or the adultery of the plaintiff, all barred separation.[65] Remarriage remained forbidden. It is reasonable to assume that, given the prevalent public opinion of the times, these requirements, which held sway over the greater part of the century, would operate against women plaintiffs.[66] It was only while the Cromwellian Marriage Act of 1653 was in force that the innocent party to divorce proceedings was, following the recommendations of the Westminster Assembly of Divines, permitted to marry again.[67] This legislation was not re-enacted after the Restoration. So, when one of Moll Flanders's beaux bewailed his lot in being married to a whore who had deserted him, his chief complaint was that he could not remarry.[68]

This harsh inflexibility was somewhat offset by the contemporary practice relating to alimony. The principle on which these arrangements was based seems to have been closely connected with a wife's dower right. During separation proceedings the husband was required to pay his wife to the tune of from a quarter to a third of his real estate. It would appear that whether a wife was 'guilty' or not, she still had legal claim to her portion.[69]

In the last decade of the century a third line of escape was introduced. This was divorce by private Act of Parliament. In our period, these very rare divorces[70] were hardly ever passed unless the plaintiff had already gone through the process of legal separation before an ecclesiastical court, and had also won an action of criminal conversation or assault and battery against the co-respondent.[71] The case of John Manners, Lord Roos, took eleven years to complete (1659–70) and was, strictly speaking, not even a divorce, but an act to allow him to marry again.[72] Only the rich need apply. The delaying powers which a determined opponent, like the Countess of Macclesfield—who was living in open adultery with Lord Rivers—could employ were almost inexhaustible. Parliamentary divorce was a purely male prerogative up to 1801.[73]

The procedure, which persisted well into the nineteenth century, is well summed up by the ironic remarks of Justice Maule to a man who had committed bigamy after his first wife had robbed and then deserted him:[74]

> But, prisoner, you have committed a grave offence in taking the law into your own hands and marrying again. I will now tell you what you should have done. You should have brought an action into the civil court, and obtained damages, which the other side would probably have been unable to pay, and you would have to pay your own cost—perhaps £100 or £150. You should then have gone to the ecclesiastical court and obtained a divorce *a mensa et thoro,* and then to the House of Lords, where, having provided that these preliminaries had been completed, you would have been enabled to marry again. The expenses might amount to £500 or £600 or perhaps £1,000. You say you are a poor man, and you probably do not possess as many pence. But, prisoner, you must know that in England there is not one law for the rich and another for the poor.

This statement, though made in 1845, is equally valid for 1700. The slender hopes of the poor man would be shared by almost all women.

There were, however, ways in which the rigour, expense and publicity could be evaded. Strype, the eighteenth-century antiquarian, reported that Tudor[75]

> Noblemen would very frequently put away their wives, and many others, if they like another woman better or were like to obtain wealth by her. And they would sometimes pretend their wives to be false to their beds and so be divorced and marry again such as they pleased.

Although Canon 107 of 1604 tried to tighten up on this evasion by requiring that parties to separation cases should give security not to marry again, it was still possible, provided a party was prepared to forfeit the security, to marry again without incurring further trouble. That this was a not uncommon practice among the rich is borne out by Godolphin in his *Repertorium Canonicum* in 1678.[76] There is also evidence that in the early seventeenth century people of puritan leanings, who, as Powell says, had a far more modernistic view of divorce than the dogmatically catholic-oriented Anglican Establishment, were prepared to go outside the law in cases of blatant matrimonial infidelity. After the reactionary Canons of 1604 were promulgated, thus ending all hope that the protestant reforms mooted in Edward VI's reign would be adopted, puritans whose spouses had deserted or committed adultery did obtain extra-legal divorces from like-minded ministers, magistrates or unofficial assemblies. Powell claims that there is 'evidence that the ancient [i.e. Hebraic] practice of private divorce existed during [the] whole period [1487–1653], especially among the Independents'.[77] Finally, there are instances of informal, private separation agreements by mutual consent. These might be agreed to before some private witnesses, or, more formally, before a well-disposed magistrate. The arrangements often included the handing over of the wife's portion and perhaps an additional maintenance.[78] Authority did attempt to discourage the worst abuses. In 1604 a statute made it a felony to run out on a family. The preamble suggests that it was common: 'Divers evil disposed persons being maried, runne out of one countie into another . . . and there become to be maried again.'[79]

Before discussing procedures in the New World, it is well to notice the divorce theories advanced by some leading puritans in England, especially in the first half of the century. Of course the greatest puritan theoretician on the question of divorce was Milton. In four books, all written in the 1640s—when he himself was weathering the difficulties of his first marriage (with Mary Powell) —he advanced what for long were taken to be the most radical proposals on the subject.[80] According to Howard, his proposals add up to 'the boldest defence of the liberty of divorce which yet appeared'.[81] In some ways Milton's most eye-catching plans were the forerunners of modern English divorce law. He advocated that as well as desertion, adultery, cruelty and impotence, evidence that the marriage had irremediably broken down should be sufficient grounds for divorce. 'What hath the soul of man deserved', he asked, 'if it be in the way of salvation, that it should be mortgaged thus, and may not redeem itself according to conscience'. He regarded divorce on the grounds of incompatibility as justified by Mosaic law, 'in nature and reason', and by the 'law of moral equity'.

There are, however, two reservations to be entered, before going overboard on Milton as the prophet of matrimony as a society 'more than human' centring in 'the soul rather than the body'—a companionship resting upon 'the deep and serious verity of mutual love' without which wedlock is 'nothing but empty husks of an outside matrimony, as undelightful and unpleasing to God as any other kind of hypocrisy'.[82] The first is that, according to Powell, Milton was not the daring innovator in divorce-thinking that he has often been called. Powell traces Milton's main arguments back to such earlier puritan thinkers as Perkins—particularly to his *Christian Oeconomy*, first published in Latin in 1590—and even to Erasmus. He points out that the editors who produced annotations to the Old and New Testaments in 1643 held many similar views, and that the very fact that Milton was aiming his propaganda at the Westminster Assembly of Divines suggests that he had hopes that his ideas might be shared, if not adopted. Powell particularly sees the writings of the early independents, Brown, Greenwood, Barrow, and Robinson, as formative.[83] This is not to deny that Milton 'exhausted the theological arguments'; but he was not a voice crying in the wilderness—of puritan thought, anyway.

The second reservation that must be made about Milton, the freedom-fighter for the maritally incompatible, is that his liberalism was much more equal for men. It was the husband's grievances that excited his compassion. It is perhaps no coincidence that he 'put away' his first wife at the very time that he was working on The Doctrine and Discipline of Divorce. Milton's most radical and contentious proposal advocated the right of self-divorce, for which he found precedent in the Old Testament. Absolute and final 'hindering of Divorce [cannot] belong to any civil or earthly power', he held. It was for the stern, unerring conscience of puritans to decide when incompatibility threatened salvation. This might be defensible when the incompatibility was mutual. But when it was not, it was the husband alone who was to be the arbiter. (Howard quotes: 'The will and consent of both parties, or of the husband alone'.) Though he might be far in advance of canonical thinking, Milton was a man of his times socially. His attitude was patriarchal. In the repudiation, or 'putting away' procedure, that he devised, after admonition from a 'minister or other grave elders' of his church, the husband would declare

> the hope he has of a happy resurrection, that otherwise than this he cannot do, and think himself and his case not contained in that prohibition which Christ pronounced, the matter not being of malice, but of nature, and so not capable of reconciling.

As the sprightly J. D. Jeaffreson remarked, 'the poet, whose Adam prayed the Almighty to give him an *equal inferior* for his companion in the happy garden, does not appear to have conceived it possible for a woman in her right mind to wish to put away her Lord and Master'. He also points out that while Milton quite genuinely saw the christian conscience as the sole guide,[84]

> no libertine, for the sake of wickedness and the gratification of low desire, ever demanded greater licence in marriage than Milton, in the name of religion, demanded for Christian men, in order that they might find meethelps, and escape the grievances of uncongenial wedlock.

To do him justice, Milton did see the possible injustice of his proposals to women. But his attempts to justify his plans led him to pathetic rationalisations, rather than admission, or even sympathy. While his argument that private divorce—with the husband acting as both prosecutor and judge—saved her from the scandal inextricably attached to cases in the 'Bawdy Courts' had some weight, his point that the woman always received justice, because she was either guilty or escaped a guilty husband, was either hopelessly naïve or culpably disingenuous. Milton might offer compassionate solace for the puritan male, but his schemes also represented a Bill of Rights for the unprincipled adventurer and of Rightlessness for the unprotected wife.[85]

The opportunities open to English women in matrimonial causes in the seventeenth century were, then, hardly enviable. Two points drawn by Powell from the drama of the first half of the century underline our argument. In discussing the common 'Patient Grissel' stereotype, he points out that the only solution available to her is to sit and wait for her errant husband to return from his waywardness. Women's only resort is suffering. Second, in his analysis of plots dealing with marital infidelity and break-down, he shows that where the wife is the culprit, the play ends in tragedy; where the husband, in reconciliation and forgiveness.[86] At the end of the century, Richard Steele and Daniel Defoe may have begun presenting persuasive arguments in favour of women's legal rights, but the evidence suggests that they were preaching to the very much unconverted.[87]

The practices concerning divorce and separation in Massachusetts and Virginia were very different. While the latter stuck to English precedents—though considerably ameliorating woman's position in practice—the former embraced completely different principles. These principles were a very significant contribution to the improvement of women's marital lot, in many ways like later reforms in the nineteenth and twentieth centuries. It is on Massachusetts, then, that we shall concentrate in this section, with little more than a glance at the Virginian deviations from English legal practice.

In his *History of Massachusetts*, Thomas Hutchinson, who himself was familiar with divorce cases as a colonial judge, wrote as follows:[88]

In matters of divorce they left the rules of the Canon Law out of the question; with respect to some of them, prudently enough. I never heard of a separation, under the First Charter, *a mensa et thoro*. Where it is practised, the innocent party often suffers more than the guilty. In general what would have been cause for such a separation in the spiritual courts, was sufficient, with them, for a divorce *a vinculo*. Female adultery was never doubted to have been sufficient cause; but male adultery, after some debate and consultation with the Elders, was judged not sufficient. Desertion a year or two, when there was evidence of a determined design not to return, was always good cause; so was cruel usage of a husband. Consanguinity they settled in the same degrees as it is settled in England and in the levitical laws.

The rather glib statement that 'they left the rules of the Canon Law out of the question' conceals the fact of radical change. The idea of a civil divorce was, of course, a natural corollary of civil marriage, and as such was the product of puritan thought going back to the middle of the sixteenth century. In fact, to a large extent the New Englanders put into practice the proposals of the *Reformatio Legum Ecclesiasticarum* commission of protestant divines and lawyers under Cranmer's chairmanship, published in 1552 but never adopted in England. There was also an element of reaction against the abuses of the ecclesiastical courts and the conservative Canons of 1604, and a belief that the New England way was closer to biblical precedents.

The major effect of this radical reform was that women were accorded nearly equal treatment in the crucial area of the breakdown of marriages. Only nearly equal, because, as Hutchinson points out, the traditional English discrimination against wifely adultery was usually retained. None the less, a wife could expect far more equitable treatment in Massachusetts than in England. If she were the innocent party, moreover, she could also remarry, and stood as good if not a better chance of having her property rights protected.[89]

Howard drew up a table—not altogether reliable—of the annulments and divorces in Massachusetts between 1639 and 1692, that is, up to the introduction of the second charter.[90] It is quite clear from his partial list of forty cases that the great majority of petitions —over three-quarters—came from the wives. The majority of causes given are desertion along with adultery, or desertion and remarriage. There is only one case of a divorce being given to a wife on the sole grounds of husband's adultery, and this decision was reversed on appeal after three years.[91] There is, however, an instance of the granting of a suit citing only the wife's infidelity.[92] In two petitions where long absence is given as cause, the General Court gave the wife leave to remarry, that is, it gave sanction to the presumption that the husband was lost either at sea or without trace.[93] There are two cases in Howard's list in which the question of the husband's impotence was a cause of the wife's petition. In the case of *Mary* v. *E. White*, the husband's 'deficiency' was not accepted as sufficient cause, and in the confused case of *Mary* v. *Hugh Drury*, where Hugh contested the suit, but Mary refused to return to him, the court seems to have finally issued a decree very similar to an English separation.[94] Morgan records a divorce being granted to Katherine Ellenwood by the Essex County Court on the grounds of her husband's impotence. The court ordered the return to her of 'her apparel and what estate she brought with her'.[95] Another case concerning a husband's impotence, not recorded by Howard, was the petition of *Anne [Keayn] Lane* v. *Edward Lane* to the Court of Assistants in March 1659.[96] The court dissolved the marriage after hearing that, despite fourteen months' 'vaine experiments' by Dr Snelling and others, Lane was still only 'a pretended husband'. The case took on a macabre quality when the couple were reconciled in 1659, after further treatment appeared to have restored 'his sufficiency as a man'. Anne Lane gave birth to two children. However, after Lane's death in 1665, and Anne's remarriage to Nicholas Paige in 1666, doubts were raised about Paige's possible fatherhood of the two children born while Lane was alive, and Anne Paige narrowly escaped a charge of adultery.

At the end of the century the Massachusetts laws were altered in two opposing directions. On the one hand the position of the forbidden degrees was clarified by a law of 1695—the so-called Bill against Incest—which prohibited marriage with a deceased wife's sister or niece, though not with a deceased husband's brother or nephew. This bill, proscribing a not uncommon practice, only squeaked through because of pressure from the clergy.[97] On the other hand, the General Court in 1698 reduced from seven to three years the period after which a husband missing at sea could be safely presumed by his wife to have been lost.[98]

The regulations in Plymouth paralleled those of the Bay Colony. There were only six cases in the seventy-two years of separate jurisdiction, according to Howard, and four of these were instituted by women. In finding for the petitioner Elizabeth Burge in 1661, on the grounds of her husband's misconduct, the court also ordered that he should be publicly whipped at Plymouth and Sandwich.[99] Plymouth seems to have been slightly more liberal and to have recognised husbandly adultery as sufficient cause for granting divorce.[100]

So far as alimony was concerned, the Massachusetts General Court codified general rules in June 1696. It granted to the Supreme Court of Judicature the power to assign to the woman 'such reasonable part of the estate of her late husband as in their discretion the circumstances of the case may admit, not exceeding the third part thereof'.[101] This clarified the law of 1641 which decreed that a divorced wife, if innocent, did not forfeit her dower rights for life. But, in practice, Massachusetts courts could be far more generous and protective of divorced women than these laws suggest. When, for instance, the wife of James Luxford, the bigamist, had her marriage declared void in 1639, she was given 'all that hee hath', and he was fined, set in the stocks, and ordered to be deported.[102] In fact, Morris quotes Peck as claiming that, even when a wife was the guilty party, this did not automatically cancel her dower rights as it did in England.[103] In the case of *Mary v. Augustine Lyndon* (1679), the petitioner was granted two-thirds of her ex-husband's lands by the General Court, along with other property.[104] In the case of *Katherine v. Edward Nailer* (1672), where the husband was found to have been both adulterous and cruel, the Court of Assistants decreed that for the petitioner's protection Nailer should be banished ten miles from Boston and should give bond for his good conduct towards his wife.[105] When the suspicion arose that John Richardson, the husband in Massachusetts of Elizabeth Fryer, might be the husband in England of somebody else, the Court of Assistants in 1644 'Ordered that John Richardson should be sequestered from Elizabeth Fryer to whom he was married the 12th of the 8th month, and neither to meddle with hir Person, nor estate, till thinges bee cleared by advice from England'. In other words, as Morris says, the court prudentially put a protection order on her and her property as a very necessary safeguarding of a potential victim's interests.[106]

The admission of divorce suits in Massachusetts overthrew to all intents and purposes the common-law myth that husband and wife were one legal person. The cool realisation of this did not come overnight. As late as the early eighteenth century, divorce proceedings could still be instituted by the wife's parents, and the question of giving evidence against her husband could still give rise to legal doubt and questioning.[107] Generally speaking, the result of clear divorce doctrines in Massachusetts was that a more rigorous attitude towards marriages could be adopted. Do-it-yourself divorces and separations could be stamped upon. Sarah Knight was shocked that in Connecticut 'those uncomely *stand aways* are too much in Vougue'. The authorities in Plymouth treated very toughly an unofficial attempt at the 'putting away' of a wife who had deserted:[108]

> William Paybody, for making a writeing for the seperating of William Tubbs, against Mercye, his wife, in reference unto theire marriage bond, is fined by the court the summe of five pounds, and Leiftenant Nash and John Sprague, for subscribing as witnesses to the said writing, are fined each 3 pounds.

The very unsatisfactory separation *a mensa et thoro* could be dispensed with, and couples could be forced to 'keep company' with each other.[109] As we have seen, the churches to which warring spouses belonged might add their pressure and disciplinary powers.[110] Where a spouse had been deserted, he or she could take protective action before the desertion became actionable in divorce proceedings.[111]

None of these expedients led to a dramatic amelioration of a woman's lot. If her husband was mentally cruel to her, for instance, but did not beat her, or commit adultery, or desert her, she could be forced to continue suffering with him.[112] None the less, if it is accepted that the wife was usually more likely to suffer from the doctrine of coverture in matrimonial causes, then the granting her of a legal *persona* in Massachusetts was equally likely to be a benefit. What we know of the procedure in the Bay Colony and in Plymouth amply bears this out. Milton, for all his radicalism in England, would probably have been taken for a reactionary, so far as women's legal rights were concerned, in New England.

We will conclude this chapter with a brief note on Virginia. In a letter to Kenelm Chiselden, the Attorney-General of Maryland, William Fitzhugh, who fancied himself as a legal authority in Virginia, set out the procedure for his sister-in-law Rose Blackston to obtain a separation from a husband 'so notorious and cruel . . . his cruelty already having occasioned her to make two or three attempts to destroy her self, which if not timely prevented will inevitably follow'. He admitted that[113]

> There in Virginia it is a rare Case, of which nature I have known but one which was between Mrs. Brent & her husband Mr. Giles Brent; the Case thus managed: She petitioned the Governour and Council, setting forth his inhumane usage, upon which Petition, the Court orders her to live separate from him, & he will allow her a Maintenance, according to his Quality & Estate, & to make his appearance at the next General Court, before which Court he dyed, & so no farther proceedings therein. . . . It cannot properly be called a Divorce but a separation rather. . . . Divorces propter Saevitiam & causa Adulterii are more properly Separations, because no Dissolutions a Vinculo Matrimonii but only a Mensa et thoro, & the Coverture continues, and consequently a Maintenance allowed her & Dower after his Decease, as is plentifully set forth by those that treat thereof.

Significantly, Fitzhugh cites 'Cooke on Littleton' and Coke's gloss on the English case of *Porter* v. *Porter* as his sources. This bears out Spruill's contention that 'there was general acceptance of the principles of the English laws governing women'.[114] Fitzhugh was right in maintaining that separations were rare in Virginia in the seventeenth century, but they were not so rare as he claims. Calhoun cites three cases which came up before county courts in which wives were allowed to live apart from their husbands and were granted separate maintenances. He also gives two examples of women who had been deserted or rejected by their husbands receiving protection from the authorities of the colony.[115] Susie B. Ames also has some details about court orders in matrimonial cases. In 1680, for instance, in Accomack County on the eastern shore of Virginia, a separation agreement laid down that the wife should forego her thirds and all claims on her husband's estate in return for the husband's quitting her of all offices and duties and giving her a house, furniture, other property, and wearing apparel. When a husband turned his wife out of doors in Northampton County, he was ordered either to 'entertain her into his house and provide for her' or 'take care that she had maintenance elsewhere and not be burdensome to the parish'.[116] In 1699, Mary Taylor was allowed to live separately with a separate maintenance, because of the persecutions of 'her cross and cruel husband'; other sadistic males were from time to time required to give bond that they would not misuse their wives. The following year, the authorities of Northumberland County gave orders that Elizabeth Windy should be awarded a separate maintenance from her husband William's estate unless he put in an appearance at court. On the other hand, courts could exert social control as stern as that of Massachusetts. The Northumberland Court Order Book for 1666–8 contains an entry about the 'returning of Sarah Littlefield to her husband by the constables'.[117]

Mrs Spruill pointed out that the number of women who separated from their husbands, either formally or informally, increased in the early eighteenth century, and she mentions twenty-six such cases. Moller comments that the female initiative was in strong contrast with male-sponsored separations in England.[118] Mrs Jester gives details of a very strange separation granted to Elizabeth Taylor, the wife of Dr James Taylor, in the middle of the seventeenth century. Mrs Taylor appears to have married Francis Slaughter, a merchant planter of Rappahannock County, while her first husband was still alive.[119]

Virginian courts seem to have been more liberal than English in their treatment of separated women's legal rights. In the case of *Richardson* v. *Mountjoy* it was held that a postnuptial separation agreement which gave the wife the legal capacity of a *femme sole* was valid and that she could therefore make contracts. This was a great improvement on English legal doctrine. The legislators went too far in trying to protect a separated woman in 1742. A bill was passed granting Frances Greenhill the right 'to dispose of her lands and other estate by deed or will notwithstanding her husband James Greenhill shall still be living'.[120] Though James Greenhill had deserted his wife twenty years previously, the Commissioners of the Board of Trade in London disallowed the bill, arguing that[121]

> This is the first instance wherein the Legislatures in any of the Colonies abroad have taken upon themselves to alter the Law in so settled and known a part as giving a power to a Feme Covert to sell or dispose of her Real or Personal Estate in the supposed life time of her husband.

The practice of the Henrico County authorities, however, suggests that at the local level the courts showed considerable favour to women's property rights, against English precedents. When Joanne Sheapard's husband left America in debt, the court excused her from all liability and gave her the full right to sole ownership of the fruits of her labour. Similarly they invested Rachell Price with the rights of a *femme sole* over her plantations and labour, because her husband was a man of violent disposition. On the other hand, they refused a similar petition from Elizabeth Hall, although her husband had squandered her estate and deserted her.[122]

Apart from the greater protection that Virginian courts tended to give to women, the other great difference from England was the absence of any system of ecclesiastical courts. In legal theory, where there were no courts to administer the law, the law itself was in abeyance. The Virginian courts, therefore, were only legally empowered to rubber-stamp separations by mutual consent or parol separations, and this accounts for their practice of awarding alimony to wives without a concomitant separation suit. This was unknown to the English law, where alimony or separate maintenance arrangements were merely incidental to the actual separation proceedings.[123] This strange gap in the legal machinery might in theory have jeopardised women's position in Virginia, had not the civil authorities in practice moved in to fill the vacuum. This, as Fitzhugh's letter to Chiselden demonstrates, they did do, not only to safeguard the wronged wife, but also to punish the husband.[124]

One of the prerequisites for genuine sexual equality that Paul Landis advances is 'equal rights in marital choice and in the dissolution of marriage'.[125] Harriet Martineau saw that, in the early nineteenth century, marriage was 'safer' for American than English women because of[126]

the greater freedom of divorce, and consequent discourage-
ment of swindling and other vicious marriages; it is more
tranquil and fortunate from the marriage vows being made
absolutely reciprocal; from the arrangements about property
being generally far more favorable to the wife than in
England; and from her not being made, as in England, to all
intents and purposes the property of her husband.

Of course this situation did not yet exist in our period. Mather's
Boston and Blair's Williamsburg were not seventeenth-century
Renos. None the less seeds of the marked differences noted by Miss
Martineau in 1837 had already germinated in colonial society by
the end of the seventeenth century.

Notes

1 Cf. G. L. Haskins, *Law and Authority in Early Massachusetts* (New York, 1960), p. 186.
2 On these points, see J. C. Spruill, *Women's Life and Work in the Southern Colonies* (Chapel Hill, 1938), p. 340, n. 2; E. A. Dexter, *Colonial Women of Affairs* (Boston, 1924), ch. 8; Haskins, op. cit., pp. 185–7. The Child petition to the General Court in 1646 that Massachusetts 'might be wholly governed by the laws of England', bears out the changes that had been wrought there. Despite the official Declaration of 1646 which set alongside English and colony law in an effort to demonstrate their similarity, Haskins shows that 'both the magistrates and the deputies were well aware . . . that the Massachusetts legal system was not that of the common law' (p. 186). Winthrop's reaction is instructive; see *Journal: History of New England,* ed. J. K. Hosmer (New York, 1946), vol. II, pp. 271–2, 297–301.
3 If she murdered her husband, however, it was petty treason.
4 Cited by Spruill, op. cit., p. 340.
5 Quoted in C. Bridenbaugh, *Vexed and Troubled Englishmen* (New York, 1968), p. 28.
6 Cf. E. J. Gagen, *The New Woman* (New York, 1954), p. 130; M. Ashley, *Stuarts in Love* (London, 1963), p. 23.
7 W. P. Rye, *England as Seen by Foreigners* (London, 1865), p. 72.
8 Wycherley, *Plain Dealer,* IV: iii, quoted in Gagen, op. cit., p. 135.
9 See, e.g., A. L. Jester, *Domestic Life in Colonial Virginia in the Seventeenth Century* (Jamestown, 1957), pp. 65–7; for a good summary of husband's common law rights, see R. Morris, *Studies in the History of American Law* (New York, 1930), pp. 166–7.
10 Ibid., p. 128.
11 Spruill, op. cit., p. 344.
12 Ibid., p. 337, quoting Blackstone, *Commentaries,* vol. IV, pp. 28–9 to this effect.
13 *Pynchon Court Record,* p. 308.
14 Spruill, op. cit., p. 339; Morris, op. cit., p. 194.
15 Ibid., p. 138.
16 A. W. Calhoun, *Social History of the American Family* (Boston, 1918), vol. I, p. 17.
17 E. S. Morgan, *Puritan Family* (New York, 1966), p. 83.
18 Ibid., p. 37.

19 W. W. Hening, *Statutes at Large . . . of Virginia* (Richmond, Va, 1809–23), vol. I, p. 451.

20 Sir William Holdsworth, *History of English Law* (London, 1922–6), vol. V, pp. 311–15; Morris, op. cit., pp. 135–6. For example, the third of the Southampton lands that were left to Rachel, Lady Vaughan, on her father's death was in trust. Gladys Scott Thomson, *The Russells in Bloomsbury* (London, 1940), p. 17. The position over the Clifford lands was more complicated, as they descended to Lady Anne by entail and were also inherited by her in reversion according to her father's will, which conflicted with the entail. By whichever means she gained title, however, she personally owned and administered the estates in the north, even though her separated husband, Pembroke, was still alive. W. Notestein, *Four Worthies* (London, 1956), Part III, *passim*. Cf. L. Stone, *Crisis of the Aristocracy 1558–1641* (Oxford, 1965), p. 661.

21 A. Clark, *The Working Life of Women in the Seventeenth Century* (New York, 1920), ch. 5; Morris, op. cit., p. 129.

22 Clark, op. cit., p. 237.

23 This paraphrases the description in Haskins, op. cit., pp. 180–2. The husband, if his wife predeceased him but had issue, had a life interest in any estates she had been seised of, 'by the curtesy of England'. Morris, op. cit., p. 164.

24 Spruill, op. cit., p. 364.

25 Stone, op. cit., pp. 643–5. Stone also claims that in the seventeenth century, jointures were generally less than dower rights.

26 This contention is supported by James Ford: 'In general the Plymouth and Massachusetts Colonies were virtually pioneers in recognising the rights of women.' 'Social Life', ch. 10 in A. B. Hart, ed., *Commonwealth History of Massachusetts* (Boston, 1928–9), vol. I, p. 280.

27 Morris, op. cit., pp. 131–4, 168.

28 Ibid., pp. 136, 138.

29 J. Demos, *A Little Commonwealth* (New York, 1970), p. 86.

30 For examples, see Morgan, op. cit., pp. 58–9; Spruill, op. cit., pp. 364–6; Calhoun, op. cit., vol. I, p. 96; Sewall, *Diary*, Vol. III, pp. 182–205, 226–33, 262–75, 299–304; Jester, op. cit., pp. 42–4; G. E. Howard, *History of Matrimonial Institutions* (Chicago, 1904), vol. II, p. 203; *Pynchon Court Record*, p. 210.

31 *Westover Diary*, pp. 441, 503.

32 Quoted in Morris, op. cit., pp. 141–2 and Howard, op. cit., vol. II, pp. 237–9. Another example of a postnuptial agreement, between the Stoevers of Virginia, is given in Spruill, op. cit., p. 353.

33 Calhoun, op. cit., vol. I, p. 96.

34 Morris, op. cit., pp. 171–3; he also gives an example from Plymouth, and cases where women sole traders brought actions which were not directly connected with their businesses.

35 Ibid., pp. 192, 195–9; Spruill, op. cit., p. 346.

36 Haskins, op. cit., pp. 180–3.

37 Morris, op. cit., pp. 144–53.

38 Demos, op. cit., p. 85.

39 Morris, op. cit., pp. 154–61.

40 Ibid., p. 196; my debt to Professor Morris's brilliant pioneering work is both obvious and heartfelt.

41 Privately communicated; cf. the will of Ralph Josselin, in A. Macfarlane, *The Family Life of Ralph Josselin* (Cambridge, 1970), pp. 64–7, 211–13.

42 For England, see note 20; for Massachusetts and Plymouth, see Calhoun, op. cit., vol. I, 120–3; for Virginia, see C. Ray Keim, 'Primogeniture

and Entail in Colonial Virginia', *3 WMQ*, vol. XXV (1968), pp. 545–86, and B. Bailyn in J. M. Smith, ed., *Seventeenth Century America* (Chapel Hill, 1959), pp. 107–15; cf. Spruill, op. cit., pp. 349–56.

43 This is borne out by the differing provisions for unborn children; if the child were a son he was more likely to inherit landed property than a daughter.

44 See especially Keim, op. cit., pp. 552–7.

45 T. Wilson, *The State of England* (London, 1660).

46 H. J. Habakkuk, 'Marriage Settlements in the Eighteenth Century', *Royal Historical Society's Transactions*, Fourth Series, vol. XXXII, pp. 18–19. Under these circumstances, the adoption of the strict settlement at least gave the younger children a legally enforceable settlement.

47 Sewall, *Diary*, vol. III, p. 65.

48 Privately communicated to the author.

49 Quoted by K. Thomas, 'Women and the Civil War Sects' in Trevor Aston, ed., *Crisis in Europe, 1560–1660* (London, 1965), p 338.

50 Ibid.

51 Keim, op. cit., pp. 585–6.

52 Bailyn, op. cit., p. 111; cf. Addison's remarks on the fate of the younger sons of gentlemen in his character of Will Wimble, *Spectator*, No. 108, 4 July 1711.

53 E.g. Rebecka Josselin had £500 as marriage portion and only 10s. for a remembrance ring on her father's death. Macfarlane, op. cit., pp. 64–5.

54 Habakkuk, op. cit., p. 27, argues that one reason for the decline in jointures was that, under the arrangements for most strict settlements, provision for children was no longer the responsibility of the widow. However, he sees 'the subordination of marriage to the accumulation of wealth' as the major reason for the decline. On this point, see also the illuminating remarks of G. E. Mingay in *English Landed Society in the Eighteenth Century* (London, 1963), pp. 26–31.

55 Quoted in G. S. Alleman, *Matrimonial Law and the Materials of Restoration Comedy* (Wallingford, Pa, 1942), p. 59; in fact, private Acts of Parliament were used at the end of the century for this purpose, as we shall see.

56 For a full list of causes voiding a marriage, see C. L. Powell, *English Domestic Relations 1487–1653* (New York, 1917), p. 10. For Essex divorce, see *The Chamberlain Letters*, ed. E. Thomson (n.p., 1966), pp. 113–16.

57 The unsuccessful suit of Henry VIII was of course bedevilled by international politics.

58 Alleman, op. cit., pp. 73–5; on Mrs Manley's case, see G. B. Needham, 'Mrs Manley', *Huntington Library Quarterly*, vol. XIV (1950–1), pp. 259–262.

59 R. B. Schlatter, *The Social Ideas of Religious Leaders, 1660–88* (London, 1940), p. 24; C. Hill, *Society and Puritanism* (London, 1964), p. 295. Cf. Dorinda in *The Beaux' Stratagem*, 'They never meddle but in case of uncleanness', quoted in Alleman, op. cit., p. 122.

60 Ashley, op. cit., p. 19.

61 Alleman, op. cit., p. 122.

62 Howard, op. cit., vol. II, pp. 78, 80–4; Powell, op. cit., pp. 80, 87, 95.

63 Cf. Mrs Friendall in Southerne's *The Wives Excuse* (1692): 'The unjust world . . . condemn(s) us to a slavery for life; and if by separation we get free, then our husband's faults are laid on us', cited with similar dramatic evidence by Alleman, op. cit., pp. 120–3.

64 Powell, op. cit., pp. 81–4.

65 Ibid., pp. 112–13.

66 In 1624, William Whately's *Care Cloth* daringly reopened the question of remarriage after separation. 'It shall be no sinne for him or her to make a new contract with another person.' To the conservative Canonists, however, the matter was closed. Whately was cited before the Court of High Commission and forced to retract his heresy. W. and M. Haller, 'The Puritan Art of Love', *Huntington Library Quarterly*, vol. V (1940–1), p. 267.

67 Powell, op. cit., p. 88.

68 Defoe, *Moll Flanders* (Signet ed., New York, 1964), p. 121.

69 Thus, when Moneylove threatens a separation in Rawlins's *Tom Essence* (1677) his wife responds, 'Fret on sir, yet 'twill not do, for your promise is good, the Portion must be paid, and Divorce when you will the Prerogative Court will give me alimony, and the Chancery separation money, enough to maintain a gallant.' It was similarly stated that 'Cuckoldom is the liberty, and a separate maintenance the property, of the freeborn woman of England'. Alleman, op. cit., pp. 117–19; cf. Stone, op. cit., p. 661.

70 Alleman, op. cit., has a list on p. 136.

71 This was necessary because of the legal fiction that husband and wife were one person, and adultery was therefore, to say the least, difficult.

72 The transitional nature of thought at this time is shown by the debate on the Cottington case. In 1671 Cottington married an Italian lady who had obtained a divorce in Italy. Three years later, claiming that his conscience was troubled over the divorce, he renounced the marriage. The ecclesiastical authorities, however, restored marriage rights to the wife, because they had no powers to review the Italian decree. The divines Barlow and Allestree, dissenting, advised Cottington to disregard the ecclesiastical court's decision. God, they argued, did not sanction divorces. Schlatter, op. cit., p. 25.

73 Alleman, op. cit., pp. 107, 114–17, 136–9.

74 Howard, op. cit., vol. I, pp. 102ff., quoting Lecky's *Democracy and Liberty*, vol. II, pp. 201–2.

75 Quoted by Powell, op. cit., p. 64; cf. Alleman, op. cit., p. 110.

76 Powell, op. cit., pp. 81–4. This seems to be the course which Moll Flanders recommended to her banker friend: 'Well, sir, you must divorce her . . . and then you are free.' Even this was 'tedious and expensive' (ed. cit., p. 121).

77 Powell, op. cit., pp. 68–9.

78 Alleman, op. cit., quotes the case of Thomas and Katherine West at the Warwickshire Quarter Sessions in 1661, p. 108. Lady Anne Clifford and her second husband the Earl of Pembroke seem also to have gone through some such arrangement in 1634; see Notestein, op. cit., Part III. Alleman, op. cit., pp. 109, 120–2, cites several cases of separation by mutual consent in stage plays of the Restoration period. Alexander Oldys has his London jilt say 'As it is the Duty of a Man and a Woman, in case of Separation, I have shared our Goods' (p. 58). Cf. Moll Flanders's separation by mutual agreement, in which her husband 'discharged me, as far as lay in him, and gave me free liberty to marry again' (p. 153).

79 Quoted in Bridenbaugh, op. cit., p. 41; he also cites examples of presentations to quarter sessions of couples living apart, and of women in London presented for having two husbands, p. 39.

80 John Milton, *The Doctrine and Discipline of Divorce, The Judgement of Martin Bucer, Tetrachordon* and *Colasterion*.

81 Howard, op. cit., vol. II, pp. 85–92.

82 The quotations in the two preceding paragraphs are all taken from Howard, op. cit., vol. II, pp. 85–92.

83 Powell, op. cit., pp. 45–55, 67–98. Other Miltonic sources seem to have been Hooper and Whately; ibid., pp. 67–9. The Hallers, op. cit., pp. 266–271, share Powell's view of Milton's position.

84 J. D. Jeaffreson, *Brides and Bridals*, vol. II, pp. 338, 333, cited by Howard, op. cit.

85 This paragraph follows the argument and citations of Howard, op. cit., vol. II, pp. 85–92.

86 Powell, op. cit., pp. 196–200.

87 A. Wallas, *Before the Bluestockings* (London, 1929), p. 210.

88 Quoted in Howard, op. cit., vol. II, p. 331. A more detailed list of grounds for annulment and divorce is in the *Magnalia*, Book V, p. 49. This is reprinted in Morgan, op. cit., pp. 35–6.

89 This section, like former paragraphs, leans heavily on the scholarship of G. E. Howard, to whom I am greatly indebted.

90 Unfortunately there is a gap between Volume I of the *Colonial Records*, ending in 1641, and the start of the relative records of the Court of Assistants in 1673 in which divorce cases would occur–a gap only very slightly filled by Whitemore's cullings from local records—so that the forty cases recorded by Howard are probably well below the total. See Howard, op. cit., vol. II, pp. 328–33, for a fuller discussion of the lacunae. See also Morgan, op. cit., p. 38, on petitions which lack a decision by the court in the extant records.

91 *Joan v. George Halsall* (1655–9), Howard, op. cit., vol. II, pp. 333–4. E. Oberholzer, *Delinquent Saints* (New York, 1956), pp. 143–9, found twelve cases of adultery, mostly male, mentioned in seventeenth-century church records.

92 Petition of Thomas Winsor (1685), Howard, *idem*.

93 *Dorothy v. William Pester* (1652); *Mary v. Henry Maddox* (1678) in ibid. Cf. Calhoun, op. cit., vol. I, pp. 147–8, on a similar Plymouth ruling on the petition of Edward Jenkins on behalf of his daughter in 1675.

94 On the Drury Case, see also 'Records of the Suffolk County Court 1671–80', pp. 837–41.

95 Morgan, op. cit., p. 36.

96 This case is discussed by E. S. Morgan in 'A Boston Heiress', *Colonial Society of Massachusetts Transactions*, vol. XXXIV (1942), pp. 500–12.

97 Sewall, *Diary*, vol. I, p. 407 and n.; see also Howard, op. cit., vol. II, pp. 213–18.

98 Ibid., p. 340; cf. Sewall, *Diary*, vol. II, p. 415.

99 Howard, op. cit., vol. II, pp. 349ff.

100 Morgan, *Puritan Family*, p. 37.

101 Howard, op. cit., vol. II, p. 339.

102 Ibid., vol. II, p. 159; Morris, op. cit., p. 163.

103 Ibid., pp. 162, 164.

104 Howard, op. cit., vol. II, p. 238.

105 Ibid.

106 Morris, op. cit., p. 153. Of course, such measures were not purely humanitarian; the court, like the English authorities at the time, would work to avoid anyone unnecessarily burdening the relief system.

107 As, for instance, in the Willis case, reported by Sewall, *Diary*, vol. II, p. 350.

108 Sarah Knight, *Journal*, ed. George P. Winship (New York, 1935), p. 39; Nathaniel B. Shurtleff, *Plymouth Colony Records* (Boston, 1855), vol. IV, p. 66.

109 E. S. Morgan, 'Puritans and Sex', *New England Quarterly*, vol. XV (1942), p. 604; Howard, op. cit., vol. II, pp. 159–61.

110 Oberholzer, op. cit., pp. 120–2; *Records of the First Church of Boston*, p. 61. An ingenious exception occurred in Plymouth. On 10 July 1686, Dorothy Clarke, having failed to prove her divorce petition against her husband Nathaniel, entered into a postnuptial agreement with him to live separately in divided quarters under the same roof. Oberholzer, op. cit., p. 122.

111 William Tubbs, already noticed, appeared in 1664 before the Plymouth Court and publicly disowned all future debts incurred by his wife who had deserted him. Morris, op. cit., pp. 139, 182. This method was commonly used in Virginia in the early eighteenth century, through the agency of newspaper advertisements of waiver of responsibility. The long-suffering Tubbs finally got a divorce in July 1668 from the ill-named Mercy, 'a woman of ill fame and light behaviour', after she had obdurately stayed away in Rhode Island for four years. Shurtleff, op. cit., vol. IV, pp. 187–92.

112 There are in fact cases where couples were unofficially living apart. The most famous is that of young Sam Sewall, who left his adulterous wife and lived with his parents in 1713 and 1714. Sewall, *Diary*, vol. II, p. 405; vol. III, p. 40; for other cases see ibid., vol. I, p. 104; vol. II, p. 216. There was, however, as Sewall makes clear, strong pressure on them to reunite; e.g. the Savages, *Diary*, vol. III, p. 286.

113 Dated 8 June 1681; R. B. Davis, *William Fitzhugh and his Chesapeake World* (Chapel Hill, 1963), pp. 97–8.

114 Spruill, op. cit., p. 340, n. 2.

115 Calhoun, op. cit., vol. I, pp. 299–304.

116 Susie B. Ames, 'Court Records of Virginia's Eastern Shore', *3 WMQ*, vol. III (1947), pp. 185–6.

117 These examples are all from Spruill, op. cit., pp. 341–4.

118 Ibid., pp. 179–84; H. Moller, 'Sex Composition and Correlated Culture Patterns in Colonial America', *3 WMQ*, vol. II (1945), p. 143.

119 Jester, op. cit., p. 46.

120 William Byrd, *Another Secret Diary*, ed. M. Woodfin (Richmond, Va, 1942), p. 28.

121 Morris, op. cit., p. 154; cf. the case of Susannah Cooper, above, p. 163.

122 These examples from the 'Henrico County Court Records, 1707–9' are taken from Spruill, op. cit., p. 361.

123 Howard, op. cit., pp. 366–9, quotes the prayer in 1691 of Ruth, the wife of John Fulcher, for separate maintenance.

124 Calhoun, op. cit., vol. I, p. 276, reports that in *Brent v. Brent*, Giles Brent was arraigned for seditious words, but died before the case could be heard.

125 P. Landis, *Social Problems* (Chicago, 1959), p. 296.

126 Harriet Martineau, *Society in America*, ed. S. M. Lipset (New York, 1962), p. 296.

Chapter 9

Women's Education in England and the Colonies

In this environmentalist age it hardly seems necessary to justify the importance of education in affecting woman's position in society. To be effective, any feminine Declaration of Independence must contain a clause demanding complete equality of educational opportunity. It is surely no coincidence that women's status and roles improved in America at the same time as higher education was being extended to them.[1] Ruth Bolton, the mildly-feminist heroine of Twain and Warner's *The Gilded Age*, tells her less advanced mamma, 'Mother, I think I wouldn't say "always" to any one until I have a profession and am as independent as he is. Then my love would be a free act, and not in any way a necessity.'[2] If, as Calhoun avers, 'economic independence is the only sure basis of equality', then educational opportunity is its handmaid.[3]

Professor Bailyn has recently warned us of the anachronistic dangers inherent in the word 'education'.[4] While we use the term to denote what used to be somewhat scornfully known as 'book-larnin' ', the seventeenth-century concept was much closer to our 'upbringing', or more pedantically 'acculturation'. In the last three centuries, the educational balance has tipped heavily from the family to the school. The illiterate has become a curiosity, but so has the son intimately versed in his father's trade. This chapter will be limited to a discussion of formal education and training, but this restriction will omit much of what was then legitimately regarded as education.

After some preliminary points, this chapter will concentrate on two closely interlinked problems: the comparative facilities for women's education in England and the two colonies, and the quality and type of education offered.

A great deal of important research has been done in recent years on the educational situation in Tudor and Stuart England, which has produced some important revisions.[5] The first major finding is that, in Stone's words, there was something of an 'educational revolution' afoot in the early part of the seventeenth century. This is reflected in the large sums given by philanthropists for the founding of schools, particularly grammar schools. W. K. Jordan's computation of one school for every 4,400 of the population in mid-century is probably an underestimate.[6] Wallis claims that there were more than 4,000 grammar schools, including private, fee-paying secondary schools, in England in the century as a whole.[7]

Second, the philanthropic provisions, and perhaps, too, the physical provisions, for elementary education were less generous than for secondary schools. This would tend to handicap girls, because they would expect to receive the bulk of their education in the petties.[8]

Third, the puritan emphasis on an educated laity, which went hand in hand with a preaching clergy, is borne out by Jordan's findings on endowments of schools and the location of many schools in puritan areas. Vincent's thesis, endorsed by Simon, is that 'if the puritan government had survived, the ideas of Comenius, Hartlib and Dury would have been put into practice, and a national system of education realised'.[9] The Restoration heralded the beginning of a decline in English educational aspirations, though there is some disagreement about the steepness of the downward path.

In the seventeenth century there was a more rigid distinction than nowadays between the rudimentary skills. Children were not allowed to start learning to write until they had thoroughly mastered reading, and mathematics tended to be similarly delayed. This created a far more marked distinction between reading and writing literacy. It was not all that abnormal to find people who could read quite fluently, but who could not write. Despite the stimulus of the commercial revolution, it is still questionable how many people in the seventeenth century *needed* to write. On the other hand, 'Reading, if for nothing else it were, as for many things else it is, is verie needeful for religion.' Printing and the use of the vernacular would likewise tend to stimulate reading, though not necessarily writing, literacy.[10] The distinction was probably further widened by the fact that writing was conceived of as an art, with various styles of orthography to match various purposes.[11] This helps to explain the curious dialogue reported by Adamson:[12]

> John. How write you, 'people'?
> Robert. I cannot write.
> John. I meane not so . . . I meane spell.
> Robert. Then I answer you p, e, o, p, l, e.

The inability to write, then, need not have meant isolation from literate society, nor need it have been the handicap or the mark of shame which it would be in advanced societies nowadays.[13]

Provision in England

Girls of the relatively well-to-do classes had three alternatives: to be educated at home, to board with another family of similar standing, or to go to boarding-school. In the first two alternatives, they might have access to a good education, particularly if they had brothers of a similar age, for whom their parents had hired tutors. There was no guarantee of this, however. Swift described girls' governesses as 'generally the worst that can be gotten for the money'.[14] Their education would be under the general supervision of their mothers, or 'foster-mothers', and its quality and structure would depend to a great extent on their predilections and intellectual outlooks.

The girls' boarding-school facilities expanded very noticeably in the seventeenth century. The reasons for this development are not altogether clear, but one seems to have been the need felt by parents of the successful middle classes and by country families to impart some social poise to their daughters. These so-called 'public schools' are usually known to us only from casual reference. It is often hard or impossible to discover how long they survived. Like the modern English preparatory school they were commercial enterprises. They could be bought and sold, and their character and quality could change rapidly with new owners or economic fluctuations. It is difficult, therefore, to be very precise about the quantity. The three suburban villages of London which boasted the majority of these establishments were Hackney, Putney and Chelsea. The first two are more often mentioned in the first half of the century in this connection, while Chelsea seems to have attracted education after the Restoration. Indeed, Hackney was known as 'The Ladies University of the Female Arts' and that great ogler, Pepys, made a special trip one Sunday to Hackney church for an eyeful of the pretty young ladies.[15] Evelyn also wrote of rowing up the river to Putney to see its schools in 1649.[16] Dr King, the rector of Chelsea from 1694 to 1732, refers to the 'several large houses taken for boarding schools for Ladies and Gentlemen'.[17] I have been able to discover references to fourteen of these schools in the London area in the seventeenth century. The first is in 1617, when the girls of Ladies Hall, Deptford, provided twelve nymphs for the masque *Cupid's Banishment* performed before Queen Anne at Greenwich. What seems to have been the largest and one of the best was Robert Perwick's at Hackney, which flourished between 1643 and 1660 and had as many as 100 girls or more at one time.[18] One of the last to be mentioned in the century was that of 'Mrs. Priest's at Great Chelsey', which had probably moved out there from Leicester Fields in 1680, and which saw the first performance of *Dido and Aeneas*.[19]

'Public schools' were also in business in provincial centres. There was one at Westerham in Kent, in 1620; two in Manchester, then a small town; two in Exeter in 1641; two in Oxford and one at Burchester, only ten miles away.[20] There was a similar school at Leicester.[21] It is more than probable that a more intensive search would throw up more names of girls' boarding-schools in London and the country. Archbishop Sheldon's order of 1665 for returns of all 'public mistresses of schools and instructors and teachers of young maids or women' possibly implies that they were quite common.[22] The same inference could be drawn from the fact that boarding-schools figure in Restoration drama. It is impossible to arrive at any precise figure of either schools or places, though it seems clear that their numbers grew as the century progressed.

The provision of educational opportunities for the poor, where it existed at all, was a very hit-or-miss affair. For families near the survival line, the children, of necessity, must start earning their keep at the age of three; Gregory King estimated that this would account for a good half of the population.[23] Richard Baxter wrote of the tenant farmers in the midlands after the Restoration: 'They cannot spare their children from work while they learn to read, though I offer to pay the schoolmaster myself . . . so that poverty causes a generation of barbarians.'[24] Another counterweight against formal literate education for the poor was the widely-held belief in the hierarchical nature of both society and creation. Modern ideas of creating a meritocracy, of attempting to cancel out the random inequalities of birth by educational opportunities, were largely alien to the seventeenth-century mind. Whatever education the poor were lucky enough to pick up would more likely equip them for lowly service to society. Needless to say, in this order of things, the poor lad had one creature below him on the social scale, and that was the poor lass.

Poor girls, then, would be dependent for any education that they might get on either charity or the social welfare of their parish. In both cases, the emphasis was on practical skills rather than on literacy. This, for instance, was the plan of John Cary's working-school for 100 girls founded in Bristol in the New Workhouse in 1697. The forty children in the London Workhouse opened in the next year worked daily for nine hours at spinning, had one hour for dinner and play, and one for learning to read and write. Thomas Tryon's scheme of the same period, while nodding in the direction of literacy and moral training for the poor, stressed that the proposed twenty free schools in London should equip their inmates with practical skills suitable for apprentices.[25] The trust which Sir William Borlase established in his will in 1628 for the support of a school for twenty 'weomen children' in Great Marlow laid it down that they were to learn spinning, knitting and lace-making.[26] Flax-spinning was favoured for the thirteen girls at Humphry Walcot's school at Lydbury, founded in 1642.[27] What happened at Christ's Hospital in the seventeenth century may well have happened elsewhere. Originally started in 1553 for boy and girl foundlings, the hospital gradually came to give preferential treatment to the boys, both in places and in benefits. None of the girls were helped by the benefactions of Charles II, and when the girls' section was moved in 1695 to Hertford, it was hardly distinguishable from an industrial school.[28] All these processes occurred in the fairly early stages of the charity school movement at the turn of the seventeenth and eighteenth centuries. This voluntary campaign, under the aegis of the S.P.C.K., to provide education for the poor, originally boasted a 'Literary Curriculum', along with a strong stress on religious and moral instruction. However, thanks to social and financial pressures, the literary side quickly gave way to learning the hard and thankless toil of domestic service, especially for girls. Although in the first decade boys outnumbered girls by only two to one, by 1730 the ratio had jumped to five to one and later in the century to eight to one. The charity schools before long closely resembled those schools which, in the larger towns of the seventeenth century, had made work for pauper children under the supervision of a poor widow or old maid.[29] Finally there were the provisions of the Poor Laws whereby children of paupers, or poor orphans, could be bound out to service with families on the payment of a relatively low premium by the overseers. Where there were any stipulations about teaching girls to read in such indentures, all the incentives on both parish authorities and masters were against the implementation of such requirements.[30] The only formal instruction that most of the poor had was probably the catechising by the minister before evensong on Sundays. Even here, it is questionable how many of the clergy fulfilled this function during the seventeenth century, and, even where they did, the girls in the class might well have inferior instruction.[31] The kind of bequest which Bartholomew Hickling made to Loughborough in 1683, of £4 for the stipend for a school-mistress and £6 to 'equip 20 girls with books, gowns, shoes and stockings' so that they could learn their 'ABC, the true spelling and reading of English, good manners and behaviour and the grounds and principles of the Christian religion', was, according to Simon, very rare. While it might be intended to give the really poor a basic literary education, it is doubtful whether their parents could spare them for such frivolities. It was the lot of the poor girl, despite efforts such as these and the charity-school movement, to remain well-nigh totally illiterate.

What of the remainder of the female school-age population? 'The instruction of girls of the middle and lower ranks, whose parents were not absolutely poor, but whose position did not afford them more than a competence, constitutes the most baffling problem of our educational history.' Adamson wrote this of preceding centuries, but it is equally true of the seventeenth.[32] For the sons there might well be grammar schools, even scholarships to the universities and careers in the church, the law, scholarship, the civil service or business. The daughters quite clearly never got within sniffing distance of a university. It seems probable that they did not enter the grammar schools proper, either, in the seventeenth century. This was rather less of a deprivation than it would appear, because first the role of the grammar school was primarily as a preparation for university, and second the grammar in grammar school was Latin rather than English.[33] That this exclusion had the effect of creating something of a cultural divide between men and women, because of the latter's ignorance of classical learning and literature, may well have been accidental rather than an intentional subordination.

Some confusion over the eligibility of girls to go to grammar schools has been created by the provisions of some founders, notably John Lyon, founder of Harrow, that girls should be excluded. This type of specific prohibition could imply that normally girls would have been admitted to endowed grammar schools. However, for the grammar course proper, silence may well represent an assumption that girls would not attend, anyway.[34] The confusion may have arisen from the fact that not all grammar schools, especially in smaller towns, were limited to a strict grammar course. For instance, the rules and orders of the market town of Alford in Lincolnshire—the home of Anne Hutchinson— were issued in the year 1599. These stipulate that none are to enter the grammar school unless they can read and write legibly. The schoolmaster is not required to teach reading and writing 'but of his own good will and gentleness'.[35] The chances are that the schoolmaster at Alford and at many other small places found it well worth his while to take in a class of 'petties', who may well have included girls.[36] This probably explains the female figures in the schoolroom scene on the common seal of Oakham and Uppingham Schools, Rutland, and in the woodcut in Edward Coote's *The Englische Scholemaister*.[37] It would also account for the short stay of the dozen or so girls mentioned as attending the grammar school at Rivington, Lancs., in 1678 and 1681.[38] Where there was an alternative elementary school, however, girls might well be kept out. The injunctions of 1598-9 which Strype ascribes to Whitgift make this clear: 'It seemeth very unfit that girles should be taught in a school within the precincts of the church, especially seeing they may have instruction by women in the town.'[39] Moreover, this interpretation would admit the truth of Mulcaster's statement that, although the country allows the education of young maidens, they are not admitted to the public *grammar* schools.[40]

The problem of the provision of elementary education, the education which girls would most likely get, is a contentious and intractable one. The petty stage was the weakest link in Stuart education. Charles Hoole, who taught in London at the time of the Restoration, complained that 'the want of good Teachers of English in most places where Grammar Schooles are erected, causeth that many Children are brought thither to learn the Latine Tongue, before they can read well'.[41] On the other hand, so far as the actual provision of facilities is concerned, there are those experts who argue that in the seventeenth century most villages had some kind of common school. These two points of view are not completely irreconcilable, since what some scholars lament is not the absence of elementary schools so much as their lack of proper endowment.[42] It was traditionally and canonically the job of the parish clerk, who ought anyway to be literate, to teach the village children their ABCs. The Canons of 1604 gave to the curate the right of first refusal of the post of parish schoolmaster.[43] Statistics of the provision of these schools are hard to come by. Jones reprints the tables of the Charity Commissioners originally published between 1818 and 1843, which show that there were 460 endowed non-classical schools in England before 1698. They also list 291 charities for elementary education.[44] Jordan describes rural districts 'precariously but bravely attempting to provide at least rudimentary education'.[45] The Visitation Returns for Cambridgeshire in 1590 and 1596 tell us more about the inefficiency of parish officials than about the provision of parish teachers. In 1590, twenty parishes are recorded as having a teacher, forty-five have 'nullus', and eighty-six are blank. In 1596, twenty-two parishes have teachers, but only nine coincide with the 1590 list.[46] From the 'Lincoln Diocesan Returns' from 1600 to 1626, and the 'Subscription Book of the Diocese' from 1626 to 1640, Simon has culled the names of seventy Leicestershire teaching clergy, schoolmasters and ushers. Several men described in the 1630s as ushers were Oxbridge graduates. 'Some village schools were, no doubt, confined to younger children and small enough, but at least two had a graduate master and a petties class under a young assistant.' The grammar schools in the market towns usually had lower schools attached to them where children could learn their ABCs and read simple books in English.[47] These elementary village schools often met in a part of the church; at Medbourne, Leics., the north transept was remodelled in the seventeenth century to form a schoolroom. Leicestershire, however, was probably one of those educationally favoured counties about which Stone writes. There was a strong puritan element in the county, and in the reign of Charles I, at least, probably a quite unusually high supply of male teachers, because of Laudian purges of the clergy. A majority of emigrants to Massachusetts Bay came from these favoured counties.[48] It was probably more normal for many of the parish schools in a county to be presided over by a dame. Hannah Woolley assumed that the village schoolteacher would be a 'mistress'.[49]

These petty schools were quasi-public, and largely supported out of the parish chest. There was also an indeterminate number of fee-paying elementary schools. Gardiner argues that these, either fee-paying dame's schools or clergy taking in pupils, were quite common.[50] Adamson makes a further suggestion of a source of instruction in the rudiments. He points to the enormous popularity of Edward Coote's *The Englische Scholemaister*, originally published in 1596 when the author was, briefly, master of the grammar school at Bury St Edmunds. It was reissued right up to 1704, and the impression of 1684 claims to be the forty-second. The preface is directed 'to such men and women of trade as Taylors, Weavers, Seamsters and such others as have undertaken the charge of teaching others'. It adds, 'Thou mayst sit on thy shop-board, at thy looms or at thy needle and never hinder thy worke to heare thy Schollers, after thou hast once made the little booke familiar to thee.' The book was 'both a text-book for the pupil and a guide to method for his instructor'. It is concerned almost entirely with reading skills. None the less, the initial publication of such a book and then its frequent republication suggest that here was another source of instruction, or perhaps in some cases, of self-instruction.[51] The British Museum's 1636 copy, which claims to be the twenty-fifth impression, has girls' names written in the margins, suggesting that it was popular for their sex.[52]

One further source of education for girls of the humbler sort was the Quaker schools. In the 1670s there were two boarding-schools specifically for girls at Brighton and Warrington, and two more which were co-educational at Ramsay and Thornbury. Smith believes that this experiment was shortlived. She points out that the school at Shacklewell had to be subsidised by the Friends' Meeting in order to keep going in 1677.

While girls below the gentle classes seem to have been pretty uniformly excluded from secondary education, the provision of instruction in at least reading skills for the humbler classes may well have been quite widespread, though of many varieties. For most of the very poor, the best that their 'education' would do for them would be to translate them from the undeserving to the deserving.

Provision in the Colonies

The cornerstone of Massachusetts's educational policy was the legal requirement from the first decade that parents should ensure that their offspring—boys or girls—should learn to read. There was never during the colonial period any legal obligation on parents to send their children to school, provided, of course, that they could make some alternative arrangements about the learning of reading— teaching them at home, for instance, or hiring a tutor. The more famous law of 1647 required towns of fifty families to support an elementary, or common, schoolmaster 'to teach *all* children as shall resort to him to read and write' (my italics). Towns of 100 families had also to provide a 'Lattin schoolemaster'.[53] These two laws between them should have ensured that all girls should at least have the opportunity to learn to read throughout the colony— provided of course that the laws were effective.

Charles Andrews claimed that the provision law was 'more honored in the breach than in the observance'.[54] The moans of later seventeenth-century divines and legislators that there was 'too general want of Education in the Rising Generation' and that the law was being 'shamefully neglected by divers towns', causing 'great decay in Inferior Schools' seems to corroborate this gloomy view. Morison describes the near-nadir of education in the 1670s, and admits that at the end of the century only eight towns appeared to him to have maintained grammar schools for any period of time.[55]

There is room for optimism, however. The fact, for instance, that the frontier township of Haverhill was presented three times for its educational shortcomings might equally well argue the very forceful execution of the 1647 law. The presenting and fining of parents for failure to teach their children to read can be similarly construed.[56]

Robert Middlekauf has recently re-examined the state of secondary education in New England at the end of the century, and claims that as many as 'about twenty-five [grammar schools] can be counted as the new century opened'. He also quotes examples of parents being fined at Hadley, Massachusetts for failing to send their sons to the endowed school in the town.[57] Even where towns did not obey the letter of the law on elementary schools they might keep its spirit by subsidising a fee-paying dame-school.[58] Finally, the practice of some towns of hiring a young Harvard graduate to teach both elementary and secondary levels might well, if he had few Latinist pupils, greatly benefit elementary education.[59]

Developments like the dispersion of population, the decline of religious zeal, and the spread of materialism undeniably had some blunting effects on the ideals of the founding generation. Furthermore, the emphasis on the provision of educational facilities and on minimal educational standards came from above rather than from below in colonial Massachusetts. Putting responsibility on perhaps apathetic or hard-pressed parents for ensuring reading literacy might appear self-defeating. Yet the enforcement of the legal requirements by a committed ruling class was probably the best insurance that the intentions and the results of the laws at least approximated.

Did girls actually go to the town schools? At the beginning of this century, W. H. Small did attempt to answer this question.[60] Out of the two hundred New England town records that Small examined, seven in Massachusetts, two in New Hampshire, and one in Connecticut explicitly required that girls should be admitted to elementary education; three, all in Connecticut, and one, the endowed Hopkins Grammar School at New Haven, specifically excluded girls. In two cases in Massachusetts, the question of admitting girls to town schools is raised, but no answer is recorded. In two other cases it is impossible to say from the evidence whether girls were admitted to the town schools or not. All of this evidence comes from the seventeenth or early eighteenth centuries. Small says nothing at all about the other 183 town records he examined. It could be argued that this massive silence means that the law, namely that *all* children be admitted to learn the rudiments, was obeyed. Small's opposite contention that 'the doors opened slowly, grudgingly' is based entirely on evidence from the late eighteenth and early nineteenth centuries.[61] There is, however, no convincing statement in the seventeen records quoted that girls were generally excluded from town schools in the seventeenth century in Massachusetts.

Along with the places in town schools for girls, there was also the private sector. Clifford Shipton claims that:[62]

> In Boston, at least, private schools [for girls] abounded, both for day and boarding students, and night sessions were early advertised. . . . To these schools, gentlemen as far away as John Stoddard of Northampton sent their daughters. Many schoolgirls lived in Benjamin Wadsworth's parsonage.

There are occasional references to private schools before the last decades of the century. In 1666, for instance, a Mr Jones was forbidden 'to keep school any longer'. In 1667, Will Howard was

licensed to keep a 'wrighting schoole'.[63] Margery Flynt, a widow of
Braintree, who died in 1687, had a considerable reputation as a
schoolmistress, with girls coming out from Boston to her school.[64]
Robert F. Seybolt reports three private secondary schools in Boston
in the 1690s. Three day- or boarding-schools for girls are mentioned in announcements in the *Boston Newsletter* between 1706
and 1714; seven private reading- and writing-schools are named in
Sewall's *Diary* in the 1680s and 1690s, and five other women are described as keeping schools—mainly dame-schools—in diaries of the
period from 1700 to 1720.[65] To this list should be added the writing-
school kept by the famous diarist, Madam Knight, around the turn
of the century in Boston. There is little doubt that girls would
have been admitted to all of these eighteen schools. Indeed, if girls
were excluded from the town secondary schools, the facilities in
Boston may well have had to cater for potential Jane Greys from
all over the colony. In describing a country bumpkin buying a
ribbon for his wife in Connecticut, Sarah Knight commented in
general terms on the rural need for education and conversation
in contrast with 'those who live in citties'.[66]

It was always possible that in certain remote areas girls might
be lucky enough to get even the beginnings of a good secondary
education. The ten daughters of Timothy Edwards—Jonathan's
sisters—attended the 'select school' in the family home in the
frontier village of Windsor, Connecticut. Mainly under the direction of their mother, Esther (Stoddard), they studied the classics
as well as English, and Jerusha Edwards had studied theology
systematically. Admittedly they completed their studies in Boston,
but the impression we are given is that they were well grounded
in the secondary stage before they ever arrived there. It also seems
highly probable that Jane Colman received a considerable amount
of intellectual stimulus from her home background, which contributed to her scholarly activities.[67]

Although it is impossible to say with any finality how good school
provision for girls was in Massachusetts, it would probably have
been better than the normal run in England. After all, sayings like
'Illiteracy and atheism go hand in hand' or 'Ignorance is a prelude
to popery' were truisms to puritans.[68]

Contemporaries could not agree about the provision of schools
in Virginia, and neither can modern scholars. Some would have
the colony an educational wilderness, peopled by tobacco-smoking
barbarians; others see it as much maligned, and, despite its environmental obstacles, quite as committed to high educational ideals as
the Bay Colony.

Although there was nothing on the Virginian Statute Book to
match the Massachusetts school-provision law, critics such as

Berkeley, Fitzhugh, 'R.G.', or Nicholson have been clearly shown to be partial or prejudiced.[69] Other contemporaries painted a rosier picture. Hugh Jones, writing in 1724, claimed that 'In most parishes are schools (little houses being built on purpose) where are taught English and writing.'[70] This confirms Robert Beverley's statement in the *History and Present State of Virginia*:[71]

There are large tracts of land, houses and other things granted to free schools for the education of children in many parts of the country . . . as well as schools founded by legacies of well-intentioned gentlemen. [Where no such schools existed, he added] the people join and build schools for their children, where they may learn on very easy terms.

Modern apologists, such as Susie Ames, argue that the novel environment dictated a completely new type of educational organisation.[72] What the dispersion of population and the lack of urban settlement required, she claims, was not a system of public education on the English or New English model, but private, community-financed, neighbourhood schools.[73] This system was what in fact Virginians gradually developed in their first generations of settlement: privately-hired tutors for the richer planters; the 'old field schools' for groups of humbler neighbours; and at least three endowed schools in favoured parishes.[74] All of these appear to have taken girls as well as boys. Surviving testamentary evidence supports this contention:[75]

When many, many persons of only moderate means directed that their children should be taught to read and write, it seems certain that the opportunity for acquiring such knowledge was available at no great cost or effort . . . The wills and inventories of the colonial period reflected a wider esteem for education than is perhaps generally recognised.

More to our purpose, there are several examples of wills in which the education of girls is a concern. Thus, John Savage arranged that the income from hiring out three servants was to pay for the hiring of a tutor for his three daughters for five years. One daughter was 'to be improved to her best advantage until she shall come to her age or till her age of marriage'. William Anderson, a merchant-planter, left the very substantial sum of £50 for his three grand-daughters' education. Similarly Francis Mackemie desired a 'sober, virtuous, religious education either here in Virginia or elsewhere' for his two daughters.[76] Another way of getting at the scale of provision is through the numbers of teachers that are mentioned in the records. (Both Ames and Bruce point out that the records of many of the seventeenth-century counties, particularly the oldest ones, have been destroyed.)[77] Ames has a list of nine men who taught in the colony up to 1700, two of whom were parish clergy.[78] Bruce has the names of seven others who were designated as schoolmasters, and a further twelve who acted in a tutorial role, including two women and two indentured servants.[79] These twenty-eight are teachers who are *named*. There are other references to unnamed teachers or tutors, including parish readers, in the pages already cited. An attempt to maintain standards was made through the regulations about the licensing of teachers by the Bishop of London, the Governor, or the county authorities.[80] That teachers were valued and respected members of their communities is suggested by waiver of taxes, by the scale of payment offered, and by the fact that some were able to buy up estates in the colony from their income.[81] There is little doubt that girls were admitted both to the old field schools and to the classes given by tutors. Indeed, five of the tutors named by Bruce were hired specifically for daughters. Where girls from a distance joined classes in the school-house or room of a large plantation they might well board there.[82] Ames's conclusion is that 'the children of the planter-merchant class had, in general, educational advantages similar to the best offered in England'.

Finally, there are good grounds for optimism about the educational opportunities available to the poor in Virginia—those, that is to say, who could not afford to pay for schooling at the old field schools or with tutors. The fact that in Surrey county between 1679 and 1684 fifty bonds were given by guardians as guarantees for providing schooling suggests that a 'comparatively large number of children were reached by Virginia's laws for compulsory primary education'.[83] It is important that the indentures for orphan girls had exactly the same educational requirements as those for boys.[84] Not only this, but from the relatively small number of extant documents of the period, there is clear evidence of a concern on the part of the more successful to help to provide for the education of the less fortunate.[85]

Considering the obstacles which contemporaries faced, and the obstacles which modern researchers face, the most reasonable conclusion from the evidence is that the provision of elementary education for girls in Virginia was surprisingly good. The Virginians appear to have developed an effective answer to the un-English environment in which they found themselves. The failure to understand the full implications of Virginian geography and settlement appears to have been a major factor in misleading the critics of their educational system.

Quality of Girls' Education in England

We turn now to the daunting task of trying to evaluate the educational 'systems' of the three areas. In the absence of achievement tests, or advanced levels, or indeed of any very reliable statistics, this will be attempted firstly by a brief review of contemporary comment and opinion on the subject of women's education, and secondly by an examination of what is nowadays—but was not necessarily so in the seventeenth century—a basic criterion: the level of literacy.

Phyllis Woodham Smith, at the conclusion of her M.A. thesis, points out the important fact that women's education in the last three centuries has been far more sensitive to prevailing moods of public—that is, to a large extent, male—opinion than has that of boys. This is probably a result of the fact that the traditional bases of male education were deeply rooted—rather too deeply rooted, as nineteenth-century reformers found—whereas the training of girls, and indeed the whole position of women in society, was more a matter of changing whim and interpretation. The various ideals of womanhood in Stuart England stressed the picturesque, the pious or the practical, but only rarely the intellectual.[86] This hardly boded well for the quality of women's education.

The vast majority of what has been written about girls' education in England in our period has been limited to the leisured classes. The general verdict is that the general intellectual quality of education for girls of the middle and upper classes was poor, and getting worse as the century progressed. Those relatively few women in England who did manage to distinguish themselves intellectually often did so by bucking the system, like Lucy Hutchinson and Elizabeth Tanfield, later Viscountess Falkland. Mrs Hutchinson's mother, 'thinking it prejudiced my health' had her books locked up from her, while Elizabeth was denied candles and had to buy them from the servants.[87] Others, like Mary Evelyn, Lady Anne Clifford, or Damaris, Lady Masham, had the benefit of enlightened parents.[88] Dorothy Osborne, Margaret Cavendish, Mary Boyle and Lettice Morison were natural rebels. Anne Kingsmill, Countess of Winchilsea or Mrs Thornton or Lady Fanshawe turned to a life of the mind as a consolation only in later years. Most of the women of any literary reputation in the period had been educated at home. The only women of any distinction educated at boarding-schools were Susannah Perwick and Katherine Phillips.[89]

More damning corroboration of the thesis that the education of girls was in decline comes from the concerted attack at the end of the century, especially against girls' boarding-schools. This campaign may have heralded the coming of the 'New Woman', but it seems quite as plausible to argue that in fact it was a desperate rearguard action against a shocking decline of standards. The quality of education offered by so-called public schools for girls was never intellectually very high, but the best of them up to the Restoration seem at least to have clung to the ideal of the practical woman, and to have tried to equip pupils for household management. Interspersed with the accomplishments of music, dancing, French, fancy needlework and handicrafts were good penmanship, accounts, cookery, preserving and medicinal knowledge. Neither was piety completely neglected, if we are to believe that *The Virgin's Pattern* and Mrs Phillips's religious education were at all typical.[90] The increasing influence of the cult of the picturesque woman after the Restoration was one cause of the catastrophic decline of standards in the boarding-schools. Of course, the needs of marriage for girls had always led to an emphasis on developing 'breeding', or social poise and attractiveness, and one role of boarding-schools had always been to turn the daughters of successful tradesmen into suitable wives for the gentry.[91] As the century progressed, the schools grew more and more like *débutante* factories, turning out mindless coquettes with no aim in life but to await proposals. 'There are too many', wrote Mr D. Bellamy, who, being the brother of 'The Mistress of a College-Boarding School' had reason to know, 'are of Opinion ... that the Ladies were design'd by Nature for the Objects of Sight only.' He quotes Fénélon in his attack on fond and foolish parents: 'That they were too solicitous about the Ornament of their Person, and too remiss, if not entirely regardless, of the Endowments of their Mind.'[92] Primping, preening and polishing were the main occupations of empty heads in idle hours. It was this decline which led to such censures of the schools as 'Academies of Vanity and Expense' or 'Schools for Wantons' or 'Breeding Grounds for frivolity and worse'.[93]

It goes almost without saying that the quality of teaching was low, especially after the Restoration.[94]

To shew how far they are from Court-breeding, their schools most commonly are erected in some Country Village nigh the Town, where to save charges, they have the worst Masters as can be got for Love or money, learning to *quaver* instead of singing, *hop* instead of dancing, and *Rumble* the *Virginals*, *scratch* the *Lute*, and *rake* the *Ghitar*, instead of playing neatly and handsomely. As for their Languages, a Magpie in a *moneth* would learn to *chatter* more than they do in a *Year*. And for their Behaviour, it is nothing else but a low Courtzie, with a bridling cast of their Chin to fetch it up agen.

Halifax warned his daughter 'Take heed [of carrying] your good Breeding to such a height as to be good for nothing and proud of it'.[95] Given this emphasis on the ornamental, it is small wonder that writers as different as Addison and Defoe, Miss Astell and Lady Masham, the poet Shadwell and Lady Chudleigh, Mrs Makin and Lady Mary Wortley Montagu, Josiah Child and Mrs Woolley should unite in condemning the slight and superficial education of girls. Small wonder, too, that marriages should too often be bereft of companionship and mutual respect, that post-marital sexual immorality should be encouraged, and that the damage to women's upbringing should be perpetuated by fools bringing up fools.[96]

The prevalence of such atrocious standards helps to explain why Mrs Bathshua Makin enjoyed such a high reputation among her more progressive contemporaries. While not denying that her *Essay to Revive the Antient Education of Gentlewomen* reflects the liberal and all too neglected views of Comenius's *Great Didactic*,[97] Bacon's *Advancement of Learning*, and Anna van Schurmann's *De Ingenii Muliebris* in its plea 'to know things [rather] than to get words' and that 'The whole *Encyclopoedia* of Learning may be useful some way or other', yet the curriculum outlined in the *Prospectus* is a bit of a comedown from her ambitious introduction. Even the generous Miss Reynolds allows that the syllabus was 'desultory, inchoate, fragmentary [and] superficial'. We may well be suspicious of the enormous range of subjects to be taught at Tottenham High Cross in 1673, especially as the accomplishments are to take up at least half the girls' time. The fact that academic subjects will be approached in 'a general way' also excites doubts. Nor are the aims of the course quite so impressive under scrutiny; they are to be an encouragement 'to polish your Souls, that you may glorify God, and answer the end of your Creation, to be meet helps to your Husbands'.[98] It may finally be significant that the *Essay* and *Prospectus* are all that has survived of the project. Perhaps it was the very isolation of the attempt amidst a vast sea of mediocrity and worse which made it appear such a bright beacon.

Much of the criticism which we have been describing referred to London boarding-schools, which were in the limelight. From what little we know about similar institutions in the provinces, they appear to have been, if possible, worse still. Though the practicalities of housewifery might be better taught, the accomplishments were often in the hands of itinerant dancing masters, an 'old hoarse singing man riding ten miles from his Cathedral' and a music master of severely limited skill and outdated music and instruments.[99] Hannah Woolley, who had some grounds for know-ing, described country gentlewomen as lacking 'any agreeable dis-course'; they were 'like so many Mutes or Statues when they have happened into the company of the ingenious . . . [they] stared like so many distracted persons'.[100] The stereotype of the utterly un-sophisticated country gentlewoman offers some support to this picture, while there is no evidence known to me to suggest the opposite result of a country boarding-school education.[101]

The luckiest girl of the wealthier classes was she who was educated at home, under the supervision of an educated mother, alongside her brothers at the feet of their tutors. When the boys had gone off to school, she might continue her studies with her father's domestic chaplain or a local clergyman. The evidence suggests that the opportunities for this kind of education were rare indeed by the end of the century.[102]

The quality of the petty and dame-schools to which the daughters of yeomen and tradesmen might most likely be sent varied enor-mously. The children of Evesham who sat at the feet of Elizabeth Elstob, the Anglo-Saxon scholar, might well have had a superb elementary education;[103] similarly with the girls who lived in the neighbourhood of Little Gidding.[104] Kamm infers from allusions in Hannah Woolley's advice to the 'Female younger sort' on their behaviour at their village school, that they would have been taught both reading and writing there. She had herself, at the tender age of fifteen, 'been intrusted to keep a little school, and was the sole mistris thereof'.[105]

There were, on the other hand, far less inspiring accounts of village education in the seventeenth century. Shenstone's character 'A Schoolmistress' describes the dame's charges as 'They grieven sore in piteous durance pent / Awed by the power of the relentless dame'. An accompanying illustration shows a seated dragon clutch-ing a birch. However, there are girls present in the schoolroom and they appear to be reading, though only boys are writing. Des-pite the birch, the boys are hardly models of classroom decorum; none the less, the pupils here appear to be beaten not *from* but *for* the Muses.[106] Bridenbaugh questions whether the usual qualifica-tions for keeping a dame-school would exclude anyone except the blatantly wicked. He gives examples from the first half of the century, where 'some poor woman of the town' is considered suit-able, or a servant woman who is unable to lift burdens is allowed to 'gett her livinge by instruccon of children'. The kind of epithets used by philanthropists to describe the sort of woman they want to run their foundations for them are 'poor, modest, discreet, grave, painful'.[107] 'It's little they pays us, and it's little we learns 'em' said one such educator.[108] Crabbe's dame, 'a deaf poor patient widow', who was little more than a child-minder, comes of course from the later eighteenth century, but it is not improbable that many of her seventeenth-century precursors were not much different. The fact that more grammar schools after 1660 were obliged to undertake elementary teaching could also mean that standards in petty-schools were in decline.[109]

The position of the poor is somewhat clearer. Even the ability to read was a real luxury. Defoe portrayed the families living near Halifax: 'The women and children carding and spinning, all employed from the youngest to the oldest, scarce anything above four years old but its hands were sufficient for its own support.'[110] The highest avocation of most poor girls would of course be some form of domestic service, or the soul-destroying, ill-paid trades connected with the textile industry. The opportunities for apprenticeship for girls to higher trades was in decline from the Elizabethan period.[111] Even when enlightened benefactors or the State attempted to give some elementary schooling to poor girls, their intentions seem too often to have been perverted. Economic exploitation was the fate of the famous 'Red Maids' of Bristol. The founder of their school, John Whitson, had decreed in 1627 that the daughters of decayed or dead freemen of the city should be taught reading and plain needlework. Since the latter was a 'laudable work towards their maintenance', it is hardly surprising to find that it took precedence, and that in the latter part of the century, the poor maids were 'slave-driven apprentices carding wool'.[112] The wink in the direction of formal education by such benefactors as William Borlase and Lady Elizabeth Hill seems likewise to have quickly waned into permanent blindness.[113] The schools attached to some bridewells and workhouses seem to have been concerned almost exclusively with industrial education. In 1675, the inmates of the Girls' Hospital at Norwich spent their time spinning wool on great wheels.

The obvious means of trying to test these conclusions would be by the quantifying of female literacy. Unfortunately, this is much easier said than done. There is first the problem of what kind of literacy is to be measured. Is it the ability to read or to write? If the former, is it reading fluency—and fluency at what level—or the ability to sound out syllables? If the latter, is it the ability to sign one's name rather than making a mark, or some clearer proof, that is needed? Here we come to another snag. The sort of people who might be called upon to sign their names on documents would tend to come from classes more likely to have writing literacy.[114] In the seventeenth century, none of the more reliable sources for quantifying literacy, like the Anglican marriage registers required by Lord Hardwicke's Marriage Act of 1753, is available. The Protestation

Oaths of 1642 and the Test Oaths of 1723 are unfortunately both defective as gauges of female literacy. Women were not required to take the former, and the numbers recorded as taking the latter are deficient.[115]

We are therefore driven back to what Schofield calls the 'traditional approaches to literacy . . . conducted on a wide, and sometimes ill-defined, front . . . which present evidence of a literary and anecdotal kind'. It was from such sources that Foster Watson derived his opinion that during the second half of the sixteenth and the first half of the seventeenth centuries 'girls could read to an extent incomparably greater than any previous century'.[116] In similar vein, J. W. Adamson, assessing national literacy in the fifteenth and sixteenth centuries, concludes, 'Though we may not accept Sir Thomas More's estimate of the proportion of the population that could read, we seem forced to believe that it was an appreciable proportion and greatly in excess of the number as frequently, perhaps, usually, assumed to-day.'[117] He cites the Act of 1543[118] which forbade women to read the Bible, except noble- and gentlewomen who could read it privately, and the statement of Richard Mulcaster that 'young maidens be ordinarily trained [in] the First Elementary'.[119] He also quotes the example of some girls of the relatively remote village of Langham on the Essex–Suffolk border, who were turned out of the church by the sidesman on Ascension Day 1534 for reciting matins from an English primer. The language used by the sidesman suggests that the offenders were of 'the humblest rank'.[120] Lawrence Stone believes that this higher level of reading literacy continued into the early seventeenth century, fostered by protestant insistence on Bible-reading by the individual. His argument that benefit of clergy—the law that a man who could read would be branded instead of, possibly, hanged, for his first offence—would stimulate reading literacy does not unfortunately hold for women, who 'had no clergy', anyway.[121] Wright's evidence is contradictory. On the one hand, Elizabeth Wallington, the wife of a turner of Eastcheap, could read the Bible, Foxe's *Book of Martyrs*, and English chronicles, and Overbury has one of his characters, the chambermaid, reading and re-reading romances.[122] On the other hand, Thomas Delony in 1598–9 suggested that it was extremely rare for servant-girls to be able to read.[123] In the wake of the transition of written works from Latin to the vernacular, and the proliferation of books after the invention of printing, it is clear that certain writers in the early seventeenth century were directing their works towards a feminine audience. This would certainly suggest that 'women of the substantial middle-class' were at least readers.[124]

In plays there are several examples of girls from relatively humble origins, like the maid Lettice in Steele's *The Lying Lover*, Biddy Tipkins in the same author's *The Tender Husband*, or Betty Goodfield in *The Woman Turn'd Bully*, who all read romances or comedies. From this, Gagen concludes that there was an 'advancing army of women readers', and that 'Increased acquaintance with the printed page was bound to emancipate women by gradual degrees.'[125]

There is considerable unanimity on the next stage up the literacy ladder—spelling-ability. Of the first half of the century, Notestein, generally an amiable witness, is forced to confess of his heroines, 'Writing was an effort; some of them did not form script easily; not many were adept at framing a good sentence; most of them wanted something in clearness and cogency of statement.' After cataloguing the remarkable later career of Anne, Lady Clifford, he is forced to admit that 'her letters, ill spelled and ill put together, reveal little of the power of her personality'. If this was the situation with such a *grande dame* as her, he concludes, 'What shall we say of the epistles of less vivid gentlewomen but that few of them repay second reading, except by the intent scholar?'[126] Certainly the spelling of the allegedly intelligent and well-educated Nancy Denton in her famous letter to her godfather Sir Ralph Verney is execrable.[127] The spelling and grammar of Brilliana, Lady Harley, were, if possible, even worse. Miss Denton's efforts remind us of the ambiguous report which Mrs Makin gave of her royal pupil, the Princess Elizabeth: 'At nine years old [she] could write, read, and in some measure understand Latin, Greek, Hebrew, French and Italian.' It is legitimate to wonder if the 'in some measure' has not been placed too late in the sentence.[128] The general decline in the quality of women's education in Restoration England is borne out by comments about the general illiteracy prevalent even among the gentle classes. Mrs Hannah Woolley wrote in *The Queen-Like Closet* in 1675:[129]

> I do daily find that in writing most women are to seek. They many times spend their time in learning a good hand; and their English and Language is, the one not easie to understand, the other weak and impertinent [i.e. 'not pertinent']. I meet with Letters myself sometimes, that I could even tear them as I read them, they are so full of impertinency and so tedious.

Miss Astell also made a plea for women to try to write good, clear English. She went on, not altogether crystal herself, to write, 'Spelling, which they are said to be very defective in, if they don't believe, as they are usually told, that it is fit for them to be so.'[130] John Evelyn's encomium on his daughter, Mary, makes her expertise seem unusual:[131]

As she read, so she writ, not only with most correct orthography, and that maturity of judgment and exactnesse of the
periods, choice of expressions, and familiarity of stile, that
some letters of hers have astonished me and others to whom
she has occasionally written.

Dr George Hickes, who was a friend of female education and
translator of Fénélon's influential *Traité de l'éducation des filles*
in 1688, inferred that it was women's education rather than their
innate intelligence that was so grievously lacking:[132]

Teach her to *Read* and *Write* correctly. It is shameful, but
ordinary, to see Gentlewomen, who have both Wit and Polite-
ness, not able yet to pronounce well what they read; they either
hesitate, or else chant, as it were, in reading. . . . They are still
more grossly deficient in Orthography, or in Spelling right,
and in the manner of forming or connecting Letters in Writing.
Accustom her then, from the first, to make her Lines strait,
and to have her Character neat and legible.

It would [he continued,] also be requisite for her to understand a little *Grammar* of her Native Language. . . . Use her
only without Affection, not to take one Tense for another;
to express herself in proper Terms; to explain clearly her
Thoughts, with Order, and after a short and concise manner.

He goes on to prescribe some elementary arithmetic, reading of
'some select prophane Authors, that have nothing Dangerous in
them for the Passions', the rudiments of Moral Philosophy, some
French, even a little Latin. That such a programme was far from
condescending is suggested by the remark in the *Guardian* of 1713,
'I am concerned when I go into a great house, there is not a single
person that can spell, unless it be by chance the butler or one of the
footmen.'[133]

None of this evidence approaches the exactitude of a literacy
rate. The chances of calculating even a moderately reliable set of
figures are, however, meagre. Even if basic reading ability was
fairly well diversified among women down to the personal-servant
class, we may wonder whether it entailed very great fluency or
linguistic mastery. As for writing and spelling, the criticisms of
the abilities of gentlewomen call in doubt the kind of skill that
women lower down the social scale could command.[134]

Quality of Girls' Education in the Colonies

It has usually been argued that puritan Massachusetts had a far
greater commitment to the education of its children than the
mother country. Certain dames were highly honoured by the

leading men of their communities, men who had reason to know of their skill in the teaching of children in the elementary skills of reading and writing.[135] The plans which Cotton Mather made for his daughters are well known:[136]

> It is time to fix my three elder daughters in the opificial and beneficial mysteries, wherein they should be well-instructed; that they may do good unto others. . . . For Katy, I determine knowledge in physic, and the preparation and dispensation of Noble Medicines. For Nibby and Nancy, I will consult their inclinations. [All were to be] very good mistresses of their pens . . . well-instructed in the art of short-hand. . . . To accomplish my little daughters for house-keeping, I would have them at least once a week, to prepare some new thing, either for Diet or Medicine.

Their education was to make them 'expert, not only at reading with propriety, but also writing a fair hand'. The proper reading was set in contrast against the temptation to 'poison themselves with foolish romances, novels, plays, songs or jests'. Mather's plans suggest that, for daughters of the intelligentsia at least, a high quality of education was available. His emphasis on his children being allowed to follow their own inclinations, and his egalitarian attitudes towards his daughters' training show that he had been influenced by Locke's *Some Thoughts Concerning Education*, published in 1693.[137] The youthful Benjamin Franklin chose for his *alter ego* Silence Dogood, a minister's widow, who is plainly liberally educated and intellectually inclined.[138]

There is, however, an obverse side to this picture. Although Perry Miller has rightly stressed the intellectualism of puritanism, and Morison has set its educational emphasis in stark contrast with the brainless fundamentalism of the wilder sects, none the less Cotton Mather himself revealed a faint anti-intellectualism towards women in his *Ornaments for the Daughters of Zion*. Although philosophers might praise exemplars like Lady Jane Grey 'who so admirably could read the Word of God in its originals' or 'the French Lady who a while since published Homilies on the Epistle to the Hebrews' or women 'who were tutoresses', for him real wisdom lay in 'the Fear of God' in the woman who would 'consider her latter end, and was wise unto salvation'.[139]

There is some reason to believe that the boarding-schools for girls in Boston were placing undue emphasis on breeding and the accomplishments. The riposte of the beleaguered Thomas Clarke when assailed by the infuriated and frustrated Mary Brattle was 'You had need to have had a £100 Bestooed upon you at a boardeing Schoole to learne manners and breeding'.[140] Abigail Adams looked back to her youth—the 1740s and 1750s—when it was 'Fashionable to ridicule female learning. . . . Female education in the best families went no further than writing and arithmetic; in some few and rare cases, music and dancing.'[141]

Recently the quality of puritan education has been questioned in another area: that of provision of high-quality, permanent teachers.[142] The theory was that bright young Harvard graduates went out from the fountainhead in Cambridge to the towns and villages of the colony, and gave their talents to the teaching even of petties in the common schools. Teaching was a relatively well-paid job for a young man who had just graduated. Elementary education, in which girls would share, would thus benefit enormously from these highly-qualified, young and enthusiastic educators. On the secondary level, the example of that great grammar-schoolmaster, Ezekiel Cheever, is usually cited. What this view evades is that the primary commitment of Harvard, however liberal its curriculum, was towards turning out future ministers, not teachers. The community and the government accorded highest esteem to ministers, rather than to schoolmasters. Cheever, great though he may have been—and greater still in Mather's telling— was untypical, the 'one exception that proves the rule of neglect by the puritans'. Schoolteaching, and even tutoring at Harvard, tended to be a temporary job for young graduates before they received a call to a congregation. The result was that towns had a series of quick-changing teachers staying only for a year or so, or even less, with at least one eye cocked for ministerial opportunities.[143] Wilson Smith concludes that 'the Puritan emphasis was upon building and maintaining institutions, rather than upon providing or attracting a supply of men to teach in them. . . . In so far as the teacher is concerned . . . the "case" in favour of Puritan educational efforts has not been wholly proved.'

Estimates of female literacy have been attempted for Massachusetts. There are, for instance, the findings of William Kilpatrick from Suffolk County deeds between 1653 and 1656, and 1681 and 1697. In the former, 42 per cent of women signed their names, in the latter 62 per cent, as opposed to 89 per cent of men in both periods.[144] Of women who left wills in Essex County, less than a third affixed signatures, and most of these were of the older, presumably English-educated, generation.[145] George Willison believed that in Plymouth few women could even read, though Alice Bradford and Bridget Fuller were exceptions. He points out that the daughters of Nathaniel Morton, the secretary of the plantation, made marks, rather than signed, as witnesses.[146]

The shortcomings of such sources for measuring female writing literacy are cruelly exposed by the findings of Clifford Shipton's analysis of the 2,729 names on petitions, addresses and other documents in the Massachusetts and Connecticut archives. The 95 per cent literacy which he discovers really tells us little more than that the vast majority who petitioned and addressed could write their own names, and, thus, also probably read. As Morison admits, 'the poorest people, indented servants and the like, had slight opportunity to sign deeds or petitions; hence any accurate estimation of total illiteracy is impossible to attain'. He was, however, more assured in his pronouncement on reading. 'It is certain that very many, perhaps a major part, of the colonists, not only in New England, but in the Middle Colonies and Virginia, who were unable to write their names, could read the King James Bible and other simple English texts'.[147] Even this is being called in doubt currently by Kenneth Lockridge, who asserts that 'the large minority of men was not literate in any sense and the overwhelming majority of women shared the same limitation'.[148] When Lockridge publishes the basis of his argument, we may be in a better position to evaluate women's education in seventeenth-century Massachusetts. At this stage, all that we can safely conclude is that, by the end of the century, around two-thirds of middle-class women in the most advanced county of the colony could at least read with considerable fluency.

The information available about the quality of girls' education in Virginia is negligible. A famous letter of 1732 from Betty Pratt to her brother at school in England, concedes that he has 'got the start of me in Learning very much'. While he can write a good hand, cypher to the power of three and speak French, she can only 'perform many dances', is learning the sibell, cannot 'cast up a sum in addition cleverly' and 'cannot speak a word of French'.[149]

The standards of the free schools were generally low. What was expected is implied by the stipulation of the Revd John Farnefold's bequest of 1702, that children should leave 'when they can read the Bible and write a legible hand'. This projected school was to be called Winchester![150]

Where a family or a community hired a tutor, or where the minister of the parish took in pupils, girls would be included in the classes. The quality of at least some of their instructors would probably have been pretty poor. It was a frequent complaint of governors and others that it was well-nigh impossible to attract an able clergy to the colony.[151] Some tutors were indentured servants, though this need not necessarily mean that they were not highly valued, or hopelessly ill-qualified.[152] Fithian's note to his successor at Nomini Hall in the Revolutionary period, stated that the 'Virginians placed a high value on mental acquirements and that a graduate of Princeton, though without any fortune was rated as

high in the social scale as a man with an estate of £10,000.' As if
to prove the point, the successor, George Peck, married one of the
girls he was hired to tutor.[153] Two great Virginian figures of the
Revolutionary period, George Wythe and George Mason, were
early educated by their mothers; this argues that the quality of some
girls' education was reasonably high. On the other hand, Morgan
believes that by the early eighteenth century many Virginians had
come round to[154]

> the generally accepted belief that the capacities of a girl could
> never equal those of her brothers. A girl was not expected to
> go beyond reading, writing and arithmetic. There was no sense
> in bothering her head with Greek and Latin, for she would
> never be able to undertake the advanced liberal education
> for which these were the foundation.

She was therefore instructed in the social graces and the domestic
skills. That this differentiation was not entirely new is borne out
by some seventeenth-century wills. William Rookings, for instance,
orders that his sons are to be 'brought up to a good education'
whereas his daughters are merely to have 'what education may be
fitting to them'.[155] On the other hand, we have seen that the seventeenth-century justices were completely unprejudiced in their
orders about the education of girl orphans, and that indentures
stipulated exactly the same educational requirements for girls as
for boys.

Bruce attempted to arrive at a writing-literacy rate for the colony
in the seventeenth century. His sources for female literacy were
some 3,000 deeds of conveyance and depositions.[156] Presumably,
women most likely to make deeds of conveyance would come from
the richer classes, whereas women making depositions could be
drawn from any class, and the sample might well number a majority
of the poorer classes. His figures of 756—or one quarter—able to
sign their names as against 2,310 who made their marks on documents between 1641 and 1700 may therefore well be skewed against
the literates, especially as the conveyance of land would more
normally be handled and signed for by men. On the other hand, he
does produce a depressing catalogue of wives and daughters of
leading landowners and clergy who signed with marks.[157] Though
it is more likely that his literates represent reading rather than
writing fluency, something nearer a half than a quarter of women
of the substantial classes may have been able to read by the end of
the century. Even this conclusion could be misleading, though.
'The fairest test of the school system of the seventeenth century',
Ames writes, is not 'the literacy of people'. In an era of massive
immigration to the colony, many girls and women arrived in the

colony too old by contemporary standards to start even a rudimentary formal education. Their illiteracy could hardly be blamed on Virginian schools or schoolmasters. 'Some immigrants were unlettered when they came, and they remained unlettered.'[158]

The educational prospects of any girl born into the English-speaking world of the seventeenth century were not particularly rosy. They would probably have been best for girls born into well-to-do families in Massachusetts or puritan-oriented families in England. The most that the great majority could hope for would be to be able to learn to read their mother tongue. On both sides of the Atlantic, the inequalities of educational opportunities between the sexes were one of the worst handicaps for women. However innately intelligent they might be, their intellectual capacities were unlikely to be fully tested or developed in their school or adult lives. We should not, however, be too gloomy. Although there was a developed literate culture in the seventeenth century, a great deal of the transmission of ideas was still by word of mouth. How else would congregations have endured three-hour sermons? The ability of women to read at least allowed them to share in the literate culture of their time, if they had less chance to add to it. So far as the colonies are concerned, we should, I think, rather applaud the efforts made towards female education amid all the other pressing tasks of settlement, than condemn shortcomings. In new, underpopulated societies, education and the leisure to apply it are great luxuries.[159] In this sense, the poems of Anne Bradstreet, the *Journal* of Sarah Knight, or even Lucy Byrd arguing over the infallibility of the Bible, are proofs of the settlers' success in their determination 'not to grow barbaric in the wilderness'. Indeed, our conclusion that the provision and quality of girls' schooling in the colonies were equal to, if not better than, those in England, suggests that concern for female education was quite probably higher in the New World than the Old.

Notes

1 Carl Degler, 'Revolution without Ideology: the Changing Place of Women in America', in Stephen R. Graubard, ed., *The Woman in America*, *Daedalus*, vol. XCIII (Spring 1964), pp. 653–4.
2 Mark Twain and C. D. Warner, *The Gilded Age* (Hartford, 1874), p. 237.
3 A. W. Calhoun, *Social History of the American Family* (Boston, 1918), vol. II, p. 80.
4 B. Bailyn, *Education in the Forming of American Society* (Chapel Hill, 1960), pp. 9–20.
5 Joan Simon, *Education and Society in Tudor England* (Cambridge, 1966), and three essays in B. Simon, ed., *Education in Leicestershire 1540–1940* (Leicester, 1968); W. A. L. Vincent, *The State and School Education 1640–1660* (London, 1950), and *The Grammar Schools; their Continuing Tradition 1660–1714* (London, 1969); K. Charlton, *Education in Renais-*

sance England (London, 1965); P. J. Wallis, *Histories of Old Schools* (Newcastle, 1966), and 'Histories of Old Schools: A Preliminary List for England and Wales', *British Journal of Educational Studies*, vol. XIV (1965); Lawrence Stone, 'Educational Revolution in England, 1560–1640', *Past and Present*, No. 28. The findings of W. K. Jordan's books on philanthropy are also crucially important in the educational area: *Philanthropy in England* (London, 1959), *The Charities of London* (London, 1960), and *The Charities of Rural England* (London, 1961). I have not had an opportunity to consult Elizabeth S. Bier, 'Education of English Women under the Stuarts' (unpub. M.A. thesis, University of California, Berkeley, 1926) and unfortunately the above-mentioned studies concentrate almost completely on the education of boys.

6 Jordan, *Philanthropy in England*, pp. 206, 283–4, 288–90.

7 Wallis, *Histories of Old Schools*, *passim*.

8 S. E. Morison, *Intellectual Life of Colonial New England* (New York, 1956), p. 62, calls elementary education 'the weak link' in the system. Vincent, *The Grammar Schools*, refers to it as 'the poor brother'. Charlton, op. cit., argues that the favouring of grammar schools reflected philanthropists' ambition and self-interest.

9 Vincent, *The Grammar Schools*, p. 16. Comenius, whose *Great Didactic* was influential in educational thought, if less so in practice, advocated, among other reforms, the equal treatment of girls with boys. He was followed in this by Harrington.

10 Roger Schofield, 'Measurement of Literacy in Pre-Industrial England' in Jack Goody, ed., *Literacy in Traditional Societies* (Cambridge, 1968), pp. 311–25. J. W. Adamson, *The Illiterate Anglo-Saxon and other Essays on Education* (Cambridge, 1946), p. 58; Vincent, *The Grammar Schools*, p. 6.

11 Phyllis Woodham Smith, 'The Education of Englishwomen in the Seventeenth Century' (unpub. M.A. thesis, University of London, 1921), p. 113, quotes detailed instructions to a waiting gentlewoman on how to cut her quill and shape her letters for the 'Roman, Italian and Mixt hands'.

12 Adamson, op. cit., p. 57.

13 That this is no mere academic point is suggested by J. Goody and I. Watt in their essay 'The Consequences of Literacy' in Goody, op. cit., pp. 67–8:

> In oral societies the cultural tradition is transmitted almost entirely by face-to-face communication; and changes in its content are accompanied by the homeostatic process of forgetting or transforming those parts that cease to be either necessary or relevant. Literate societies, on the other hand, cannot discard, absorb or transmute the past in the same way. Instead, their members are faced with permanently recorded versions of the past and its beliefs; and because the past is set apart from the present, historical enquiry becomes possible. This in turn encourages scepticism, not only about the legendary past, but about received ideas about the universe as a whole.

14 Quoted in Woodham Smith, op. cit., p. 87.

15 John Evelyn, *Diary*, 20 April 1667.

16 Quoted in D. Gardiner, *English Girlhood at School* (London, 1929), p. 214.

17 Quoted by Woodham Smith, op. cit., p. 79 from MS. Account of the Parish in Chelsea Public Library.

18 Gardiner, op. cit., pp. 209, 211–12.

19 The references to the others are mainly from Gardiner, op. cit. Some of them like De la Mare's, Challoner's or Papillon's are known only by name. Others, pp. 209–17, are: Friend's Boarding School, Stepney,

mentioned in 1628 and 1638, which specialised in embroidery and may have been named after an anglicisation of the Huguenot L'Amy; Mrs Winch's at Hackney, from which an heiress was abducted in 1637. Mrs Salmon's, also at Hackney, educated Katherine Phillips and the daughters of Sir John Bramston, around 1634 and 1649 respectively. Schools mentioned after the Restoration are Mrs Slater's, Mrs Playford's at Islington, Mrs Crittenden's (c. 1682), Hazard's School in Kensington (1682) and Mrs Kilvert's, where Claude Manger taught. Reynolds adds Gorges House, Chelsea (1676–1726), Mrs Overing's at Hackney, and Mrs Elizabeth Tutchin's at Highgate, both advertised in Queen Anne's reign.

20 Gardiner, op. cit., pp. 217–18; Mrs Isley owned the Westerham school; Mrs Parnell Amye one in Manchester (1638–73); one of the Oxford schools was run by a Mrs Waver. M. Reynolds, *The Learned Lady in England 1650–1760* (Boston, 1920), p. 258. Ralph Thoresby, the diarist, talked of his sister going off to Madam Falkland's school in 1684.

21 Josephine Kamm, *Hope Deferred* (London, 1965), p. 76.

22 Gardiner, op. cit., p. 276.

23 Gregory King's total of those decreasing the wealth of the kingdom is 2,825,000 against 2,675,520 who are increasing it.

24 J. Simon, 'Post Restoration Developments' in B. Simon, op. cit., pp. 32, 53.

25 J. Simon, 'Was there a Charity School Movement?' in ibid., pp. 60–3.

26 Jordan, *The Charities of Rural England*, p. 56.

27 Woodham Smith, op. cit., pp. 96–7.

28 Ibid., p. 99. The free school established by the yeoman William Elmer in 1653 which had specifically educated girls as well as boys, had, by 1832, been almost taken over by the males; the few girls in the school had to pay fees. *The Charities of Rural England*, pp. 57–8; Woodham Smith, op. cit., p. 97.

29 M. G. Jones, *The Charity School Movement* (London, 1938), pp. 74–88. On Bridewells see Gardiner, op. cit., pp. 276–8; Woodham Smith, op. cit., p. 98, quotes the overseers of the poor in Aylesbury paying out 5s to Mary Sutton in 1672 for teaching workhouse children lace-making.

30 D. Marshall, *English Poor in the Eighteenth Century* (London, 1926), pp. 195–6. Such arrangements were a forcing ground for prostitution.

31 Woodham Smith, op. cit., p. 95 quotes Mrs Thornton's *Autobiography*. John Barnard describes Mr Ratcliffe's catechising at Rotherhithe, c. 1710. Girls remained with the younger boys. The charge of $\frac{1}{2}d$ or $\frac{1}{4}d$ might have excluded the poor. Mass. Hist. Soc. Colls, Third Series, vol. V (1836), pp. 201–2.

32 Adamson, op. cit., p. 57.

33 Latin was in a transitional stage. Despite both the secularisation of education, and the rise of the vernacular, Latin was still viewed in a vocational light. Since women were traditionally excluded from the careers which would use Latin, there seemed little point in their learning it. Even among the gentle or noble classes it was extremely rare for women to have Latin. Exceptions were Lucy Hutchinson, Anne Baynard, Susannah Evelyn, Nancy Denton and the nieces of Charles Hatton (Gardiner, op. cit., p. 260). Lady Mary Wortley Montagu only managed to learn Latin by secretly buying books and hiding in the library to evade her governess (R. Halsband, *Life of Lady Mary Wortley Montagu* (London, 1961), p. 7).

34 Vincent accepts the opinion of the Royal Commission of 1868: 'Founders had taken for granted that only those who could profit by grammar school learning would come, or stay for long, to be taught, that thus the grammar school population would be determined, as it were, by natural selection,

and that since men rather than women were in a position to make good use of this sort of education in the world and in the service of Church and State, school regulations were addressed to boys rather than girls.' *The Grammar Schools*, p. 48. Other schools from which girls were expressly excluded were Manchester Grammar School (1519); Tiverton (1599); Queen's School, Canterbury (1598); St Olave's, Southwark (1561) and Felsted (1564). Adamson, op. cit., pp. 60–1. Vincent, op. cit., p. 47, also mentions John Sampson's foundation at South Leverton, Notts., in 1691.

35 Adamson, op. cit., p. 47.

36 At the school endowed by William Smyth of West Chiltington, Sussex, the schoolmaster was to teach 'all youth, as well poor as rich, either male or female'. The expected clientele suggests that this would be mainly a petty school. C. Bridenbaugh, *Vexed and Troubled Englishmen* (New York, 1968), p. 354.

37 Adamson, op. cit., p. 60. In both, the pupils seem to be reading.

38 Vincent, *The Grammar Schools*, p. 47. In 1645 at Madeley in Staffs., Sir John Offley founded two schools, one for boys, one for girls, divided by a partition. The girls had their own schoolmistress. At Banbury Grammar School, Cheshire (1594) and Nicholas Latham's three foundations in Northants (1619), girls were admitted to learn up to the ages of nine and ten respectively. The regulations of the school at Uffington forbade girls, though this was 'the common and usual course' (ibid., p. 46); Bridenbaugh, op. cit., p. 334.

39 Adamson, op. cit., p. 61.

40 Cited by T. Woody, *Women's Education in the United States* (New York, 1929), p. 25.

41 Let alone write. Hoole's *New Discovery of the Old Art of Teaching* was published in 1660, though written in 1637. Vincent, *The Grammar Schools*, p. 71.

42 J. Simon, 'Town Estates and Schools in the Sixteenth and Early Seventeenth Centuries' in B. Simon, op. cit., p. 25, quotes W. G. Hoskins's view that 'Besides the established grammar schools, a great number of villages had schools of their own, run by a schoolmaster in the village church, whose salary was paid by the villagers out of the church rate.' Stone, op. cit., p. 42 concurs.

43 Adamson, op. cit., p. 52. G. F. Wells, *Parish Education in Colonial Virginia* (New York, 1963), p. 17, suggests that the calibre of parish clerks declined in the seventeenth century, and that some were illiterate. Canon 78 quoted by J. Simon, op. cit., p. 20.

44 Some of the commissioners' figures have been shown to be inaccurate, and we have already seen that endowments in the elementary sector were low. Jones, op. cit., appendix I.

45 *The Charities of Rural England*, p. 58. Wells, op. cit., pp. 18–19.

46 *Victoria County History of Cambridgeshire*, vol. II, p. 338.

47 J. Simon, 'Town Estates and Schools', pp. 19, 26, appendix I.

48 Bridenbaugh, op. cit., p. 332, claims that half of the English grammar schools were in great migration areas. His total number of grammar schools is probably an underestimate.

49 Ibid., p. 334; Kamm, op. cit., p. 66.

50 Gardiner, op. cit., p. 279; cf. Vincent, *The Grammar Schools*, pp. 71–2.

51 Adamson, op. cit., pp. 56–7.

52 Kamm, op. cit., p. 66.

53 Morison, op. cit., p. 76.

54 Charles Andrews, *Pilgrims and Puritans* (New Haven, 1919), part I, pp. 83–5; part II, pp. 130–3.

55 Morison, op. cit., pp. 58–68, 72–6.
56 Marcus Jernegan, *Laboring and Dependent Classes in Colonial America,* *1607–1783* (New York, 1960), pp. 121–5.
57 Robert Middlekauf, *Ancients and Axioms: Secondary Education in Eighteenth Century New England* (New Haven, 1963), pp. 8, 18.
58 Woody, op. cit., p. 138 describes this as the practice of Springfield in 1682, Woburn, Winchenden and Weymouth around 1700, and Haverhill in 1707.
59 Morison, op. cit., pp. 92–4, 99.
60 W. H. Small, 'Girls in Colonial Schools', *Education,* vol. XXII (1902), pp. 532–7. Cf. George H. Martin, 'The Early Education of Girls in Massachusetts', ibid., vol. XX (1900), pp. 323–7, which Small demolishes.
61 He even tries to use the actions of the Dorchester selectmen in 1770 to provide the answer to a question raised at a town meeting in 1639!
62 Clifford Shipton, 'Puritan Secondary Education', *New England Quarterly.* vol. VII (1934), p. 649.
63 Morison, op. cit., p. 77.
64 C. F. Adams, *Three Episodes in Massachusetts' History* (Boston, 1896), vol. II, p. 604.
65 R. F. Seybolt, *Private Schools in Colonial Boston* (Cambridge, Mass., 1936), pp. 5–11. It is unlikely that all the eighteen secondary schools and primary schools were in operation at one and the same time.
66 Sarah Knight, *Journal,* ed. George P. Winship (New York, 1935), pp. 41–3.
67 Mary S. Benson, *Women in Eighteenth Century America* (New York, 1935), pp. 110–14, 116–17.
68 R. B. Schlatter, *Social Ideas of Religious Leaders, 1660–88* (London, 1940), p. 38.
69 W. W. Hening, *Statutes at Large . . . of Virginia* (Richmond, Va. 1809–23), vol. II, p. 517; R. B. Davis, ed., *William Fitzhugh and his Chesapeake World* (Chapel Hill, 1963), p. 15; P. Force, *Tracts,* vol. III, No. 15; Wells, op. cit., p. 20. Cf. Hartwell, Blair and Chilton, *The Present State of Virginia and the College,* ed. Hunter D. Farish (Charlottesville, 1964), p. 68. For comments on these, see P. A. Bruce, *The Institutional History of Virginia* (Gloucester, Mass., 1964), vol. I, pp. 360–1, and Susie B. Ames, *Reading, Writing and Arithmetic in Virginia, 1607–99* (Williamsburg, 1957), pp. 9, 20; and Hugh Jones, *The Present State of Virginia* ed. Richard L. Morton (Chapel Hill, 1956), vol. I, p. 338. Other contemporary criticisms are found in Francis McKemie (1705) in *Va Mag.,* vol IV (1896), p. 255 and *Virginia's Cure* in Force, *Tracts,* vol. III, p. 6.
70 In Morton, op. cit., pp. 108ff.
71 Robert Beverley, *History and Present State of Virginia,* ed. Louis B. Wright (Chapel Hill, 1947), pp. 275–6. Wright's favourable assessment of Beverley's objectivity is on pp. xxv, xxxiii.
72 Cf. Bruce, op. cit., vol. I, pp. 293–4; Louis B. Wright, *The First Gentlemen of Virginia* (Charlottesville, 1964), ch. 4.
73 Ames's essay implicitly attacks the basis and findings of Wells's monograph. His evidence is drawn from only five of the fifty Virginian parishes and the twenty-nine replies to the Bishop of London's questions which refer only to the year 1724. The extant parish records are Christ Church, Middlesex, 1663–1787; Petsworth, Gloucs., 1677–1793; St Peter's, New Kent, 1687–1789; Kingston, Mathews Co., 1679–1796; and Hungar's, Northants, 1634—1700; Wells, op. cit., pp. 12, 15–16.
74 Syms School, endowed by Benjamin Syms, or Symmes, in 1641; Eaton School, founded by Thomas Eaton's bequest in 1659, both in Elizabeth City parish; Peasley School, in Gloucester County, founded in 1675. Two

others which survived were Sandford's, in Accomac County, 1710, and William Horton's, c. 1700. William Gordon's in Middlesex, end of the 1680s, also probably continued into the eighteenth century. Nothing is known about the fate of the plans for endowed schools of Henry King, Nansemond, 1668; the Revd John Farnefold, Northants., 1702; Henry Lee, Northumberland, 1652; or Mary Whalley, Bruton parish, 1706. The College of William and Mary, founded in 1693, had a grammar school attached. The only other of the free schools which certainly had a grammar course was Eaton, Bruce, op. cit., 7, 8; Wright, op. cit., pp. 102–5.

75 Cf. ibid., p. 101, 'in the extant records of the seventeenth century, bequests for educational purposes are fairly frequent, and undoubtedly other schools were established, though the records have disappeared.'

76 Bruce, op. cit., pp. 297–307, lists twelve other bequests for girls' education. Where the term 'children' is used in others, girls may have benefited.

77 Ibid., p. 358.

78 Ames, op. cit., pp. 13–15, 17, 35–6.

79 Bruce, op. cit., pp. 324–30, 352–5, 335–9. He also, over-optimistically, suggests that 'Among the persons residing in the colony in the latter part of the seventeenth century were a large number of youths, who, having been educated at Christ's Hospital in the City of London had afterwards found employments as regular apprentices with different masters in Virginia. . . . These boys had, before leaving England, received such an extended course of instruction that they would have been fully competent to serve as [elementary] schoolmasters' (p. 314).

80 Bruce, op. cit., 334–5.

81 Ames, op. cit., p. 14, speaks of 'numerous schoolmasters' accumulating enough by their profession to purchase estates. Bruce, op. cit., p. 342, believes that the 300 acres bought by Samuel Coats in 1691 was quite typical. On pp. 341–2, he lists fees owed to a deceased schoolmaster of Isle of Wight County in 1698 which amounted to 2,139 lbs. of tobacco.

82 Bruce, op. cit., pp. 324–9. In two cases, tutors were hired for only one year to teach the girls. Girls' instruction was probably only in reading, with perhaps writing. The swashbuckling Col Daniel Parke wrote to his daughter Frances: 'Mind your writing and everything else you have learnt. . . . Mind reading and carry yourself so that everyone respects you.' Wright, op. cit., p. 80.

83 Ames, op. cit., p. 12; Bruce, op. cit., p. 308, contends that justices seem to have been scrupulous in enforcing educational requirements for orphans.

84 Ibid., p. 311. Hening, op. cit., vol. I, p. 261 (1643); vol. II, p. 298 (1672); vol. III, p. 375 (1705); vol. IV, p. 212 (1727). 'The rudiments of learning' are further defined to 'Read and write' by 1705.

85 Wright, op. cit., pp. 102–5, details six bequests intended to help the poor.

86 Reynolds, op. cit., p. 24 quotes Powell's *Tom of All Trades* (1631):

> Let them learne plaine workes of all kinds, so they take heed of too open seaming. Instead of Song and Musicke, let them learne Cookerie and Laundrie. And instead of reading in Sir Philip Sidney's Arcadia, let them read the grounds of good huswifry. I like not a female poetresse at any hand.

A. Wallas, *Before the Bluestockings* (London, 1929), p. 98, quotes Lady Masham on the religious education of many girls, which she illustrates with the example of the Catholic mother whose response to her daughter's doubts about transubstantiation was, 'What? You are a naughty Girl, and must be whip'd.' Cf. 'She is, it may be, taught the Principles and Duties of Religion, but not acquainted with the Reasons and grounds for them; being told, 'tis enough for her to believe; to examine why, and wherefore, belongs not to her.' Mary Astell, *Serious Proposal*, quoted Woodham Smith, op. cit., p. 113.

87 Reynolds, op. cit., pp. 33–4, 70–1.

88 Ibid., pp. 142, 102; Wallas, op. cit., ch. IV; Notestein, *Four Worthies*, Part III, esp. pp. 141, 179.

89 The reputation of the former is almost certainly greatly inflated by the hyperbole of her biographer, John Batchiler, in *The Virgin's Pattern* (London, 1661).

90 See M. Phillips and W. S. Tomkinson, *English Women in Life and Letters* (Oxford, 1927), p. 70, for Evelyn's encomium on the girls' education during his youth. Cf. Wallas, op. cit., ch. I; Kamm, op. cit., ch. 5. The wild and wilful Betty Verney was finally tamed, after all home remedies had failed, at a girls' boarding-school. The 'Antient Learning' that Mrs Makin was trying to revive may have been that of her own youth, rather than early Tudor times. Reynolds, op. cit., pp. 280–1.

91 See Reynolds, op. cit., p. 259, on the finishing-school role.

92 Ibid., p. 265.

93 Jane Barker, in ibid., p. 162; Aubrey, in Gardiner, op. cit., p. 220; Striller, *The Humourists*, in ibid.

94 Quoted from Shadwell's *Characters*, no. 57, by Phillips and Tomkinson, op. cit., p. 95. Some émigré teachers might have minimal English. Cf. D'Urfey's *Love for Money, or The Boarding School* (1690).

95 Quoted in Wallas, op. cit., p. 61. Cf. the nine-year-old prodigy, quoted from the *Tatler*, No. 141, in ibid., p. 214.

96 In the *Tatler*, No. 79, Steele described Sir Harry Willit reading 'a grave author' in his study, when in rushes his wife 'in a playing humour [and] claps the [pet] squirrel on his folio'. A major row ensues. She accuses Sir Harry of being 'a sower Pedant', and he defends his rage by claiming that 'he was in the highest Delight with that Author'. One of the main culprits was educational incompatibility. Wallas, op. cit., pp. 201–2.

97 Her brother, Dr Pell, knew him through their mutual friend Hartlib. Aubrey, *Brief Lives*, ed. Oliver L. Dick (Harmondsworth, 1962), p. 296.

98 Reynolds, op. cit., pp. 280–1.

99 Ibid., p. 264, has a dialogue between town and country girls, the latter unimproved by rustic education.

100 Quoted from *The Gentlewoman's Companion* (London, 1675), by Wallas, op. cit., p. 44.

101 Wycherley's Mrs Margery Pinchwife in *The Country Wife* (1675), is fairly typical.

102 The faithful Thornton, tutor in the Russell family for two generations, is a good example. Even this stout nonconformist, however, was much less stringent in his demands on the girls than the boys. Gladys Scott Thomson, *Life in a Noble Household*, (London, 1937), pp. 72–8; *The Russells in Bloomsbury*, p. 77. In some families, on the other hand, it might be one of the duties of a mere servant maid to hear the children read. P. Woodham Smith, op. cit., p. 113.

103 Wallas, op. cit., pp. 145ff.

104 P. Woodham Smith, op. cit., ch. 2, on the Ferrars.

105 Wallas, op. cit., p. 20.

106 Phillips and Tomkinson, op. cit., p. 95. Shenstone, born 1714, modelled this character on his own childhood experiences. *D.N.B.*; Reynolds, op. cit., p. 300.

107 Op. cit., pp. 334, 337.

108 F. W. Tickner, *Women in English Economic History* (London, 1923), p. 104.
109 Adamson, op. cit., p. 57, quotes Coote on the mispronunciation taught by both dames and parish clerks around 1600. Vincent, *The Grammar Schools*, pp. 70–1.
110 Quoted from Defoe, *A Tour through the Whole Island of Great Britain* (1724–6) by Tickner, op. cit., p. 82.
111 Gardiner, op. cit., p. 294, on the process in Bristol. Cf. A. Clark, *The Working Life of Women in the Seventeenth Century* (New York, 1920), pp. 9–12, 291–306; Bridenbaugh, op. cit., p. 169.
112 Gardiner, op. cit., p. 278; Bridenbaugh, op. cit., p. 337; Kamm, op. cit., p. 65.
113 Bridenbaugh, op. cit., p. 337.
114 Schofield, op. cit., pp. 310–25. He cites jurors in manorial courts, usually substantial tenants, as an example. Cf. Lockridge to Demos in *A Little Commonwealth* (New York, 1970), p. 22, for bookowners and men known to be writers signing with marks.
115 Schofield, op. cit., p. 321 and n. 1.
116 *Encyclopedia and Dictionary of Education* (London, 1921), vol. II, p. 711.
117 Adamson, op. cit., pp. 38–61. More's 1533 estimate is 'Far more than four parts of all the whole [population of England] divided into ten could never read English yet, and many now too old to begin to go to school.'
118 34–5 H. VIII, c. 1.
119 *Positions*, ed. R. H. Quick (London, 1887), ch. 38, pp. 166ff.
120 Pp. 44, 45, 46, 58.
121 Stone, op. cit., p. 42. For Benefit of Clergy, see Adamson, op. cit., p. 42.
122 Cf. the description in the Duke of Newcastle's *Humourous Lovers* (1667) of 'a Bible under every chambermaid's arm', cited by Stone, op. cit., p. 43. Similar examples in Woodham Smith, op. cit., p. 113 and E. J. Gagen, *The New Woman* (New York, 1954), pp. 95–100.
123 Louis B. Wright, *Middle-Class Culture in Elizabethan England* (Chapel Hill, 1935), pp. 103–18.
124 Ibid.; Bridenbaugh, op. cit., p. 335.
125 Gagen, op. cit., pp. 95–100. An unadulterated diet of romances could have exactly the opposite effect.
126 W. Notestein, 'The English Woman 1580–1650' in *Studies in Social History Presented to G. M. Trevelyan*, ed. J. H. Plumb (London, 1955), p. 80.
127 Margaret M. Verney, *Memoirs of the Verney Family* (London, 1894), vol. III, pp. 72–3, 327. While it could reasonably be objected that Nancy was only nine, she had not greatly improved by her late teens.
128 Clark, op. cit., pp. 15–16; cf. Bridenbaugh, op. cit., p. 335, on the spelling and style of Margaret Winthrop and Katherine Oxinden.
129 *Supplement*, p. 104, quoted in Wallas, op. cit., p. 24.
130 Ibid., p. 126.
131 Quoted in Woodham Smith, op. cit., p. 31. Evelyn does not mention the subject-matter.
132 Quoted by Reynolds, op. cit., pp. 292–3; on Hickes, see pp. 290–2.
133 Quoted from Nos 155 and 165 by Reynolds, op. cit., p. 329. Defoe, Swift and Lady Montagu were, among others, similarly caustic. Wallas, op. cit., p. 112.
134 Ability to write one's name does not necessarily reveal an ability to write anything much else. A signature is more likely in many cases to equate with the ability to read with some fluency. Schofield, op. cit., pp. 323–4. This is a nineteenth-century equation, but should apply to the seventeenth.
135 Sewall, *Diary*, vol. I, pp. 164, 417.

136 E. B. Schlesinger, 'Cotton Mather and His Children', *3 WMQ*, vol. III (1953), pp. 186–7. Katy would need some knowledge of Latin.

137 Locke's influence on education in England in the seventeenth century was probably negligible. M. L. Clarke, *Classical Education in Britain* (Cambridge, 1959), pp. 44–5.

138 Benson, op. cit., pp. 127–8. *The Dogood Papers* appeared in 1722.

139 P. Miller, *The New England Mind: The Seventeenth Century* (Boston, 1961), ch. 3; Morison, op. cit., pp. 31–3; Mather, *Ornaments for the Daughters of Zion*, p. 36.

140 Shipton, op. cit., p. 649.

141 A. W. Calhoun, *Social History of the American Family* (Boston. 1918), vol. I, p. 83. Of her own education, she wrote, 'I was never sent to any school. I was always sick.' She was taught mainly by her grandmother at Mount Woolaston. *D.A.B.*

142 Wilson Smith, 'The Teacher in Puritan Culture', *Harvard Educational Review*, vol. IV (1966), pp. 394–411.

143 Morison, op. cit., p. 93.

144 Quoted from *Dutch Schools of New Netherlands* (1912), p. 229, in Morison, op. cit., p. 83. Martin arrived at an average of 40 per cent women signing their names. Ibid.

145 H. S. Tapley, 'Women of Massachusetts, 1620–89', in *Commonwealth History of Massachusetts*, ed. A. B. Hart (Boston, 1928–9), p. 316. The ability to sign a will, often made on the death-bed, is probably not a very reliable gauge; even the shakiness of the mark, sometimes taken as proof of writing illiteracy, could obviously in such circumstances have physical causes.

146 George Willison, *Saints and Strangers* (New York, 1945), p. 385. Plymouth only copies Massachusetts's educational requirements in 1677.

147 Morison, op. cit., pp. 84–5. He could have cited Franklin and Adams in support. Neither suggested that a high literacy rate was new in mid-eighteenth century women. Wilson Smith, op. cit., p. 395.

148 Communication to Demos, op. cit., p. 22.

149 *Va Mag.*, vol. XXVI (1918), p. 288.

150 Wells, op. cit., p. 43; Wright, *The First Gentlemen*, pp. 102–4. Farnefold was an original trustee of William and Mary.

151 R. Morton, *Colonial Virginia* (Richmond, Va, 1960), vol. I, pp. 350–1. Bruce, op. cit., vol. I, p. 331, dissents: 'There could hardly, in those times, have been found outside the great seats of learning a class more competent to teach than those early Virginian clergy.'

152 Ibid., pp. 328–9.

153 E. S. Morgan, *Virginians at Home* (Williamsburg, 1952), pp. 54–5.

154 Ibid., p. 17.

155 Bruce, op. cit., p. 302. He gives many other examples of bequests designed to cover the education of sons and daughters.

156 He does not give the ratio of the one source to the other.

157 Bruce, op. cit., pp. 454–7. The majority of cases given occurred in or before the 1670s.

158 Ames, op. cit., p. 67.

159 Even the wealthy William Byrd II had to do his reading in the early morning.

Chapter 10

The Vote

The Representation of the People Act of 1918, and the 19th Amendment of 1920 are rightly enshrined in the United Kingdom and the United States as monumental landmarks in the history of the emancipation of women in modern times. Experience may indeed have shown that the effectiveness of these measures was a great deal less than had been anticipated.[1] The suggestion that women have failed to use their voting power, even if true, should not, however, be allowed to shade into an argument that votes for women were themselves relatively unimportant.

In recent years, Robert and Katherine Brown in America, and J. H. Plumb in England, have done signal service in refocusing the eyes of historians of the seventeenth and eighteenth centuries on the grassroots aspect of politics.[2] On both sides of the Atlantic there was a strong urge towards extending voting rights, certainly as far as the lower-middle classes. Robert Brown's study of the franchise in Massachusetts starts only at the granting of the second charter, when the franchise was made to conform with the traditional English requirements. His arguments—greater affluence and a higher cost of living effectively enfranchising the great mass of the male population in Massachusetts in the eighteenth century—obviously would not apply to the first charter period, where the vote in colonial—though probably not local—elections was tied to church membership. None the less, there seems little reason to doubt that the similar picture of 'democracy' for Virginia can be projected back perhaps as much as half a century from the Browns' starting point in 1705.[3] Dr Plumb presents a very persuasive argument in support of his hypothesis that, in the seventeenth century generally and particularly between 1614 and 1628 and between 1688 and 1715, the electorate was very markedly expanded, to include 'a very significant proportion of the male population'. He suggests that England may have been 'far more democratic between 1688 and 1715 than immediately after 1832'. He also emphasises the point made by both Bailyn and Pole that 'the American colonies shared a common political . . . culture with Britain. They were parts of the same polity.'[4] There is a strong probability that this democratic urge in England was a major cause for the demands of early settlers in Massachusetts to have the constitution of the colony changed in favour of representative government for freemen in the 1630s and 1640s.[5]

This background information, which does not have any direct reference to women, indicates that on both sides of the Atlantic there was a groundswell in the direction of more representative institutions. We must now concentrate on the question of whether or not women shared in the benefits of this movement.

On the national and provincial level it can be fairly safely said that they did not. *The Lawes Resolutions of Women's Rights* published in 1632 in London laid it down unequivocally that 'Women have no voice in Parliament. They make no laws, they consent to none, they abrogate none.'[6] During the unstable period of the Civil War and its aftermath women did petition Parliament and on occasions almost besieged it.[7] In the Suffolk election for the Long Parliament in 1640 some women tried to vote, but D'Ewes the High Sheriff disallowed 'what might in law have been allowed'.[8] None the less, I have been able to find no evidence that women ever voted in national elections in England in our period. Women like Lady Anne Clifford might have great influence over elections in areas where they were landowners,[9] but the suffrage was a male prerogative.

So far as the colonies were concerned the picture is not quite so clear, though we can assume that female voting on the provincial level was a rarity. The only woman voter that Albert E. McKinley was able to discover in the seventeenth century was Lady Deborah Moodey, late of Massachusetts, who in the summer of 1655 voted in a New Netherlands election. She was, of course, a woman of very high social standing, and was furthermore the oldest patentee of Gravesend, Long Island, and its civic leader.[10] In 1623 William Bradford and Isaac Allerton found it necessary, because of the rumours circulating in England, to stress that 'Touching our governmente you are quite mistaken if you thinke we admite weomen . . . to have to do in the same, for they are excluded, as both reason and nature teacheth they should be.'[11] Similarly, a Virginian statute of 1699 denied 'undue election by voice or vote of women sole or covert'.[12] Whether this can be taken as a presumption that this measure countered the previous practice of women voting is unclear, though the wording of a similar Act of 1705 suggests that in some cases they may have done. They shall not 'be obliged to appear and give his or her vote at any of the said elections; neither if they do appear, shall they have liberty to vote'. The case of Margaret Brent in Maryland is also significant. A businesswoman who had come to the colony in 1638, she was entrusted with the management of the Calvert estates in the infant colony. On 21 January 1647 she petitioned the assembly, demanding a seat in that body. After her petition had been denied she moved south to Virginia where she founded the Peace plantation in Westmorland County.[13] It is less surprising that her petition should have been denied than that she should have presented it in the first place.

Just because women could not vote on the national or colonial level did not necessarily mean that they were disfranchised on the local level. So far as local affairs in England are concerned, the evidence is rather slight. Notestein, who is concerned with the first half of the century, claims that[14]

> When we look over the records of boroughs, more of which are being published, we find women increasingly mentioned. They complained of abuses in the town; they asked for a better schoolmaster; they proved themselves sometimes zealous puritans and an embarrassment to the vicar.

Where women were allowed to vote in local elections, it was either because they happened to live in particular houses, or because the office was of no importance. Where they held minor offices, the first reason again held, or else the office was so unpopular that the men evaded their responsibilities. For instance, in the judgement on the case of *Olive* v. *Ingram* in 1739, the court held that 'in the absence of proved local custom to the contrary, women rate-payers might vote at the election of sexton, "this being an office that did not concern the public, or the care and inspection of the morals of the parishioners".' That this was not uniform national custom is borne out by some vestry minutes for 1735, denying women any vote, though they might be ratepayers, 'there being no precedent in this parish for the same'. Parishes where women were allowed to serve in minor offices were often equated with incompetent management of their affairs. Where women served as overseers of the poor, so too did poor labourers and even temporary inhabitants. When in Ribchester, Lancashire, in 1674 and 1675, women were appointed overseers because of their 'particular hereditaments', they appointed male deputies to carry out their duties for them.[15] All in all, this evidence does not add up to a very sunny picture for women's political rights, even at the local level. We have already seen William Byrd's sister-in-law bewailing the fact that the menfolk were excluding the ladies from conversation because they were obsessed with 'Politicks and Elections'.[16] At the opposite chronological pole, Joseph Hall in his *Mundus Alter et Idem* (London, 1605), sarcastically pictured Viraginia, or She-Land, where there was that ultimate shambles, full adult suffrage and perpetual sovereign parliaments. It was not, to Hall or to most of his contemporaries, a pretty sight.[17]

I have not been able to find any evidence about women's participation in local elections in Virginia, but there is reason to believe that they were not inactive in New England. Despite the blanket statement in 1639 that 'women do not vote in our church concerns'[18] some churches did indeed allow the female elect a say in their affairs, culminating in the Manifesto of the Brattle Street church in 1699, which quite unequivocally allowed women the vote.[19] Even the proposal by John Cotton that women should be treated unequally over their confessions was not immediately accepted by the Boston congregation.[20]

This seems to have carried over into civil government, to the town meeting. In the early years, church and town meetings might well have had virtually identical memberships.[21] In Sudbury, two women, Jane Goodnow and Mary Loker, who held strips of meadow of the town, were allowed to vote in the crucial debates which led to the emigration of a group of younger men to Marlborough. Both were widows, and so technically could have been regarded as heads of households. The result of the vote was a draw, twenty-seven-all, but there is no record of any protest against the women voting.[22] A woman voted on the question of dividing woodland in Dedham in 1645.[23] The town records of New Haven for 1674 show that women certainly attended town meetings, even though men were allowed preference in seating.[24] In some cases the vagueness of terms makes it unclear whether women voted or not. For example the 'Records of Worcester for 1722' speak of 'all freeholders and inhabitants of ye town be assembled on the last Wednesday of November . . . to chuse all Town Officers. . . .'[25] It seems incontestable that certain women had great influence in town affairs. Elizabeth Poole, for instance, is described on her gravestone at Taunton, Mass., as 'A great proprietor of the township of Taunton, a chief promoter of its settlement.'[26] Similarly, as we saw, Mary Starbuck was 'esteemed as a Judge among' the islanders of Nantucket, and Mary Woodbery of Beverley held a position of great influence in the town in mid-century.[27] Leading women of Boston could make their weight felt in affairs which directly concerned them. When the midwife Alice Tilly was charged with professional incompetence, they petitioned the General Court on her behalf. The petitioners included Ann Cotton, Elizabeth Winthrop, Mary Coggan, Margery Colborne, Lydia Oliver and Elinor Shrimpton.[28]

It has to be admitted that the hard evidence of women voting in town meetings is meagre. This does not necessarily mean that they did not vote. It is very rare in town records of the seventeenth century to be able to discover either who voted, or indeed who was present. The clerks were not recording for distant posterity.

There are, however, one or two suggestions, with which we may conclude this chapter, which imply a tendency towards greater influence for women. The first is the findings of Kenneth Lockridge and Alan Kreider in their article on 'The Evolution of Massachusetts Town Government, 1640–1740'.[29] Their investigations of who really ran the towns of Dedham and Watertown reveal that, up to about 1680, control tended to be in the hands of a fairly small oligarchy, and that much of the crucial town business was decided by this powerful group. After the 1680s, however, they detect a strong democratising process taking place, with many more of the important decisions being taken by the town-meeting itself instead of being merely ratified by it, and the self-perpetuating oligarchy being replaced by a much broader spectrum of townsmen. Something of the same process is recorded by Powell.[30] If this process of the democratisation of the town-meeting is found to be general, it is possible that women may have shared in this opening-up of control. It may be, furthermore, that the granting of the vote in the newly founded Brattle Street church may have been a reflection of this process. In 1733, the *New York Journal* published a letter which read:[31]

> We, the widdows of this city, have had a Meeting, and as our case is something Deplorable, we beg you will give it Place in your *Weekly Journal*, that we may be Relieved, it is as follows.
>
> We are House keepers, Pay our Taxes, and most of us are she Merchants, and as we in some measure contribute to the Support of Government, we ought to be Intituled to some of the sweets of it; but we find ourselves entirely neglected, while the Husbands that live in our Neighborhood are daily invited to Dine at Court.

Now it is, of course, quite possible that John Peter Zenger, the editor, had concocted this epistle himself. But if he had, the question arises why he should have chosen this subject to fill out a column with. It is certainly possible that what appeared mirrored some legitimate female demands. True, they only appear to want to go to dinner, but there is some resemblance to the 'no taxation without representation' principle. It is also worth mentioning that during the Revolution this same principle did not escape the attention of some women. Mrs Corbin, the sister of Richard Henry Lee, presented a protest in 1778 about her having to pay taxes without having the vote, and she proved so forceful in her argument that her brother became an advocate for women's votes. Less persuasive was Abigail Adams who wrote to her husband, John[32]

Remember the ladies and be more generous and favorable to
them than your ancestors. Do not put such unlimited power
into the hands of husbands. Remember all men would be
tyrants if they could. If particular care and attention are not
paid to the ladies, we are determined to foment a rebellion,
and will not hold ourselves bound to obey any laws in which
we have no voice or representation.

Finally, it is the case that the granting of emancipation to women
has often occurred after periods of social upheaval—in the case
of the United Kingdom and the United States after the First
World War. In America, women first generally achieved the franchise in western states and territories, where society was volatile.[33]
Historians are of course by no means agreed on the stability or
instability of colonial societies in the seventeenth century, but it
is worth considering whether the frontier communities of seventeenth-century Massachusetts, and even Virginia, may not have
given women a greater voice in local affairs than was their lot in
England.

Notes

1 Carl Deglar, 'Revolution without Ideology: the Changing Place of Women
in America', in Stephen R. Graubard, ed., *The Women in America,
Daedalus*, vol XCIII (Spring 1964), p. 664; William L. O'Neill, 'Feminism
as a Radical Ideology' in Thomas R. Frazier, ed., *Underside* (New York,
1971), pp. 139–46.
2 Robert E. Brown, *Middle-Class Democracy in Massachusetts, 1691–1780*
(Ithaca, N.Y., 1955); Robert E. and B. Katherine Brown, *Virginia 1705–
1786: Democracy or Aristocracy?* (East Lancing, 1964); J. H. Plumb, 'The
Growth of the Electorate in England from 1600 to 1715', *Past and Present*,
No. 45 (1969), pp. 90–117. See also n. 5 below.
3 Brown and Brown, op. cit., pp. 125–6.
4 Plumb, op. cit., p. 90.
5 Winthrop, *Journal: History of New England*, ed. J. K. Hosmer (New York,
1946), vol. I, pp. 74–5, 77–8, 79, 122–3, 125, 142–3, 302–5; vol. II, pp. 170–4,
116–21. See also Michael Kammen, *Libertyes and Deputyes* (New York,
1969), pp. 20–4. For a full list of recent articles on the vexed question of
the Massachusetts local franchise, see Timothy H. Breen, 'Who Governs:
The town Franchise in 17th Century Massachusetts', *3 WMQ*, vol. XXVII
(1970), p. 460.
6 Quoted in J. C. Spruill, *Women's Life and Work in the Southern Colonies*
(Chapel Hill, 1938), p. 340.
7 Ellen MacArthur, 'Women Petitioners and the Long Parliament', *English
Historical Review*, vol. XXIV (1909), pp. 698–709; Patricia Higgins,
'Women in the Civil War' (unpub. M.A. thesis, Manchester, 1965),
pp. 145–60.
8 Ibid., p. 109.
9 W. Notestein, *Four Worthies* (London, 1956), pp. 158–60.
10 Albert E. McKinley, *The Suffrage Franchise in the American Colonies*
(Philadelphia, 1905), pp. 192–3.

11 *American Historical Review*, vol. VIII (1902–3), p. 299. On the background to this see G. Langdon, *Pilgrim Colony* (New Haven, 1966), p. 79 and 'The Franchise and Political Democracy in Plymouth Colony', *3 WMQ*, vol. XX (1963), pp. 513–26; George Willison, *Saints and Strangers* (New York, 1945), pp. 334ff.

12 W. W. Hening, *Statutes at Large . . . of Virginia* (Richmond, Va, 1809–23), vol. III, pp. 172, 238.

13 Spruill, op. cit., pp. 236–9.

14 W. Notestein, 'The English Woman 1580–1650' in *Studies in Social History Presented to G. M. Trevelyan*, ed. J. H. Plumb (London, 1955), p. 94.

15 Sidney and Beatrice Webb, *English Local Government* (London, 1906), vol. I, pp. 15n., 107, 31, 64, 17.

16 *Va Mag.*, vol. XXXVII (1929), p. 112.

17 C. Hill, *Intellectual Origins of the English Revolution* (Oxford, 1965), E. J. Gagen *The New Woman* (New York, 1954), pp. 163–77 on Amazonian Utopias.

18 H. S. Tapley, 'Women of Massachusetts, 1620–89', in A. B. Hart, ed., *Commonwealth History of Massachusetts* (Boston, 1928–9), p. 309.

19 S. K. Lothrop, *History of the Brattle Street Church* (Boston, 1851), p. 25.

20 D. Rutman, *Winthrop's Boston* (Chapel Hill, 1965), pp. 106, 130.

21 Ibid., p. 65.

22 S. Powell, *Puritan Village* (New York, 1963), pp. 160–1, 204.

23 B. Katherine Brown, 'Democracy in Dedham', *3 WMQ*, vol. XXIV (1967), pp. 387–8.

24 'Records of New Haven', vol. II, p. 319, cited by R. Morris, *Studies in the History of American Law* (New York, 1930), p. 134.

25 *Worcester Historical Collections*, vol. II, p. 9.

26 A. M. Earle, *Colonial Dames and Goodwives* (Boston, 1895), p. 51.

27 A. Starbuck, *The History of Nantucket* (Boston, 1924), p. 520; A. Lapham, *Old Planters of Beverley and their Lands* (Cambridge, Mass., 1930), pp. 68–9.

28 Rutman, op. cit., p. 231.

29 Kenneth Lockridge and Alan Kreider, 'The Evolution of Massachusetts Town Government, 1640–1740', *3 WMQ*, vol. XXIII (1966).

30 Powell, op. cit., chs 7–9.

31 Quoted in E. A. Dexter, *Colonial Women of Affairs* (Boston, 1924), p. 18.

32 A. W. Calhoun, *Social History of the American Family* (Boston, 1918), vol. II, p. 114.

33 A. Sinclair, *Emancipation of American Woman* (New York, 1966), pp. 204–219: 'The early legislators were also ignorant of the prejudices of settled lawmaking bodies; they had not represented others so long that they could feel sure that their own opinions were those of the voters; they were open to intellectual persuasion.' (p. 210) cf. A. P. Grimes, *The Puritan Ethic and Woman Suffrage* (New York, 1967), pp. 8, 9, 13, 76, who argues that western women got the vote because some western men needed it to boost their power.

Chapter 11

The Moral Tone of Society

In this concluding chapter we deal with a vast subject, which helps both to summarise our preceding argument and also to break new ground in two specific areas. We shall not be taking the moral temperature of our three societies at hourly intervals. We shall merely be interested in the ways in which the moral tone of a society affects the status and role of women and vice versa.

The position of women in any society can be both cause and effect of that society's moral values. If women are generally held in low esteem, not only would we reasonably expect male promiscuity, prostitution, exploitation, and a general prurience, but also, conversely, there would be little opportunity for women to reform or influence their unappealing world. Alternatively, if women are generally respected, protected, needed and heeded, then their influence on their milieu will be very powerful. Can we assume, though, that it will be benevolent? Notwithstanding the examples of certain houris, until recent times women, through the very force of their circumstances, have been on the side of respectability. Where women are likely to be left holding the baby, all their influence will work towards its being a legitimate baby. This may depreciate morality to mere expediency, but of such coarse metals are social standards made. In short, as de Tocqueville realised, 'Morals are the work of women.'[1]

Morality in Stuart England

If we examine general statements about the relative moral elevation of English and colonial society in the seventeenth century, we find a highly confusing and contradictory picture. The greatest degree of unanimity lies in the common view that English society in the Stuart period is scandalously corrupt morally, and is daily becoming more so. It is a lament which swells in volume from the beginning to the end of our period, with only a partial intermission half-way. If Queen Elizabeth would have turned over in her grave at the lowered standards of Jacobean times, she would have risen from it at the contemplation of Restoration London. But here the first *caveat* must be entered: London was not England. This is dramatically illustrated by the scene in Shadwell's *The Squire of Alsatia* (1688), in which Belfond, the innocent squireen from the country reacts to London women in conversation with his guide, Shamwell:[2]

> *Belfond*: Sweet rogues! While in the country a pies (pox) take them! There's such a stir with 'Pish! fy! nay, Mr Timothy! What do you now!' I vow I'll squeak, never stir; I'll call out! Ah, ha!—
>
> *Shamwell*: And if one of them happen to be with child, there's straight an uproar in the country, as if the hundred were sued for robbery!

It is certainly hard to imagine Dorothy Osborne's innocent country milkmaids sitting unaccosted and unsullied for long in the shade of the trees in Hyde Park or Mile End Green. To her, the 'Towne Gallant that lives in a tavern or ordinary . . . [and] makes court to all the women he sees . . .' was even viler than the cloddish country gentleman, who might be interested in 'nothing but hawks and dogs and bee fonder of either than of his wife'.[3] Indeed, it was the dullness of country life, and the vacuity of country ladies that contemporaries commented on, rather than rustic vice.[4] Although Roger Lowe was an active and promiscuous country wooer, there is never any suggestion that his courting of local wenches went beyond the bounds of propriety.[5] Finally, the well-established paradigm of the country girl corrupted by London, always has her arriving innocent and virginal. When William Byrd paid visits to the country, the almost nightly bouts of copulation stop, only to start again with renewed vigour on his return to the city.[6]

There are grounds for believing that innocence did not thrive unchecked or unchoked even in the country. It is hardly realistic to separate the capital from the rest of the nation as far as manners and morals were concerned. Not only would we expect London modes to percolate down at least as far as the country gentry, but modern demographic research suggests that a remarkable proportion of the population in the seventeenth century may well have had first-hand experience of London life.[7] There is, furthermore, considerable direct evidence of rural vice. The churchwardens of Thame presented Thomas Heath in 1698 for unlawfully cohabiting with the wife of George Fuller 'having bought her of her husband at 2¼d the pound'.[8] The court records of the first forty years of the century show a high incidence of immorality in the countryside, exacerbated, no doubt, by such frolics as maying, church ales, harvest homes and weddings. In the seventeenth century the number of inns and taverns increased dramatically, and, since in country districts inns served as places of assignation, it seems not unlikely

that their multiplying encouraged rural immorality.[9] Another encourager of promiscuity was almost certainly the Act of Settlement
of 1662, which hindered young men in rural districts from settling
permanently in parishes as cottagers or labourers. Indeed Dorothy
Marshall suggests that the whole operation of the Poor Laws in
England in the seventeenth and eighteenth centuries worked to
undermine the morality of the lower classes.[10] The pastoral idyll
seems more likely to have been a product of romantic imaginations
than an accurate description of country life. *Cold Comfort Farm*
is probably nearer the mark.[11] This is not to deny that morals in
London were more disreputable than elsewhere in the country, but
merely to point out that some of the wide-eyed lads and lasses who
found themselves in the city for the first time were not quite so
ingenuous as tradition would have us believe.[12]

Though criticism of the moral state of the nation was persistent,
it reached its highest pitches at the beginning and the end of the
century. No doubt the reputation of the courts of both James I
and his grandsons had much to do with this. The relief which
courtiers and Englishmen generally felt at the end of 'petticoat
government' in 1603 quickly turned to nostalgia for the dignity,
regality and respectability of the old queen's times.[13] The court
stank of the drunkard's spew, of cloying sexuality, of lavatorial
humour and of reeking, mindless self-indulgence.[14] What went on
at court was then, paradoxically, a good deal more public than
nowadays in an age of mass communications, and if corroboration
were needed of the gossip and rumour circulating, scandals like
the Essex divorce, with its unsavoury revelations about the crimes
of royal favourites, provided it.[15] In 1605, the king comforted
himself with the thought that, if he had not escaped the Powder
Plot, 'It should never have been spoken or written in ages succeeding that I had died ingloriously in an Ale-House, a Stews, or such
vile place.'[16] This, to some, was exactly what his court became.
'The world', lamented Chamberlain, 'is become a brothell house
of sinne.'[17] The controversy over women in the second decade threw
up many attacks on the general decline of respectability of the
times.[18] The criticisms continued up to the Civil War. Quite apart
from being a celebration of chastity, Milton's *Comus* is also a tract
for the times. The tempter Comus, with his orgiastic court and his
worship of sensual pleasures, echoes the mood of the Cavalier
poets of the Caroline period and the coterie theatre then developing.
This, in turn, was the precursor to the more uninhibited lustful-
ness of the Restoration. Laud, who in the moral sense was just as
puritan as a Prynne or a Winthrop, was equally concerned about
the backsliding of his fellow countrymen,[19] and used the High
Commission as a moral as well as a theological censor. Edward

Johnson and other puritan critics used epithets denoting immorality, like 'lascivious' or 'lecherous', in their attacks on their adversaries in England. It is not just Philistia that is being left behind by the new Israelites, but also Sodom and Gomorrah.[20]

The period of the Commonwealth and Protectorate has been described as an interlude in a lecherous century. Certainly reform of manners was seen as a major purpose of government in the 1650s. The campaign against playhouses, alehouses, gaming-houses and other meeting-places with shady reputations was, in part at least, a blow struck for respectability. In 1650 adultery became a crime, a capital one for wives. The apogee of moral rearmament was the rule of those 'satraps' and 'bashaws', the Major-Generals. The detailed instructions in Thurloe show quite clearly that the Lord Protector had mucking-out in mind.[21] In London, brothels were raided and 400 whores transported to the West Indies.[22] In Coventry Major-General Whalley reminded the magistrates of their duty: 'Viz. depress sinn and wickedness, and incourage godlynes.' Worsley was active in the west midlands against drunkenness, swearing and loose living. In Cheshire alone, 200 alehouses were suppressed and couples living in sin punished.[23] Cromwell hailed the work of the Major-Generals as being 'more effectual towards the discountenancing of vice . . . than anything done these fifty years'.[24]

Yet there is grave doubt whether Cromwell's vaunted 'Reformation of Manners' was more than skin-deep. There is the suggestion of this in one of the Protector's later speeches:[25]

> As for profane persons, blasphemers, such as preach sedition; the contentious railers, evil-speakers, who seek by evil words to corrupt good manners; persons of loose conversation— punishment from the magistrate ought to meet with these. Because if they pretend conscience; yet walking disorderly and not according but contrary to the Gospel, and even to natural lights they are judged by all. And their sins being open make them subject of the magistrate's sword, who ought not to bear the sword in vain. The discipline of the army was such that a man would not be suffered to remain there, of whom we could take notice that he was guilty of such practices as these.

England, perhaps fortunately, was not the New Model Army, and the letters of the Major-Generals make it all too clear that what magistrates ought to do was not what they did. The intended millennium of moral uplift seems in retrospect to have been a brief interlude when middle-class respectability tried to drive out the underworld, and only succeeded in pushing it a little deeper.[26]

Among the many things that the Restoration is alleged to have restored, the old cynicism was one. The age of Charles II is almost a byword for lechery. 'At the court of Charles II . . . debauchery was almost a proof of loyalty. . . . Francis North, Lord Guildford, was seriously advised to "keep a whore" because, we are told, "he was ill looked upon for want of doing so".'[27] When Lord Sandwich took a mistress, Pepys recorded the event as his lordship allowing 'himself the liberty which everyone else at court takes'.[28] Of a Sunday, the king would sit and toy publicly at Whitehall with his current mistresses.[29] That court values affected the thinking of the rest of the age is suggested by the derisory award of 100 marks damages to the Duke of Norfolk against the adulterer Germain in 1692, made by the King's Bench jury.[30] The kind of corruption of morals which infected the primly-raised Pepys[31] is even detectable in the writings of nonconformists like John Dunton.[32] As Sedley's Merryman opined, ' 'Tis a mad Age, a Man is laught at for being a Cuckold, and wonder'd at if he takes any care to prevent it.'[33] Evelyn despaired that 'innocence is reputed a mere defect of wit and weakness of judgement'.[34] It is a fitting epitaph to the period, that when the mob was pelting her coach, Nell Gwynne stopped them by yelling 'Peace, good people! I am the *protestant* whore!'[35]

What of women in all this degradation? To read some dramatists and wits, one would think that they, and especially ladies of the court circle and the wives of citizens, were responsible for it. There were of course some notorious libertines among their sex. Yet, to blame women for offering opportunities to gallants is to wield the double standard like a bludgeon. If women as a sex enjoyed very low esteem in England in the seventeenth century, they would hardly have much influence on the deplorable state of moral standards. In that short-lived, cyclonic movement variously called the Reformation of Manners and the Moral Revolution of 1688, in which middle-class respectability grappled with the Medusa's head of vice up and down the land, women played hardly any visible part. Despite the patronage of Queens Mary II and Anne, the reformation societies were dominated by men, as were the S.P.C.K., the S.P.G., and the religious societies formed after 1678.[36] This was in spite of the fact that middle-class woman probably stood to lose most by the prevailing debauchery of the age.[37] This masculine domination of the Societies for the Reformation of Manners is borne out by the suppressive and superficial methods which were favoured. As William Bisset contentiously but accurately claimed about the reformed, 'They may be secretly wicked, lewd and worldly as they please; we won't force them to a heavenly mind. . . . But we would oblige them to be civil upon Earth.'[38] The virtues that the men aimed at spreading were the negative virtues of not swearing, not whoring, not profaning the Lord's day.[39] We may well wonder whether the venom with which they prosecuted prostitutes rather than their customers or masters was not yet another muted example of the double standard. Middle-class respectability, especially on this kind of superficial and nega-tive level, was not likely to be of great benefit to women. On this note, it is also significant that the project of a ladies' college advanced by Mary Astell, which would have provided a real sanc-tuary from gallantry and male licentiousness, was squashed by the opposition of Gilbert Burnet and the sarcasm of Jonathan Swift, both of whom were enthusiastic for a reformation of manners.[40] In the main, women had to remain a silent majority, providing whispered encouragement for male champions like Jeremy Collier, Sir Richard Steele or Daniel Defoe. They supported Collier's campaign against the depravity of the stage; they read the good-humoured barbs against contemporary morals in the *Spectator* and the *Tatler*.[41] Occasionally a still, small voice, like that of Anne Killigrew or the Countess of Winchilsea, was heard amid the masculine hubbub, criticising the profligacy of their times, but it was quickly drowned in the male ridicule of any woman who could wield a pen.[42] Most women with any social awareness presumably confined their activities to the home, where their husbands told them they belonged, and either devoted themselves to private piety or attempted, like Susannah Wesley, 'the mother of Methodism', to educate their children in the direction of virtue.

Colonial Morality

The relative unanimity on the subject of England's, or, at the very least, London's creeping depravity is shattered when we turn to a review of the colonial situation. In Massachusetts the confusion is caused partly by the sharp distinction between contemporary Cassandras, and the praise of more modern commentators. The latter find that the general standard of sexual morality in Massachu-setts was 'unusually high' among the vast majority of inhabitants,[43] and even Thomas Hutchinson, in the middle of the next century, wrote 'we have no evidence of any extraordinary degeneracy' in our period.[44] Yet men at the time, from Edward Johnson and William Bradford to the Mathers, the Pynchons, Samuel Willard or Benjamin Wadsworth, painted a picture of licentiousness on the march. The domestic reasons for this paradox are highly complex, and need not detain us here. It is true that society in Massachusetts was, particularly during the Matherarchy, undergoing a gradual change, so that the Boston described by a visitor like Francis Goelet in 1750 is hardly recognisable as the home of Samuel Sewall, and that *mores* were adapting to a more comfortable, less strato-spheric ideal.[45] None the less, for our comparative purposes, the crucial question is: Were the critics of morality in Massachusetts—the founders there of Societies for the Reformation of Manners,[46] the Synodalists of 1679 or the preachers of Jeremiads—were they attacking a situation similar to that in England? The answer seems to me to be a resounding no. First, if we examine what the New England critics were complaining about, it transpires that it was a great deal more innocent than what worried English counterparts —mixed dancing, the wearing of periwigs, a certain amount of labouring on the sabbath, some extravagance of dress and the use of cosmetics, playing at ninepins and cards, stage-plays and the reading of romances. There had been, in the last decades of the century, some increase in drunkenness and a modest increase in sexual offences.[47] What was being bewailed as profane and profligate was not a land crawling with whores, lechers, sodomites, bastards, sots and blasphemers, but a colony growing more prosperous, worldly, secular and self-indulgent. Even the critics in their saner moments recognised that Massachusetts was still highly respectable by international standards. In a famous passage 'Marvilous it may be to see and consider how some kind of wickedness did grow and breake forth here', William Bradford concedes that[48]

> hear (as I am verily perswaded) is not more evills in this kind, nor nothing nere so many by proportion, as in other places; but they are here more discover'd and seen, and made publick by due serch, inquisition, and due punishment; for ye churches looke narrowly to their members, and ye magistrats over all, more strictly then in other places. Besids, here the people are but few in comparison of other places, which are full and populous, and lye hid, as it were, in a wood or thickett, and many horrible evills by yt means are never seen nor knowne; whereas hear, they are as it were, brought in ye light, and set in ye plaine feeld, or rather on a hill, made conspicuous to ye view of all.

Similarly Cotton Mather accepts that 'New England, being under the greatest "obligations", was to be held criminal for "omissions" which in other countries were more or less normal "commissions".'[49] When New Englanders paused in their orgy of self-criticism, and looked about to see how other societies behaved, they probably agreed with Nathaniel Mather's epitome of them:[50]

> This character may be justly given to them, that they are the best people under Heaven; there being among them, not only less open Profaneness, and less of Lewdness, but also more of

the serious Profession, Practice and Power of Christianity, in proportion to their number than is among any other People upon the Face of the Whole Earth.

This complimentary view is borne out by comparing the 'arm-chair' view of Boston by the English scatologist, Ned Ward, with what the most censorious Bostonian could dream up against his city. Ward's *Trip to New England* is really *The London Spy* with a little New England dressing. His jokes about adultery as revenge on marriage; about fines for public kissing leading to kinder kissing in corners; about women relieving nature in corners; about easily lost virginity; about the industry of the males in bed; about 'Whore Fair' after meeting; and the rest, all fit into the well-worn English anti-puritan convention. It is so much more scurrilous and scabrous than anything that the most querulous local cleric could imagine.

Further corroboration comes from the impact of Englishmen on Massachusetts society, especially during the Restoration period, though we may note in passing the short shrift that such dissolute Englishmen as Thomas Morton or Sir Christopher Gardiner, complete with his whore, received from the authorities in earlier years.[51] The reputation of Massachusetts as a respectable and reformative society in contrast with England seems to have been established as early as the 1640s. The preamble of a law of 1647 reads: 'Whereas sundry gentlemen of quality and others, ofttimes send their children unto this country, to some friends here, hoping (at least) thereby to prevent their extravagant and notoris courses. . . .'[52] The most obvious incursion of English *mores* occurred during the Dominion of New England experiment under the governorship of Andros. The clash of cultures, of reprobate Old England against respectable New England, comes out clearly. The charges against Andros include his implied debauching of Indian squaws after making them drunk and the robbing of Casteen's house; one of his followers admitted his own lechery at Billings's tavern.[53] Sewall infers that Andros, and particularly his followers, introduced a quite unfamiliar wild and ribald element into colony life.[54] We have already seen how such unsuitable immigrants as Laurence Vanderbosk, the renegade Huguenot minister, and Samuel May, the would-be seducer of Boston matrons, were summarily despatched.[55] A final example, slightly reminiscent of Falstaff's confrontation with Justices Shallow and Silence, occurred during the visit to Boston in 1714 of British troops under the command of General Nicholson. About 9 p.m. on a Saturday night, that is, according to Boston practice, part of the sabbath, Sewall, as J.P., with Mr Bromfield and the constable, were summoned to Wallis's tavern in the South End.

There they found soldiers in rumbustious mood, drinking healths to the queen. The ringleader in this fracas, which seems to have been a quite new encounter for Sewall, was the general's secretary, one John Netmaker, who was so insulting and contemptuous in his behaviour that he had to be sent to the cooler for the weekend.[56]

It would be wrong to give the impression that the people of Massachusetts were narrow-minded. Edmund Morgan has persuasively argued that as far as sex was concerned they were the opposite.[57] To them sex did not occupy the almost sacred position which twentieth-century man accords it. John Demos has remarked on the sexual gossip which at times led to civil actions for slander. He sees it as 'an unavoidable part of the larger social atmosphere'.[58] The same impression could be gained from the 'Pynchon Court Record', with its accounts of people calling each other 'base bawdy rogue'; or claiming that a man tried 'to play the rogue' with someone else's wife; or a wife was 'a light woman and that he could have a leap on her when he pleased' or of a young man penning a 'foolish and reprochful Rime upon the Towne and the Maides in Towne'.[59] None the less, it is obviously dangerous to judge a society from the behaviour of its deviants, and the very fact that these cases appear in the records at all suggests that people were considerably more sensitive about sexual innuendo than they were in England.

A good deal more could be said on the subject of respectability in Massachusetts. The fact, for instance, that women could and did regularly travel unaccompanied without fear is surely significant.[60] Puritan teaching about the duty to love Christ above one's fellow men, or women, may also have acted as a form of sublimation for some.[61] However I do not believe that there can be room for much doubt that, while domestic critics might have feared that Massachusetts would slip into the grossness of contemporary English morals, the slide was unslippery, inordinately long and of almost imperceptible gradient.

What of Virginia? To John Winthrop in 1641 it already had a reputation for drunkenness.[62] Half a century later, Durand, himself an abstemious man, was shocked at the amount of beer, cider and punch which the men put away at a wedding breakfast, sousing far into the night until they fell like dead men.[63] We have already met Governor Spotswood having to bribe his servants to remain sober during a formal celebration. Mrs Spruill talks in general terms about men dying in their prime because, among other things, they were 'weakened by intemperance'.[64] Turning to other vices, there was a certain amount of sexual promiscuity among Virginian males, especially with negresses and Indians. At the time of Bacon's Rebellion, the Queen of Pamunkey had had a child by an English colonel.[65] The author of the *Narrative of the Indian and Civil War in Virginia in the Years 1675 and 6* wrote of Lawrence of Jamestown 'and his negress concubine' and of 'soldiers wenches'.[66] A clergyman and burgess with the unlikely name of Bosomworth was married to an Indian.[67] William Gooch wrote to his brother that he had discovered a negro slave who had a cure for venereal disease, 'even the most inveterate pox'.[68]

There were, of course, all sorts of reasons why Virginian society might be expected to fall short of the high standards set by Massachusetts. Already by the end of the century the colony was becoming recognised as a useful dumping ground for 'the wretched refuse' of England. Narcissus Luttrell described how, in November 1692, ' a ship lay at Leith, going for Virginia, on board which the magistrates had ordered 50 lewd women out of the houses of correction and 30 others who walked the streets after ten at night'.[69] This was where Moll Flanders and her highwayman friend ended; in real life their kind was doubtless a good deal less sympathetic than Defoe depicted. Then again, the existence of large numbers of indentured servants was not calculated to improve the tone of society. The fact that, while indentured, they were unable to marry might well encourage already developed vices. The status of servitude would allow a girl poor defences against the advances of her master or his sons. Beggars for labour could not be choosers; any hands—no matter what pockets they had been in, or pistols they had held, or customers they had stimulated—any hands were better than none. When these unfortunates and reprobates had worked out their indentures, they might settle or drift in frontier regions where social control was lax.[70] It is possible, too, that life on isolated, far-flung plantations away from churches and courthouses, where the climate and natural affluence encouraged indolence and leisure, may have been an added spur to low standards. No wonder, then, that Hugh Jones should speak of the people as 'the poorest, the idlest, and worst of mankind, the refuse of Great Britain and Ireland, and the outcast of the people' or that William Byrd should talk of scapegrace 'sotting about with the Dregs of the People'.[71] No wonder either that the government should be concerned about a reformation of manners.

Yet before we see Virginia as a little England, peopled with cuckolders, drunkards and whores, we should look at the other side of the coin. The reports of the two early eighteenth-century governors, Spotswood and Gooch, expatriate Englishmen both, are complimentary of the manners and morals of the colonists. Writing to the Bishop of London in the year of his arrival as governor, Spotswood reported: 'I have observed here less Swearing and Prophaneness, less Drunkenness and Debauchery, less uncharitable feuds and animositys, and less Knaverys and Villanys than in any part of the world where my lot has been'.[72] Gooch, writing privately to his brother, declared that 'the Gentlemen and Ladies here are perfectly well bred', a comment admittedly only on superficial manners rather than the state of morality. Yet later he writes of a young man called Cannon, who had arrived in Virginia with recommendations from the Bishops of Norwich and Salisbury, but who turned out to be 'a shocking bear' and as such was despised by the local gentry.[73] Furthermore, when a tutor called Lefevre arrived from England to take up his appointment at William and Mary in company with an idle hussy, and generally misbehaved himself, drinking and swearing, he was himself discharged and his hussy sent back alone to England. This summary treatment appeared to work a wonderful reformation on him.[74] The contrast between English and Virginian morals seemed, according to Morgan, to work in the opposite direction as well. 'The eighteenth century was an era of great licentiousness and corruption in England', he writes, 'and the boys and girls who were educated there frequently returned with dissipated health, corrupt morals and bad manners.'[75] Perhaps this was one reason why the colony obtained the reputation for reformatory qualities among concerned Englishmen. If much of the vice of England was encouraged by inequalities of wealth and by real economic suffering, then Hammond may have been right in his claim that 'Many, who in England have been lewd and idle, there in emulation or imitation (for example moves more than precept) of the industry they find there . . . grow ashamed of their former courses.'[76] The staggering change in the behaviour of William Byrd on his return to Virginia from the carnalities of London is eloquent witness to a less arrogantly immoral society. It also appears from his diary-entries that the improvement is not merely a superficial one, brought about by lack of opportunity. His private penitences in Virginia, unlike the mere formalities of the London period, are accompanied by virtuous resolutions, which have all the appearance of deep conviction.[77] Though Byrd appears to have been very discreet with the servant girl, Annie, whom he brought to Virginia with him from London, his relations with her, which were, so far as we can tell, pretty innocent, excited comment and criticism in the colony.[78]

The Virginians also give the impression of being more concerned about protecting social morality, both by laws and enforcement, than were authorities in England.[79] For instance, Mrs Spruill shows that successive authorities were worried about the problem of masters of servant girls taking sexual liberties with them, and lists laws and decisions of county courts which were designed to protect these vulnerable women.[80]

Finally, stray hints from many sources suggest that there was a certain innocent and relaxed quality about relations between the sexes which contrast favourably with the innuendo and suspiciousness of English society, where the tendency seemed to be to think the worst. There was far less of that Sicilian atmosphere, where men were assumed guilty of vicious intentions and women must be protected by duennas and incarceration. The Parke sisters, who in many ways were spoilt and self-willed—in London, easy prey for gallants—give every evidence of being chaste. Indeed, when Byrd tried to take liberties with Mrs Chiswell, he was left in no doubt at all by either her or his wife that this was not on. There was gossip among the women, but it was frowned on. When Frances Custis was to go to Mrs Harrison's in the coach, she refused to go alone with Dr Cocke, 'out of her great modesty'. It seemed not at all unusual for men to visit women innocently while their husbands were absent, or for women to drive or ride unaccompanied by men. The master and mistress at Westover kept a close watch on the morals and manners of their slaves and servants and punished backslidings.[81] Foreign visitors remarked upon the unabashed hospitality which women in Virginia offered them; there was none of the slur which might well have accompanied such invitations in England.[82] Even the freedom accorded girls in their courtship argues for a far healthier and trustful social atmosphere.

We can clearly only come to very tentative conclusions about the moral state of Virginian society in the face of this conflicting evidence. There do seem grounds for thinking, with Bailyn, that the community was by the turn of the century achieving a social stability which it had lacked earlier in its development.[83] It also seems likely that by this time the families that were to form the great eighteenth-century aristocracy were exhibiting fairly high standards of personal and group conduct, which could be expected to percolate downwards. There were, it is true, 'dregs', many inveterately vicious from their English schooling, but economic opportunity and the example of superiors could be expected to redeem all but the utterly unreclaimable. Around 1700, slaves were beginning to be imported in greatly increased numbers, but that particular cloud in the moral climate was only hand-sized for most of our period. All in all, it appears that Virginia occupied a middle ground between England and Massachusetts, but that to equate its standards with those of England would be a serious insult.

Sexual Promiscuity

Two aspects of the moral tone of a society which may help to corroborate these rather impressionistic findings in a more quantitative way are the comparative incidences of prostitution and of fornication. Neither is, of course, an infallible yardstick, even if anything like accurate figures are available. Societies may well not regard certain kinds of fornication as immoral at all, and where it is thus approved or winked at, prostitution may decline.[84] However, for the seventeenth century, on both sides of the Atlantic, it is safe to say that there was pretty general social disapproval for both extra-marital and commercialised sex activities.

There is a great deal of evidence to support the contention that prostitution in London—and to a lesser extent, in the country at large—was a major social problem throughout the seventeenth century. Writing in 1609 of his visit to the capital, the German, Offenbach, noted that in Southwark[85]

the continuous row of houses which exists to the west was formerly given over to Brothels, but in the time of Henry VIII they were prohibited. . . . We are not ignorant that in various places whole streets are found to be full of such wares [whores] and, officially prohibited, these quarters are tolerated by con-niving eyes.

In his *Christs Teares* (1598), Thomas Nashe was far more out-spoken.[86]

London, what are thy suburbes but licensed stewes? Can it be so many brothel-houses of salary sensuality and sixepenny whoredome (the next doore to the Magistrates) should be sett up and maintained, if brybes did not bestirre [?] them. . . . Whole Hospitals of tenne times a day dishonest strumpets have we cloystered together. Night and day the entrance is as free as to a Tavern. Not one of 'em but has a hundred retayners, Prentises, & poore Servaunts they encourage to robbe theyre Maisters. Gentlemens purses and pockets they will dive into and picke, even while they are dallying with them. . . . Halfe a crowne or little more (or sometimes less) is the sette price of a strumpet's soul.

On 20 August 1620, true bills were found against nineteen women brothel-keepers in the Middlesex Quarter Sessions.[87] Certain areas of London were notorious for prostitution in the age of James I. One of these was Saffron Hill, especially Charterhouse Lane, where 'notorious and common whores . . . are entertained into divers houses for base and filthy lucre sake to the private benefitt of Landlordes and Tennanters', and where 'infamous queanes' sit at doors and 'by their Wanton and impudent bahaviour doe allure . . . such as passe by that way'.[88] The borough of Southwark, despite the actions of Henry VIII, also retained its low reputation, especially the Paris Garden area. Here was the famous brothel with its Dutch madam which was the inspiration for Nicholas Goodman's salacious comedy *Hollands Leaguer* (1632). Here also it cost £20 for gentlemen merely to have dinner with the queen of queans, Bess Broughton—let alone postprandial exercise.[89] The Strand and Fleet Street were also, according to Vaughan, red light districts:[90]

> . . . riotous sinful plush and tell-tale spurs Walk Fleet Street and the Strand, when the soft stirs Of bawdy ruffled silks turn night to day.

It says something about this pre-Civil War era that one of its heroines was Moll Cutpurse, a notorious baggage christened Mary Frith, whore, pick-pocket, forger and fortune-teller, immortalised by Dekker and Middleton as Mad Merry Moll in *The Roaring Girl* (1610).[91] So far as I have been able to ascertain, there are no figures for prostitutes in the earlier part of the century, but there seems little doubt that the statement that there had been a 'great increase and frequency of whoredoms and adulteries', made in the *First and Large Petition of the City of London* in 1641, is probably justified.[92] Prostitutes seem to have been a commonplace sight. Bridenbaugh, in discussing country vice in the earlier Stuart period, suggests that the incidence of prostitution there was also rising. The operation of the Poor Laws of the end of Elizabeth's reign would encourage the growth of the profession, and the declining economic opportunities available to women exacerbated the situation.[93] In 1640, Exeter even went to the length of ordering the provision of a cart for punishing whores.

Although the Restoration period affords copious references to the superfluity of prostitutes in London in general terms,[94] the earliest suggestive figures I have found are in the Black Lists compiled by the Societies for the Reformation of Manners. Of course, in their eagerness to advertise their success, the members may have somewhat inflated their totals, and anyway, in their early campaigns, they attacked not only brothel-keepers and bawds, but also those who profaned the sabbath or swore. However, some of the Black Lists are very detailed, and were often drawn up by men who, in their normal businesses, placed high premiums on accuracy and careful recording. In their *Twenty-Sixth Account of the Progress Made* (1719), they claimed that 'the total number of Persons prosecuted by the Society in and around London only, for Debauchery and Prophanity, for the Thirty Years last past are calculated at 75,270'. One of the earliest groups to get the reforming bug was in the Tower Hamlets region. They claimed that in less than two years they had 'routed those naughty houses, which formerly abounded amongst them and brought to due punishment seven or eight hundred criminals'.[95] In the early Black Roll of 1694, 103 keepers of bawdy houses are named and 197 night-walkers and pliers in bawdy houses.[96] Woodward's *Account of Societies for Reformation of Manners* speaks of forty or fifty 'of that pestilent generation of night-walkers' being sent to bridewells in a single week.[97] The 1698 Black List contains 752 lewd and scandalous persons successfully prosecuted. The overwhelming majority of names are those of women, and the great majority of these are prostitutes or madams —over 90 per cent of the total. The *Eleventh Blacklist* contains 830 names, again almost entirely female and bawdy. Admittedly some are repeaters: Hannah Hussey, for instance, had six convictions during the year and Mary Sanford ten. None the less, the number of different names is over 700.

These totals may at first glance appear to be very low, and to suggest that the problem was exaggerated by the craze for reformation of manners. The population of London has been estimated at 575,000 in 1700, and these few hundred annual convictions seem a drop in the ocean of humanity. Yet there are several reasons for believing that the total numbers caught were only a fraction of the total. First, prostitution is a notoriously difficult offence to detect or to prove, especially when its practitioners are forewarned that a campaign is being launched against them. Second, the activities of the Reformation Societies—eight at the height of the movement —could not hope to cover the whole city and suburbs. Most important, the methods used by the societies to achieve convictions would rapidly tend to become counter-productive. They relied, after the first flush, on using constables and paid informers to furnish evidence for their prosecutions. But, as Ned Ward—who in this area had some claims to expertise—pointed out in 1698, the constable or informer might well find it more profitable and comfortable to become a protection racketeer, only turning in the poor whore who could not afford the 2s 6d hush money. By 'squeezing whores' financially, the searcher actually 'puts them upon fresh villainies to keep themselves from starving'. He continues, 'Each bawdy house they break into is a weekly stipend taken out of their own pocket. . . . The only good the constables have done is to put a sort of socket money upon whoring, and themselves are collectors of the tax'. Ward describes the searchers as easily corruptible; they are 'a parcel of loose fellows and self-serving profligates'.[98] Ward, of course, had little time for the whole campaign. He may, in a formal and feigned kind of way, admit that 'vice, 'tis true, is grown to a great and lamentable pitch in this wicked age we live in', but as a publican and debunker of puritanism, he had little to gain from a thorough-going disinfection of the stews. What is certain is that the campaign was a failure in the long term; indeed, from the number of repeaters on some of the Black Lists, it does not seem to have deterred even for short periods. *A View of London and Westminster, Or The Town Spy,* whose second edition was published in 1725, claimed that

There are reckon'd to be 107 Pleasure-Houses within and about this settlement [the hundred of Drury] the Ladies whereof ply the Passengers at Noon-day. . . . A Romish Priest, who has lodged here many years, assures me that to his Knowledge the Societies for the Reformation of Manners have taken more pains and expended as large sums to reclaim this Sodom as would have fitted out a Force sufficient to have conquered the Spanish West Indies.

But all this internal defence expenditure was about as lastingly fruitful as that expended on the Cartagena expedition. Later in the eighteenth century, Saunders Welch, a reforming J.P., wrote of the fact that 'Prostitutes swarm in the streets of this metropolis to such a degree, and bawdy houses are kept in such open and public manner, that a stranger would think that . . . the whole town was one general stew'. He went on to voice his conviction that a computation of 3,000 prostitutes from information in the Bills of Mortality for the city 'falls far short of the truth'.[99] In George III's reign, the philanthropist Jonas Hanway computed that 3,000 Londoners died annually of venereal diseases.[100] In 1770 it was stated that there were 50,000 prostitutes in London, and in the same year John Fielding listed the numbers of brothels and 'irregular taverns' in various parts of the city—about thirty, for instance, in St Mary-le-Strand alone, or twenty in Hedge Lane.[101]

Unfortunately I have not been able to discover any figures for the incidence of prostitution outside London. Only one provincial reformation society, that of Bristol, kept minutes which have been recovered. These record information about several bawdy houses and prostitutes in the city and possibly in the surrounding country, but there is nothing so detailed as the London Black Lists.[102] It does, however, seem likely that provincial towns, and especially the outports, shared the social problems of London, only to a lesser extent. The number of whores who were seized at Leith in one swoop in 1692—eighty—is staggering.[103] Something between 9,000 and 12,000 women were transported to the American mainland colonies alone in the first seventy-seven years of the eighteenth century. A large majority of these included prostitution among their crimes, and a sizeable minority were non-Londoners.[104] From this admittedly very sketchy material, it seems safe to conclude that prostitution was a scandal in the capital, and a serious social problem in certain parts of the provinces.[105]

Hunt the whore was not the test for Londoners that it was for colonists intent on a lecherous adventure.[106] Indeed, whore-hunting in Boston in the seventeenth century was like trying to find a nettlehead in a haystack. The word 'whore' defined in its non-commercial sense is quite commonly used;[107] it was often thrown around in neighbourly feuds: thus, Widow Hale was charged with slander for 'saying that the wife was a whore and that shee had severall children by other men, and that Cuckoldlay old Rogue her husband owned them',[108] but there is very little evidence that prostitution existed, let alone flourished, even in the ports of the Bay Colony. Josselyn, it is true, suggests that there was prostitution, but Parkes, I think rightly, regards his evidence on this point as unreliable.[109] There is some suggestion that one Alice Thomas in 1672 kept a whore-house in Boston, but, if indeed the entertainment she allegedly provided was of a bawdy nature, it was quickly suppressed by the General Court.[110] There are other examples of promiscuous women in the colony, but no evidence at all that they traded for cash or walked the streets.[111] Two other tenuous pieces of evidence for the seventeenth century come from church records. The Boston church in 1653 dealt with one James Everill for, among other things, frequenting a house of ill report and in 1694 a woman was excommunicated from the Roxbury church for bawdery.[112] In neither case, however, is there any evidence of follow-up by either the church or civil authorities. Brothels and prostitutes did appear in Boston in the eighteenth century,[113] but what is remarkable is that this thriving seaport, with a population approaching 10,000 by the end of the seventeenth century, should have managed to maintain such high standards of public respectability for so long.[114]

About Virginian prostitution there is little direct evidence. On the two occasions when William Byrd tried to find a woman on the streets of Williamsburg, in 1720 and 1721, he was unlucky. When he made an assignation at the old plantation with Jenny, who had already endured two hours' kissing and breast-pawing, 'the whore did not come'.[115] It seems reasonable to assume that the absence of cities and the dispersion of settlements would have militated against prostitution, even though female immigrants may have arrived with pretty shady pasts. There was probably some exploitation of female indentured servants and of slave-girls, but it is very difficult to estimate its frequency.

Some very interesting research has been done in recent years on the subject of premarital fornication in pre-industrial England by Dr P. E. H. Hair.[116] His inquiries cover the period from the beginnings of registration in parish records in the sixteenth century to the second half of the eighteenth century, and his second paper attempts to deal more thoroughly than the first with the sixteenth and seventeenth centuries.[117] The two main findings which concern us are first that the average numbers of pregnant brides—based on baptism within eight-and-a-half months of marriage—runs in the earlier two centuries at a fairly steady 20 per cent. Hair's earlier suggestion that there was a markedly higher rate of bridal pregnancy in northerly parishes is largely refuted by his later findings. He also implies that there does not seem to have been any very noticeable increase over this two-century period. His second conclusion is that the eighteenth century saw a very striking increase in bridal pregnancy rates to between 30 and 40 per cent.[118]

In his second article, Hair briefly examines the possible causes for this seventeenth-century English rate of bridal pregnancy. There are two plausible theories to explain the situation. One, which is supported by Laslett in *The World We Have Lost,* is that there were social dispensations to betrothed couples permitting, or at least, condoning sexual intercourse.[119] This betrothal-licence theory is borne out, according to Laslett, by the relatively low bastardy rate, and more strongly, according to Hair, by the fact that before 1700 a majority of early babies had been conceived within three months of the marriage ceremony. None of this, however, rules out the shotgun wedding theory, that is, that betrothal *followed* pregnancy rather than vice versa. It is, from the extant evidence, almost impossible to choose between the two, but, even if the shotgun theory is preferred, it does argue that the custom of making an honest woman out of a pregnant girl-friend may have persisted to the end of the period, although the evidence is relatively scanty.

There are two contributory factors raised by Hair which also concern us. He tends to reject the theory that the traditionally prohibited seasons of marriage, Lent, Whitsuntide, Advent and Christmastide, operated in the seventeenth century as a frustrater of legitimate sex for the hot-blooded. There does still seem to have been considerable hostility to Lenten marriages throughout the seventeenth century, but prohibitions of Advent marriages were already being lifted in the early decades, thus removing the opening months of what could, with an early Lent, be an almost continuous five-month closed season on matrimony.[120] Second, he is not able to show the correlation, if any, between bridal pregnancy revealed in church records, and presentments for fornication made subsequently by the churchwardens to the ecclesiastical courts, because the extant printed records only rarely coincide. His suspicion is that churchwardens tended to turn a blind eye towards offenders;

that there was little shame attached to bridal pregnancy in English communities; and that the penance which 'luckless pairs' had sometimes to perform in churches was little more than a formality, simply because in most communities the fact of the sin would long have been common knowledge.[121]

Hair's investigation deals only with the most easily quantifiable area of premarital immorality. Even here, of course, his figures can only, as he admits, be approximations; the nature of the records makes it difficult to allow accurately for girls who married outside their families' parishes, or for those whose first babies were stillborn, or who miscarried, and his percentage of the total does not take into account those women who were childless, which would raise the percentage of fertile women who were pregnant brides. Maurice Ashley has done some sampling of Quarter Sessions and Church Court Records in an effort to look at the problem in the broader area of extra-marital fornication, whether it led to early babies or to bastards. He finds that bastardy and premarital intercourse were a 'widespread evil'. The 'Oxfordshire Records' suggest that a potent cause of the trouble was male breach of promise. In the 'Wiltshire Quarter Sessions Records' for the year 1578 there were eighty-four bastardy cases. The annual averages of bastardy cases in the records that he has examined vary from thirty to eighty. In a six month period from September 1623 to April 1624 there were sixty cases of immorality from twenty-nine parishes in the Archdeacon's Court at Taunton; twelve of these were for prenuptial intercourse. Ashley concludes that it would be wrong to think that sexual offences were 'extremely common' or that 'illegitimacy in the sixteenth and seventeenth centuries exceeded that of, say, the Victorian age'.[122] This view seems to be corroborated by Laslett and Oosterveen's work on illegitimacy, as reported in the second edition of The World We Have Lost.[123] Their figures from twenty-four parishes show that the percentage of baptisms marked 'illegitimate' in the records was 4.3 in the decade 1601–10, dropping gradually to 2.1 in 1641–50 and then dramatically to 0.5 in 1651–1660. Surprisingly, the percentages for the last four decades of the century rose only from 1.6 to 1.9 in the sample. Locally, the bastardy ratios of the west and north were higher in the early decades of the century than those of central, southern and eastern England. However, there is some evidence that women who had a series of bastards may have had a considerable effect on 'fluctuations in the illegitimacy rate'. Although these figures are the most precise that we currently possess, we must suspend both judgement and disbelief until the publication of the full study. As they stand, these data certainly conflict with the conclusions of other scholars on the illegitimacy situation.

Bridenbaugh argues that bastardy was on the rise as the century progressed, and that it was not confined to the lowest orders in town or country. It was not uncommon among the yeomanry, and clergy were not altogether free from suspicion in several cases. In 1609 a statute complained that 'great charge ariseth upon many places within this realm by reason of bastardy'. The country wench with 'the mischance of a great belly caught at a Whitsun-ale' was a commonplace type of the whole period.[124] Dorothy Marshall links the startling rise in the illegitimacy-rate in the eighteenth century with the harsh Settlement Act of the Restoration and argues that the number of bastards was most probably on the increase well before the end of the Stuart century. She claims 'that the habit of disregarding marriage became common' then, and that the problems of marrying and finding accommodation for the poor were greatly exacerbated by a lowering of real wages—further deferring the age at which people could afford to marry—and by the inhuman actions of parish officials who were concerned above all else to keep down the Poor Rates—which might well be inflated by a rash of 'fatherless' bastards. The hovels in which the unsettled poor had to live, the workhouses to which they might be condemned, or the common lodging-houses, especially in London, to which they were forced to resort, were all encouragements to promiscuity and sexual vice. Henry Fielding described a typical lodging-house in the London slums in the eighteenth century:[125]

> These beds, several of which are in the same room, men and women, often strangers to each other lie [in] promiscuously, the price of a double Bed being no more than 3d. [single beds cost 2d.] as an Encouragement to them to lie together: That as these places are adapted to Whoredom.

Finally, the pernicious system of binding out pauper children, bastards and orphans to unsupervised masters in the interests solely of reducing the Poor Rate, meant that large numbers of poor girls would be at the sexual, as well as economic, mercy of their 'guardians'. The same lamentable results were also likely to occur from the operations of the double standard and the hierarchical class system. As Defoe, Steele and Jeremy Collier pointed out at the end of the century, the aristocratic or middle-class seducer would retire, unscathed or with his reputation enhanced by his exploits, while his big-bellied victim would be condemned first to the bridewell, and ultimately to a life of prostitution and early death.[126]

The situation in the colonies was, predictably, a great deal less distressing. It would have been superhuman, even of the Pilgrim Fathers or the builders of a 'cittie upon a hill', to have expected to suppress fornication altogether in their settlements, and cases occur from the early days of both plantations. None the less, the frequency does appear to have been a good deal lower than in England, and this despite the fact that betrothal licence was incorporated into the laws of Plymouth, and was the accepted practice of the courts in fornication cases in Massachusetts.[127] Despite this 'open invitation to sexual licence', however, there were only twenty-four cases of premarital fornication in Plymouth, between the years 1633 and 1661. The next seventeen years saw a rise in this very low average, with forty-one cases, several of which involved such important families in the plantation as Whites, Robinsons and Cushmans. Had the criterion been the fortnight short of nine months that Hair uses, the total might have been higher, but in Plymouth action was only taken if the birth occurred within seven-and-a-half months of marriage.[128]

Both the church and the court records of Massachusetts provide figures for fornication. As Oberholzer warns, the church records must be handled with care, since not only are they sometimes incomplete and refer to church members rather than the whole congregation, but also in a significant number of cases, later generations performed atavistic whitewashing jobs by excising their ancestors' sins from the records. From this source, he arrives at an overall annual average for all sexual offences of 5.64 over the period 1620–1839—including Plymouth churches. For the period 1730–1769, where the records are particularly complete for the same areas, the average works out at slightly less than seventeen cases a year. There is, however, considerable danger in trying to project this average back to the previous century, because it is well known that this period of the eighteenth century saw a very marked rise in sexual misdemeanours, and it may well be that the seventeenth-century average was less than half of this.[129]

This rise is reflected in Henry Bamford Parkes's studies of the secular court records in the seventeenth and early eighteenth centuries. He finds that the annual average number of fornication cases in Essex county before 1660 was two, rising to ten in the later part of the century and to twenty-six between 1700 and 1740.[130] Similarly in Middlesex county, the annual average for the whole seventeenth century was five, but after 1719 it rose to twenty-two. The Hampshire average of one a year rocketed to ten after 1711.[131] The incidence of fornication in the 'Suffolk County Court Records' between 1671 and 1680 is somewhat higher, but this is to be expected, because it was an area of relatively high population-density and the period was one of grave disquiet in the colony, a disquiet which culminated in the Synod of 1679. There are twenty cases of premarital fornication and forty-three other cases of fornication between couples who did not subsequently marry, and who received markedly harsher punishments. Only thirteen men were brought to trial as the putative fathers of the children borne by the forty-three girls, and they, of course, were required to give bond for maintaining the bastards that they had sired. One can only speculate on the reasons for this. In some cases the girls probably concealed their lovers' names, in the manner of Hester Prynne. It is not impossible that in some cases the fathers were transient visitors, like seamen or militiamen during King Philip's War. At least four of the girls charged with fornication were negresses, and many more were probably indentured servants, who dared not ascribe their children to their masters or masters' sons. Within the nine-year period of the published records, the average for the first four years was just over six cases a year, and for the last five just under eight.[132]

Assuming that the number of cases did not increase in the next decade, it is possible from these figures to compute a very crude illegitimacy rate for Suffolk County, which makes a useful comparison with the Laslett-Ooversteen figures for England. The population of Suffolk in 1690 was probably in the region of 12,000.[133] Assuming a birth-rate of thirty-five per thousand, the number of births each year would be in the region of 420. This would render the illegitimacy rate for the county around 1·6 per cent. Remembering that Suffolk was not only the most populous county, but also that most exposed to vice, including as it did the international port of Boston and the large maritime town of Dorchester, our initial claim is probably borne out. It is given greater credibility by the fact that the percentage of illegitimate births in the fishing-port of Ipswich was 0·5 for the seventeenth century.[134]

Averages within other townships in or bordering on the colony vary considerably. In Bristol, Rhode Island, for instance, there were no cases of premarital fornication discovered between 1680 and 1720.[135] It was a new settlement in 1680, and seems to have had a majority of middle-aged couples in its population of seventy-odd households. The mean age of marriage up to 1750—23·9 for men and 20·5 for women—seems to have been somewhat lower than in other towns. Greven finds that the rate of premarital intercourse in Andover between 1658 and 1699 averaged 9·4 per cent, but his criterion is marriages which produced offspring within nine months of the wedding, which might therefore include a significant percentage of premature babies conceived in wedlock.[136] Charles Francis Adams's study of sexual morality in Braintree, with a population of around 700 in the last quarter of the seventeenth century, turns up only four cases of sexual immorality among church members in thirty-six years, and one of these was a case of technical incest, that is marrying a deceased wife's sister. Of course, the morality of saints would be expected to be of a far higher standard than that of the unregenerate.[137] Finally, the 'Pynchon Court Record Book' (1639–1702) contains eleven fornication cases occurring between 1655 and 1686. Two of these were premarital cases, and another was belatedly converted into one by the father agreeing to marry the mother. The distribution of these cases is markedly heavier at the end of the period.[138]

Although it has not always been possible to convert totals into the rates as given by Hair, there seems none the less little doubt that the rate of fornication, including premarital intercourse, was markedly lower in Plymouth and Massachusetts than it was in England. In this connection, it is perhaps significant that Hair finds that the corresponding rate for Scotland, another puritan-dominated area, in the same era was around 7 per cent, compared with 20 per cent for England.[139] It is more than likely that the recorded number of cases in Massachusetts would be much nearer the total number of actual breaches of the moral code than in England. The church members, or, after 1662, owners of the half-way covenant, frequently confessed their sins in order to obtain baptism for their children.[140] The authorities were also more constantly vigilant in bringing sinners to book, and were deeply concerned throughout our period with any declension of manners. The earlier marriage age, and the greater freedom of choice of marriage partner, both reflections of greater economic opportunities, would discourage fornication caused by sexual frustration. The balance of the sex ratio and the strong popular pressure in favour of marriage would act in similar directions. All in all, the evidence on fornication goes far to buttress the conclusion that the moral tone of the Bay Colony provided an object-lesson to Old England.

It is more difficult to reach such firm conclusions on the frequency and rate of fornication in Virginia. There seems good reason for believing that it occupied a middle ground, as in other subjects of this book, between England and Massachusetts. It seems likely that a very significant number of offences were either never presented by the churchwardens, or were dealt with by the courts in the form of bastardy cases, because of concealment. Many, perhaps even most, of the women guilty of fornication were indentured servant-girls. Their masters had strong motives for reporting their offences if the father was another servant or came from off the plantation, because the master could legally claim extra service from the girl for the time that had been lost through her pregnancy, confinement and nursing. In mid-century this extra service was often as long as two years, but it was reduced by the statute of 1696 to one year.[141] By the statute of 1657–8 and by the practice of many county courts, the master might be required to pay the fine on behalf of his female servants, who recompensed him by further service. Similarly, the churchwardens had the motive of 'saving the parish harmless' from supporting the child, by discovering the reputed father and extracting some kind of security for the child's maintenance. In these cases, the motives for uncovering fornication were strong, and detection likely. But it is probable that a large number of fathers of the bastards born to indentured servant-girls were in fact either their masters or masters' kin. Governor Nicholson referred to this practice as 'a serious grievance', even after the legislature had, in 1672, closed the loophole which allowed a master to claim extra service from the girl, even though he had fathered the child on her. If the master himself, or one of his sons, or even his overseer, had had intercourse with the girl, his motive veered sharply from detection to concealment. He stood not only to be fined or flogged for his own sin, but also to have to give bond to maintain the bastard. Above and beyond this was the moral obloquy which he was likely to incur from his own class. Even if a charge were preferred against the girl for bearing a bastard, the master could exert great pressure on her to withhold the father's name, and it seems to have become the practice of several county courts by the end of the century not even to bother to discover the reputed father. Bearing in mind the general shortage of women in Virginia, and the probable moral background of many of the women who migrated to the colony, and the fact that indentures prevented servants from marrying, we should reasonably expect a pretty high rate of extra-marital intercourse. However, the factors cited above make it extremely difficult to compute with any accuracy what the fornication-rate was.

Bruce did attempt to gather together the extant evidence on bastardy and fornication in those county court records of the seventeenth century that have survived.[142] He insists that the relatively common breaching of the law 'was not due to any lack of strictness on the part of the authorities in enforcing the laws designed to discourage this form of immorality'. From eight county records, some of which only span short periods, he lists about 120 cases of fornication and bastardy and sexual immorality. Some of these were certainly cases of premarital fornication; of the twelve indictments for incontinence in Lower Norfolk in 1654, for instance, nine of the consequent children were born in wedlock. At least two of those indicted were negresses. In 1688, Colonel Custis had three servant girls who had had bastards. The frequency of cases does seem to have risen after mid-century, when the number of immigrant indentured servant-girls greatly increased.

It is, unfortunately, impossible to compute a rate for the colony comparable with the figures we have given for England and Massachusetts. We must make do with Bruce's conclusion:[143]

> When we consider on the one hand, the size of the Colony's population, and, on the other, the comparatively small number of prosecutions for offences of this character, in spite of the extraordinary watchfulness of the authorities, an impression is created that the communities of Virginia, during the Seventeenth century, were proportionately far more exempt from these forms of viciousness than contemporary England itself.

The ingredients which go towards the concoction of the moral tone of a society are many and of often subtle flavour. Indeed it may well be misleading to write of moral tone as though it were a monolithic, universally held concept. Who and what form the opinion-formers is still very much a live issue today. Plainly, many of the subjects which we have been discussing throughout this book would have some effect on the prevailing moral tone—however this may be subdivided among different classes, different areas, different religious, political or ideological affiliations. Religious beliefs, the economic situation, the proportion or disproportion of the two sexes, the role and effectiveness of government, the quality and availability of education, and the philosophy and precedents of the law all spring to mind as conditioning agents. Nor do developed societies exist in vacuums of time or space. Inherited traditions and imported customs play a vital part in their development.

Yet to accept this multiplicity of factors does not, I think, invalidate our initial contentions that women may have a very marked impact on the moral tone of a society, and that the esteem or contempt in which they are held at any given time will be reflected in the relative respectability or licentiousness of accepted standards. The evidence that we have presented strongly suggesting that both commercialised and extra-marital sex were more common in seventeenth-century England than in either of the colonies under study gives weight to our general thesis that women enjoyed a higher social standing in America than they did in England. What motives lead a woman to a life on the streets or a leap between the sheets will obviously vary widely with the individual and with the times. Individual motives will, however, be encouraged or restrained by the trends of the times. The economic influences on the prevalence of prostitution—and to a lesser extent on fornication—which the sociologists and economic historians stress are plainly important. Yet they should not be exaggerated. Strong religious beliefs in societies with low economic expectations may well outweigh economic forces encouraging the sexual exploitation of women.

Death may be a real alternative to dishonour. Anyway, a society so economically organised as to encourage such exploitation can hardly be seen to hold women in high esteem. Arguments that prostitution protects the morals of a society are, as Keith Thomas points out, both male-oriented and appear to treat women as a species of property.[144] Similarly, pre-contraceptive societies which fail to curb fornication will almost always be male-dominated societies, where the double standard rules. A society which condones the use of women as a satisfier of the male libido is by definition an anti-feminine society.

Notes

1 A. de Tocqueville, *Democracy in America* (New York, 1947), p. 391.

2 Thomas Shadwell, *The Squire of Alsatia* (1688), Act I, scene i.

3 M. Phillips and W. S. Tomkinson, *English Women in Life and Letters* (Oxford, 1927), p. 52.

4 Cf. W. Notestein, 'The English Women 1580–1650' in *Studies in Social History Presented to G. M. Trevelyan*, ed. J. H. Plumb (London, 1955), p. 80.

5 Roger Lowe, *Diary*, ed. W. L. Sachse (London, 1938), *passim*.

6 *London Diary*, e.g. pp. 147, 176. He was staying with friends and therefore under the frustrating obligations of a guest.

7 H. Moller, 'Sex Composition and Correlated Culture Patterns in Colonial America', *3 WMQ*, vol. II (1945), p. 142, argues that the moral tone of English society was largely set by the aristocracy well into the eighteenth century; Keith Thomas, 'Double Standard', *Journal of the History of Ideas*, vol. XX (1959), p. 205, likewise comments on the limited influence of middle-class respectability. On contact with London, see E. A. Wrigley 'A Simple Model of London's Importance in Changing English Society and Economy, 1650–1750', *Past and Present*, No. 37 (1967), *passim*.

8 Thomas, op. cit., p. 213. Cf. the opening chapter of Hardy's *The Mayor of Casterbridge*.

9 C. Bridenbaugh, *Vexed and Troubled Englishmen* (New York, 1968), pp. 366–72; *Past and Present*, No. 29 (1964), p. 63; A. M. Everitt, 'The Marketing of Agricultural Produce' in Joan Thirsk, ed., *The Agrarian History of England* (London, 1967), vol. IV, pp. 559–62, 588–90.

10 Dorothy Marshall, *English Poor in the Eighteenth Century* (London, 1926), pp. 161–232.

11 Thomas, op. cit., p. 206, has some general remarks about the 'tradition of promiscuity' among the lowest classes. The need for a general reformation of manners seemed to be felt throughout the country in the 1690s.

12 London was rapidly becoming the 'pleasure capital' of the country—the focus for leisure entertainment, the season, and attendant high-jinks. Added to this, the large number of young domestic servants, whose employment was often seasonal or erratic, and always poorly paid, created a situation attractive to the aspiring pimp. Bridenbaugh, op. cit., pp. 372ff.; Conrad Russell, *Crisis of Parliaments* (London, 1972), pp. 173ff.

13 L. Stone, *Crisis of the Aristocracy 1558–1641* (Oxford, 1965), p. 665.

14 For a *tour de force* on this subject see J. P. Kenyon, *The Stuarts* (London, 1958), ch. 2, especially the orgy at Theobalds, 1606, pp. 50–2. Cf. Robert Ashton, *James I by his Contemporaries* (London, 1969), pp. 228–45.

15 Cf. the anger of the common people at Lady Essex's lenient sentence, reported in *The Chamberlain Letters*, ed. E. Thomson (n.p., 1966), p. 121. Notestein, op. cit., p. 76.

16 Quoted by Kenyon, op. cit., p. 47.

17 Quoted by Bridenbaugh, op. cit., p. 361; cf. p. 193.

18 C. L. Powell, *English Domestic Relations 1487–1653* (New York, 1917), pp. 164–70. E.g. *My Ladies Looking Glass* (1616) or Barnabe Rich, *Honestie of This Age* (1614).

19 C. V. Wedgwood, *The King's Peace* (London, 1955), p. 101.

20 E. Johnson, *Wonderworking Providence of Sion's Saviour*, ed. J. F. Jameson (New York, 1937), pp. 23–5.

21 T. Birch, ed., *The State Papers of John Thurloe* (London, 1742), vol. IV, p. 341.

22 W. H. Blumenthal, *Brides from Bridewell* (Rutland, Vt, 1962), pp. 55–6. There is possibly some significance in the fact that Instruction 19 referred to houses of ill-fame in London and Westminster only.

23 Margaret James, *Social Policy during the Puritan Revolution* (London, 1930), pp. 12–14; Ivan Roots, 'Swordsmen and Decimators' in R. H. Parry, ed., *The English Civil War and After, 1642–58* (London, 1970), pp. 78–92; D. W. Rannie, 'Cromwell's Major-Generals', *English Historical Review*, vol. X (1895), pp. 471–506.

24 Sir Charles Firth, *Oliver Cromwell* (London, 1924), pp. 342–6.

25 Ibid., p. 357.

26 James, op. cit., pp. 14–15: 'So long as a man was not a notorious drunkard or profligate his morals were regarded as his private concern.' Paradoxically, the activities of some of the extreme sects, who redefined sin, sanctioned polygamy or encouraged bigamy for the 'new born', undermined the moral revolution from within. R. Knox, *Enthusiasm* (Oxford, 1950), pp. 160–6; P. M. Higgins, ' Women in the Civil War' (unpub. M.A. thesis, Manchester, 1965), pp. 70–1, 95.

27 Thomas, op. cit., p. 195.

28 Samuel Pepys, *Diary*, 10 August 1663.

29 John Evelyn, *Diary*, 4 February 1685.

30 G. S. Alleman, *Matrimonial Law and the Materials of Restoration Comedy* (Wallingford, Pa, 1942), pp. 121, 140.

31 Above, p. 68.

32 E.g. *Letters from New England*, ed. W. H. Whitmore (Boston, 1867), pp. 64ff.

33 *Bellamira* (1687), quoted by E. J. Gagen *The New Woman* (New York, 1954), p. 181.

34 Cf. Sir Matthew Hale's call for 'a return to ancient order from modern extravagance, dissipation and idleness'. D. Gardiner, *English Girlhood at School* (London, 1929), p. 274.

35 I have not dwelt on the mass of evidence on this point. For a brief discussion and further evidence, see Dudley Bahlmann, *The Moral Revolution of 1688* (New Haven, 1957), ch. 1.

36 Bahlmann does not mention the name of one woman reformer throughout his account.

37 A. Wallas, *Before the Bluestockings* (London, 1929), ch. 6.

38 William Bisset, *Plain English* (London, 1704), p. 28; cited by Bahlmann, op. cit., p. 43.

39 Ibid., p. 101.

THE MORAL TONE OF SOCIETY

40 M. Reynolds, *The Learned Lady in England 1650–1760* (Boston, 1920), pp. 300–6.
41 Ibid., p. 118; Wallas, op. cit., ch. 6.
42 On these and other female critics, see Reynolds, op. cit., pp. 139ff.
43 Henry Bamford Parkes, 'Morals and Law Enforcement' *New England Quarterly*, vol. V (1932), p. 943; C. F. Adams, *Three Episodes*, vol. II, pp. 795–9; and *Some Phases of Sexual Morality in Colonial New England* (Boston, 1891), p. 11; E. S. Morgan, 'Puritans and Sex', *New England Quarterly*, vol. XV (1942), pp. 606–7. P. Greven, *Four Generations* (Ithaca, 1970), p. 113, similarly finds that 'normal behaviour reflected continence'.
44 Quoted by P. Miller, *From Colony to Province* (Boston, 1961), p. 47.
45 Goelet's *Journal* is reprinted in the *New England Historical and Genealogical Register*, vol. XXIV (1870).
46 On 'Do-Good', see Miller, op. cit., pp. 395–416.
47 A compendium appears in George P. Winship's introduction to *In Boston in 1682 and 1699* (Providence, 1905), pp. ix–xxviii; see also Cotton Mather, *Magnalia*, Book V, pp. 88ff.; Book VI, pp. 37ff.; on the Synod of 1679, see Miller, op. cit., pp. 33–9. The 'Result', i.e. the report of proceedings, must not, he argues, 'be taken too seriously'.
48 *Bradford's History 'Of Plimouth Plantation'* (Boston, 1898), pp. 460–1.
49 Miller, op. cit., p. 33; cf. Mather's admission of the virtue of many women in the Bay in *Ornaments for the Daughters of Zion* (Boston, 1691), p. 31.
50 *Magnalia*, Appendix to Book II; also K. B. Murdock, *Selections from Cotton Mather* (New York, 1960), p. 151.
51 On Morton, see Bradford, op. cit., pp. 284ff.; and his own *New English Canaan* (1637), ed. C. F. Adams in *Publications of the Prince Society*, vol. IX (Boston, 1883); on Gardiner, see John Winthrop, *Journal: History of New England*, ed. J. K. Hosmer (New York, 1946), vol. I, p. 63; and J. Josselyn, 'Chronological Observations' in *Two Voyages to New England* (London, 1674; repr. Boston, 1865), under 1632; also Thomas Dudley's letter to the Countess of Lincoln in Alexander Young, ed., *Chronicles of the First Planters* (Boston, 1846), p. 334.
52 Cited in A. W. Calhoun, *Social History of the American Family* (Boston, 1918), vol. I, p. 120.
53 *Andros Tracts*, ed. W. H. Whitmore (Prince Society, Boston, 1868), vol. V, pp. 101, 168.
54 Sewall, *Diary*, vol. I, pp. 122–231, *passim*.
55 Ibid., vol. I, p. 98; and *Magnalia*, Book VII, p. 36.
56 Ibid., vol. II, p. 419. The practice of toast-drinking, a well-known excuse for communal inebriation, had been banned as such in the early years of the colony.
57 Morgan, op. cit., *passim*.
58 J. Demos, *A Little Commonwealth* (New York, 1970), p. 153.
59 J. H. Smith, *Colonial Justice in Western Massachusetts* (Cambridge, Mass., 1961), pp. 236, 237, 247, 259, 273, 287.
60 Johnson, op. cit., p. 191; Sarah Knight, *Journal*, ed. George P. Winship (New York, 1935), pp. 2, 3.
61 E. S. Morgan, *Puritan Family* (New York, 1966), p. 165, cites Anne Bradstreet's poem 'I have a more beloved one/Whose comforts far excell'. Cf. Shepard's 'sensuality delighting my soul more in my dear wife than in God' in Young, op. cit., p. 529; and Sewall's widower's wish 'Oh that I . . . might be married to CHRIST.' *Diary*, vol. III, p. 180; Mather made much of the 'match with the Lamb' when he wrote his *Ornaments for the Daughters of Zion*, pp. 72, 36.
62 Winthrop, op. cit., vol. II, pp. 20–1; referring to Nathaniel Eaton, late of

Harvard, he wrote that, in Virginia, he is 'usually drunk, as the custom is there'.

63 J. Durand, *A Frenchman in Virginia*, trans. and ed. by Fairfax Harrison (privately printed, 1923), pp. 33–5.

64 J. C. Spruill, *Women's Life and Work in the Southern Colonies* (Chapel Hill, 1938), p. 156.

65 'Bacon's Rebellion' by T. M. (almost certainly Thomas Mathews), reprinted in Peter Force, *Tracts*, vol. I, No. 8, p. 14.

66 Ibid., No. 11, pp. 27, 46. It is worth mentioning that T.M., who also mentions Lawrence enjoying 'the darke embraces of a Blackamoore, his slave', alludes to it with real distaste.

67 Spruill, op. cit., p. 176, ch. 15; Moller, op. cit., p. 134.

68 *Gooch Letters*, p. 16. On the general theme of miscegenation in the colonial period see W. D. Jordan, *White over Black* (Baltimore, 1969), ch. 4.

69 Quoted, along with other examples, in Blumenthal, op. cit., pp. 25–9.

70 Spruill, op. cit., p. 176, ch. 15.

71 Hugh Jones, *Present State of Virginia*, ed. Richard L. Morton (Chapel Hill, 1956), p. 130; *Va Mag.*, vol. XXXVII (1929), p. 30; cf. Robert Beverley, *History and Present State of Virginia*, ed. Louis B. Wright Chapel Hill, 1947), Book III, section 7.

72 R. A. Brock, ed., *The Official Letters of Alexander Spotswood* (Richmond, Va, 1882–5), vol. I, p. 28.

73 *Gooch Letters*, pp. 4, 132–5.

74 Spotswood's letters, ed. cit., pp. 4, 157.

75 E. S. Morgan, *Virginians at Home* (Williamsburg, 1952), p. 10.

76 J. Hammond, 'Leah and Rachel', in Force, *Tracts*, vol. III, No. 14, p. 17.

77 Cf., e.g., entry on p. 140 of *London Diary* with p. 491.

78 Ibid., p. 500.

79 One of the main butts of Reformation Societies' attacks in England was lax magistrates who lamentably failed to enforce laws against immoral conduct. Bahlmann, op. cit., pp. 14–15, 18, 25–6, 29.

80 Spruill, op. cit., pp. 320–4.

81 *Westover Diary, passim*, and especially pp. 7, 30, 31, 101, 192, 221, 323, 340, 387, 433, 436, 469, 476, 508, 551, 583.

82 E.g. A. Maury, *Memoirs of a Huguenot Family* (New York, 1872), pp. 261, 262, 267; cf. *London Diary*, pp. 626, 625, 628. Cf. the situation in Wycherley's *The Country Wife*.

83 B. Bailyn, 'Society and Politics in Colonial Virginia' in J. M. Smith, ed., *Seventeenth Century America* (Chapel Hill, 1959), *passim*.

84 Alternatively, other societies may positively defend prostitution as an oatfield for young or not so young men and a sustainer of virtue for respectable women. Thomas, op. cit., pp. 213–15.

85 G. P. V. Akrigg, ed., 'Offenbach's Journal', *Huntington Library Quarterly*, vol. V (1940–1), p. 86.

86 Thomas Nashe, *Christs Teares* (1598), vol. II, pp. 148–54, quoted in Bridenbaugh, op. cit., p. 373. Cf. F. Bamford, ed., *A Royalist's Notebook* (London, 1936), p. 229.

87 Bridenbaugh, op. cit., p. 373.

88 M. D. George, *London Life in the Eighteenth Century* (London, 1925), p. 83; Bridenbaugh, op. cit., p. 373.

89 C. V. Wedgwood, op. cit., p. 66.

90 Quoted in ibid., p. 31.

91 Gagen, op. cit., p. 109; Bridenbaugh, op. cit., p. 372.

92 Quoted by C. Hill, *Society and Puritanism* (London, 1964), p. 301.

93 Bridenbaugh, op. cit., pp. 367ff.

94 Cf. 'The ordinary discourse of the world', which held in 1661 that 'a great part of men have, at one time or the other, had some species of this [Venereal] Disease.' Graunt, in C. H. Hull, *The Economic Writings of Sir William Petty* (New York, 1964), p. 356.
95 *Proposals for a National Reformation of Manners* (London, 1694), p. 24.
96 Ibid., p. 34; some have such ironic christian names as Temperance and Christian; one madam gave her name in the sessions as Charity Squish.
97 (London, 1700), p. 18.
98 *The London Spy*, pp. 276–9.
99 *A Proposal to Render effectual a Plan to remove the Nuisance of Common Prostitutes from the Streets of the Metropolis* (London, 1758), pp. 1, 13n.
100 In Dorothy Marshall's *Dr. Johnson's London* (New York, 1968), p. 236.
101 Ibid., p. 235, quoting Archenholz, George, op. cit., p. 400. In his *Plan for preserving those deserted girls who become Prostitutes from the Necessity* (c. 1758), Fielding, himself a Bow Street magistrate, pointed out that the forty odd girls who might be brought in after a search-night would mostly be under eighteen, and many not above twelve years old. Ibid., p. 324, n. 12. Paul Landis, *Social Problems* (Chicago, 1959), p. 301, quotes a figure of 275,000 prostitutes for the whole United States in 1951, an era, admittedly, of relative prosperity.
102 Bahlmann, op. cit., pp. 44–6.
103 Blumenthal, op. cit., p. 25. There were alleged to be twenty-six whores in Deal in 1703. Bahlmann, op. cit., p. 104.
104 Blumenthal, op. cit., pp. 36, 52.
105 The number and popularity of reform societies throughout the country seems to support this contention. See Bahlmann, op. cit., pp. 38–41, 52–4.
106 William Byrd only very rarely failed to pick up a girl to his liking in his almost nightly sorties.
107 For instance, Mather speaks of the Huguenot minister Vanderbosk, 'baptising a noted whore or two of his acquaintance' in 'A Vindication of New England', in *Andros Tracts*, vol. II, pp. 36–7.
108 'Records of the Suffolk County Court', p. 818.
109 Parkes, op. cit., p. 443.
110 Miller, op. cit., p. 36.
111 Mather, for instance, cites a girl who had had two base children, the second of whom she murdered, and who had intercourse with another prisoner when she was in the condemned cell. *Magnalia*, Book VI, p. 49. Cf. Morgan, 'Puritans and Sex', p. 602. 'Records', p. 914.
112 *Records of the First Church of Boston*, vol. I, p. 54; E. Oberholzer, *Delinquent Saints* (New York, 1956), p. 142.
113 Cf. C. Bridenbaugh, *Cities in the Wilderness* (New York, 1960), pp. 388–9.
114 We should be somewhat suspicious of references in Cotton Mather's diary in 1712, 1713 and 1714 to 'wicked houses'. They are always linked with proposals for activities for the Society for the Suppression of Disorders, and may well have been merely copying the procedures of London societies. W. C. Ford, ed., *The Diary of Cotton Mather* (New York, n.d.), vol. I, pp. 160, 229, 234, 284.
115 *London Diary*, pp. 484, 505, 506–7.
116 P. E. H. Hair, in *Population Studies*, vol. XX (1966), pp. 233–43; vol. XXIV (1970), pp. 59–70.
117 The sample for his first article is seventy-seven parishes in twenty-four counties, and for his second eighteen parishes in eight counties.
118 An increase in the fornication figures of several colonies in the eighteenth century has given rise to some rather inconclusive hunches about causes for this phenomenon. See Adams, *Some Phases*; Parkes, op. cit., refutes

the argument that the increase in confessions was connected with the Great Awakening. It may be useful to give some twentieth-century figures, from Hair. A group of 1,000 women married between 1900 and 1924, voluntarily providing information, produced a percentage of twenty-two admitting to bridal pregnancy. In 1938, 18 per cent between fifteen and forty-five were pregnant. In the 1960s the figure was above 20 per cent. According to Kinsey and his associates, some 50 per cent of American brides in 1950 were non-virgins. Hair, op. cit., vol. XX, p. 240; vol. XXIV, p. 66.

119 This, as we shall see, was legally recognised in Massachusetts.

120 I.e. from November to March, with only about a week in January open for weddings.

121 On penance procedures, see M. Ashley, *Stuarts in Love* (London, 1963), p. 57. Cf. P. Laslett, *The World We have Lost* (London, 1971), ch. 6. Laslett's figures, on p. 148, appear to corroborate Hair's. See also p. 302.

122 Ashley, op. cit., pp. 56–60.

123 Laslett, op. cit., pp. 135–45, 298–301.

124 Bridenbaugh, *Vexed and Troubled Englishmen*, pp. 367–70.

125 Quoted by Marshall, op. cit., p. 232; her general discussion cited here covers pp. 161–7, 180–1, 195–222, 226.

126 This, it will be remembered, was how Moll Flanders entered on the primrose path; see Thomas, op. cit., pp. 203–4.

127 The fine for 'carnal copulation' by a betrothed couple was 50s., as opposed to £10; on the other hand, copulation with a third party during the engagement period was treated as adultery. G. E. Howard, *History of Matrimonial Institutions* (Chicago, 1904), vol. II, pp. 180–1; for the sentencing record of Suffolk Court judges, see Howard's analysis, ibid., pp. 187–8.

128 Ibid., pp. 186–7.

129 Oberholzer, op. cit., pp. 150–1.

130 H. W. Lawrence, *The Not-Quite Puritans* (Boston, 1928), p. 173, who reports thirty-four fornication cases in Essex, between 1680 and the end of 1683.

131 Parkes, op. cit., p. 443.

132 'Records', *passim*; cf. Howard, op. cit., vol. II, p. 188.

133 E. B. Greene and V. Harrington, *American Population before the Federal Census of 1790* (New York, 1932); we take 1690 as the year, because there are no reliable figures for the previous decade, and the rate of population growth for the county is unclear.

134 Susan Norton, 'Population Growth in Colonial America', *Population Studies*, vol. XXV (1971), p. 443.

135 J. Demos, 'Families in Colonial Bristol', *3 WMQ*, vol. XXV (1968), p. 56.

136 Greven, op. cit., p. 113.

137 C. F. Adams, *Some Phases*, pp. 6–11; the fornication cases recorded in the church records were all premarital.

138 J. H. Smith, op. cit., pp. 103ff.

139 Hair, op. cit., vol. XX, p. 241; the impetus to confess the fornication often seems to have come from the mother.

140 Oberholzer, op. cit., p. 139.

141 Spruill, op. cit., p. 318, n. 13.

142 P. A. Bruce, *Institutional History of Virginia* (Gloucester, Mass., 1964), vol. I, pp. 45–54.

143 The offences mentioned are all moral cases, including profanity, drunkenness, sabbath-breaking and slander.

144 Thomas, op. cit., pp. 197–9, 209–14.

Epilogue

The compartmentalisation that the deployment of any complex thesis imposes leads to a certain unhistorical neatness, which contemporaries would not have recognised. The sex ratio was closely bound up with economic opportunity. To Frederick Jackson Turner one concept of the frontier—the most vital, according to David Potter—was almost synonymous with a low threshold to success and plenty. We have noted a similar blurring between our so-called causes and results. Educational possibilities cannot be glibly docketed as either cause or effect. When girls have the chance of a better education their position in society tends to improve, but they will not get that chance if society persists in regarding women as little better than village idiots or child-minders and sink-servers, or as delicate plants whose bloom is all-important. The same kind of inter-reaction operates over the areas of civil and political rights, the setting of the moral tone, and the general position of women in the family. The pretty patterns which the analytical historian delights to trace traduce the real past, which, as we are so often reminded, was such an unpredictable and unfathomable mess.

The last question we shall raise here is 'How long did it last?' Was this early freeing of American women in the first century of settlement another of those colonial legacies which helped permanently to shape the American national character, like the establishment of representative government or the cult of worldly success? Did the lead of American women in the long-distance and still unfinished race to full sexual equality start here? Or was women's emancipation in the Stuart colonies a temporary phenomenon, like the early Tudor flowering, later to wither? Was it just a brief concomitant of a shocked and disordered frontier situation, before new traditions were firmly bedded and old certainties reimposed?

It would take another book to answer this question fully, but a few pointers can at least be given. We can look at what have emerged as the important factors and indices of women's emancipation in the seventeenth century and see whether they were still present and operative in the following century. Little work has been done on the eighteenth-century sex ratios of either England or the colonies. There are no very compelling reasons for thinking that the sex ratio in England turned very spectacularly in women's favour. True, there were fewer wars and no plagues to destroy men, and women may have become more liable to industrial accidents as the factory system and mechanisation progressed. On the other hand, emigration from England, so far as we know, continued to soak up more surplus males than females, and men were more likely to die as a result of criminal activities or the wages of sin. In the colonies, however, we would expect the advantageous sexual balance of men to women to swing away from the latter. As the population grew and multiplied, producing roughly equal numbers of recruits to either sex, the effects of male-dominated immigration would become less noticeable. The swing away from male surplus would be hastened by the decimations of war and dangerous masculine jobs. We would, of course, expect to find considerable local variations; frontier regions, like new colonies, would be likely to have male surpluses. The evidence suggests, however, that in the more settled areas where the great majority of the population would live—and from which males bound for new settlements on the frontier might migrate—the sex ratio was no longer a strong factor favouring the position of women in the eighteenth century; indeed, in eastern Massachusetts it probably operated to the advantage of men.[1]

There is considerable evidence to suggest that the striking contrast between economic opportunities for women became less marked in the eighteenth century. It has, for instance, been recently shown that in Boston the wealth, that had in the first century been fairly evenly spread, was by about 1765 becoming far less equally distributed. A wealthy class had emerged, and alongside it was a significant number of really poor people. The westward exodus of the 1790s arose from the push of eastern want rather than from the pull of western opportunity.[2] The number of propertyless adult males in the city had quadrupled in 1771 in comparison with 1687, though the population had only doubled. By the latter date, almost one-third of the adult male population was landless and poor. This picture is endorsed by the findings of Kenneth Lockridge on the availability of land. By 1787 New England was an overcrowded society and the average of 150 acres which the original settlers had been granted had fallen to about 40. Land prices had risen between two and three times between 1660 and 1760. 'Amicus Patriae', writing as early as 1721, complained that 'many of our old towns are too full of inhabitants for husbandry. . . . Many of our people are slow in marrying for want of settlements.'[3] Probably Virginian society was tending in the same general direction, though less drastically. The establishment of a more settled social order, the increased control over land resources by the aristocracy, and the enormous increase in the number of slaves imported and naturally multiplying in the colony could be expected to reduce the economic opportunities of the humbler classes of the white population.[4]

The economic opportunities offered to women in England in the eighteenth century probably did not improve. The conditions decried by Alice Clark were exacerbated, and they operated most powerfully against women. Though the onset of mechanisation in the textile industry may have provided women with employment, it is highly questionable whether this could be rated as an improvement in their lot; more likely it was the opposite. Although, therefore, the situation in Massachusetts and Virginia was less promising than it had been for women—these two colonies were not necessarily any longer so typical—it was probably still better than what prevailed for the majority of women in England.

While it is safe to say that the kind of influence that the puritan church exerted in its seventeenth-century heyday was much less in the eighteenth, Perry Miller has wisely warned against too facile assumptions that Georgian New England was taken over by secularism.[5] It is beyond the scope of this brief essay to examine the effects of either the growth of toleration or such movements as Methodism and the Great Awakening on the position of women in English and colonial society. If the example of the more 'enthewsiasticall' sects of the seventeenth century is anything to go by, it is possible that the eighteenth-century revivalist movements accorded women a more pronounced role in religious life, on both sides of the Atlantic. Whether widespread female participation would heighten women's esteem in society at large is more open to doubt.[6]

The fourth differentiating factor was the frontier. Lockridge's figures for land shortages in New England towards the end of the eighteenth century suggest that the frontier there was hardly fulfilling its function as provider of economic opportunity and low threshold to affluence. The same may well have been true for piedmont Virginia. The whole question of the eighteenth-century frontier is a vast and all too little examined one. Factors like land speculation, lack of communications, imperial settlement and Indian policies, the Indian trade, and colonial domestic politics all played their part. What kind of influence the frontier had on later colonial society, and what its effects were on the role of women both on the frontier and in the colonies at large I am not qualified to say. My guess would be that in both areas it was less in the eighteenth than in the seventeenth century.[7]

This reduced influence can be detected in what has been loosely lumped together as 'effects'. For instance, as the colonies became more firmly established, the legal rights which women had been accorded during the 'do-it-yourself' period of colonial juridical rulings were eroded as American practice fell more in line with that of the imperial power. True, divorce continued to be obtainable in Massachusetts, but other property rights in both New England and Virginia were less tenaciously maintained. Again, it seems that women's education in both colonies tended to follow the enervating English model in the eighteenth century, with accomplishments and good breeding increasingly emphasised at the cost of intellectual stimulation and training.[8] In both colonies the relatively high moral tone of the Stuart years also suffered a slide. Certainly the Boston of 1750 would have seemed like Sodom or Gomorrah to John Winthrop or John Cotton. In Massachusetts there was a marked rise in bastardy and fornication in mid-century, and prostitution was added to the other mercantile occupations of the seaport towns. The same process took place in Virginia. After the English legislation of 1718, transportation, previously slight, provided thousands of migrants of both sexes every decade. Virginia, a frequent dumping-ground, almost certainly suffered from this immoral or demoralised influx. Cases of bastardy became much more common, and newspaper sources point to an increase in marital infidelity. The inrush of slaves probably encouraged the indolence of Virginian women and allowed their husbands fresh fields for extra-marital adventures.[9]

In New England the old-maid problem suggests that women's bargaining power in courtship and marriage would be seriously affected. The same goes for Virginia, though more gradually. As landed wealth was accumulated in fewer hands, the freedom of daughters to marry whom they wished would be curtailed by parents concerned about the future and the further increase of family estates. Shortage of land in certain areas might also lead to delayed marriage, which would have subtle effects on the structure of the family. Finally, although there were outstanding women in eighteenth-century America, like Eliza Pinckney and Abigail Adams, it is worth reiterating Mrs Dexter's supposition about colonial women of affairs that 'conditions were worse then [in the eighteenth and early nineteenth centuries] than they had been in the previous century'.[10]

If we are to accept Mary Benson's account of women in eighteenth-century America, culled mainly from literary sources and private correspondence, attitudes towards women reflected colonial 'dependence on the upper and middle classes of the Old World'. Paradoxically, the growth of sophistication and a more leisured class seem to have meant an ebbing of those specifically American values which we have described. 'The truly American woman, uninfluenced by European ideas, if she existed at all, was to be found on the frontier, not in the comfortable homes of the Atlantic seaboard'.[11]

It is always tempting to try to find a neat and logical line of progress running through the history of any particular social group, political party, constitutional theory, even civilisation. 'The Rise of . . .' and 'The Decline and Fall of . . .' are concepts of great attraction. It seems unlikely, however, that the path of women towards liberation and equality can be so tidily and straightly drawn. More probably, it was a meandering route that was followed, a route which sometimes lost itself, doubled back, stopped dead or edged slowly sideways. Rather than representing a mere acceleration in progress towards the promised land, feminist movements may well be the result of frustration and anger at ground lost and worsening prospects. None the less, throughout her history, American woman has enjoyed a more attractive position in society than her English counterpart, of whatever class. Although all the gains of the seventeenth century were not maintained, this superiority, like so many other lasting American characteristics, was founded during the early generations of the New World.

Notes

1 On Massachusetts, see J. H. Benton, *Early Census-Making in Massachusetts*, (privately printed in Boston, 1905), *passim*; on both colonies, see E. B. Greene and V. Harrington, *American Population before the Federal Census of 1790* (New York, 1932), pp. 14ff.; on England, see C. M. Law, 'Some Eighteenth Century Censuses', *Population Studies*, vol. XXIII (1969), pp. 87–100.

2 J. A. Henretta, 'Economic Development and Social Structure in Colonial Boston', *3 WMQ*, vol. XXII (1965), pp. 77–85.

3 K. Lockridge, 'Evolution of New England Society 1630–1790', *Past and Present*, No. 39 (1968), pp. 62ff. Both Lockridge and Greven have drawn attention to something of a population explosion in the third and fourth generation Dedham and Andover respectively.

4 C. Ver Steeg, *The Formative Years* (London, 1965), pp. 58, 135–8.

5 'From the Covenant to the Revival' in James Ward Smith and A. Leland Jamison, eds, *The Shaping of American Religion* (Princeton, 1961), pp. 322–68.

6 The role of certain noblewomen like the Countess of Huntingdon in the Methodist movement in England is well known. Philip Greven is currently working on certain social aspects of the Great Awakening.

7 On the eighteenth-century Virginian frontier, see some suggestive remarks in R. Morton, *Colonial Virginia* (Richmond, Va, 1960), vol. II, pp. 540ff.

8 Cf. Benjamin Rush, *Thoughts upon Female Education* (Boston, 1787), reprinted in Frederick Rudolph, ed., *Essays on Education in the Early Republic* (Cambridge, Mass., 1965), pp. 27–35.

9 J. C. Spruill, *Women's Life and Work in the Southern Colonies* (Chapel

Hill, 1938), pp. 76, 179–80, 323. W. D. Jordan, *White over Black* (Baltimore 1969), pp. 137ff. argues that 'it seems likely there was more miscegenation in the English colonies during the eighteenth century than at any time since.'

10 Cf. William L. O'Neill, *Everyone Was Brave* (Chicago, 1969), pp. 3–14.
11 M. Benson, *Women in Eighteenth-Century America* (New York, 1935), p. 11.

Index